THE GOVERNMENT OF
THE OTTOMAN EMPIRE
IN THE TIME OF SULEIMAN
THE MAGNIFICENT

AMS PRESS
NEW YORK

THE GOVERNMENT OF
THE OTTOMAN EMPIRE
IN THE TIME OF SULEIMAN
THE MAGNIFICENT

BY

ALBERT HOWE LYBYER, Ph.D.
PROFESSOR OF EUROPEAN HISTORY, OBERLIN COLLEGE

"Our empire is the home of Islam; from father to son the lamp of our empire is kept burning with oil from the hearts of the infidels."　　　　MOHAMMED II, THE CONQUEROR.

"A lord and his bondsmen."　　　　RANKE.

"Les Turcs . . . nées de la guerre et organisées pour la conquête."　　　　CAHUN.

"The Ottoman government . . . seems to have attained during the sixteenth century the highest degree of perfection of which its constitution was capable."　　　　ROBERTSON.

CAMBRIDGE
HARVARD UNIVERSITY PRESS
LONDON: HENRY FROWDE
OXFORD UNIVERSITY PRESS
1913

Library of Congress Cataloging in Publication Data

Lybyer, Albert Howe, 1876-1949.
    The government of the Ottoman Empire in the
time of Suleiman the Magnificent.

    Reprint of the ed. published by Harvard Univer-
sity Press, Cambridge, which was issued as v. 18
of Harvard historical studies.
    Includes bibliographies.
    1. Turkey—Politics and government—1453-1683.
    2. Turkey—History—Süleyman I, 1520-1566.
    I. Title. II. Series: Harvard historical
studies; v. 18.
DR507.L8   1978   320.9′561′01   75-41305
ISBN 0-404-14681-3

Reprinted from an original in the collections
of the University of Iowa Libraries

From the edition of 1913, Cambridge
First AMS edition published in 1978

Manufactured in the United States of America

AMS PRESS INC.
NEW YORK, N.Y.

PREFACE

The Ottoman Turks, after the world had long despaired of them, have in these last years shown signs of renewed vigor. The time is, then, perhaps not inauspicious for an examination of the structure of their organization in the period of its greatest power and prestige. It is not easy for the present age to realize how large the empire of Suleiman bulked in the eyes of contemporaneous Europe. Amid the vast energies and activities, the magnificent undertakings and achievements, of the marvellous sixteenth century, nothing surpassed the manifestations of power that swept forth from Constantinople. The following pages will have been worth while if their incomplete presentation shadows forth, however dimly, the secrets of Ottoman greatness and success.

This book was originally prepared in partial fulfilment of the requirements for the degree of Doctor of Philosophy in Harvard University, and was subsequently awarded the Toppan Prize. The writer desires to acknowledge his very great indebtedness for advice, suggestion, and criticism to a number of kind friends with whom he has consulted, but especially to Professor A. C. Coolidge and Professor G. F. Moore. Nor can he let the book go to press without recording his extreme obligation to his wife for unwearying assistance at every stage of its preparation.

A. H. L.

Oberlin, Ohio, 1912.

CONTENTS

INTRODUCTION

CHAPTER I

THE CHARACTER OF THE OTTOMAN STATE IN GENERAL

CHAPTER II

THE OTTOMAN RULING INSTITUTION: AS A SLAVE–FAMILY

CHAPTER III

THE RULING INSTITUTION: AS MISSIONARY ENTERPRISE AND EDUCATIONAL SYSTEM

CHAPTER IV

THE RULING INSTITUTION: AS AN ARMY

CHAPTER V

THE RULING INSTITUTION: AS A NOBILITY AND A COURT

CHAPTER VI

THE RULING INSTITUTION: AS GOVERNMENT

CHAPTER VII

THE MOSLEM INSTITUTION OF THE OTTOMAN EMPIRE

CHAPTER VIII

COMPARISON OF THE TWO GREAT INSTITUTIONS

APPENDICES

THE GOVERNMENT OF THE OTTOMAN EMPIRE

THE GOVERNMENT OF THE OTTOMAN EMPIRE

INTRODUCTION

IDEAS CONSTITUTE A NATION

A nation, when considered from its earliest to its latest days, is much more a body of ideas than a race of men. Men die, families decay, the original stock tends to disappear; new individuals are admitted from without, new family groups take the lead, whole tribes are incorporated and absorbed; after centuries the anthropological result often bears but slight resemblance to the original type. Undoubtedly the fabric of ideas which a nation weaves as its history develops also undergoes changes of pattern; old principles pass out of sight, and new ones, born of circumstance, or brought in from without, come to controlling influence. But ideas are not, like men, mortal: they can be transmitted from man to man through ages; they can be stored in books and thus pass from the dead to the living; when built together into a solid and attractive structure, they impart to the whole something of their individual immortality. Singly they pass as readily to strangers as to kindred; when organized to rounded completeness as the culture of a great living nation, they have a power which lays hold of men of many races, alone or in masses, and in the absence of strong prejudice compels acceptance.

Such an assimilative force can clearly be seen in vigorous operation in the United States of America today. A system of ideas, woven of countless threads spun by Egyptian, Babylonian, Hebrew, Greek, Roman, and Teuton, preserved and enlarged by Frank, Anglo-Saxon, Norman, and Englishman, recombined in a new and striking pattern by the founders of the republic, is thrown over men from every nation under heaven, who under its influence all become of one type, not to be mistaken wherever it is seen.

3

The history of the Ottoman Empire reveals the constant working of a like assimilative force. It was not merely, and not even mainly, the compulsion of the sword that built up and maintained the strongest national power of the sixteenth century. Swords must be wielded by men; and how were enough strong and capable men found and bound together in willing coöperation to conquer large sections of Europe, Asia, and Africa, to organize and govern their conquests in a fairly satisfactory fashion, and to establish a structure which, after more than three hundred years of decay, disaster, and disintegration, has yet enough strength to form the basis for a new departure? The only answer possible is that the attraction of a great body of national ideas gathered men from every direction and many races to unite in a common effort. Although much violence, injustice, and destructive passion was involved, the result was a great and on the whole a durable and useful empire.

The government of the Ottoman Empire when at the height of its power cannot be understood from a description of its court, costumes, ceremonies, and officials, with a catalogue of their provinces and duties. A thorough comprehension of the main political ideas that constituted the life of the empire is essential. Since most of these ideas were old and tried, and were wrought in a thousand ways into the general scheme, a complete treatment would demand that they should be considered historically from the time of their adoption. Nor would it be sufficient to go back to the beginning of the house of Osman. The Turkish nucleus which gathered around him, and the Mohammedans and Christians from near and far who joined his rising fortunes were already in possession, in a fairly systematic form, of most of the ideas of the completed Ottoman government. The inquiry should be begun farther back, among Byzantine Greeks, Seljuk Turks, Mohammedans of Persia and Arabia, and Turks of Central Asia. Many of the ideas, indeed, can be traced yet farther, through Tartary to China and through Parthia and Rome to Babylon and Egypt.

These origins, however, cannot be considered here except in the briefest possible fashion. All that can be done is to outline the background of Ottoman history, the general character of the Ottoman Empire and its service to the world, the racial descent of the Ottoman Turks, and the main influences which affected their institutions and culture.

THE BACKGROUND OF OTTOMAN HISTORY

From early times the developing Chinese civilization in the valley of the Yellow River had to contend with intermittent attacks from the barbarians of the north and west. In the latter half of the third century B.C. China's work of domestic consolidation and centralization reached completeness, and foreign conquest began. The policy was then initiated which has never since been departed from, — the subjugation of the outlying lands and the cultural assimilation of their inhabitants.[1] Following up with armies, governors, and garrisons the nomads who fled to the west, by the beginning of the second century A.D. China held vassal all the population of the steppe country from the Great Wall to the Caspian Sea; her frontiers marched with those of Parthia. Early in the third century she entered upon four hundred years of weakness, and her western possessions fell away; but she regained strength and restored her western dominion just in time to confront the rising Saracen flood. During three brilliant centuries, the seventh, eight, and ninth of our era, she held the nomads in fairly constant subjection, and presumably taught them many of her orderly, organized ways. It was probably in part by the strength of her discipline that in the succeeding half-millennium the descendants of these nomads, Turks and Mongols, wrought their will from the Sea of Japan to the Adriatic, over most of Asia, half of Europe, and a goodly portion of Africa.

From the eighth century Turks drifted southwestward in ever-increasing numbers out of Chinese territory into the declining Saracen Empire. Early in the eleventh century an army followed this course and set up the vast but short-lived empire of the Seljuk Turks. These broke the eastern frontier of Asia Minor, which had protected the Greeks and Romans for fourteen

[1] Cahun, *Introduction à l'Histoire de l'Asie*, 90.

hundred years, and pushed on until they could see the domes of Constantinople. The eastward pressure of the crusading period kept them from European shores for two centuries, near the close of which the Mongols overran their disintegrated lands. A remnant, the Seljuk Sultanate of Rûm, struggled on in Asia Minor until the close of the thirteenth century, when it fell into ten parts. The East Roman, or Byzantine Empire, had by that time also been thoroughly wrecked, and the Balkan Peninsula was divided among Frank, Italian, and Catalan, Greek, Serb, Albanian, Wallach, and Bulgarian.

The people of one of the ten fragments of the Seljuk Sultanate of Rûm took the name of Osmanlis from their chief Osman. Located on the border of the Greek and Turkish groups of principalities, they drew men and governmental ideas from both. The rapidity of their growth from so small a beginning, and under such apparently unfavorable circumstances, into a durable state is one of the marvellous things of history. In about two and a quarter centuries from the time of their independence they were able to attempt for the last time to unite the entire Mediterranean civilization into one empire. North Africa, Egypt, Syria, Arabia, the Tigris-Euphrates valley, Armenia, Asia Minor, Greece, the Balkan Peninsula, a large part of modern Austria-Hungary and of modern Russia, were theirs; they threatened Italy, Central and Eastern Europe, and Persia. They thus held all three of the earliest centers of Mediterranean civilization, the western half of the Old Persian Empire, and all the dominions of Rome except the northwestern one-third. Apart from Spain and the lands east of the Zagros Mountains, they ruled the Saracen Empire. With the exception of Italy (with Illyricum and the adjacent islands) and the short-lived Byzantine conquests in Spain, the empire of Justinian lay within their boundaries. The later Byzantine Empire became the heart of their dominions, and its two chief supports — the trade which passed through the Bosphorus and the products and men of Asia Minor — became their own principal supports. The inheritance of lands and of institutions by the Ottoman Turks from the two great medieval empires of the Levant, the Saracen and the East Roman, is by all odds the most pregnant fact of their existence. They were the immediate heirs of a part of the territory and of the whole of the culture of the Seljuk Turks. The scene of the " world's debate " formed but an insignificant part of their dominions. They gathered into one net all the shoal of feudal, royal, and imperial powers which made the Levant of the thirteenth century as decentralized as the Holy Roman Empire or the Italy of the fifteenth century.

CHARACTER AND MISSION OF THE OTTOMAN EMPIRE

This rapid survey leads to a number of significant observations. First, the Ottoman Turks of the sixteenth century ruled countries wholly within the sphere of the Mediterranean civilization. The only possible exception was the steppe lands north of the Black Sea; but these had been almost as much under the sway of Rome and Constantinople as they ever were under that of Stamboul. Even communication with Eastern and Southern Asia was well-nigh cut off. The road to China north of the Caspian Sea alone remained open, but after the break-up of the Mongol Empire it had become long and dangerous. The rival and hostile New Persian power firmly closed the southern land route to India and China; and even the sea-way from Egypt eastward was blockaded by the newly-arrived Portuguese. Thus the Ottoman Empire, except in remote origins, which, indeed, profoundly influenced it, grew and flourished within what is commonly considered the main field of history. Accordingly, it has a greater claim upon the Western world on the score of kinship than has hitherto generally been allowed.

Second, within the Mediterranean civilization the Ottoman Empire combined regions of both Orient and Occident. The classical world knew chiefly Romans, Greeks, and Orientals. The Ottoman Turk succeeded to two-thirds of this world, the lands of Greece and the East. From the day of Issus to the day of Menzikert, Asia Minor had to all intents and purposes been a part of Europe. After Menzikert it became a center of Turkish rule, to which, in the course of time, territories from both Asia and Europe were added in widening circles. No deep knowledge of historical forces is necessary to suggest that neither in Southern Europe nor in Asia Minor itself could the teachings of fourteen centuries or more be obliterated in five centuries or less, or even in an eternity; nor would they fail to exert a profound influence from the moment of conquest. To regard the Ottoman Empire as a mere Oriental state would be to misread history and to misunderstand human nature. Its lands were of both Orient and Occident, so also were its people, so also were its culture and its government.

Third, the Ottoman Turks drew men and ideas from both Mohammedans and Christians. They have commonly been regarded as wholly Mohammedan, 'and therefore they have been shut off by a well-nigh impenetrable barrier from the sympathies of a world still possessed by the prejudices of crusading days. The foundations of such prejudices are easily open to attack. The main religious ideas of Mohammedanism are not, except as to the divinity of Christ, inharmonious with those of Christianity; they were, indeed, in all probability drawn chiefly from the religious teachings of the Old Testament. The social system of Mohammedanism is also much like that of the Old Testament. Its most objectionable features, the seclusion of women, polygamy, and slavery, may be regarded as survivals from an older condition of mankind out of which a portion of the human race has emerged — not without frequent cases of atavism — and which Mohammedans themselves are tending to abandon. But, leaving aside the question of the kinship of Christianity and Mohammedanism, no one can deny that the Ottomans ruled over many Christians, that many of their ablest men and families were of Christian ancestry, and that, according to the nature of humanity, as much of their civilization and ruling ideas may have come from Christian as from Mohammedan sources.

It is true that as a nation the Ottoman Turks remained Mohammedan; this has constituted the real " tragedy of the Turk." Bound hand and foot by that scholastic Mohammedanism which was reaching rigid perfection at the time when the Turks first became prominent in the Saracen Empire, and which only in very recent days seems tending toward a Reformation, they could not amalgamate the subject Christian peoples, already confirmed in nationalism by the events of centuries. The deadening system stilled their active spirits, imprisoned their extraordinary adaptability, and held them at a stage of culture which, though in some respects it distinctly led Europe in the sixteenth century, was before long passed through and left behind by the progressive West. Nevertheless, the Turks were no more limited to Mohammedan ideas than to Mohammedan men, and they are entitled to be considered in the light of their double origin.

Fourth and last, the great task before the Ottoman Turks was a work of unification. Lands which had been united under the great Theodosius, and then during eleven centuries had been more and more disintegrated by invasion of German, Slav, Arab, Tatar, and Turk, by war of Byzantine, Persian, Moslem, Crusader, and Mongol, by destruction of roads and safe water-routes, and by general decay of civilization, until confusion and disorder reigned and anarchy seemed not far ahead — these lands were once more brought under a single control. Was it their destiny to be genuinely reunited, not merely in a common subjection, not merely by an external shell of authority, but in the pulsing life of a vigorous nation, harmonious in every part and run through by patriotism? This was the well-nigh insoluble problem which the Ottoman Turks attempted bravely. How they solved the administrative and governmental phase of it the present treatise will try to show. Religious unity was out of the question; and in the sixteenth century, in East and West alike, social and cultural unity waited upon the religious. Had the Ottoman Empire been able four hundred years ago to set apart religious considerations as matters for the individual — a process which affords the chief hope of the new Turkey of the twentieth century — her whole subsequent history must have been very different.

But in the measure in which unity was attained in the Levant under the Ottoman authority, in that measure did the Ottoman Empire render service to civilization and humanity. After the close of the thirteenth century Western Europe, absorbed in its own affairs, was able to give little attention to the East. Two centuries were taken up with the consolidation of national powers, chiefly at the expense of feudalism and the medieval church. By the sixteenth century a measure of internal solidarity had been attained and the struggle for external supremacy over the West had been begun. The whole situation was complicated by the actively leavening force of the New Learning and the explosively rending force of the Reformation. Under such circumstances even the advance of the Turks into Central Europe could only temporarily divert attention from absorbing problems and direct it toward the East. To what a state of minute division and infinite disorder the Levant would have come by that time, had the Ottoman Empire not grown up, can only be imagined. Egypt, the only Levantine power of consequence after the close of the crusades, had reached the natural limits of her dominion, and had she aimed at wider conquests the Mameluke government would scarcely have been capable of imperial sway. No other of the countless principalities of the eastern Mediterranean showed enough life to accomplish unity. But the Ottoman Turks, cruelly and destructively, imperfectly and clumsily, yet surely and effectively, built up and maintained a single authority, to which the world probably owes most of that measure of enlightenment, culture, and order which can be found in the Levant today.

The Racial Descent of the Ottoman Turks

The question as to the origin of the Ottoman Turks was raised in Western Europe as soon as the race began to appear upon the stage of history. There seemed to be something mysterious and uncanny about their rise to power. If an innumerable horde of strange barbarians, a second invasion of Attila, had overrun the Levant and settled down to rule its conquests, cause and effect would have been apparent. But this nation seemed to arise out of the earth. Organized and disciplined beyond any parallel in the West, it seemed to come from nowhere and to begin at once to take a very real part in human affairs.[1] The problem of its origin is by no means completely solved as yet, but the main elements can perhaps be outlined. A search for these carries the inquiry to the steppe lands.

The great band of open country which stretches with hardly a break across the whole of Asia and far into Europe resembles the ocean both in its vastness and in its character as an intermediate region through which the travel of commerce, statesmanship, religion, learning, and curiosity can pass between more thickly-settled lands. It differs from the ocean, however, in being everywhere more or less habitable. The ethnic relations of its families, tribes, and nations are by no means clear. China, with a markedly Mongolian population, lay at the east and southeast; Indo-Europeans of the Caucasian race dwelt at the southwest and west. The tribes between seem from the earliest recorded times to have presented every intermediate stage of physical type, as they do now; and in general the shading from yellow to white appears to have proceeded regularly from east to west, a circumstance that may have been due largely to climatic influence, but was probably far more the result of admixture.[2] These peoples were given to frequent warfare, one of whose objects was the capture of men, women, and children as the most valuable booty. They seem to have had no race aversions that

[1] The West was much concerned in the sixteenth century with the problem of ascertaining the origin of the Turks. Balbus gives an idea how difficult it was to reach a definite opinion: "Some count the Turks among the Asiatic Sarmatians, and say that they were expelled by their neighbors from the Caspian mountains into Persia, and descended into Asia Minor. Others, following the name, perhaps, think that this people had its beginning in Turce, a great and opulent city of the Persians. Others consider them the progeny of the Parthians. Some think the Turks had their origin in Arabia, and some in Syria. But it is more likely that they were Scythians by origin, and (as we said above) from the foot of Mount Caucasus, and that they formerly inhabited vast deserts." See also Knolles, 1–2.

[2] Keane, *Man, Past and Present,* 268, 314–315. Holdich (in *Encyclopaedia Britannica,* 11th ed., ii. 749 b) says, "As ethnographical inquiry advances the Turk appears to recede from his Mongolian affinities and to approach the Caucasian." Keene (*Turks in India,* 1 ff.) is inclined to consider the Turks a mere mixture of Mongols with Caucasians. So bald a theory does not account for the group of Turkish languages.

would hinder inter-mixture, and no race pride that would prevent captives, in the course of time, from attaining full equality in any rank to which their abilities could carry them. Accordingly, the process of admixture that can be observed in historic times has probably been followed from the remote past.

The name Tatars may be used to designate all the inhabitants of the steppe-ocean who were not distinctly Caucasian. By geographical designation they are properly called the Ural-Altaic peoples, while ethnically they constitute the Mongolo-Turki group.[1] Included perhaps among those unclassified peoples who were known of old to the Greek as Scythians, to the Persians as Turanians, and to the Chinese as *Hiung-nu*, the Tatars, despite many differences, show unmistakable kinship, usually in their physical features, always in their language and institutions. They have been grouped since medieval times into two great divisions, the Mongols and the Turks. This division may be said to correspond in a very general way to their greater and lesser resemblance to the Chinese, and to a narrower and wider geographical separation from China. Many tribes possess such intermediate characteristics that they cannot easily be classified as Turks or Mongols;[2] but a tribe that is markedly like the Chinese is clearly Mongol, and a tribe that differs widely from the Chinese is clearly Turkish. If these explanations be adopted, the Turkish peoples are then in general those Tatars who have had the greatest admixture of Caucasian blood. Their original seat seems to have been in Mongolia, but in historic times they had come to occupy the whole central part of the steppe region, from the Desert of Gobi to the Volga, in contact with their Mongol kindred on the east and with Iranians on the south and Slavs on the west. The theory of admixture receives support from the fact that the peoples of the Mediterranean civilization found Mongolians repulsive in appearance, but prized Turkish slaves for their beauty.[3]

The name Turk does not appear prominently in the Byzantine and Chinese annals before the fifth century A.D., when the people

[1] Keane, 267.
[2] *Ibid.* 317.
[3] *Ibid.* 322; Hammer, *Geschichte,* i. 3.

of a Tatar empire were designated Τοῦρκοι and *Tu-kiu*.[1] The word *Turcae* was used by classical writers soon after the beginning of the Christian era.[2] The name has been suspected of lying hidden in the *Targitaos* of Herodotus and the *Togharmah* of Scriptures. However this may be, ancestral peoples possessing the characteristics of the Turks of course existed, and perhaps appeared in history, in very early times.

Some have suggested that the Sumero-Accadians of Babylonia were Turks, but this question hardly bears on the present subject. The relations of Turks and Persians on the Central Asian frontier is much more apropos. The legends of the long wars of Iran and Turan, however little detailed historical value they may have, illustrate the circumstances of continual contact both in war and in peace.[3] Princes and nobles whose lives were forfeit in their own country fled over the border; princesses were exchanged in marriage; and unnumbered thousands of less exalted folk passed the frontier as captives or slaves. The frontier itself was not fixed, but left great regions now to the rule of the Persian and now to the rule of the Turk. The Parthians may have been Turks.[4] After their downfall the lines

[1] Keane, 322; Hammer, *Geschichte*, i. 2; etc.

[2] Hammer, *Geschichte*, i. 1. This fact, known to Knolles (p. 2), seems to have escaped the attention of Sir Charles Eliot (*Encyclopaedia Britannica*, 11th ed., xxvii. 470 d).

[3] The older view, that Iran represented peoples of Indo-European stock, and Turan peoples of Ural-Altaic stock, though once so generally adopted as to sanction the bestowal of the names Iranian and Turanian upon these groups of peoples, has been abandoned as regards the original legends, in which Turan seems to have represented ruder tribes of Indo-European lineage (Meyer, *Geschichte*, i. pt. ii. 814-815). But the Greeks from their first acquaintance with the name identified Turan with the Scythians, and at about the same time the Persians began to apply it to the Northern peoples of alien stock. The conditions of frontier contact between Turks and Persians during many centuries were undoubtedly as described in the legends.

[4] Rawlinson, *Parthia*, 33-35; Keane, 319. Meyer (in *Encyclopaedia Britannica*, 11th ed., xxi. 214 c) regards the Parni or Aparni, who became the conquering tribe in Parthia, as Iranian nomads; but Peisker (in *Cambridge Medieval History*, i. 332) asserts that the nomads of the Asiatic background all belong to the Altaian branch of the Ural-Altaian race. The fact that the Parthian army was a slave army (see Meyer, as above, 217 a) is perhaps the strongest piece of evidence that the original Parthians were Turks.

of Persian and Turk were drawn sharply by the nationalist Sassanians. From the middle of the fifth century, indeed, the Persians had their fill of wars with the Ephthalites, whose appellation of White Huns may indicate their mixed Mongolian and Caucasian origin; the Chinese annals specify the kinship of the *Tie-le* with the *Tu-kiu*. No sooner had the Arabs engulfed Persia than they began to welcome the Turks whom they found to the north, and whose semi-nomadic culture was singularly like their own. The Saracen Empire was administered for about a century chiefly by Arabs, for another century chiefly by Persians, and after that chiefly by Turks, who rose rapidly through slavery and military service to the rule of provinces and even of kingdoms. Thus great numbers of Turks came or were brought into many parts of Western Asia. When Toghrul, grandson of Seljuk, led the first great Turkish invasion into the heart of the Saracen Empire, he found his kindred everywhere. Under the Seljuk Sultans large numbers of Turks streamed in and were settled in Persia, Azerbaijan, Syria, and Asia Minor.

The Turkish occupation of Asia Minor has been called the most thorough piece of work done by the race.[1] Few details of it have been recorded, but one great fact stands out: under the Byzantine Empire, Asia Minor was Greek, Christian, and the home of the empire's most vigorous and loyal citizens; under the Ottoman Empire, Asia Minor is Turkish, Mohammedan, and the home of the empire's most vigorous and faithful subjects. The process of this transformation, so far as it is known, deserves examination.

Seljuk and Ottoman Turks in Asia Minor

The Seljuk Turks were orthodox, and often fanatical, Moslems; accordingly they put great pressure upon the inhabitants of the peninsula to make them exchange Christ for Mohammed. " Great numbers apostatized, ' many thousand children were marked by the knife of circumcision; and many thousand

---

[1] Keane, 327. Asia Minor is here used in the larger sense, as denoting in general the Asian territory which lies west of a line drawn from the eastern end of the Black Sea to the head of the Gulf of Alexandretta.

captives were devoted to the service or the pleasures of their masters.[1] ' "

The Seljuk Turks were already a mixed race, and had no greater objection than their ancestors to the reception of new members. They had come as a Turkish army followed by a host of Turcoman nomads.[2] The soldiers took wives from the women of the land and servants from the men and children, and the nomads filled the gaps left among their women and children after the long, hard journey. Those of the adult Anatolians who were left free found a thousand temporal advantages in following the Prophet, whose simple faith and consoling doctrines, moreover, suited both their temperament and their circumstances. Christianity had sat lightly upon many of them, and Mohammedanism seems to have been accepted as lightly; for traces of Christian and perhaps of pre-Christian practices and beliefs can be seen among the Moslems of Asia Minor today.[3] To turn Moslem was then, as ever since, to turn Turk. In the course of three centuries the process of settlement and conversion reached virtual completion; nearly all the plateau of Asia Minor became Mohammedan and Turkish. Nothing approaching the nature of statistics is available for determining what the proportion was between invading Turks and converted Christians. The probabilities, based on the known character of Turkish invasions and the length and difficulty of the journey from the steppe lands, point to a relatively small number of Turkish settlers.[4] Yet this doubly-mixed people has contributed those subjects of the Ottoman Empire who are accounted the most characteristically Turkish.

The invasion of Western Asia by the Mongols of Genghis Khan in the early part of the thirteenth century drove an un-

---

[1] Quoted in Keane, 328, from Gibbon (ed. Bury), vi. 250.

[2] Vambéry, *Die Primitive Cultur*, 47; Keane, 328; Cahun, *Introduction*, 169 ff.; Ramsay, *Studies in Eastern Roman Provinces*, 295.

[3] Ramsay, *Studies in Eastern Roman Provinces*, 297. This statement has been confirmed by conversation with other persons well acquainted with conditions in Asia Minor. See also E. Huntington, in *National Geographic Magazine*, September, 1910, p. 767.

[4] Vambéry (*Die Primitive Cultur*, 47) expresses the opinion that the Ottomans never received, all told, more than 25,000 men of Turkish blood.

known number of Persians and Turks to take refuge in Asia Minor. Among these is said to have been a group led by a chief named Suleiman, whose grandson Osman gave the Ottomans their name.[1] This group reached the Seljuk kingdom of Rûm, and was allowed by good custom of the time to proceed to the Christian frontier and conquer what it could. About the time of settlement tradition specifies the number as four hundred families, or 444 horsemen, a figure which has clearly been shaped with reference to the sacred number four, but which shows the belief that the group was not large.[2] The growth of this band was far more rapid than could have been accomplished by natural increase. A part of the additional membership was supplied by Turks and other Moslems of adventurous spirit who sought the fighting and booty of the border-land. But these were by no means all. The Ottoman traditions and history reveal at countless places the hospitable incorporating spirit of the embryonic nation, which rapidly increased its numbers from the Christian population by conversion, marriage, and capture, and most strikingly by the tribute tax of Christian male children. The Ottoman conquests to the eastward brought gradually into the brotherhood all the Seljuk Turks of Asia Minor, and as many as were or became Mohammedan from the various conquered peoples — Greeks of Trebizond, Armenians, Syrians, and others. The conquests in Europe converted *en masse* some sections of Bulgarians and Albanians, who still show evidence of their origin; a very great number of individuals among the subject Christians, however, were so completely incorporated as to lose all trace of their source. Thousands upon thousands of captives from the whole of Southeastern Europe, from all of Southern Russia and Poland, from the Caucasus region, from Central Europe as far as Regensburg and Friule, and from the shores and islands of the Mediterranean were likewise incorporated; till, as a result of all this Western admixture, the ruling nationality of the Ottoman Empire,

---

[1] *Ottoman* is an attempt to pronounce *Othman* by those who pronounce *th* like *t*; *Osman* a similar attempt by those who pronounce *th* (as in " thin ") like *s*.

[2] Hammer, *Geschichte*, i. 42–43.

though called Turkish today, retains no physical trace whatever of Mongolian ancestry.[1] Many of its members undoubtedly have no Tatar blood in their veins; as for the rest, they are, if the above discussion be well founded, a mixture of Europeans chiefly with Turks of Asia Minor, who were themselves a mixture of the former Christian population with Seljuk Turks, while these again were a mixture dating back through countless ages of contact between the white and the yellow races. A simple computation will illustrate the matter. Osman is said to have captured a fair Greek lady named Nenuphar, or Nilufer, the Lotus-flower, and to have given her as bride to his son Orhan, *Orhan* the first of the Ottoman sultans.[2] From that time it became increasingly the policy of the sultans to take their wives from the Caucasian race.[3] If Orhan be set down as of pure Mongolian descent, and if it be supposed, as is certainly very near the truth, that all the mothers of succeeding sultans were not of Turkish blood, and if the mother be assumed to contribute to the child an influence equal to the father's, the proportion of Mongolian blood in the veins of the reigning sultan, who is of the twentieth generation from Orhan, can readily be calculated, — about one part in one million.[4] Similar proportions would hold good

[1] Keane, 268, 316. Peschel, 380, says, "The Turks of the west have so much Aryan and Semitic blood in them that the last vestiges of their original physical characters have been lost, and their language alone indicates their previous descent." On the other hand, E. Huntington (in *National Geographic Magazine*, September, 1910, p. 767) expresses the opinion that the inhabitants of the central part of the plateau of Asia Minor are "almost purely Turkish in race." He does not say, however, that this opinion is based on observation of physical appearances.

[2] Hammer, *Geschichte*, i. 59.

[3] Keene, 2, makes the interesting suggestion that this custom, followed *mutatis mutandis* by the Moguls of India, was a survival of exogamous conditions among the ancestors of the Turks.

[4] The twentieth power of $\frac{1}{2}$ is $1/1,148,576$. The description given of Orhan, furthermore, shows scarcely a discernible trace of Mongolian ancestry. Compare Hammer, *Geschichte*, i. 158: "Mit demselben [Osman] waren ihm zwar die Bocksnase und die schön gewölbten schwarzen Augenbrauen gemein; aber er hatte blonde Haare und lichte Augen, die Statur und die Stirne hoch, die Brust breit, die Faust kräftig wie die Klaue des Löwen, das Gesicht rund und die Farbe desselben weiss und roth; der Körperbau stark, der Bart und Knebelbart dicht und wohlgenährt." Murad II showed a little more evidence of Tatar descent. He "is," says La Broquière, 181, "a man of stout build and short body, and he

for many of the Osmanli Turks. Probably the nation as a whole has no more of Tatar blood than the American nation has of Norman.

THE SOURCES OF OTTOMAN CULTURE

The question at once arises: What significance, then, has the name Turk as applied to modern Turkey ? To this query a general answer only can be given here, as part of a rough statement in regard to the derivation of the main elements of Ottoman culture.

Of the whole body of ideas and institutions and intangible inheritances possessed by the Ottoman Turks in the sixteenth century, no small number of the most fundamental ones were derived from the remote Tatar ancestors of a part of the nation, from whom even this part was far separated in time and space. Foremost among these inheritances is the Turkish language, which in its principles of monosyllabic stem, inflexion by post-fixes alone, and assonance, and in its general system of grammar and body of words of ordinary life, has survived from the early days through all vicissitudes.[1] Old Turkish is the Anglo-Saxon of the Osmanli, as Persian is his Greek and Arabic his Latin. Somewhat more hospitable than those who use Western languages, the Turk has nearly always accepted with a foreign thing its foreign name; and the great majority of the foreign words and phrases so accepted he has not changed in any way, except to modify the pronunciation of some sounds about which the tongue does not readily curl. Among other Tatar bequests to the Osmanlis may be named the hospitable assimilative tendency to which reference has already been made; a predisposition to war and conquest, accompanied by an openness of mind as to the best methods and means of prevailing; an ability and inclination to govern, combined with great adaptability as to methods and means; and some acquaintance with systematic

has something of the broad face of a Tatar's physiognomy, and he has a rather large hooked nose and rather small eyes, and he is very brown in the face, and he has plump cheeks and a round beard."

[1] Keane, 266.

and bureaucratic methods of government impressed upon the nation by the Chinese. Again, the Tatars, possessed of the tenacious conservatism of a primitive people, predisposed the Ottomans to a close adherence to custom — to the doctrine that, when a thing had been done once in a certain way, it should always thereafter be done in the same way. Finally, the Tatars contributed various elements of the national character, such as a touch of the old love of nomad life, a certain stolidity of spirit and calm sobriety of temper (taught, perhaps, by the vastness of the steppe in comparison with the littleness of man), and a lack of originality which hindered the construction of freely-borrowed ideas into new forms of higher relation. In general, therefore, the foundations of the national character of the Ottomans were laid in the early days, in a body of ideas which was passed down continuously from man to man, not so much through blood-relationship as through willing acceptance or enforced adoption.

The nature of a Tatar nation in the steppe lands, manifesting many of the elements mentioned above, is extremely significant as foreshadowing some features of the Ottoman government. A Tatar nation was a voluntary association, independent of kinship, formed about a promising leader, and interested in war and conquest; thus it might grow with extreme rapidity until the geographical extent of its dominion would be marvellous. The empire of the *Tu-kiu*, for example, gathered in about twenty-five years after its foundation territories which reached from China proper to the confines of the Byzantine Empire. The leader of such a nation maintained his control by the right voluntarily given him to punish treason and conspiracy by death;[1] when his controlling hand grew weak, the nation went to pieces. "A Turkish tribe could maintain a political organization and a compact grouping only by war; without benefits from pillage and tributes, it would be obliged to dissolve and to disperse by clans, whose fractions would group themselves anew, and form another nation about the strongest man. . . . In regard to

---

[1] Compare the election of Sebuktegin, in Schéfer's edition of the *Siasset Namèh*, 158.

empires like those of the Huns, or the Turks, military associations without ethnic bonds, one cannot say that they dissolve; they disband.   Reversing the custom of other peoples, with the Turks it is the king who feeds his people, who clothes them, who pays them." [1]   Add to this system a loyalty to a hereditary leader which makes the bonds of union permanent, and the description would apply fairly well to the growing Ottoman nation.   A passage from the *Kudatku Bilik* applies yet more closely, since it shows a military government in the midst of a subject population: [2] —

> "In order to hold a land one needs troops and men;
> In order to keep troops one must divide out property;
> In order to have property one needs a rich people;
> Only laws create the riches of a people:
> If one of these be lacking all four are lacking;
> Where all four are lacking, the dominion goes to pieces."

The ancient Persian seems to have given the Ottoman at long range a number of his ideas of government, such as the exaltation of the monarch, the separation of officials of the court from those of the government proper, the division of the ministry into five departments, the council of state, the giving of large powers to local governors, and the beginnings of the so-called "legal" system of taxation. [3]   From him also seems to have come the policy of allowing subjects who professed alien religions to form separate organizations, which lived in a measure under their own laws.   One writer goes so far as to say: " All investigations into the oldest state regulations of the Orient, into the origin of monarchical forms and constitutions, into the ceremonial of courts and the hierarchy of officials, lead back to the great kingdom of the ancient Persians, from whom they have come down more or less modified, to the Arabs, who sat as

---

[1] Cahun, *Introduction*, 79.

[2] Vambéry, *Uigurische Sprachmonumente und das Kudatku Bilik*, 118. This passage closely resembles the words attributed to Artaxerxes I, first king of the Sassanian Persian line: " There can be no power without an army, no army without money, no money without agriculture, and no agriculture without justice " (Rawlinson, *Seventh Great Oriental Monarchy*, i. 61).

[3] Hammer, *Staatsverfassung*, 36–45.

caliphs on the thrones of the three continents, to the Seljuk Turks and the Byzantines, who at the same time grew up on the ruins of the Saracen and Roman kingdoms in Asia and Europe, and through both to the Ottomans who swallowed up the kingdoms of Iconium and Byzantium." [1] The Sassanian Persians handed down through the Moslems the completed " legal " system of a land tax of two sorts based on cadasters, and a capitation tax levied on those who practised a foreign religion. They may also have contributed many features of the Ottoman feudal system. During the Abbassid period the Persians and the Turks who gradually displaced the Arabs in the civil and military administration of the Saracen Empire were thrown into very close contact with each other. It was only natural, therefore, that the Persians, who possessed the more advanced culture, should influence the Turks in many directions. Their chief direct gift lay in the domain of poetry and literature, a field in which they added a vast number of words and ideas to the original Turkish stock.

The Saracens gave the Ottomans a complete religious and social system, united under a Sacred Law which professed to provide for all relations of life, and which became more and more rigid as time went on. Into this had been wrought slowly by generations of learned men most of the Persian governmental ideas that have been mentioned, together with others from Arabian and Byzantine sources, such as a species of laws of inheritance and a system of juristic responses. The Saracens gave also their alphabet and a large stock of Arabic words. All that the Moslems gave the Ottomans was embodied in one great, complex institution, which was founded upon an elaborate system of education and supported by the revenues from a large part of the land of the empire, and which possessed great solidity and an almost changeless permanence, In the Ottoman Empire, as in all other Moslem lands, the influence of this completed institution was ultimately very injurious; when added to the Tatar love of custom, it laid a heavy hand on all movements toward improvement and progress. Its ultimate attitude

---

[1] *Ibid.* 36.

toward earthly affairs is well expressed in the following couplet: —

> " To build in this world palaces and castles, there is no need;
> They will at last be ruins: to build cities, there is no need."[1]

A development which took place among the Turks within the Saracen Empire was of the profoundest significance to Ottoman history. From some date in the early ninth century, Turkish youth were brought to Bagdad in large numbers as purchased, but by no means unwilling, slaves. Having been trained as soldiers, they became generals and local governors, and after no great length of time the central government also passed into their hands. The training of such young Turkish slaves in the palaces of caliphs and governors clearly foreshadowed Ottoman methods. The account that perhaps looks farthest back in relation to the Turks is found in the *Siasset Namèh*, and refers to the time of the Samanid dynasty, which ruled in East Persia from 874 to 999. It describes the external aspect of the system of education, such as promotion and marks of honor, but leaves the severe work which lay behind to be inferred: —

" This is the rule that was followed at the court of the Samanids:

" They advanced slaves gradually, taking account of their services, their courage, and their merit. Thus a slave who had just been purchased served for one year on foot. Clothed in a cotton tunic, he walked beside the stirrup of his chief; they did not have him mount on horseback either in public or in private, and he would be punished if it were learned that he had done so. When his first year of service was ended, the head of the chamber informed the chamberlain, and the latter gave the slave a Turkish horse which had only a rope in its mouth, a bridle and a halter in one. When he had served one year on horseback, whip in hand, he was given a leathern girth to put about the horse. The fifth year they gave him a better saddle, a bridle ornamented with stars, a tunic of cotton mixed with silk, and a mace which he suspended by a ring from his saddle-bow.

---

[1] Quoted by Cahun, in Lavisse and Rambaud, iii. 964.

In the sixth year he received a garment of a more splendid color; and in the seventh year, they gave him a tent held up by a pole and fixed by sixteen pegs: he had three slaves in his suite, and he was honored with the title of head of a chamber; he wore on his head a hat of black felt embroidered with silver and he was clothed with a silk robe. Every year he was advanced in place and dignity; his retinue and his escort were increased until the time when he reached the rank of chief of squadron and finally that of chamberlain. Though his capacity and merit might be generally recognized, though he had done some noteworthy deed and had acquired universal esteem and the affection of his sovereign, he was obliged nevertheless to wait until the age of thirty-five years before obtaining the title of *emir* and a government." [1]

In this system of the training of slaves for war and government lay the nucleus of the fundamental institution of the Ottoman state, which, together with the institution based on the Sacred Law, was to sum up practically the entire organized life of the Ottoman nation. Under the Samanids it was Turkish boys who were thus educated by Arabs and Persians, but the Ottomans were later to apply the same principle to the education of Christian youth.

The Seljuk Turks brought most of the ideas that have been mentioned into Asia Minor. They served chiefly as mediators between the older Turkish, Persian, and Mohammedan systems and that of the Ottomans. Besides adding some features out of their own experience, such as a method of book-keeping, and handing on a taste for constructing public buildings like caravanserais, khans, and mosques, they gave rise to several important religious orders which were to have a place in Ottoman life.

What was left for the Byzantines to contribute to the Ottoman ? He had received already the main features of his national character, — language, literary influences, law, and religion. One of his two leading institutions was already almost fully developed in Moslem lands, and required only transplantation. The other, however, the institution of war and government,

---

[1] Schéfer, *Siasset Namèh*, 139.

could still be modified considerably; and this was to incorporate much from the Byzantines.[1] Many details of governmental organization, both imperial and local, a supplementary system of taxation, a greatly elaborated taste for court ceremonial and splendor, a plan of organizing foreign residents under a special law, and a host of lesser usages and customs were to be taken over by the Ottomans. The Ottoman feudal system also probably owed its final form to the Byzantines; and perhaps it was from them that the Ottomans learned their abnormal love for fees and gifts. The matchless structure of Saint Sophia served as a model for the superb mosques that lift the shapely masses of their great gray domes, supported by clusters of semidomes and lesser domes, above the cypress tress and gardens of the rounded hills which in Constantine's city slope down to the blue waters of the Sea of Marmora, the Bosphorus, and the Golden Horn.

This sketch of the origin of the elements of Ottoman culture does not profess to be in any sense complete. So great a subject is worthy of separate and extended treatment. No more has been attempted here than partly to prepare the way for an understanding of the strange system of government which the Ottoman Turks developed, and to show that that system was no new creation, but was made of elements which in their origins reached far back into the past. Out of old and tried ideas was built up a double structure which was individual, conservative, and efficient, strong, durable, and useful.

[1] Bérard, 4 ff.

CHAPTER I

THE CHARACTER OF THE OTTOMAN STATE IN GENERAL

DEFINITION

THE Ottoman Turkish state of the sixteenth century was a despotism, limited and supported by the Mohammedan Sacred Law; it governed a vast territory, which had been gathered by the progressive conquest of many separate lands, and which was consequently held in many diverse relationships; it ruled a multitude of peoples, some of which were favored as holding to the state religion, and others of which, though in an inferior position, had yet the right by sacred compacts to practise other religions and obey other laws.

This description reveals at once the complex and parti-colored character of the Ottoman Empire at the period when its power and prestige were greatest, when its armies were feared from the shore of the German Ocean to the borders of India and its fleets from Gibraltar to Bombay, and when its favor and good-will were sought by powers great and small in Asia, Africa, and Europe. For the state as for the individual, the penalty of greatness is increase of responsibility and care. In any conquering nation the growth of governmental institutions must keep pace with increase of territory and population, or advance will be stifled by confusion. The growth may, however, be too rapid to be intelligently directed. Most great institutions, in fact, tend to develop a separate life of their own which may become too vast and powerful for human comprehension and control; for political, religious, economic, and social forces proceed out of and act upon them in numerous and unexpected ways. In the case of the Ottoman Empire the situation was rendered more difficult by the presence in its territory of stable and vigorous institutions centuries older than its own. These were profoundly hostile to its inner spirit, far too powerful and individual to be destroyed or absorbed by it, and therefore an eternal obstacle to unity. In addition, the Ottoman institutions themselves grew more and more apart into two unified groups, which were in striking contrast in many ways; dwelling together, they acted upon each other continually; and unfortunately they were so constituted that their reciprocal influence was to the injury of both. A fuller explanation will make the complicated situation clearer.

The Limitations on Despotism

It may seem a contradiction in terms to speak of a despotism as limited; yet a little reflection will show that there never has existed and never can exist a despotism that is not limited. In what land has the will of one man been obeyed instantly, everywhere, and by all ? In what land have there not been stubborn traditions, ineradicable prejudices, and powerful organizations, which have blocked the way of the despot as effectively as lofty mountains and stormy channels ? The great limitation upon the power of the Ottoman sultan was the *Sheri*, or Sacred Law of Islam, which claimed to be wholly above him and beyond his alteration.[1] He might by act of violence transgress its provisions, but he had even then done it no damage; it was still what it had always been. And he knew well that his transgressions must not be too many, and must not at all touch certain matters, else he would be declared to have forfeited the throne.[2] The Sacred Law divided with him the allegiance of his Mohammedan subjects; it demanded to be consulted before he removed the head of a criminal,[3] or went to war with an enemy;[4] it took for itself the revenues of a large share of his lands, and so controlled the imposition of general taxation as seriously to embarrass his finances; it even protected his Christian subjects from all efforts of his to bring them forcibly under its sway;[5] it entered into his very spirit and persuaded him to relinquish

---

[1] Hammer, *Staatsverfassung*, 30; D'Ohsson, v. 7; Heidborn, III
[2] D'Ohsson, i. 291; Hammer, *Staatsverfassung*, 32.
[3] D'Ohsson, vi. 253.
[4] *Ibid.* v. 53.   [5] *Ibid.* 109.

harmless pleasures,[1] while it supported him in the execution of able and worthy brothers and sons.[2] The *Sheri* was a form of rigid constitution which by its own provisions was incapable of amendment. It purported to regulate for all time the matters included in its scope. Open to a small measure of modification by juristic interpretation, it was probably on the whole as changeless a system as has ever prevailed among men. The sovereign had no right to modify it in the least respect.

Nor was the Sacred Law the only real limitation upon the sultan's power. Although he was not bound to observe the legislation of his ancestors or maintain their institutions,[3] yet he could not lightly destroy what he must at once replace. Some of their laws he might cease to observe, some institutions he might neglect, improve, or reform; but the main substance of their work was too useful and too well-established to be undone. Suleiman bears the name of Legislator (*El Kanuni*); but in his case it was even more true than in similar instances in other lands that he did not so much ordain and create anew as rearrange and put in order, reorganize and regulate.

Again, few other peoples in the world, perhaps, have been so much under the power of custom as was the Ottoman nation.[4] That which had been once done in a certain way must always be done in the same way, or in what was believed to be the same way, unless a change had been accomplished by the distinct intervention of fully recognized authority. The inertia of the

---

[1] *Ibid.* iv. 280; Busbecq, *Life and Letters*, i. 331; Erizzo, 137.

[2] This was based upon a passage of the Koran, " Sedition is worse than execution " (Sura 2: 187): Hammer, *Geschichte*, i. 216. Professor G. F. Moore points out that in this passage (and in Sura 2: 214, which is substantially identical) the text refers to Mohammed's war with the Meccans, or to fighting in the sacred months. The word *fitnah*, here translated " sedition," has various meanings: first of all, " trial," as gold and silver, for example, are tried by smelting; then, " successful temptation, leading or turning a man astray, error, discord, dissension, sedition, etc." The context indicates clearly that Mohammed had in mind the leading or turning of people from the true religion as that which is " worse than killing." The other meanings would, however, allow some accommodating jurist or theologian to make this a plausible proof-text for authorizing the killing of the sultan's brothers, who might become seditious or furnish cause for dissension.

[3] Hammer, *Staatsverfassung*, 31.

[4] *Ibid.* 32; D'Ohsson, vii. 150.

people was so marked that the sovereign power seldom found it worth while, and then only when driven by necessity, to put forth the great exertion required to make a change in the established order.

Restricted thus by an unchangeable constitution, by the presence of deep-rooted laws and institutions, and by the settled customs of a highly conservative people, the power of the Ottoman sultan could be exerted freely in certain directions only. What these were will appear as the scheme of the government is unfolded.

THE TERRITORIAL BASIS

A fundamental characteristic of the modern state is considered to lie in the fact that its power is territorial, that it exerts equal authority over every part of a certain territory, and over every human being and every material object upon, above, or under the surface of that territory. Although an authority so evenly applied may be possible theoretically, it is never in actual existence in any particular state; for special laws and arrangements always modify the situation. For example, lands and property devoted to religious or educational uses, or owned by a foreign nation for its ambassador, are regularly exempted from taxation. Or, again, the government of the United States of America stands in different relations toward the soil of the District of Columbia, the state of Massachusetts, the territory of Alaska, the Philippine Islands, and the Panama Canal Zone.

By the laws of Islam the soil of a conquered land is granted by God as the absolute possession of the *Imâm*, or divinely commissioned prince, who commands the conquering army.[1] Apart from the question as to where the sovereignty rests, this theory of ownership is substantially that of the modern state. The fact that the soil of the Ottoman Empire came into highly complex relationships with the government, therefore, arose not so much from a different fundamental theory as from a greater number of special arrangements based on circumstances and on the personality of religion and law.

---

[1] Hammer, *Geschichte*, iii. 478, and *Staatsverfassung*, 340.

The Ottoman Empire consisted, first, of a great body of lands which were directly administered according to a system that was exceedingly intricate but approximately uniform; second, of a number of regions less directly administered under special regulations; third, of numerous tributary provinces; and fourth, of certain protected or vassal states.   Outside the whole, except where the frontiers were natural, lay a belt of neutral or disputed territory, which tended to be depopulated by continual raids from both sides, only less frequent and terrible in time of peace than in time of war.[1]   The great significance of this belt to the Ottoman people and government was that it furnished a continuous supply of captives for the enormous slave-trade of the empire.   Outside of the raided belt, again, lay the *Dar-ul harb*, or land of war, inhabited either by peoples whose religions were regarded as inferior, or by heretics, whom it was a duty to conquer, at least when practical.[2]   The order in which these several regions are mentioned, an order based on progressive diminution of control, corresponds in general to an increasing distance from Constantinople.   While the Ottoman Empire was growing, each sort of territory tended to absorb the next, proceeding from the center outward.

These lands may be considered rapidly in the reverse order. The territory in which raiding was frequent consisted of a strip extending across Austria-Hungary from the head of the Adriatic in a northeasterly direction, and another band stretching eastwardly across Southern Poland and Russia in the edge of the forest region.   The latter was separated from Crimean Tartary by the steppe land, which the Tartars kept uninhabited in order to afford a free passage to their light horse.   The Persian frontier also lay waste; but the country was too much broken for easy raiding, and Mohammedans, even though heretical, could not

[1] For the Tartar method of raiding in the seventeenth century, see Ricaut, book i. ch. xiii.   This may be compared with Turkish methods in the fifteenth century, as described by the author of the *Tractatus*, ch. v.

[2] D'Ohsson, v. 50.   Orthodoxy in the Moslem religion was by no means an insuperable obstacle to attempts at conquest.   The Mamelukes whom Selim I overthrew were Sunnites, and Malekite Morocco was long a land coveted by the Ottomans.   A desire for the unification of orthodox Islam came into play here.

lawfully be enslaved.[1]   Similar conditions existed on the Moroccan frontier, except that the majority of the inhabitants of Morocco were orthodox Moslems.   Another section that may properly be regarded as one of the raided regions from which slaves and booty were drawn was the Christian shipping on the Mediterranean Sea, and the islands and shores of that sea so far as they were held by Christians.   Crimean Tartary, Georgia, Mingrelia, and parts of Arabia were vassal territories, more or less lightly attached and paying no regular tribute.[2]   Venice's island of Cyprus, the Emperor Ferdinand's possessions in Hungary, the territories of Ragusa, Transylvania, Moldavia, and Wallachia, all paid regular tribute with occasional presents, for the privilege of maintaining their own administrations.   Egypt was under a special government, adapted with slight changes from that of the Mamelukes, headed by a pasha sent out from Constantinople for a term of three years, and delivering a large part of its annual revenue to the imperial treasury.   The Holy Cities of Mecca and Medina, far from paying tribute, received a large annual subsidy at the cost of Egypt.[3]   North Africa, conquered by the Corsairs, was brought into the empire by Khaireddin Barbarossa principally for the sake of prestige and support; but, though in its organization it imitated the parent government, it was seldom in close obedience.

The regions directly administered were divided into districts, or *sanjaks*, each of which had a separate law or *kanun-nameh*, of taxation, which rested upon terms made at the time of conquest.[4]   Parts of the mountain lands of Albania and Kurdistan, and the desert of Arabia, though nominally under direct administration, were in very slight obedience; they retained their ancient tribal organizations, under hereditary chieftains who were invested with Ottoman titles in return for military service, and whose followers might or might not submit to taxation.[5]   The remaining

[1]   D'Ohsson, v. 86.

[2]   The Turks laid claim also to Morocco, but they never exercised abiding authority there: Knolles (ed. 1687), 987.

[3]   Hammer, *Geschichte*, ii. 520–521.

[4]   These are given in detail in Hammer's *Staatsverfassung*, 219–327.

[5]   *Ibid.* 251 (*Kanun-nameh* of the *sanjak* of Kurdistan).

sanjaks, more closely under control, were yet organized in no simple way.

Parcels of land in the great central portion of the Ottoman Empire were in three classes, — the tithe lands (*ersi 'ushriyeh*), the tribute lands (*ersi kharâjiyeh*), and the state lands (*ersi memleket*).[1] The tithe lands had been granted to Mohammedans in fee-simple (*mulk*) at the time of conquest, on condition of paying a relatively small portion (not more than one-tenth) of the produce to the state. The tribute lands had been granted or left to Christians in fee-simple at the time of conquest, on payment of one of two taxes — either a fixed sum for the land itself or a share of the produce — the latter ranging in amount from one-tenth to one-half.[2] The state lands were such as had never been granted in fee-simple, and hence their title remained in the sultan. He received the revenue, however, from only a part of them; for a very large portion had been given to mosques as endowment (*vakf*) for their maintenance and the support of their attendants, or for the benefit of the schools, hospitals, and other buildings attached to them; and another large portion had been granted in fief to Mohammedans, who in return rendered military service on horseback.[3] The comparatively small remainder of the state lands was held as crown domain, administered in a special way by the sultan as owner. The tenants of state lands held title only by lease, or *tapu,* and paid both money and crop rent to the church, the fief-holder, or the crown.[4] All the lands in Europe were regarded as state land,[5] for the Ottomans gave out in fee-simple few lands that were conquered from Christians. Asia Minor was also largely state land; but Syria, Mesopotamia, and Egypt were held under older arrangements, and were mainly tribute lands. Arabia and Bosra were almost wholly tithe lands, as being the oldest Arabian possessions.[6] The fundamental quality of all tribute

---

[1] Hammer, *Geschichte,* iii. 478, and *Staatsverfassung,* 343 ff.; Heidborn, 320 ff.

[2] Hammer, *Staatsverfassung,* 344.

[3] D'Ohsson, vii. 372 ff.; Hammer, *Geschichte,* iii. 475 ff., and *Staatsverfassung,* 337 ff.

[4] Hammer, *Staatsverfassung,* 345.

[5] *Ibid.* 347.   [6] *Ibid.* 344.

land was unchangeable;[1] but original tithe lands which had come into the hands of Christians were temporarily regarded as tribute lands,[2] and lands in fee-simple (tithe and tribute lands) might be devoted by their owners as religious endowments (*vakf*).[3] Original small fiefs might be made into one large one; or a number of persons might come to hold a fief without division of it, provided they jointly furnished the required military service.[4] Many endowments (*vakf*) were made by private individuals for various public purposes; in time, through the attachment of pension provisions and by other devices, a system was built up which had many of the features of the employment of uses under English law.[5]

No small amount of land of every sort went out of cultivation, and after a certain time had elapsed, if the owner was unknown, became state land. If this or any other unoccupied land was brought again under the plow, it might be granted to the new cultivator.[6]

This rapid survey is sufficient to reveal the tangled nature of the Ottoman land system in both its farther and its nearer aspects, and to show why the administration had to become markedly and increasingly bureaucratic. Such a multiplication of relations acted powerfully toward decentralization, since the regulation of countless details could be attended to better from points near at hand; and the immense amount of adjustment to which officials and clerks must devote their time afforded infinite opportunities for corruption and extortion. Suleiman, in his legislation, made a series of efforts to simplify and systematize the situation, and with some success; but he could not remove the causes of the complications, or arrange matters so that they would not eventually become worse than before.

[1] D'Ohsson, v. 96.
[2] *Ibid.*
[3] Belin, *La Propriété Foncière*, 88 ff.
[4] Hammer, *Geschichte*, iii. 476; D'Ohsson, vii. 374.
[5] D'Ohsson, ii. 523 ff., especially 552–557.
[6] Belin, *La Propriété Foncière*, 104 ff.

THE PEOPLES

The wide Ottoman territory held a great number of peoples, marked off by differences of race, language, religion, and customs. The raided belt was inhabited chiefly by Southern Slavs, Germans, Hungarians, Poles, and Russians; and the Christian shores and islands of the Mediterranean chiefly by Greeks, Italians, French, and Spaniards. Accordingly, slaves from all these peoples were constantly forwarded to the center and distributed widely — in the service of the sultan, in the households of the great, and on the estates of country gentlemen. They were treated without prejudice in accordance with their abilities, and in the end the great majority were brought into the Moslem fold, many of them rising to the highest positions. The inhabitants of the tributary states were left in possession of most of their own institutions, but whether to their advantage in the long run is a question open to debate.[1] They were plundered directly by their own princes and indirectly by the Turks, and they had almost no part in the work and life of the empire. The Mingrelians and Georgians captured and even raised children for the slave-trade of the empire proper and of Egypt.[2] The Egyptian fellahs toiled, as they have done through all ages, to produce wealth for their masters, who were now in two bodies — the Mamelukes, recruited as always from slaves of many races, and the group of officials and Janissaries who aided and sustained the Ottoman pasha. The Berbers of North Africa furnished a sufficient task of government to their rulers, who consisted of a body of officials and Janissaries recruited from captives and from the Turks and other inhabitants of southwestern Asia Minor,[3]

[1] Ricaut, 112.

[2] Bernardo, 387 (" like a mine of slaves for the service of the Turks "); Ricaut, 123; Chardin, 85, 90 (" sometimes they will sell their own children "), 94, 114, 192. It is said that the practice of raising Circassian girls for sale is still carried on in Asia Minor (Heidborn, 81).

[3] Ricaut, 138; Postel, iii. 71; Nicolay, 10 (" The most of those who are called Turks in Algiers, whether in the king's household, or on the galleys, are Christians of all nations who have denied their faith and turned Mohammedan — sont Chrestiens reniez et Mahumetizez de toutes nations "); Lavisse and Rambaud, iv. 816, 820.

but connected only at the top with the central government of the empire.

In the region which was under more or less direct administration, Albanians, Servians, Croatians, Bulgarians, and Greeks — in general, the Christian subjects in the Balkan Peninsula — furnished most of the tribute children; but some were taken from the Christians of western and northeastern Asia Minor and the Caucasus region.[1] Kurds and Arabs, being Moslems, could not be enslaved, but they fought for the empire on the eastern frontiers. Armenians and Jews were, by ancient privilege, exempt from both blood tribute and military service.[2]

The principle of the personality of law and religion came most visibly into play in the heart of the empire. Prevalent in the Orient from the time of Assyria's greatness to the present day, it is not easily to be understood in a land that has wholly separated religion and law. Where these two ideas are united, two men who hold different faiths must perforce live under different laws.[3] Islam inherited the idea of the personality of law through the Sassanian Persians, and endeavored to apply it with simplicity by drawing a single line between Moslem citizens (*Muslim*) and non-Moslem subjects (*Zimmi*).[4] The Ottomans adopted the idea unreservedly and worked it out into a complicated system: each considerable body of their non-Moslem subjects, Greek Orthodox, United Greek, Armenian, and Jewish, they left, in time, not merely to its own religion, but to its own law and the administration of its law in all matters that did not concern Moslems.[5] Proceeding yet farther with the same prin-

[1] Nicolay, 83. Jorga, iii. 167–189, has taken note of the ancestry of many of the high Turkish officials of the sixteenth century; he finds no Roumanian among them.

[2] In regard to the Armenians, see Schiltberger, 73; Chalcocondyles, 53. As to both Armenians and Jews, see Navagero, 42; Postel, i. 34. Morosini, 294, makes mention of an Armenian who was in 1585 the *Beylerbey* of Greece by special favor of the Sultan.

[3] Pélissié du Rausas, i. 21–22.

[4] D'Ohsson, v. 104. Visiting foreigners (*muste emin*) who might remain more than one year became tributary subjects (*zimmi*): Belin, *La Propriété Foncière*, 57.

[5] For the times when these different " communities " were formed within the Ottoman state, see Steen de Jehay, *passim*. In brief, the Greek community was

ciple, they granted even greater privileges to foreigners who wished to reside within the empire. Except for a tax upon the land which they might occupy, for the necessity of paying customs duties, and for responsibility to Ottoman courts of justice in civil cases in which Ottoman subjects were concerned, such foreigners were almost wholly free from Ottoman control, freer far to do as they pleased than they could be in their native lands.

Regions existed where nearly all the inhabitants obeyed one law. In Bulgaria and Greece few were not Greek Orthodox. In the interior of Asia Minor few were not, at least legally, Mohammedan. But in the great cities of the empire, and especially in the capital, there was an immense variety of obedience. Not only did the various colonies of foreigners and the various subject nationalities have their separate rights under different systems, but individuals among them, such as ambassadors and clergymen, had special privileges and immunities. Even among the Mohammedans there were various distinctions. Several large classes were privileged, and in different ways, including all the people of court and church, of the army and the law, of government and education. The social and legal structure was thus scarcely less complicated than that of medieval Western Europe, with its interlocking of feudal and official and royal privilege, of clergy and nobility, of free and chartered cities.

INSTITUTIONS OF GOVERNMENT

In the midst of so much territorial complexity and among so many peoples which enjoyed different rights, what unifying institutions did the Ottoman Empire possess? In the largest sense, the government included every organization that could lay claim to any public character, and all of these must be brought into view if there is to be a complete understanding of the conditions. In the first place, however, it is necessary to discover and

organized in 1453 and the Armenian in 1461. The latter was at first supposed to include all subjects who were not Moslem or Greek Orthodox; those who were not Gregorian Armenians were gradually separated off by a process of differentiation which may be said to be active still. With the growth of the spirit of nationalism in the nineteenth century, the Greek Orthodox community has also been divided.

comprehend the genuinely great and powerful institutions. These were two, and not, as is essential to the modern conception of the state, a single one. Each was, it is true, composed of several parts, which may be regarded as distinct institutions in themselves; and yet each had an inherent unity that must be firmly grasped and held if the situation is to be understood.

If names must be assigned to these two great composite institutions, the nearest approximation would perhaps be to call them State and Church. But these words give no adequate idea of them, since each embraced a little less and at the same time far more than is included in the conception of the corresponding Western institutions. They will therefore be described and discussed as the " Ottoman Ruling Institution," and the " Moslem Institution of the Ottoman Empire." The character of each and the distinction between them will become clear as they are explained in detail. For the present, a brief statement of the composition of each and of its function in the government of the empire will suffice.

The Ottoman Ruling Institution included the sultan and his family, the officers of his household, the executive officers of the government, the standing army composed of cavalry and infantry, and a large body of young men who were being educated for service in the standing army, the court, and the government. These men wielded the sword, the pen, and the scepter. They conducted the whole of the government except the mere rendering of justice in matters that were controlled by the Sacred Law, and those limited functions that were left in the hands of subject and foreign groups of non-Moslems. The most vital and characteristic features of this institution were, first, that its personnel consisted, with few exceptions, of men born of Christian parents or of the sons of such; and, second, that almost every member of the Institution came into it as the sultan's slave, and remained the sultan's slave throughout life no matter to what height of wealth, power, and greatness he might attain.

The Moslem Institution of the Ottoman Empire included the educators, priests, jurisconsults, and judges of the empire, and all who were in training for such duties, besides certain allied groups, such as dervishes or monks, and emirs or descendants of the Prophet Mohammed. These men embodied and maintained the whole substance and structure of Mohammedan learning, religion, and law in the empire. They took part in the government by applying the Sacred Law as judges assisted by jurisconsults, and in these capacities they paralleled the entire structure of administration to the remotest corner of the empire.[1] In fact, their system extended to regions where direct administration was not exercised. In the Crimea, for example, the rendering of justice was in their hands, while the other functions of government were performed by a vassal state in light obedience. The situation in Arabia and in North Africa was somewhat similar, though complicated by the presence of rival systems of jurisprudence. In direct contrast to the Ruling Institution, the personnel of the Moslem Institution consisted, with hardly an exception, of men born of Moslem parents, and born and brought up free.

Both these institutions, while uniquely powerful and independent within the empire, were paralleled by lesser institutions, but in different ways. The Ruling Institution was followed closely by the governments of Egypt and North Africa, and less closely by those of the tributary and vassal states; but all these were strictly subordinate, and exercised what authority they possessed only within definite territorial limits. The Moslem Institution was followed closely by the Greek and Armenian and Jewish national institutions, and to some extent by the organization of the foreign colonies. Each of these various institutions rested on a religious organization or theory, cared for the learning, religion, and law of its people, and rendered justice in matters not covered by the Ottoman administration; but all were wholly independent of the Moslem Institution, and, since they were based on personality instead of territory, they exercised jurisdictions which were territorially co-extensive with its jurisdiction and often with the jurisdictions of each other.

[1] Hammer, *Geschichte*, ii. 237.

The two great institutions and the lesser parallel ones included practically all the government of the empire when regarded in its widest aspect.   In the time of Suleiman the Ruling Institution was perhaps of greater power and influence than the Moslem Institution, but the tendency of the latter was to gain upon the former.   Notable progress in that direction was made during his reign, and indeed through his personality.   The policy of both toward the parallel lesser institutions was to prevent them from gaining in power, and, so far as possible, to weaken them. In the former aim this policy succeeded with all but two classes, — the governments of North Africa, which were separated by a sea under their own control, and the organizations of the foreign settlements, which were supported by active and increasing powers outside of the empire.   But the two great institutions were restrained by circumstances and their own inherent structure from extirpating the parallel institutions, and in time they were to cease to weaken them.   The greatest dangers to the whole Ottoman system lay, however, in the rivalry of the two great institutions and in a tendency of the Ruling Institution toward decentralization and division into its component parts.

CONTEMPORARY DESCRIPTIONS OF THE TWO GREAT INSTITUTIONS

Few writers on the history and government of the Ottoman Empire since the sixteenth century have grasped the individual unity, the parallelism, and the contrast of its two leading institutions.   D'Ohsson and Von Hammer understood the Moslem Institution, but missed the conception of the Ruling Institution, the unity of which had disappeared long before their time. Ranke obtained from a few of the Italian writers a very vivid conception of the Ruling Institution, particularly as a slave-family and an army; but he did not see the Moslem Institution in its due proportion and importance.   Zinkeisen, making wider use of the Italians, came nearer than any other to a clear understanding of the whole scheme; yet his exposition does not leave a distinct impression.   Bury, in his lucid chapter in the *Cambridge Modern History*, describes well the *Spahis* and the Janissaries, and notes that many tribute children rose to high positions; but he does not grasp the unity of the Ruling Institution, and he seems hardly at all to see the Moslem Institution. Jorga, the latest to write a general history of Turkey, makes it his avowed purpose to exhibit cultural and institutional growth; he comes near, but does not attain, a distinct conception of the Ruling Institution; while giving especial attention to the renegades who reached high position in the fifteenth and sixteenth centuries, he seems not to recognize how definite, and how intelligently constructed and directed, were the policy and organization which raised them to power.[1]

In order to show how clearly some of the Italian writers of the sixteenth century understood the two institutions, though not under any particular names, translations of certain quotations are subjoined. Since they will serve also to justify the present writer's point of view, no apology need be made for their length.

Andrea Gritti, Venetian orator extraordinary to Bayezid II, in his report to the Venetian senate on December 2, 1503, mentions the highest Turkish officials as follows: — "For affairs of state and every other matter of importance His Majesty is wont to take counsel with the pashas. . . . These are ordinarily four in number, who reside in Constantinople; they are born of Christian parents, seized from the provinces while small, and educated in different places by men delegated for that purpose; raised then to certain positions either through the affection which the Grand Signor bears for them, or by some enterprises valorously carried through, they quickly become very rich, selling, among matters of importance, justice and favors; but when they find themselves at the summit of felicity they live in great danger." [2]

Antonio Barbarigo, Venetian *Bailo* at Constantinople from 1555 to 1560, speaks further of the high officials: " Nor does there exist in this so great empire either superiority or illustriousness of blood, so that any one can glory in his descent, but all

[1] See Jorga, iii. 167 ff., especially 174, 188.
[2] Gritti, 24–25.

are in an equal condition, and they themselves wish to be named and called slaves of the Grand Signor, and their greatest pride is when they say that they are slaves of the Signor; and all his chief men and governors are slaves, and Christian renegades, and sons of Christians brought up from an early age in the seraglio, and then in time, according to their worth, exalted and rewarded and made great by His Majesty." [1]

Marcantonio Barbaro, *Bailo* of Venice at Constantinople from 1568 to 1573, seems to have been the first to discern clearly the contrast of the two institutions.

" It is a fact truly worthy of much consideration, that the riches, the forces, the government, and in short the whole state of the Ottoman Empire is founded upon and placed in the hands of persons all born in the faith of Christ; who by different methods are made slaves and transferred into the Mohammedan sect.   Then whoever will carefully direct his attention to this principal consideration, will come more easily to an understanding of the government and nature of the Turks. . . .

" Other sorts of persons are not ordinarily admitted to the honors and the pay of the Grand Signor, except the above-mentioned, all Christian-born. . . .

" The emperor of the Turks has ordinarily no other ordinances and no other laws which regulate justice, the state, and religion, than the Koran; so that, as the arms and the forces are wholly reposed in the hands of persons all born Christians, so, as I have already said, the administration of the laws is all solely in the hands of those who are born Turks, who bring up their sons in the service of the mosques, where they learn the Koran, until being come of age they are made *kazis* of the land, who are like our *podestas*, and administer justice, although the execution remains in the hands of those who wield arms. . . .

" I have taken much space to demonstrate to your most excellent Signory how the government of this empire is wholly reposed in the hands of slaves born Christians, this appearing to me a matter for much consideration. . . ." [2]

[1] A. Barbarigo, 149–150 (from a summary of his *Relazione*).
[2] Barbaro, 315–329, *passim*.

Gianfrancesco Morosini, Venetian *Bailo* at Constantinople from 1582 to 1585, later made a cardinal of the Roman church, yields to none in the fulness and depth of his observation of the Turks. He too distinguishes clearly the great institutions: —

" There are two sorts of Turks: one of these is composed of natives born of Turkish fathers, and the other of renegades, who are sons of Christian fathers, taken violently in the depredations which his fleets and sailors are accustomed to make on Christian territories, or levied in his own territory by force of hand from the subjects and non-Moslem tax-payers (*carzeri*) of the Signor, who while boys are by allurement or by force circumcised and made Turks. . . . Not only does the greater part of the soldiery of the Turks consist of these renegades, but in yet greater proportion all the principal offices of the Porte are wont to be given to them, from the grand vizier to the lowest chief of this soldiery, it being established by ancient custom that the sons of Turks cannot have these positions. . . .

" To the native Turks are reserved then the governing of the mosques, the judging of civil and criminal cases, and the office of the chancery: from these are taken the *kazis* and the *kaziaskers*, the teachers (*hojas*), and their *Mufti*, who is the head of their false religion; and the *kazis* are like podestas, and render justice to every one, and the *kaziaskers* are like judges of appeal from these *kazis*. . . ."

"_The renegades are all slaves and take great pride in being able to say, ' I am a slave of the Grand Signor '; since they know that this is a lordship or a republic of slaves, where it is theirs to command." [1]

Lorenzo Bernardo was *Bailo* of Venice in Constantinople from 1584 to 1587. After a second period of service in 1591 and 1592 he presented the longest extant report to the Venetian senate on the Ottoman Empire. After describing the principal officers of the Ottoman government at the time he says in his involved style: —

" These are they, in whom is reposed not only the whole government of the state, but also the command of all the arms

---

[1] Morosini, 263–267, *passim*.

of this so great an empire; and yet these are neither dukes, nor marquises, nor counts, but all by origin are shepherds, and persons base and vile; wherefore it would be well if this most serene republic, imitating in this direction the Grand Signor, he who from this sort of persons, his slaves, creates and makes the best captains, *sanjaks* and *beylerbeys*, giving them in this way credit and reputation. . . . .

" Just as the whole government of the affairs of the state and the command of its arms is reposed in the hands or the control of slaves by origin Christian, and then made Turks by various accidents; so the government of the affairs which look toward justice, and all the charge of affairs of religion are located in the hands of native Turks, sons of Turks, who having been educated in the universities instituted by the Grand Signor and the present ministers, and made learned in their laws, which consist, both civil and criminal, in no other teaching than that of the sole book, the Koran, become *imâms*, or priests, who govern mosques; *kazis*, or podestas; *hojas*, or preceptors of great men; and finally *kaziaskers*, or judges of supreme appeal, of whom there are only two, the one in Asia and the other in Europe; and the head of all these and supreme in their religion is the *mufti*, like the pope among us, who is chosen by the Grand Signor." [1]

Lastly, Matteo Zane shall speak, Venetian *Bailo* in Constantinople from 1591 to 1597. In the imperfect record of his vigorous report, the illustrious diplomatist says: " The Turks are partly natives and partly renegades; the natives, who live for the most part in Asia, are in comparison with the renegades less depraved and less tyrannous, because they still have in them some religion, which the others have not, — the most arrogant and scoundrelly men that can be imagined, having seemingly with the true faith lost all humanity. This alienation from religion is fitting in desperate characters, who are induced to it by licentious freedom of life, and by seeing placed in their hands the arms, the government, the riches, and in short the whole empire, excluding the native Turks, who are admitted only to the careers of justice,

---

[1] Bernardo, 358–364, *passim.*

as that of *kazi* and the like, and to those of religion, such as *mufti, hoja,* and *imâm,* as is very well known." [1]

The impending break-down of the system near the close of the sixteenth century is also set forth clearly by Zane: " The government of the Turkish Empire is suffering within itself so many and such great alterations, that one may very reasonably hope, divine aid mediating, for some notable revolution within a short time, because the native Turks continue to sustain the greatest dissatisfaction, from seeing all the confidence of the government reposed in the renegades, who, at a tender age for the most part, are taken into the seraglio of the king or of private citizens, and made Turks.   To the renegades is committed not merely the care of arms, but the entire command and the execution of the acts of justice of the *kazis* (although they do not allow appeals), and the superintendence of religion; whence one may say that they rule everything and that the native Turks are their subjects as are servants to their masters; which was not true in other times to such excess as at present." [2]

To these testimonies from Italian writers may be added a paragraph written about 1603 by the great English historian of Turkey, Richard Knolles.   Knolles shows no acquaintance with the Moslem Institution, but his recognition of the Ruling Institution is good: —

" The *Othoman* Government in this his so great an Empire, is altogether like the Government of the Master over his Slave, and indeed meer tyrannical; for the Great Sultan is so absolute a Lord of all things within the compass of his Empire, that all his Subjects and People, be they never so great, do call themselves his Slaves and not his Subjects; neither hath any man power over himself, much less is he Lord of the House wherein he dwelleth, or of the Land which he tilleth, except some few Families in *Constantinople,* to whom some few such things were by way of reward, and upon especial favour given by *Mahomet* the Second, at such time as he won the same.   Neither is any man in that Empire so great, or yet so far in favour with the Great Sultan, as that he can assure himself of his Life, much less

---

[1] Zane, 389.   [2] *Ibid.* 414.

of his present Fortune or State, longer than it pleaseth the Sultan. In which so absolute a Sovereignty (by any free born People not to be endured) the Tyrant preserveth himself by two most especial means; first, by taking off all Arms from his natural Subjects; and then by putting the same and all things else concerning the State and Government thereof into the Hands of the Apostata, or Renegade Christians, whom for the most part every third, fourth, or fifth Year (or oftner, if his need so require) he taketh in their Child-hood, from their miserable Parents, as his Tenths or Tribute Children; whereby he gaineth two great Commodities: First, For that in so doing he spoileth the Provinces he most feareth, of the flower, sinews, and strength of the People, choice being still made of the strongest Youths, and fittest for War; then, for that with these, as with his own Creatures, he armeth himself, and by them assureth his State; for they, in their Child-hood, taken from their Parents Laps, and delivered in Charge to one or other appointed for that purpose, quickly, and before they are aware, become Mahome-tans; and so no more acknowledging Father or Mother, depend wholly on the Great Sultan; who, to make use of them, both feeds them and fosters them, at whose hands onely they look for all things, and whom alone they thank for all. Of which Fry, so taken from their Christian Parents (the only Seminary of his Wars) some become Horse-men, some Foot-men, and so in time the greatest Commanders of his State and Empire, next unto himself; the natural Turks, in the mean time, giving them-selves wholly unto the Trade of Merchandise, and other their Mechanical Occupations; or else to the feeding of Cattel, their most ancient and natural Vocation, not intermedling at all with matters of Government or State." [1]

[1] Knolles (ed. 1687), 982.

CHAPTER II

THE OTTOMAN RULING INSTITUTION: AS A SLAVE-FAMILY

I. General Description

Perhaps no more daring experiment has been tried on a large scale upon the face of the earth than that embodied in the Ottoman Ruling Institution. Its nearest ideal analogue is found in the Republic of Plato, its nearest actual parallel in the Mameluke system of Egypt; but it was not restrained within the aristocratic Hellenic limitations of the first, and it subdued and outlived the second. In the United States of America men have risen from the rude work of the backwoods to the presidential chair, but they have done so by their own effort and not through the gradations of a system carefully organized to push them forward. The Roman Catholic church can still train a peasant to become a pope, but it has never begun by choosing its candidates almost exclusively from families which profess a hostile religion. The Ottoman system deliberately took slaves and made them ministers of state; it took boys from the sheep-run and the plow-tail and made them courtiers and the husbands of princesses; it took young men whose ancestors had borne the Christian name for centuries, and made them rulers in the greatest of Mohammedan states, and soldiers and generals in invincible armies whose chief joy was to beat down the Cross and elevate the Crescent. It never asked its novices, " Who was your father ? " or " What do you know ? " or even " Can you speak our tongue ? "; but it studied their faces and their frames and said, " *You* shall be a soldier, and if you show yourself worthy, a general," or, " *You* shall be a scholar and a gentleman, and if the ability lies in you, a governor and a prime minister." Grandly disregarding that fabric of fundamental customs which is called " human nature," and those religious and social prejudices which are thought to be almost as deep as life itself, the Ottoman system took children forever from parents, discouraged family cares among its members through their most active years, allowed them no certain hold on property, gave them no definite promise that their sons and daughters would profit by their success and sacrifice, raised and lowered them with no regard for ancestry or previous distinction, taught them a strange law, ethics, and religion, and ever kept them conscious of a sword raised above their heads which might put an end at any moment to a brilliant career along a matchless path of human glory.

The members of this system were, in a general way, as long as they lived, at once slaves, proselytes, students, soldiers, nobles, courtiers, and officers of government. To be understood fully, the institution should be considered from each of these points of view. The aspects which were of central and controlling importance, however, were those of war and government; the others were preparatory or accessory. Furthermore, the sultan was the head and center of the institution in every one of its aspects. He gave it its unity, its vigor, and its propelling force. Although his despotic power was limited in many directions, it knew no limits with regard to the members and the mechanism of this institution. The person, the fortune, the property, and the life of every member lay in his hand.[1]

The absolute character of the sultan's authority was an element of great strength to the institution, but it contained also the possibility of a great danger. To manage the system well required an almost superhuman intelligence. The sultan held the position of Deity toward his slaves, and he needed the omniscience and benevolence of Deity to exercise his power wisely and justly. Unfortunately, his position, which controlled the whole scheme, was the only one that was filled by the uncertain lot of heredity. While strong men came to the throne, the system worked out marvellous results. When weak men were to come, as happened immediately after Suleiman, the system was to begin to fall apart into dangerous fragments. Yet its

[1] Ricaut, 14–15.

vitality was so strong that it lived on through nearly three centuries of alternate decline and rehabilitation, and its spirit may almost be said to abide still.

The Ruling Institution contained certain component parts, which were capable of separate existence, and some of which at times tended to escape complete control. Among these the best-known, though not intrinsically the most important, was the body of permanent infantry known as the Janissaries. They represented the brute force of the system and its most dangerous element. Another component institution was the permanent cavalry, the *Spahis* of the Porte.[1] These were more numerous than the Janissaries, but being better educated and encouraged by the presence of greater opportunities, they were not so dangerous. A third important sub-institution was the hierarchy of governing officials. Although these had great power, they could be dealt with individually; and the sword was never far from their necks. Subordinate bodies of a secondary influence were the *Ajem-oghlans*, or apprentice Janissaries, and the colleges of pages, which trained many of the *Spahis* of the Porte and most of the officers of government. Each of these component parts will be dealt with in its proper place. Theoretically, and except at certain junctures practically, they were strictly subordinated to the main institution and yet fully incorporated with it. The Ruling Institution as a whole will be considered as a slave-family, a missionary institution, an educational system, an army, a court, a nobility, and a government.

II. THE SLAVE-FAMILY

Every one who belonged to the Ruling Institution in any capacity from gardener to grand vizier, save only the members of the royal family, bore the title of *kul*, or slave, of the sultan.[2]

---

[1] These *Spahis* of the Porte are to be distinguished from the body of feudal *Spahis*. See below, pp. 98–105.

[2] This is illustrated by the quotations in the last section of Chapter i, above. See also Menavino, 138 (referring to the pages, he says " Tutti sono suoi schiaui & figlioli Christiani "); Ricaut, 14 (all who receive pay or office from the sultan are called *kul*); D'Ohsson, vii. 203 (" Les employés civils de même que les mili-

Nor was this title a mere form: with few exceptions, all members entered the system as actual slaves, and there was nowhere along the line of promotion any formal or real process of emancipation. The power of the sultan over the lives, persons, and property of the members of the institution, and his right to their absolute obedience, bear every mark of having been derived from the idea of slavery. The very word despot means by derivation the master of slaves, and it was only over his *kullar* that the sultan's power was despotic in the fullest sense.[1]

Entrance to the system came by the door of slavery, which was open regularly only to Christian boys from ten to twenty years of age. It is an error, found in some writers even lately, to name eight years as the usual age.[2] The correct limits are given approximately by many contemporary writers.[3] It is probable that the preferred ages were between fourteen and eighteen, and that only in exceptional cases were boys taken before the age of twelve or after the age of twenty.

taires, suivant l'antique usage de l'Orient, sont assimilés aux esclaves du Souverain, et qualifiés de ce nom — couil — dans toutes les pièces publiques "). In D'Ohsson's time the term had acquired such a general usage as in the English phrase " your obedient servant." Della Valle, i. 44, speaking of the entry to the Divan, says, " Tutti sono schiavi; " and Ranke, 9, says, " All were slaves."

[1] D'Ohsson, vii. 149, 207.

[2] For example, Lodge, *The Close of the Middle Ages* (1906), 500; Myers, *Medieval and Modern History* (1905), 165.

[3] The *Tractatus*, ch. viii, says simply 20 years and under; Zeno, 128, says above 10 years. Ramberti and Junis Bey (below, pp. 244, 263) mention pages from 8 to 20 years old; Navagero, 49, says between 12 and 15 years, Trevisano, 229, says that they were taken not at the age of 6 or 7 years as formerly, but at 10 or 12 years. Postel, iii. 23, sets between 12 and 14 as the lower limit, and 18 and 20 as the upper limit. Nicolay, 62, says that the pages were from 8 to 20 years of age; Garzoni, 396, says that they ranged from the tenth to the thirteenth year; Ricaut, 74, fixes the age at 10 or 12 years. Too much reliance should not be placed on Trevisano's statement as to former times, since hearsay evidence as to Turkish affairs is unreliable. Considering the rougher life in earlier times, it is likely that levies would then have been made of older, rather than younger, boys. The presence of young boys among the pages was due to the selection of unusually promising captives.

METHODS OF RECRUITING

Four methods were employed for obtaining recruits for the system, — by capture, purchase, gift, and tribute. Of these only the last is commonly considered;[1] but it was originally, and probably always, merely supplementary to the others.[2] The four methods ultimately rested on two. Slaves who were bought for the sultan or given to him had nearly all been either taken as captives or levied illegally with the tribute boys; there was hardly any other way, since slaves passed too rapidly into the Moslem fold to have their children available for the system. As to the comparative numbers obtained by the different methods there are few data for calculation. Probably about three thousand tribute boys was the annual average in the sixteenth century,[3] but there is no reason to think that this was a majority in the number of annual recruits. The whole number in the system may be estimated at about eighty thousand.[4] Since the losses by war were sometimes tremendous, it is probable that the average annual renewal required was as much as one-tenth, or between seven and eight thousand. On this basis the tribute boys furnished somewhat less than one-half of the whole number. These calculations are, of course, more or less arbitrary.

It is true that children of *Spahis* of the Porte might be admitted to the college of pages at the pleasure of the sultan, but their

[1] Myers (as above) mentions the two methods of capture and tribute as successive.

[2] Djevad Bey, i. 26: "Ces prisonniers ou esclaves étaient d'ailleurs incorporés dans l'armée des Janissaires, et alors l'effectif qui manquait était complété par la voie de la levée de troupes parmi les sujets chrétiens."

[3] Ramberti and Junis Bey (below, pp. 254, 270) say that 10,000, or 12,000 were taken every 4 years. Geuffroy, 242, and Postel, iii. 23, give the same estimate. Ricaut, 74, says he is "given to understand" that about 2000 were collected yearly in the middle of the seventeenth century. The exigencies of war probably increased the number greatly at times. Bérard, 12, naming no authority, says that in some years Suleiman took 40,000 boys.

[4] 20,000 *Ajem-oghlans*, 12,000 to 14,000 Janissaries, 10,000 of the auxiliary corps, grooms, etc., 40,000 *Spahis* of the Porte (including the 12,000 members of the four corps and the followers they were obliged to bring), 2000 pages and high officials. Suleiman took with him on his last campaign 48,316 men under pay (Hammer, *Staatsverwaltung*, 181). Morosini, 259, says that in 1585 the sultan had under pay 80,000 men. This is exclusive of about one-half of the *Ajem-oghlans*.

grandchildren and the children of all other Moslems were excluded by rigid rules.[1] These rules began to be invaded about the close of Suleiman's reign by the admission of the sons of Janissaries,[2] an innovation that was of ultimately fatal import to the system. A certain number of adults were also received and some of these were sons of Moslems; exceptional individuals from among the irregular troops were admitted to the *Spahis* of the Porte by way of reward,[3] and that body contained a Foreign Legion of about two thousand, composed of renegade Christians, Arabs, Nubians, and the like.[4] Occasionally, also, some high official of Suleiman's government had been born a Moslem.[5] But the total effect of all these exceptions was so slight as to cause them to be disregarded by more than one contemporary observer.[6]

The original homes of the captives have been described.[7] By the Sacred Law the sultan was entitled to one-fifth of all captives taken in war;[8] and he chose as his share, through agents, such young men as seemed suitable for a place in his system.[9] Since by special Ottoman regulation the sultan's fifth belonged to the church, he was accustomed to pay twenty-five aspers to the church for each slave that he took.[10] His officers also purchased in the public slave-market of the capital such youths as were available.[11] These came from the captives that the Tartars of the Crimea took in great numbers, from the quasi-slave-farms of the Caucasus,[12] from the irregular raids in

---

[1] Postel, i. 20.

[2] See below, p. 69, note 3.

[3] Postel, iii. 36.

[4] See below, p. 99, note 1.

[5] For example, Piri Mohammed, a descendant of the thirteenth-century poet, Jelal ad-din Rumi. Cf. Hammer, *Geschichte*, iii. 18.

[6] Notably Junis Bey, who says (below, p. 265), "None can be a pasha except a Christian renegade." This custom is said to have been established by Bayezid II (Angiolello, 74, quoted by Jorga, ii. 306, note 2). For further instances, see the last section of Chapter i, above.

[7] See above, p. 33.

[8] D'Ohsson, v. 91.

[9] Schiltberger, 5, gives an early example. See also *Tractatus*, ch. viii.

[10] Hammer, *Geschichte*, i. 167.   [11] Zeno, 127.

[12] Zeno is strongly impressed by these two sources.

Austria, and from the corsair expeditions. The sultan received a large number of boys as gifts, since it was well known that no presents were more acceptable.[1] Those who desired his favor kept a lookout for such as would please him.

THE TRIBUTE BOYS

Although the levying of tribute boys in the Christian provinces of the empire seems not to have produced the majority of neophytes for the system, the practice has always received a share of attention far beyond its numerical importance. Several reasons for this suggest themselves. In the first place, it rested on a unique and almost unparalleled idea; then, it involved an extraordinary disregard of human affection and of the generally acknowledged right of parents to bring up their children in their own law and religion;[2] and, finally, it produced the ablest and highest officials of the system.[3] In the latter respect its youth seem to have borne some such relation to those obtained by capture as the cultivated fruits of the garden do to those gathered in the woods.

The levying was accomplished by a regular process, the *devshurmeh*. Normally every four years, but oftener in case of need,[4] a body of officials more skilled in judging boys than trained horse-dealers are in judging colts were sent out by the government to the regions from which tribute was taken.[5] The whole of the Balkan Peninsula, Hungary, the western coast of Asia

[1] Postel, iii. 17–18. It was in this way that Menavino entered the system (see his *Trattato*, 10).

[2] Cf. Postel, iii. 23.

[3] A study of the nationality of the high officials of the sixteenth century gives evidence of this. For example, Ibrahim was an Albanian (Junis Bey, below, p. 265); Rustem Pasha was a Croat (Hammer, *Geschichte*, iii. 268); Ferhad was a Hungarian (*ibid.* 365); the grand vizier Ali, whom Busbecq (*Life and Letters*, i. 157) calls "a thorough gentleman," was a Dalmatian; Ayas was an Albanian, and Kassim a Croat (Junis Bey, p. 265); etc. For many other examples, see Jorga, iii. 167–189.

[4] The *Tractatus*, ch. viii, says every 5 years; Spandugino, 102, says once in 5 years or oftener; Zeno, 128, says each year; Ramberti and Junis Bey (below, pp. 254, 270) say every 4 years; Postel, iii. 22, says every 3 or 4 years.

[5] *Tractatus*, ch. vi.

Minor, and the southern and eastern shores of the Black Sea were included in the territory visited; but the strongest and ablest youths came from the mountain regions inhabited by Albanians and the Southern Slavic peoples.[1] The recruiting officers were commissioned each to bring in a certain number, which had been apportioned to them out of a total determined at the capital.[2]   There was no principle of tithing, and no fixed proportion or number of boys was levied from each village or family;[3] the quota desired from each district was obtained for the government by selection of the most available youths.   The recruiting officers sometimes collected a larger number than was asked for, and sold the surplus on their own account to high officials or wealthy private citizens.[4]   A regular procedure was followed.   The officers obtained from the Christian priest of the village a list of the boys whom he had baptized, and who were between the ages of twelve and twenty years or thereabouts.[5] All these were brought before the officers, who selected the best.[6] Parents who had strong and well-favored sons might lose them all, while those who had weaklings would lose none.[7]   On leaving each village, the officer took with him the boys whom he had

[1] Giovio, *Commentarius*, 75; Zeno, 128; Nicolay, 83.   Jorga, iii. 188, finds no Roumanian among the high Turkish officials of the sixteenth century.   Roumania, being a vassal state, was not exposed to the *devshurmeh*.   Knolles (ed. 1687, pp. 984–985) says that the tribute boys from Asia were not advanced to become Janissaries, because they were not of sufficiently high quality.   They are not found in positions of prominence.

[2] Navagero, 48.

[3] Menavino's translator says *quasi decimatione* (Lonicerus, i. 140).   Postel, iii. 22–23, says expressly that the children were not tithed; Nicolay, 83, however, states that one in three were taken, as does J. Soranzo, 245.   Morosini, 264, speaks of a tithe (*decima*).   Gibbon (ed. Bury), vii. 79, says that a fifth of the boys were taken; see also Lavisse and Rambaud, iv. 758.   The latter statements seem to be based theoretically on the fifth of the captives to which the sultan was entitled. The differences among those who profess to fix a proportion are evidence that there was none.

[4] Spandugino, 103.

[5] Postel, iii. 22.   Navagero, 49, says that the officers summoned the heads of families and commanded them to present their sons.

[6] Navagero, 49.

[7] Postel, iii. 23.

selected; and, when his quota had been gathered, he took them to the capital.[1]

ESTIMATE OF THE SYSTEM

This levying of boys as tribute has always elicited a great amount of moral indignation, as representing an extreme of oppression, heartlessness, and cruelty. The religious factor has increased the odium of the custom. Certainly no argument can be found which will justify it to those who believe in the liberty of the individual, the absolute right of parents over minor children, and a complete withdrawal of human beings from the category of property, — principles which seem in the sixteenth century to have had no place in Ottoman philosophy or jurisprudence, at least as regards Christian subjects. It may be said at once that the custom cannot be brought into harmony with Western ideas. So much being granted, how did the system bear upon the parents who were despoiled and the boys who were taken ?

In the midst of the conflicting testimony of reputable witnesses, it is evident that the parents of tribute boys did not all feel alike. The grief at parting was often a heart-breaking thing to witness; [2] the mother whose son was taken by force to an unknown life among enemies of all that she had been taught to hold dear would hardly have suffered more at the death of her son. At the same time, she might hope to see him one day in the possession of great wealth and power. It is not to be supposed that youth taken at from twelve to twenty years of age would ever forget their parents; and, if they lived and prospered, they would sometimes seek them out, as did Ibrahim, even though they might not try his unfortunate experiment of bringing them up to the capital.[3] Fathers would appreciate the opportunities

---

[1] Navagero, 49.   [2] Postel, iii. 23.

[3] Geuffroy, 240. Bragadin (1526), 103, says: " Ibrahim has his mother and two brothers in the palace. He does much good to Christians. His father is *Sanjak* in Parga." And again, 104: " Ayas has three brothers. His mother at Avlona is a Christian, and he sends her 100 ducats annually." Nicolay, 86, says, on the contrary, that the tribute boys are never afterwards willing to recognize father, mother, or relatives. He cites the case of an uncle and nephews of Rustem Pasha, who begged in Adrianople, but received no aid from him. Cf. Zane, 438.

which arose before their sons much more than would the mothers. Both would be more or less reluctant to let them go, according as their Christian religious convictions were deep or shallow. Parents who wished to keep their sons would sometimes marry them in tender years, since married boys were ineligible; those who had means bought exemption for their sons from the recruiting officers, who thus reaped great rewards.[1]   On the contrary, many parents were glad to have their sons chosen, knowing that they would thus escape from grinding poverty,[2] receive a first-rate training suited to their abilities, and enter upon the possibility of a great career.   Some parents, in fact, came to regard the process as a privilege rather than a burden;[3] and they had reason to do so, since Turkish parents envied them the opportunity, and sometimes tried to evade the regulations by paying Christians to take their Moslem sons, and declare them as Christian children, so that they might be enrolled as the sultan's slaves.[4]   Apart, then, from political theory and religious prepossession, the levying of tribute children was by no means a mere evil to the parents.

The situation of the boys themselves, considered under the same reservations, was almost wholly favorable.   They were taken at an age when they would not feel the parting as they might have felt it in earlier or later years, when their attachment to things and places would be at its weakest, and before their religious convictions were likely to have become fixed.   They were taken from the narrow mountain valleys and the labor-hungry plains.   They were taken at the age when the bounding pulse and the increasing strength of youth suggests great hope and promises great achievement.   They were taken to opportunities as great as their utmost abilities, greater often than they could possibly imagine.   They might still have to labor for a time, but a distinct career lay ahead.   The best military educa-

---

[1] Spandugino, 144, 145.

[2] Trevisano, 130.

[3] *Ibid*.

[4] Bernardo, 332, says in 1592, after the system had been dislocated, that the greater part of the recruits were then sons of Turks.

tion in the world would certainly be theirs. If their abilities lay in that direction they could have a finished and thorough, though specialized, education of the mind. They could look forward to travel, wealth, power, and all else that human ambition desires. In that land and that age of the world, the question of the religious and social systems being laid aside, an unprejudiced observer could hardly imagine a more brilliant opportunity than that which lay before the tribute boys.

THE SLAVE STATUS

Whether captured, purchased, presented, or levied, the young men who entered the system were the slaves of the sultan, the personal property of a despot. They were his slaves for life, and, though they felt honored by the title,[1] they were never allowed to forget the responsibilities of their condition. They must to the end of their days go where the sultan chose to send them, obey his slightest wish, submit to disgrace as readily as to promotion,[2] and, though in the highest office of state, they must accept death by his order from the hands of their humblest fellow-slaves.[3] If one of them was executed, all his property went to his master. The time had not yet come when heads would be removed for the sake of the owner's possessions; yet Suleiman profited greatly by the death of several of his slaves, in particular from the estates of the *Defterdar* Iskender Chelebi and the grand vizier Ibrahim.[4] When one of the sultan's slaves died leaving sons or daughters, the master sealed up his property, and took the tenth part for himself before distributing the rest to the children;[5] the nine-tenths was, indeed, given to the children rather by the favor of a bountiful and wealthy master than as a right. If the slave had no sons or daughters, the sultan took his whole estate;[6] and a day was to come when his

---

[1] Erizzo, 131; Morosini, 267; Ricaut, 14.

[2] Spandugino, 180.

[3] *Ibid.* 183; J. Soranzo, 250.

[4] Hammer, *Geschichte*, iii. 144, 156, 162.

[5] Postel, iii. 68.

[6] *Ibid.* G. Soranzo (1576), 197, says that the Grand Signor is heir of all the pashas.

empty treasury would demand the whole estate under all circumstances.[1] Thus in all essential respects the eighty thousand *kullar* of the sultan constituted one great slave-family.

THE HAREM, THE EUNUCHS, AND THE ROYAL FAMILY

Two or three less numerous but highly important groups may properly be discussed in the present connection. The imperial harem and the imperial family itself were virtually parts of the same slave system.[2] The harem of Suleiman was not the large and costly institution that was maintained by some of his successors; like his father Selim,[3] he was not given to sensuality, but is said to have been faithful to Khurrem from the time that he made her his wife.[4] The character of an Oriental royal harem has often been set forth incorrectly. While it may contain hundreds or even thousands of women, a very few of these are the actual consorts of the monarch. A large number are the personal servants and entertainers of himself, his mother, his consorts, his daughters, and his infant sons. Another section consists of those who are being educated for the same personal service. A fourth group, probably the great majority, are mere house-servants, who attend to all the domestic labors of the harem and are seldom promoted to more honorable positions. There is, finally, a group of older women who preserve order and peace, teach, keep accounts, and manage the establishment generally.[5]

Suleiman's harem contained about three hundred women, who were kept in a separate palace well fortified and guarded.[6] His harem fully deserves to be reckoned as part of the great slave-family, since all its inmates except his children were pur-

---

[1] D'Ohsson, vii. 147. In the seventeenth century the sultan allowed the children of pashas only what pleased him (Ricaut, 131). Morosini, 274, refers to a similar practice in the latter part of the sixteenth century.

[2] Ricaut, 16, calls the Turkish court " a prison of slaves."

[3] Hammer, *Geschichte*, ii. 379.

[4] Busbecq, *Life and Letters*, i. 159.

[5] D'Ohsson, vii. 61 ff.

[6] Spandugino, 77; Ramberti, below, p. 253; Junis Bey below, p. 268; Nicolay, 64.

chased or presented slaves.[1] These women, brought for the most part from the region of the Caucasus,[2] and including in their number some of the fairest female captives of many lands, were nearly all daughters of Christians. Khurrem herself was a Russian, while the rival of her youth seems to have been a Circassian.[3] In another respect the harem deserves to be reckoned with the Ruling Institution, in that its inmates, upon attaining the age of twenty-five, were, if they had not attracted the sultan's special attention, as a rule given in marriage to distinguished *Spahis* of the Porte.[4]

A comparatively small group, not hitherto mentioned, of the attendants at the sultan's palace and harem belong within the slave-family. Although the Sacred Law strongly disapproved of the employment of eunuchs, that unfortunate class was thought too useful to be dispensed with entirely. Some were white, brought mainly from the Caucasus region; but the great majority were negroes brought from Africa. Tribute children seem rarely to have been made cunuchs.[5] The class deserves mention because several of the important offices of state among the " men of the pen " were held by eunuchs, and now and then one rose to high place in the army or the administration.[6]

The royal family also may rightly be included in the slave-family. The mothers of the sultan's children were slaves; the sultan himself was the son of a slave; and his daughters were married to men, who, though they might be called vizier and

---

[1] Spandugino, 78, is probably wrong in his statement that the girls of the harem were recruited from gifts, *tithes*, and *tribute*. The small number of women in the harem would make the elaborate process of tribute-taking unnecessary.

[2] Postel, i. 34.

[3] Navagero, 75; Jovius, *Historiarum*, ii. 371. But Bragadin, 101, calls her a Montenegrin, and Ludovisi, 29, an Albanian; while Busbecq (*Life and Letters*, i. 178) says that she came from the Crimea. Gomara indicates that her Turkish name was Gul-behar, the Rose of Spring (Merriman, *Gomara's Annals of Charles V*, 141). This confusion of knowledge in regard to so important a personage gives evidence of the secrecy which surrounded the sultan's harem.

[4] See below, p. 79, note 2.

[5] Hammer, *Geschichte*, i. 232. Spandugino, 69, says that many were made such. Menavino, who was himself a page, says that very few were so treated, and only for punishment (*Trattato*, 138).

[6] Spandugino, 69; Busbecq, *Life and Letters*, i. 237.

pasha, wore these titles at the sultan's pleasure, whereas they bore indelibly the title of *kul*, or slave.[1] The sultan's sons, though they might sit upon the throne, would be the consorts of none but slaves. Long before Suleiman's time, the sultans had practically ceased either to obtain brides of royal rank, or to give the title of wife to the mothers of their children.[2] Suleiman, given to legality and religious observance, and greatly devoted to the lovely Roxelana, made her his lawful wife. Since, by the Sacred Law, the status of the mother as wife or slave does not affect the legitimacy of the children if the father acknowledges them,[3] all children born in the harem were of equal legitimacy and rank.

OTHER OTTOMAN SLAVE-FAMILIES

The ruling institution of any state is apt to be copied in miniature by many organizations within the same state. The municipalities of Rome, and the state and city governments of the United States, were each modeled after the central government. In a similar way, every great officer of the Ottoman court built up a slave-family after the model of the Ruling Institution. The grand vizier had a very large establishment; the viziers had somewhat smaller ones; the governors of provinces had households in proportion to their incomes;[4] and each adult prince kept a miniature government. Not only the slave-

---

[1] Menavino, 143; " Schaiui chiamati Bascia [pasha]."

[2] Busbecq, *Life and Letters*, i. 112. Selim I, married a princess, daughter of the Khan of the Crimean Tartars. This appears to have been the last of such alliances, of which there were a number in earlier times.

[3] D'Ohsson, vi. 9.

[4] *Ibid.* vii. 177. In 1537, Junis Bey (below, p. 265) says that Ayas had 600 slaves, Mustapha 200, Kassim 150, Barbarossa 100. But this account must contain misprints or errors; for Ramberti (below, p. 246) says that in 1534, Ibrahim had more than 6000 slaves, Ayas 2000, Kassim 1500, and Barbarossa about 4000. Bragadin, 103, said in 1526, that Ibrahim had 1500 slaves. Mustapha 700, Ayas 600. Junis Bey (256-258) says further that the *Beylerbeys* of Rumelia and Anatolia and Caramania had 1000 slaves each, the *Beylerbey* of Syria 2000, the *Beylerbey* of Cairo 4000, etc. Iskender Chelebi had 6000 slaves (Hammer, *Geschichte*, iii. 144). Geuffroy, 240, says of the viziers: " Tous ont saray de femmes et d'enfans comme ledict grant Turc." See also Menavino, 143; and Ramberti's description of Alvise Gritti's household at the close of his third book.

family feature but all the other features of the Ruling Institution were imitated. All deemed it meritorious to purchase Christians and turn them into Moslems. Iskender Chelebi had a highly successful educational system;[1] he also kept a little standing army, and at a later time so did Rustem.[2] Each great officer protected his slaves, each kept them about him like a court, each used them as a little government to rule his affairs. Such imitation might easily become a danger to the state, but ordinarily a prompt remedy could be applied. Every such household was strictly personal; it was gathered about a living man; that man was ordinarily himself a slave of the sultan: let him show the least movement toward treason, and his head would be removed, his property would come to his master, his household would be incorporated with the central slave-family, all danger would be at an end, and the sultan would only be the stronger. Further safeguards lay in the close relations of the head of each slave-family to the sultan, and in the fact that some *Spahis* of the Porte and other imperial *kullar* of inferior position seem usually to have been attached to the suite of each great official.[3] Moslem private citizens also kept slave-families as numerous as they could afford,[4] but these could hardly become dangerous under any circumstances. They might emulate the missionary and educational character of the greater households, but they would not dare attempt any imitation of the military features. Further, the whole Ottoman system so discouraged great accumulations of wealth that private citizens could never hope to compete with the power of officials and of the sultan.

---

[1] Hammer, *Geschichte*, iii. 157. Seven of his slaves became viziers and grand viziers, among them Mohammed Sokolli.

[2] Iskender Chelebi was followed to war by 1200 horsemen (Hammer, *Geschichte*, iii. 144). Rustem trained 200 carbineers as part of his household (Busbecq, *Life and Letters*, i. 242).

[3] Garzoni, 413, says that 1000 *Spahis* were assigned to the retinue of the grand vizier, and 500 to those of each of the other pashas.

[4] *Tractatus*, ch. vii.

CHARACTER OF OTTOMAN SLAVERY

Ottoman slavery was a very different institution from that which Anglo-Saxons have practised. In it there could ordinarily be no color-line, and therefore no ineffaceable distinction. Where difference in color existed it counted for nothing, by old Islamic customs. Nor did the fact of slavery impart any indelible taint. Islam knew slave and free; [1] in the Ottoman Empire, at least, it knew no intermediate class of freedmen. [2] The sultan seems never to have emancipated his slaves, probably because of a lingering Oriental theory, foreign to Mohammedanism, [3] that all his subjects were his slaves. Private citizens had the power of emancipation, [4] and they often exercised it as a meritorious act. The slave who was set free was immediately in possession of full rights. [5] Slavery had therefore no inherent quality. It was merely an accidental misfortune from which complete recovery was possible. The idea of Aristotle, that some men are born to be slaves, was wholly absent.

Where no permanent wall of separation exists, natural human affection can have free play. The Moslem religion teaches kindness and benevolence to all but armed enemies of the faith. [6] Moslem masters, in constant personal association with persons whose condition led them to strive to please, were apt to become very friendly toward them. Such friendliness often led to warm affection and the bestowal of benefits. Emancipation was one of these; and, further, not only the sultan but many of his subjects did not hesitate to give their daughters in marriage to worthy slaves. [7] A slave was often beloved above a

---

[1] D'Ohsson, i. 49.

[2] In the early days non-Arab converts held a position of clientage, but they had never been slaves. In the Ottoman Empire new converts were particularly honored, so that this distinction was lost. A partial enfranchisement was possible, and might sometimes resemble the condition of a Roman freedman. Cf. D'Ohsson, vi. 28 ff.

[3] According to D'Ohsson, v. 86, no free-born Moslem could ever lawfully become a slave.

[4] D'Ohsson, vi. 24.   [5] *Ibid.*   [6] *Ibid.* iv. 300 ff.

[7] Spandugino, 180. It may be observed that Ottoman slavery bore no slight resemblance to the method of bondage which brought from Europe many ancestors of present-day Americans. " In the year 1730," says Mrs. Susannah Willard

son;[1] it was felt that, while a son possessed a character which was more or less a matter of chance, a slave had been selected. Thus it is clear why the sultan's slaves were sometimes called his children,[2] and why the title of *kul* was prized.[3] Suleiman was a stern, and sometimes a cruel parent to his great family; but he was as just in rewarding as in punishing, and it is not surprising that all his slaves were true to him.[4]

Thus was woven what has well been termed " a wonderful fabric of slavery." [5] History may have known as large a slave-family, but certainly none that was more powerful and honorable, better provided for and rewarded, more obedient and more contented.

Johnson (in her *Narrative of Captivity* reprinted Springfield, 1907, pp. 5–6) " my great-uncle, Colonel Josiah Willard, while at Boston, was invited to take a walk on the long-wharf, to view some transports who had just landed from Ireland; a number of gentlemen present were viewing the exercise of some lads who were placed on shore to exhibit their activity to those who wished to purchase. My uncle spied a boy of some vivacity, of about ten years of age, and who was the only one in the crew who spoke English: he bargained for him. I have never been able to learn the price; but as he was afterwards my husband, I am willing to suppose it a considerable sum. . . . He lived with Colonel Willard until he was twenty years of age, and then bought the other year of his time." In this account a number of the characteristics of the Ottoman system can be observed. Young boys of Caucasian blood are taken from their native land; they are bought and sold; they are judged like young animals by appearance and physical activity; no taint attaches to their bondage; they may marry into the master's family. The one noteworthy difference is that the bondage terminates at a definite age.

[1] *Tractatus,* " Oratio Testimonialis ": " Denique domino meo ita carus eram, ut saepius in collocutione plurium, plusquam filium suum, quem unicum habebat, me diligere assereret," etc.

[2] Postel, iii. 20, says that all the pages were considered children of the sultan, and were truly his adopted sons.

[3] Ricaut, 14.   [4] Postel, iii. 21.   [5] Ricaut, 16.

CHAPTER III

THE RULING INSTITUTION: AS MISSIONARY
ENTERPRISE AND EDUCATIONAL SYSTEM

I. The Missionary Motive

ALTHOUGH almost every member of the governing group in the Ottoman Empire had been born a Christian, it was absolutely necessary for his advancement that he should profess the Moslem faith. A keen contemporary observer knew of only one Christian who had been entrusted with great power. Alvise Gritti was allowed to hold special command in Hungary, but this appointment was made outside the system, as a personal affair of the grand vizier Ibrahim, without the concurrence of the sultan.[1] Various Christians were employed in such matters as the superintendence of ship-building and cannon-founding;[2] but this was a purely commercial relationship, and such a man had no place in the *cursus honorum*. The fundamental rule, open to the few exceptions previously described, was very simple. Every member of the Ruling Institution must have been born a Christian and must have become a Mohammedan.

A number of questions arise at once. 'Why were none but sons of Christians admitted ? Why was conversion essential to promotion ? What was the process of accomplishing conversion ? How thorough was the conversion ? Why were the sons of most of the converts, and the grandsons of practically all, carefully pushed out of the system ?

The first of these questions might be answered in terms of policy of state; but since, in all Moslem thinking, church, state, and society form one undivided whole, such an answer would be inadequate. Conversion to Mohammedanism meant much more than an inward change and an outward association for religious purposes with a new group of worshippers. It meant

---

[1] Postel, iii. 21.   [2] *Ibid.* 71–72; Ramberti, below, p. 255.

the adoption of a new law for the whole of life, beginning with the religious and ethical, but including as equally essential portions the regulation of all social, commercial, military, and political relationships.[1] It meant admission to a new social system, naturalization in a new nation, an entire separation from the old life in all its aspects and a complete incorporation with the new. Expansion of membership was always a cardinal principle of Mohammedanism; and the expansion was to be not merely by the aid of the sword, but far more by peaceful means. The sword took the land and sometimes the body of the unbeliever; but his soul was to be won by the benefits of the system, first religious, then social, financial, and political.[2] Every nation that has reached eminence has believed firmly that its general system was immensely the superior of every other in the world, and no nations have been more thoroughly convinced of this than those of Moslem faith. Accordingly, their desire to convert the unbeliever was founded primarily on benevolence. Closely connected with this motive was a burning interest in the grandeur of Islam as a militant, expanding system; and subordinate thereto was a purpose to increase the wealth, numbers, and power of the state.

The Ottoman Attitude

The Ottoman system incorporated young Christians not merely to obtain more faithful, more obedient, and more single-hearted servants, but, before and beyond this, to obtain new members of the Ottoman nationality, new believers in the Moslem faith, and new warriors for the Ottoman Empire as representing Islam. This missionary purpose stands out very clearly in the words attributed to Kara Khalil Chendereli, the traditional founder of the corps of Janissaries, by a poet-historian of the early sixteenth century, who no doubt here, as elsewhere in his writings, introduced the ideas of his own day: " The

---

[1] Hammer, *Staatsverfassung*, 12.

[2] According to Sale's translation, the Koran says (Sura 2: 257), " Let there be no violence in religion." Palmer translates, " There is no compulsion in religion." See D'Ohsson, vi. 59; Schiltberger, 73.

conquered are slaves of the conquerors, to whom their goods, their women, and their children belong as a lawful possession; in converting the children to Islam by force, and in enrolling them as soldiers in the service of the faith, one is working for their happiness in this world and their eternal salvation. According to the words of the Prophet, every infant comes into the world with the beginnings of Islam, which, developing in an army formed of Christian children, will encourage even in that of the infidels the ardor of conversion to Islam; and the new troop will recruit itself not merely with the children of the conquered, but also with a crowd of deserters from the enemy, united to the believers by common origin or pretended opinions."[1] The sentiment of this declaration is woven of two strands, both ultimately religious, — a desire to convert great numbers to Islam, and a purpose to strengthen the army which wars for the faith.

Mohammed the Conqueror expressed the same idea poetically in a letter to Uzun Hassan: " Our empire is the home of Islam; from father to son the lamp of our empire is kept burning with oil from the hearts of the infidels." [2]   This declaration seems to reveal two things. First, the Conqueror asserts that, since by Moslem theory there can be but one *Dar ul-Islam*, or land of Islam, his empire is the sole lawful Moslem state; second, he declares that, by the policy of his house, the empire derives its strength from the ever-renewed supply of Christians. Whether this exegesis be exact or not, the fact is indisputable that the fundamental missionary spirit of Islam was strong in the Ottomans of the sixteenth century,[3] and that the Ruling Institution was deliberately conducted for the purpose, among others, of transferring the ablest and most useful of the subject Christians in each generation into the dominant nation. As the first Western observer who comprehended the system remarked,

---

[1] Idris, fol. 107, quoted in Hammer's *Geschichte*, i. 91.

[2] Quoted *ibid*. ii. 117.

[3] Ricaut, 147–148: " No people in the World have ever been more open to receive all sorts of Nations to them, than they, nor have used more arts to encrease the number of those that are called *Turks*."

" This comes from no accident, but from a certain essential interior foundation and cause, which," he feels it his Christian duty to say, with a helpless admiration, " is desperation of good, and obstinacy in evil, and . . . is the work of the devil." [1] Not only did Mohammedanism encourage the practice of taking in outsiders to serve, fight, and aid in ruling, but this practice was thoroughly in harmony with the old Turkish spirit which prevailed in the steppe lands, and a similar policy had been followed by the Byzantine Empire. Thus, in encouraging the incorporation of foreigners the three great influences which met in the Ottoman state had exerted a combined activity as perhaps in no other direction. The Ruling Institution acted for centuries as a great steadily-working machine for conversion.

Other Motives for Incorporating Christians

Besides the combined religious and national purpose which led to the introduction of Christian youth into the system, other motives helped to give it definite shape. That purpose alone would hardly have caused a rigid rule to be laid down which would exclude Mohammedans. Here, undoubtedly, the well-known tendency of governments that rest on force to rely upon servants brought from a distance and owing all to their favor came strongly into play.[2] The sultan's *kullar* were uniformly faithful to the hand that had raised them from poverty to high position. " Being all slaves by condition, and slaves of a single lord, from whom alone they hope for greatness, honor, and riches, and from whom alone on the other hand they fear punishment, chastisement, and death, what wonder that in his presence and in rivalry with each other they will do stupendous things ? " [3] Having expected ill treatment from the enemies of their nation, they were drawn by the surprising contrast to deep gratitude and boundless devotion;[4] they were not attached to interests and traditions of family and property which would prevent full and loyal obedience; they learned what was taught

---

[1] *Tractatus*, ch. viii.　　[3] Bernardo, 369–370, and see also 359.
[2] Ricaut, 46.　　[4] Postel, iii. 21.

them by their master's command, and were not possessed by ideas and prejudices that would make them independent in mind and intractable. On the contrary, Moslems born and bred in pride of religion and nationality could not easily be moulded to the shape desired; the very title of *kul* was out of harmony with their beliefs; hence they were inherently unavailable for the system, and the recognition of this fact led to their rigid exclusion. An important reason for excluding children of renegades was that heredity of privilege and office was against Ottoman policy. The immunity from taxation that was enjoyed by the sultan's officials would tend to the building up of vast fortunes that would be beyond the reach of public taxation;[1] and the power of great families entrenched behind large property interests would in time endanger the supremacy of the throne.[2]

THE REQUIREMENT OF CONVERSION

Conversion was a principal object of the system, and favor and promotion waited as rewards upon acceptance of the Moslem faith. In fact, a young man was not fitted to participate in the system until he had turned Moslem. He could not be an Ottoman warrior and statesman and fail to profess and practise, in most respects, at any rate, the system which inspired his fighting and on whose principles the state rested. The garment was seamless: it must be either worn or not worn.

At the same time, conversion of the neophytes of the Ruling Institution seems not ordinarily to have been forcible.[3] The

---

[1] *Ibid.* 20.   [2] Ricaut, 128 ff.

[3] The general Ottoman attitude on this point is shown by Schiltberger, 73: Mohammed " has also ordered, that when they overcome Christians, they should not kill them; but they should pervert them, and should thus spread and strengthen their own faith." *Tractatus*, ch. xi, says, " Turci neminem cogunt Fidem suam negare, nec multum instant de hoc alicui persuadendo, nec magnam aestimationem faciunt de his qui negant." The last clause of this testimony, however, is contrary to practically all other sources. Conversion seems sometimes to have been forced as an alternative to death when a Christian had offended greatly against the Mohammedan faith (Lonicerus, i. 123; see also D'Ohsson, vii. 327). Some writers, however, assert that circumcision, the outward mark of acceptance of Islam, was regularly enforced upon the tribute boys (Chesneau, 41; J. Soranzo, 245; Morosini, as quoted above, p. 41). Heidborn, 128, says that conversion was not anciently enforced on a large scale, *except* for the recruiting of Janissaries.

Ottomans were too wise to believe that the best results could be accomplished by such means. Their policy was rather to throw every difficulty in the way of remaining a Christian, and to offer every inducement to make the Moslem faith and system seem attractive. To this end their educational scheme helped greatly;[1] for it involved complete isolation from Christian ideas of every sort, and complete saturation in all the ideas of Mohammedanism, religious, moral, social, and political. Even those whose education was mainly physical were isolated from Christians in a strict Moslem environment. No doubt there were special rejoicings and rewards when a *kul* was ready to declare, " There is no God but Allah and Mohammed is His Prophet," as there were in like circumstances in the rest of the Ottoman world.[2] But the *kullar* seem not to have been urged to change their faith; on the contrary, an attitude of apparent indifference was sometimes taken with them.[3] Probably, however, few who remained long in the system failed to surrender sooner or later. Prejudices of childhood would in time be overcome; what the majority did would tend to act powerfully upon the individual; the reward of a brilliant career would take clearer and more alluring shape, until in time, in the absence of all contrary suggestion, the real truth and value of the Mohammedan religion would make it appear to be the only worthy system. It is not surprising that the scheme seemed to Christians one of diabolical ingenuity.

What went on in the sultan's slave-family in regard to the conversion of slaves went on in every Mohammedan household. Conversion was desired but not compelled, and reward awaited it.[4] Among female slaves also, even in the imperial harem, the same process was employed. Not merely the imperial slave-family, but the entire system of slavery that existed in the Otto-

---

[1] Ricaut, 46 ff.

[2] Schiltberger, 74; La Broquière, 219; Spandugino, 249. Ricaùt, 152, says that great inducement was offered the common people to become Turks; they obtained honor and the privilege to domineer and injure with impunity, and they became in the fashion.

[3] *Tractatus*, ch. xi, quoted above.

[4] D'Ohsson, vi. 59; Ricaut, 148.

man Empire, was thus a great machine for the conversion of Christians into Turks.

SINCERITY OF CONVERSION

It is not easy to learn what thoughts possessed the hearts óf the members of the Ruling Institution. Enough is recorded, however, to show that not all who turned Moslem did so without mental reservation, and to prove that it was possible to hold fast to an inward belief in the superiority of Christianity through many years spent in the sultan's service. It has been said sometimes that the converted Christians were more severe than the Moslems toward their brethren who remained steadfast.[1] This would be natural both because of the zeal of new converts, and because Christianity is intrinsically less tolerant than Mohammedanism; but the accusation does not seem to be supported as against the members of the Ruling Institution. A distinction must be drawn between behavior in time of war and in time of peace. The Janissaries were fierce fighters and terrible enemies; but religiously they belonged to a sect which was so liberal as to be accused of rank heresy, and even, it is said, to have been denied the name of true believers.[2] Many of the renegades were persons who held no sort of religion.[3] The grand vizier Rustem told Busbecq, after offering him great rewards if he would turn Moslem, that he believed in the salvation of those of other faiths;[4] and a *deli*, or scout, in his service confided to a French gentleman that, while he pretended to follow Mohammedanism, he was a Christian at heart.[5] The fact that a Genoese boy, taken at twelve years of age, educated as a favored page for eight or nine years, and evidently trained carefully in Mohammedan beliefs, would seize the first opportunity to escape shows what was possible beneath the surface.[6] Two generations earlier there was a renegade who cursed the day when he had

---

[1] *Tractatus*, ch. v; Nicolay, 86.
[2] Ricaut, 284.
[3] Bernardo, 367; Zane, as quoted above, p. 42. See also Jorga, iii. 188.
[4] Busbecq, *Life and Letters*, i. 235.
[5] Nicolay, 160–161.   [6] Menavino, 244.

turned Turk, but who felt that he could not go back.[1] Nor were the members of the system always submissive to the stricter rules of Mohammedan ethics. The Janissaries, for example, forced Bayezid II to reopen the wine shops of the capital, which in the religious fervor of his later years he had ordered closed;[2] and the members of the government were led by fondness for display and lavish expenditure into shameless venality, the cause and the effect being equally contrary to the teachings and example of Mohammed. The probability is that large numbers of the sultan's slaves were merely nominal Mohammedans in religious belief, though they necessarily followed the larger part of the Moslem scheme of life.

EFFECT OF THE PROCESS

Sons of Janissaries were not allowed to become Janissaries, although the rule began to be infringed about the end of Suleiman's reign.[3] Sons of *Spahis* of the Porte might be admitted as pages and to the corps of *Spahi-oghlans*, but their grandsons were rigidly excluded.[4] Sons of great officials were provided with fiefs, or pensions, and so usually passed out of the Ruling Institution into the territorial army.[5] Thus few were allowed in the scheme beyond the first generation in the Moslem faith, and almost none beyond the second. The explanation of this has been given already: descendants of renegades were Moslems, and hence subject to the same disqualifications as members of Mohammedan families of long standing. Not all Moslems of the empire were counted Ottomans, or, as they called themselves, Osmanlis, or, as they are commonly called nowadays, Turks;

---

[1] *Tractatus*, ch. xxi.

[2] Hammer, *Geschichte*, ii. 351.

[3] Georgevitz (before 1552), 40, " De Ordine Peditum "; Ranke, 19–20; Barbaro (1573), 305, 317. Selim II, on his accession granted to the Janissaries the formal privilege of entering their sons in the corps; for the Persian war of 1594 the corps was opened to other Turks and all Moslems. By 1592, the majority of the Janissaries were said to be sons of Turks; Bernardo, 332. See also Knolles (ed. 1687), 985.

[4] Postel, iii. 20.

[5] *Kanun-nameh* of Mohammed II, printed in Hammer's *Staatsverfassung*, 94.

for Arabs, Kurds, and other Mohammedans who had not adopted the Turkish language did not bear the Turkish name. But all the descendants of members of the Ruling Institution were added to the Ottoman-Turkish nationality. The total number of Janissaries in the three centuries during which they were recruited from Christian children has been estimated at five hundred thousand;[1] but, as reckoned above, the tribute boys furnished less than one-half of the recruits of the institution,[2] and the page system persisted in its original form after the Janissaries had become hereditary. From one to two millions of the flower of the Christian population must have been brought into the Ottoman nation by the operation of the Ruling Institution.

It does not necessarily follow that a like number of new Turkish families were thus founded. The Janissaries were not supposed to marry, although the rule was not strictly enforced;[3] a hundred years later, at any rate, the majority are said to have been unmarried.[4] As the *Spahis* of the Porte probably married late, when they married at all, the whole system had thus something of a monastic aspect.[5] High officials, it is true, were apt to keep harems of some size; yet the children even of these were ordinarily few in number.[6] Furthermore, the frequent fierce wars carried off many of the sultan's slaves, and the danger of execution and of confiscation of property put a check on their establishment of families. It is probable, therefore, that the Ruling Institution, like most great slave-families, was wasteful of human life.[7] But although its Christian-born members may not have

[1] Hammer's *Geschichte*, i. 94.

[2] See p. 49.

[3] Spandugino (1517), 108, says that the Janissaries are not allowed to marry. He was probably wrong. Certainly some were married soon after his time: Ramberti (1534), below, p. 249; Junis Bey (1537), below, p. 267; Nicolay (1551), 92.

[4] Ricaut, 366.

[5] The resemblance of the Janissaries to monks is noticed by Busbecq, *Life and Letters*, i. 88, and Tavernier, 12.

[6] Ricaut, 151.

[7] One careful observer thought that this might be true of the whole Ottoman nation. *Ibid.*, but in the middle of the fifteenth century contrary testimony was given (*Tractatus*, ch. xi).

perpetuated their numbers, they nevertheless increased the Ottoman nation by the addition of such children as were born to them; and the Moslem descendants of these, sailing in quieter waters, doubtless became, both numerically and otherwise, a great strength to the nation.

II. THE EDUCATIONAL SCHEME

Plato would have been delighted with the training of the sultan's great family, though his nature would have revolted from its lowliness of birth. He would have approved of the life-long education, the equally careful training of body and mind, the separation into soldiers and rulers (even though it was not complete), the relative freedom from family ties, the system's rigid control of the individual, and, above all, of the government by the wise. Whether the founders of the Ottoman system were acquainted with Plato will probably never be known, but they seem to have come as near to his plan as it is possible to come in a workable scheme. In some practical ways they even improved upon Plato, — as by avoiding the uncertainties of heredity, by supplying a personal directing power, by insuring permanence through a balance of forces, and by making their system capable of vast imperial rule.

In the largest sense the Ruling Institution was a school in which the pupils were enrolled for life. Constantly under careful drill and discipline, they advanced from stage to stage through all their days, rewarded systematically in accordance with their deserts by promotions, honors, and gifts, and punished rigorously for infraction of rules, while both rewards and punishments increased from stage to stage until the former included all that life under the Moslem scheme could offer, and the latter threatened to take away the life itself. The system also cared for all sides of the nature of its pupils, subject to the considerable limitation that it was especially a school of war and government. The bodies of all were trained as thoroughly as were the minds of the best. Though all received some mental training, including at least an acquaintance with the Moslem mode of life, the ablest were put through a severe course in Oriental languages and Moslem and Ottoman law, which embraced ethics and theology. Thus both body and mind, as well as the religious nature, were provided for systematically and through life. Looked at thus, the Ottoman educational scheme, in its relations to the whole lives of those under instruction, was more comprehensive than any Western institution of learning. The officers of a Western army are educated and organized in a life-long system which provides for both body and mind; but they do not learn theology and they do not govern the nation. Great American railroads and manufacturing corporations possess schemes of education and advancement which bear comparison to the Ottoman system in life-long scope, promotion for merit, and the possibility of rising from the bottom to the top; but the mental training which they give even to their ablest helpers is of a highly technical sort, which bears no comparison to the general learning and finished culture bestowed upon the most studious in the Ottoman scheme. In general, Western universities and educational systems, although they far surpass the Ottoman scheme in the scope and character of the intellectual training which they give, do not provide a comparable systematic training of the body; and their control over the lives of their students ceases early. The superior comprehensiveness of the Ottoman system was, of course, based upon the fact that its members were slaves. Their master could keep them at school all their lives, in order that they might become better and better trained to serve him. At the same time, reward was considered more potent than the rod. Unequalled prizes were offered in this school, so skilfully disposed and graded as to call out the utmost strivings and the best work of every pupil.

The first stages of the wide scheme, which constitute the educational system in its narrower sense, were a fitting introduction to the rest. All the recruits for the sultan's slave-family, whether captured, bought, presented, or levied, to the number of probably three or four thousand annually, with an addition of ten or twelve thousand in the years of the *devshurmeh*,[1] were brought by a regular process before trained officials, carefully

---

[1] See the calculation above, p. 49.

registered, and divided into two classes.[1] Those who best satisfied the criterions of bodily perfection, muscular strength, and intellectual ability so far as it could be judged without long testing,[2] — about one in every ten of the whole number, — were chosen for a superior quality of training, especially on the intellectual side. The remainder were destined for a different education, which was mainly physical.[3] The first regularly became pages and *Spahis* of the Porte, and the ablest of them rose to the great offices of the army and the government. The others regularly became *Ajem-oghlans* and Janissaries, but the ablest of these might also rise to positions as *Spahis* of the Porte and even as generals and officers of state.[4] Failure to be selected for the higher school was not, therefore, a final restriction to low position. Merit was recognized everywhere, and regularly led to promotion. At the same time, it was a distinct advantage to a young man to be chosen for the higher training, since he would receive greater care, would acquire more of both ornamental and useful learning, and would associate with those already great, and perhaps with the sultan himself.

THE COLLEGES OF PAGES

Of those selected for the higher training, a portion were distributed among the households of the provincial governors and high officers at the capital.[5] These were probably brought up in much the same way as if they had remained with the sultan. The very choicest of the recruits, to the number of perhaps two hundred annually, or twelve to fifteen hundred in all,[6] were

---

[1] Navagero, 50; Barbaro, 316; Nicolay, 84. J. Soranzo, 245, states that the tribute boys were all brought to Constantinople, circumcised, and brought before the *Agha* of the Janissaries. Record was made of the name of each, of his father's name, and of his native place. Soranzo's accuracy is questionable, as when he says that the greater part were put into palaces in Constantinople.

[2] Postel, iii. 17; Ricaut, 46.

[3] Ricaut, 74: "In whom appearing more strength of body than of mind, they are set apart for labor and menial services."

[4] Busbecq, *De Re Militari*, 260.

[5] Spandugino, 104: the emperor chooses a few and sends the rest to the towns of the Turks of Anatolia to live with the lords and gentlemen.

[6] Spandugino speaks of 900; Junis Bey and Ramberti, 1400; Geuffroy, 1200; Postel, 1300 to 1500.

taken into three palaces of the sultan as *Itch-oghlans*, or pages. Three or four hundred were in the palace at Adrianople,[1] a like number in one at Galata,[2] and from five to eight hundred in the principal palace at Stamboul.[3] These were all handsome boys, physically perfect, and of marked intellectual promise. An excellent idea of the international character of the college is given by a Venetian writer, who said that the pages of the palace included Bulgarians, Hungarians, Transylvanians, Poles, Bohemians, Germans, Italians, Spaniards, a few French, many Albanians, Slavs, Greeks, Circassians, and Russians.[4]

The *Itch-oghlans* were dressed in suitable raiment and were well cared for without luxury.[5] That the sultan took a particular interest in the arrival of excellent specimens is evident from the reception that Menavino received.[6] The general Ottoman attitude toward the pages, and indeed toward all recruits, has been well expressed by a thoughtful observer: " The Turks rejoice greatly when they find an exceptional man, as though they had acquired a precious object, and they spare no labor or effort in cultivating him; especially if they discern that he is fit for war.   Our plan [that is, in Western Europe] is very different; for if we find a good dog, hawk, or horse, we are greatly delighted, and we spare nothing to bring it to the greatest perfection of its kind.   But if a man happens to possess an extraordinary disposition, we do not take like pains; nor do we think that his education is especially our affair; and we receive much pleasure and many kinds of service from the well-trained horse, dog, and hawk; but the Turks much more from a well-educated man (*ex homine bonis moribus informato*), in proportion as the nature of a man is more admirable and more excellent than that of the other animals." [7]

---

[1] Junis Bey and Ramberti, 300; Geuffroy, 300.

[2] Junis Bey and Ramberti, 400; Geuffroy, 400; Postel (iii. 20), 600 or 700.

[3] Junis Bey and Ramberti, 700; Geuffroy, 500; Postel (iii. 3), 700 or 800.

[4] Navagero, 42. See also Tanco, 205.

[5] Menavino, 13. Postel, iii. 17, says that, when presented, they were clothed in silk and cloth of gold or silver; but Ricaut, 49, says that their clothing and diet were simple.

[6] Menavino, 11 ff.

[7] Busbecq, *De Re Militari*, 262–263.

That the primary object of the page system was educational appears from all contemporary observations. Not merely are their palaces termed " places for nourishing youths," [1] but Menavino calls the place where he was taught " the palace school." [2] Another writer gives chapters on " The Education of Young Men in the Seraglio," and " The Studies and Learning in the Seraglio," [3] and speaks of the young men as " designed for the great offices of the empire." Another says, " And the said emperor does this good for the profit of his soul, and when they are grown up he takes them from there and gives them dignities and offices, according as it seems to the emperor they have deserved." [4] Some of the pages were the personal servants of the sultan, and a band of thirty-nine constituted his gentlemen of the bedchamber, or *Khas Oda*.[5] These were the élite of all, chosen by selection after selection; and, though young, they ranked very high in the system. Since only a few of all the pages could attain to this honor, the remainder were at school for outside service.[6]

Besides many less direct descriptions of the course of training, two exist which are derived from men who passed through the palace school. Menavino tells his own story; [7] and Ricaut

[1] Postel, iii. 2.

[2] Menavino, 126.

[3] Ricaut, chs. v–vi.

[4] Spandugino, 63. See also Nicolay, 84; and the quotations in the last section of Chapter i, above.

[5] D'Ohsson, vii. 34.

[6] Hammer (*Geschichte*, i. 232), by a singular perversion of the truth, asserts that the page system had its origin and primary purpose in the satisfaction of the unnatural lusts of Bayezid I and his successors. Not only does the whole structure and organization of the system disprove this, but the absence of reference to such a purpose in all contemporary writers is sufficient to settle the matter. The vice which takes its name from Sodom was very prevalent among the Ottomans, especially among those in high position (Spandugino, 186; Busbecq, *Life and Letters*, i. 232; Ricaut, 151, 211; D'Ohsson, iv. 473). The pages were apt to be afflicted by it, and were carefully watched to prevent it, and terribly punished if discovered (Ricaut, 60). Occasionally a sultan became enamored of a page (Ricaut, 61); but Suleiman seems to have been free from this vice (Busbecq, i. 159; Marini Sanuto, *Diarii*, December 6, 1523).

[7] Menavino, 126–128. He was a page from about 1505 to 1514 (*ibid.* 243–245).

records what he learned from a Polish captive who had spent nineteen years in the sultan's service and had reached high position.[1] Although these accounts were written one hundred and fifty years apart, they agree in essentials. Menavino does not refer to the physical training in arms and horsemanship; but at the time of his escape he showed himself, if not a courageous, yet an accomplished horseman. Postel, some twenty years after Menavino's time, describes this training in some detail. He probably had his information from a French page named Cabazolles, whom he quotes as authority on one point.[2]

The pages were trained in the art of war, the use of all sorts of arms, and good horsemanship.[3] Suleiman took especial delight in watching their cavalry evolutions, and occasionally summoned a page who pleased him, conversed with him, and dismissed him with presents.[4] Also, by old Oriental custom, every page was taught some handicraft useful in his master's service, and, no doubt, intended to provide for his own support in case of need.[5]

Menavino describes the course of study in the so-called *Yeni Oda*, or New Chamber, which contained from eighty to a hundred boys. " When a boy has remained five or six days in that school, they set him to learning the alphabet. There are four teachers in the school. One drills the boys in reading during their first year. Another teaches the Koran in the Arabic (*Moresco*) language, giving explanations of the different articles of their faith. After this a third teaches books in the Persian tongue, and some write a little, but they do not teach writing willingly. A fourth teaches Arabic books, both vulgar and literary." It is interesting to notice that, from the first, rewards in the form of

[1] Ricaut, " To the Reader," 45–62. This describes the system as it was about 1650.

[2] Postel, iii. 11.

[3] *Ibid.* 19; Ricaut, 50.

[4] Postel, iii. 10; Ricaut, 50.

[5] Ricaut, 51. The same custom was observed in the education of the princes and of all children of great officials (Spandugino, 179). Tanco, 197–198, says he has heard that Suleiman himself labored daily at a trade, so that even the Prince should earn his bread by the sweat of his brow; see also Jorga, ii. 343.

pay were given for labor. " These boys," continues Menavino, " have a daily allowance of two aspers during the first year, three during the second year, four during the third year, and thus their allowance increases each year. They receive scarlet garments twice a year, and some robes of white cloth for the summer." [1] Postel describes how they learned with great diligence Arabic and Turkish letters and the law.[2] Ricaut explains 'in more detail that the chief object of the course of study was to teach reading and writing for the purpose of giving inspection into the books of law and religion, especially the Koran. He says that Arabic was taught to enable the boys to inspect the writings of the judges and to have knowledge of religion, Persian to give them quaint words and handsome and gentle deportment, and adds that both tongues might be needed in governing Eastern regions. He gives a list of their text-books, and remarks that those who wished to become men of the pen studied with greater exactness. They were not, he says, taught logic, physics, metaphysics, mathematics, or geography, and their knowledge of ancient history was much mixed. " Yet as to the successes and progress of Affairs in their own Dominions," he adds, " they keep most strict Registers and Records, which serve them as Presidents and Rules for the present Government of their Affairs." [3] This shows that the pages were instructed in Turkish history and the various *Kanun-namehs*, or imperial laws. Most of the teachers were Anatolian Turks,[4] chosen no doubt, as imparting better pronunciation and more orthodox religious views.

Discipline was severe,[5] but was kept within bounds. A page could be beaten on the soles of his feet with no more than ten strokes, and not more than once on any one day.[6] The boys, organized in groups of ten, were watched carefully by eunuchs, both day and night.[7] Absolute obedience, modest behavior and

---

[1] Menavino, 126, 127.
[2] Postel, iii. 10.
[3] Ricaut, 59.
[4] Navagero, 43.
[5] Ricaut, 48, says that in the three colleges of education the eunuchs exercised very severe discipline beyond that of monks.
[6] Menavino, 127.
[7] Ramberti, below, pp. 244, 245; Junis Bey, below, p. 263; Ricaut, 49.

decorum, and good manners were taught with great insistency.[1] The two sections, or *odalar*, at the palace seem to have been of equal rank,[2] while the schools in Pera and Adrianople ranked lower.[3] Select boys who had finished their studies were promoted through the different chambers of the personal service of the sultan to the Inner Chamber,[4] where twelve or fifteen of the thirty-nine held titular offices.[5] On reaching the age of twenty-five every page was sent out from the school.[6] Those from the Inner Chamber passed at once to places in the Noble Guard (*Muteferrika*), or to governorships of towns.[7] Ibrahim passed almost directly to the place of grand vizier;[8] but he was the first to break the regular order of promotion, and in after times much evil was held to date from the precedent.[9] The majority passed into the regular cavalry, or *Spahis* of the Porte.[10] Those who left the school were honored by a ceremony of farewell. The sultan personally commended each one, and gave him encouragement for good conduct in his new position. He presented each with an embroidered coat and one of his most beautiful horses, and often a gift in money. The young man, with all the presents he had received during his stay, was escorted to the great gate, where he mounted his horse triumphantly, and departed from the palace forever.[11]

THE HAREM

Probably because of the tendency of the human mind to construct along parallel lines, the imperial harem partook of the characteristics of the schools of pages. There were two

[1] Ricaut, 49: " Their first Lessons are silence, reverence, humble and modest behaviour, holding their heads downwards, and their hands across before them."
[2] *Ibid*. 48.   [3] D'Ohsson, vii. 47.
[4] Ricaut, 51; D'Ohsson, vii. 34 ff.   These chambers were the *Kiler-odassi*, or Pantry; the *Khazineh-odassi*, or Treasure Chamber; the *Khas-odassi*, or Inner Chamber.   See below, pp. 126–128.
[5] Ricaut, 52.   [6] Postel, iii. 11.   [7] Spandugino, 62.
[8] Hammer, *Geschichte*, iii. 32.   [9] *Ibid*. 490.
[10] Ramberti (below, p. 244) says that they became *Spahi-oghlans*, *Silihdars*, and officials of higher degree according to their worth and to the favor which they had gained with the sultan; Junis Bey, below, p. 263.
[11] Menavino, 138.

odalar, or rooms, for the recruits of the harem, in which they were taught housework, sewing and embroidery, manners and deportment.[1] They were organized in groups of ten, each group under a matron. Those with a taste for music and dancing learned those accomplishments, those who were studious learned to read and write. All were carefully instructed in the system of Islam. Like the pages, nearly all of them passed out of the palace at the age of twenty-five, being given in marriage to *Spahis* of the Porte or to other officials.[2] Thus the harem might be considered a training-school of slave-wives for the sultan himself and for the most highly honored of his *kullar*.

THE AJEM-OGHLANS

The term *ajemi-oghlanlar* signifies "foreign youth," and was sometimes applied to all the young recruits. Ordinarily, however, it was given only to the remainder left after the pages had been selected. These, for the most part destined to become Janissaries, probably numbered about twenty thousand.[3] Their training was largely physical, industrial, and military, with oral instruction in the Turkish language and the principles of the Mohammedan system. The *Ajem-oghlans* usually passed through two or three stages. Unless they knew Turkish and something of Turkish ways, they were first scattered through Asia Minor in the service of Moslem country gentlemen.[4] There they were set at hard agricultural labor, to strengthen their bodies to the utmost. They were expected to learn to speak and understand the Turkish language and to learn the faith, the laws, and the customs of the Turks. The sultan allowed them no pay. The

---

[1] Ricaut, 71; Postel, i. 33; Nicolay, 64; D'Ohsson, vii. 64.

[2] Ramberti, below, p. 254 ("he marries them to Spahi-oghlans, or to others of the slaves of the Porte according to the degree and condition of both parties "); Junis Bey, below, p. 269; Geuffroy, 244; Chesneau, 40; Nicolay, 64.

[3] Trevisano, 130, speaks of 16,400; but this number does not seem sufficient to account for all.

[4] Chalcocondyles, 97; Spandugino, 103; Ramberti, 255; Junis Bey, 270; (they are sent "to dig earth in order to learn Turkish "); Zeno, 127; Geuffroy, 243: Navagero, 50. Chesneau, 44, states that those *Ajem-oghlans* who were levied in Anatolia were sent to gentlemen in Rumelia.

gentlemen whom they served, responsible for them to the sultan, supplied them with food and clothing and whatever else they were pleased to give.[1]   The number of these *Ajem-oghlans* of the first stage may be estimated as ten thousand.[2]   At the end of two or three years, or perhaps at about the time for a new *devshurmeh*,[3] officers came to examine them.   If they knew enough Turkish and were strong and well-grown, they passed to the next stage.

Having been brought to Constantinople, and once more carefully inscribed and estimated,[4] the *Ajem-oghlans* were again distributed, but now in groups.   About two thousand were assigned to service with the fleet at Gallipoli.[5]   Another two thousand, probably the most intelligent, were appointed as gardeners, or *Bostanjis*, to the sultan's palaces in Stamboul, Adrianople, Brusa, and Magnesia;[6] and five hundred or more served in other capacities about the palaces, as wood-cutters, helpers in the kitchen, and the like.[7]   Five or six thousand were kept in Constantinople and employed in the shipyards or on public buildings,[8] or were hired out in bands of one hundred or more to private citizens for hard labor of various sorts.[9]   Some were hired out similarly in other cities.[10]   In the midst of such a variety of occupations, two objects seem always to have been kept in mind, — the *Ajem-oghlans* were to develop the utmost strength of body, and they were to learn some trade useful in war.[11]   In this stage they were normally organized in groups or

[1] Ramberti, below, p. 255; Junis Bey, below, p. 270; Nicolay, 86.

[2] Giovio, *Commentarius*, 78; Junis Bey, as above.

[3] Ramberti and Junis Bey, as above, say after three or four years; Geuffroy, 243, after four years.   Navagero, 50, says that every two or three years, as the service demands, an officer takes those who are ready; some have served two or three, some four or five years.   Trevisano, 130, says that they are left six or seven years.

[4] Ricaut, 77.

[5] Chalcocondyles, 97; Spandugino, 104; Navagero, 52.

[6] Navagero, 52; Postel, iii. 22, 25.

[7] Spandugino, 76.

[8] Ramberti, 254, says 5000; Junis Bey, 269, says 4000 or 5000; Geuffroy, 242, says 5000 or 6000; Trevisano, 129, says 6800; Garzoni, 415, says 6000; Postel, iii. 25, says 5000 to 7000; D. Barbarigo, 33, says 7600.

[9] Junis Bey, 269; Navagero, 51; Trevisano, 129; Postel, iii. 25.

[10] Trevisano, 129.   [11] Giovio, *Commentarius*, 77.

messes of ten. The gardeners were under the charge of an official of high rank and great authority, who bore the humble title of *Bostanji-bashi,* or head gardener; he was aided by under officers and an administrative staff. Those in Constantinople were under the orders of an *Agha,* or general officer, with a staff of under officials, clerks, and accountants.[1] Being filled with the spirit of youth, conscious of their superior physical strength and privileged position, gathered together in large groups, and unrestrained by substantial mental instruction, the *Ajem-oghlans* were by no means easy to manage. They frequently raised great disturbances in the city, in emulation perhaps of the Janissaries.[2] Those who wished were allowed to learn to read and write, but they were not obliged to do so.[3] They received a small amount of pay, with food and clothing.[4]

After a certain time spent in this stage of development, the majority of the *Ajem-oghlans* were assigned, one by one as each seemed ready, to the service of the *odalar,* or messes, of the Janissaries.[5] The latter then became responsible for their training in the art of war, and discharged this duty with much zeal. In the course of time, as the *Ajem-oghlans* acquired sufficient skill, and as vacancies occurred, they were enrolled as full-fledged Janissaries.[6] The gardeners of the sultan's palaces and the palace servants seem not ordinarily to have become Janissaries, but to have been advanced toward the directing of the transport, commissary, and artillery services, the oversight of the imperial stables, and like positions in the administration

---

[1] Ramberti, below, p. 254; Junis Bey, below, p. 269; D'Ohsson, vii. 28.

[2] Postel, iii. 25.

[3] Postel, iii. 22, says that only those who had special privilege from the sultan were allowed to learn letters. Ricaut, 76, says that some of those in the palace service were taught to read and write. In D'Ohsson's time (vii. 327), each *oda* had a *hoja* to teach reading and writing to those who wished.

[4] Junis Bey, 269, 270, says that they had 2 or 3 aspers per day at first, and more as they advanced, and that their chief was allowed 100,000 aspers a year for their food and clothing. Postel, iii. 23, says that their chief was allowed 10,000 aspers a day to keep them and pay them, and other money for their clothing.

[5] Ramberti, 254; Junis Bey, 270; Postel, iii. 25.

[6] Spandugino, 104. Trevisano, 130, says that they became such at from 20 to 25 years old, according to their mind, value, or favor.

of the army and the great household.[1]   No doubt some of those
assigned to the fleet were promoted in the navy, but most of
them seem to have become Janissaries.[2]   Thus a large number
and variety of openings lay before the *Ajem-oghlans*, who as
they became ready were advanced into them.   The ordinary age
of graduation from the corps was twenty-five years,[3] which may
be regarded as the age of majority for all the sultan's slaves.
At times war caused such depletion of the upper service that
Ajem-oghlans were promoted before they had reached the desired
age or were thoroughly ready.[4]

Advancement Based on Merit

The entire system from start to finish was designed to reward
merit and fully to satisfy every ambition that was backed by
ability, effort, and sufficient preparation.   Two parallel lines
of reward were established, the honorable and the financial.
In the page school the first was represented by promotion from
class to class, and, in the case of those who were observed to be
the most suitable, by advancement through the chambers of
personal service to the *Khas Oda*.   In this *oda* they were promoted in regular order through the twelve or more special
offices.[5]

Among the *Ajem-oghlans* the process seems to have been carried
on by carefully observing and testing individuals, by advancing
them from stage to stage on this basis, and by entrusting them
in the later stages with greater and greater responsibilities.
The financial reward began for the pages immediately upon
admission to the school.   It was then probably about equal to
the daily wages of an unskilled laborer.   This was increased
regularly year by year, and in the *Khas Oda* reached the propor-

---

[1] Ricaut, 76.   But those of the principal palace in Constantinople had greater
opportunities; they might become Janissaries, *Solaks*, *Kapujis*, etc.   (Ramberti,
below, p. 245.)

[2] Chalcocondyles, 97.

[3] Trevisano, 130; Barbaro, 316; Garzoni, 397.

[4] Zinkeisen, iii. 228.

[5] Ricaut, 53; D'Ohsson, vii. 34–39.

tions of a handsome salary.[1] The *Ajem-oghlans* depended during the first stage on the rewards assigned by their temporary masters. After that stage they began to receive a small amount of pay from the sultan, which was gradually increased.[2] All were provided with food, lodging, and at least a part of their clothing, and individuals might hope to obtain special gifts.

This double system was continued without a break through the entire institution. The lowest Janissary might hopefully aspire to promotion, either through the hierarchy of office in his own corps, or by being lifted out of it for service in the cavalry or the active administration.[3] The pages who had passed out of the school were already well up in the scale of advancement, and every place except the sultan's own was within their grasp. The grand vizier, indeed, might wield almost the whole of the sultan's power, a fact which Ibrahim, shortly before his fall, realized so fully that he added to his title of *Seraskier* the word Sultan.[4] The losses occasioned by fierce and frequent wars, and by not infrequent depositions and executions, gave abundant opportunity for men to rise from below. Conquest was continually adding new offices and commands. The whole Ruling Institution was, so to speak, in a constant state of boiling, in which the human particles were rapidly rising to the top, and, alas, disappearing, while others rose as rapidly behind them.

The figure just employed is applicable, however, only to the mere phenomenon of rising: the upward movement was not in the least accidental or automatic; it was conducted with keen intelligence at every stage. Now and then, as in the case of Ibrahim, favor disturbed the scheme; but this happened very seldom before the end of Suleiman's reign. Sometimes a temporary confusion resulted from extraordinary losses in war, but order was soon restored. There is reason to believe that human history has never known a political institution which during so long a period was so completely dominated by sheer

---

[1] Ramberti, below, p. 244; Junis Bey, below, p. 263; Ricaut, 53.

[2] Junis Bey, as quoted above, p. 81, note 4.

[3] Chalcocondyles, 171; Barbaro, 305; Nicolay, 89 ("the wages of each are increased, according to the merit of their military valor ").

[4] Hammer, *Geschichte*, iii. 160.

intellect, and thereby so unerringly held to its original plan and purpose, as was the Ottoman Ruling Institution. The democracy of Athens attained an unexampled level of average intelligence, but under its sway the exceptional mind received discouragement rather than exceptional training. The free democracies of the present age allow the gifted individual opportunities to fight his way upward, but against obstacles which sometimes become insuperable. These systems are unquestionably superior on the whole to the Ottoman scheme, because of their inclusiveness and individual freedom; but as regards sheer efficiency, unobstructed opportunity, and certainty of reward, their operation is wasteful, clumsy, and blind by comparison.

Some testimonies of shrewd contemporary observers will show how they regarded the Ottoman scheme of promotion both in itself and in comparison with Western ways. The intelligent author of the *Tractatus* is impressed by the unity and control of the scheme. " Out of the aforesaid slaves," he writes, " promotions are made to the offices of the kingdom according to the virtues found in them. Whence it comes about that all the magnates and princes of the whole kingdom are as it were officials made by the king, and not lords or possessors; and as a consequence he is the sole lord and possessor, and the lawful dispenser, distributer, and governor of the whole kingdom; the others are only executors, officials, and administrators according to his will and command. . . . Whence it follows that in his kingdom, although there is an innumerable multitude, no contradiction or opposition can arise; but, united as one man in all respects and for all purposes, they look to his command alone, they obey and serve unwearyingly." [1]

Postel says: " The Seigneur [or sultan] has four or several principal personages for all the business of his empire, whether in war or justice, and they are promoted to this honor by degrees from lower offices, always mounting and giving good examples of living, unless by some extraordinary favor the prince raises them from some low place, which is very perilous." [2] Speaking of the pages in the palace, he adds: " When they have lived

---

[1] *Tractatus*, ch. viii.   [2] Postel, i. 121.

there a long time and done well, they are given a place where they receive pay, and they are made Castellans and given other offices used among them. If there are some who have the ability to make themselves known, they may have the best fortune in the world, and become governors of the land and Pashas; for there they judge of nobility by the worth which they see appearing in a man, and they give honors according to the evidence of his past." [1]   Of Suleiman, Tanco says, " He sows hope of certain reward in all conditions of men, who by means of virtue, may succeed in mounting to better fortune "; and of the Janissaries, " Each has his good and real fortune in his hand." [2]

Among all observers, Busbecq seems to have been most impressed with the system of advancement by merit. " The Turks," he tells us, " do not measure even their own people by any other rule than that of personal merit. The only exception is the house of Ottoman; in this case, and in this case only, does birth confer distinction." [3]

Referring to his audience with Suleiman, he says: " There was not in all that great assembly a single man who owed his position to aught save his valour and his merit. No distinction is attached to birth among the Turks; the deference to be paid to a man is measured by the position he holds in the public service. There is no fighting for precedence; a man's place is marked out by the duties he discharges. In making his appointments the sultan pays no regard to any pretensions on the score of wealth or rank, nor does he take into consideration recommendations or popularity; he considers each case on its own merits, and examines carefully into the character, ability, and disposition of the man whose promotion is in question. It is by merit that men rise in the service, a system which ensures that posts should only be assigned to the competent. Each man in Turkey carries in his own hand his ancestry and his position in life, which he may make or mar as he will. Those who receive the highest offices from the sultan are for the most part the sons of shepherds or herdsmen, and so far from being ashamed of their parentage,

---

[1] *Ibid.* iii. 19.

[2] Tanco, 197, 206.

[3] Busbecq, *Life and Letters*, i. 105.

they actually glory in it, and consider it a matter of boasting that they owe nothing to the accident of birth; for they do not believe that high qualities are either natural or hereditary, nor do they think that they can be handed down from father to son, but that they are partly the gift of God, and partly the result of good training, great industry, and unwearied zeal; arguing that high qualities do not descend from a father to his son or heir, any more than a talent for music, mathematics, or the like; and that the mind does not derive its origin from the father, so that the son should necessarily be like the father in character, but emanates from heaven, and is thence infused into the human body.   Among the Turks, therefore, honours, high posts, and judgeships are the rewards of great ability and good service. If a man be dishonest, or lazy, or careless, he remains at the bottom of the ladder, an object of contempt; for such qualities there are no honours in Turkey!

" This is the reason that they are successful in their undertakings, that they lord it over others, and are daily extending the bounds of their empire.   These are not our ideas; with us there is no opening left for merit; birth is the standard for everything; the prestige of birth is the sole key to advancement in the public service." [1]

Finally, Ricaut, after describing the *Ajem-oghlans*, declares that this part of the system " is one of the most Politick Constitutions in the World, and none of the meanest supports of the *Ottoman* Empire." [2]

Financial rewards paralleled advancement in office with great exactness.   When a man came to high position, he was provided with the means to live splendidly in proportion to his rank. In addition to his salary, many opportunities of increasing his income presented themselves; and though some of these would be considered undignified in Western eyes,[3] and others were undoubtedly stained with rapacity and extortion,[4] they were

---

[1] Busbecq, *Life and Letters*, i. 154–155.
[2] Ricaut, 77.
[3] Spandugino, 185; Busbecq, *Life and Letters*, i. 108.
[4] Spandugino, 132.

allowed to be enjoyed under all ordinary circumstances. The sultan's higher officials not only lived in great splendor, with a numerous retinue, a large harem, and many costly garments, dishes, gems, and the like, but they often accumulated great wealth in money, houses, lands, mills, horses, cattle, sheep, and everything else that is considered worth collecting.[1] Thus, as men were promoted, they were enabled regularly to proportion display of wealth to rank and office.

The example of one of Suleiman's chief servants will illustrate the *cursus honorum* in the Ottoman system. Ali Pasha was a native of Dalmatia. Levied with the tribute boys, he was admitted to the principal palace at the time when Ibrahim was *Oda-bashi*, or head of the Inner Chamber of pages. In the course of time he was made *Kapuji*, or gatekeeper. When Ibrahim became grand vizier, Ali became *Chasnejir*, or chief taster, to Suleiman, and held that office during the expedition to Vienna in 1529. In due course he was discharged from the palace, and appointed to high office outside. He soon reached the grade of *Agha*, or general or the *Ghurebas*, the lowest of the four divisions of the regular cavalry, and was then promoted to be *Agha* of the *Spahi-oghlans*, the highest of the cavalry divisions. Next he became second equerry and later first equerry (*Emir-al-Akhor*), then *Agha* of the Janissaries, then *Beylerbey* of Rumelia. In the last capacity he attended the sultan in the Persian war of 1548–1549. As a reward for special services in the war he was made pasha of Egypt in 1549, and at the time of his departure was

---

[1] The grand vizier Rustem's wealth is summed up in detail in Hammer's *Geschichte*, iii. 386: " He himself left at his death an immense fortune; no grand vizier before him had amassed so much wealth. His estate consisted of 815 farms in Rumelia and Anatolia, 476 water mills, 1700 slaves, 2900 war horses, 1106 camels, 5000 richly embroidered coats and robes of honor, 8000 turbans, 1100 caps of cloth of gold, 2900 coats of mail, 2000 cuirasses, 600 saddles finished in silver, 500 others adorned with gold and precious stones, 1500 helmets plated with silver, 130 pairs of golden stirrups, 760 sabres adorned with precious stones, 1000 lances trimmed with silver, 800 Korans, 130 of which were set with diamonds, 5000 volumes of various works, 78,000 ducats, 32 precious stones representing a value of 112 donkey-loads (that is to say, 11,200,000 aspers); the ready money which was found in his house was estimated at 1000 loads (100,000,000 aspers, or 2,000,000 ducats."

nominated vizier. Returning to Constantinople in 1553, he was made third vizier, and upon the death of Rustem in 1561, he became grand vizier. Because of jealousies and enmities caused by his promotions he had hardly a friend left; nevertheless, he was able to hold the favor of Suleiman until his death in 1565.[1]

PUNISHMENTS

The system did not attempt to rely wholly upon the glittering attractions of indefinite promotion and enormously increasing wealth. Not all men çan be allured to remain unswervingly within a narrow path of strict obedience and whole-hearted service. Pages and *Ajem-oghlans* were held to severe discipline by sufficient and certain punishment; but their teachers and eunuch masters were required to keep that punishment within bounds by the certainty of yet severer punishment.[2] *Ajem-oghlans* might be beaten, or sold out of the sultan's service. After the close of the strictly educational period, punishment, like reward, followed continuously the law of proportionate increase. The higher the position, the heavier the punishment of being passed over in promotion, or of being actually degraded. Fines and confiscations also grew with rank. At no great height in the scale, the personal punishments reached that of death, and death was always very near the highest officials. Any tendency toward treason or revolt, any act of disobedience, sometimes a plot against a higher official, sometimes even a disagreement with the sultan in a matter of policy,[3] would lead to sudden execution. The viziers of Selim I carried their wills in their bosoms; and well they might, since the heads of seven are said to have fallen at his command.[4]

Thus was the system carefully kept clear of all the human material that seemed to endanger its working or threaten its unity. There was no sympathy for weakness, no accepting of excuses, no suspension of sentence, no mercy. Suleiman did

---

[1] D. Barbarigo, 30–33.   [2] Menavino, 128.

[3] The cause of the execution of Junis Pasha by Selim I. Cf. Hammer, *Geschichte*, ii. 524.

[4] Halil Ganem, i. 169.

not always have the heart to execute promptly; but in the end he had no alternative, so remorseless was the system. Even his best friend, Ibrahim, went too far and had to be removed. Two of his sons, the oldest and ablest, threatened the system in turn, and one after the other suffered the bow-string. Small wonder that Suleiman's soul was not filled with joy at the victory of Jerbé. " Those who saw Solyman's face in this hour of triumph," says Busbecq, " failed to detect in it the slightest trace of undue elation. I can myself positively declare, that when I saw him two days later on his way to the mosque, the expression of his countenance was unchanged; his stern features had lost nothing of their habitual gloom; one would have thought that the victory concerned him not, and that this startling success of his arms had caused him no surprise. So self-contained was the heart of that grand old man, so schooled to meet each change of fortune however great, that all the applause and triumph of that day wrung from him no sign of satisfaction." [1] Arbiter of the destinies of so many men, compelled to be remorseless as fate, Suleiman could allow joy no place in his soul. He who wielded as severe a rod as ever man held must maintain over himself the sternest discipline of all.

[1] Busbecq, *Life and Letters*, i. 322.

CHAPTER IV

THE RULING INSTITUTION: AS AN ARMY

THE MILITARY ASPECT

THE Ottoman government had been an army before it was anything else. Like the Turkish nations of the steppe lands, the Ottoman nation was " born of war and organized for conquest." [1] Fighting was originally the first business of the state and governing the second. As time went on, and particularly after the capture of Constantinople, the necessity of administering immense territories transferred the preponderance to the governmental aspect; but even in Suleiman's time the two great functions of the Ruling Institution were very closely united. War carried practically the whole government into the field.[2] Of course substitute officials had to be left behind to attend to what public business was absolutely necessary, but these were paralleled by, and indeed were usually identical with, the officers and soldiers who had to be left behind to preserve public order. So completely was the government an army, that the more important judges, who did not belong directly to the Ruling Institution, were taken into the field. Suleiman on his last campaign had 48,316 men under pay.[3] Acceptance of the sultan's pay by ordinary usage signified that the recipient was a *kul*.[4] Evidently, then, almost the entire personnel of the Ruling

---

[1] Cahun, *Introduction*, p. vii: " Les Turcs et les Mongols . . . nées de la guerre et organisées pour la conquête."

[2] This was true even in D'Ohsson's time (vii. 399).

[3] Hammer, *Staatsverwaltung*, 181.

[4] Curiously enough, the oldest sense in which the Turkish word *kul* was used as a term denoting relation to a prince, was in reference to soldiers (Vambéry, *Uigurische Sprachmonumente und das Kudatku Bilik*, 113, stanza 12b). At that time the word was applied to the foot-soldiers as distinguished from the cavalry, who were then volunteer knights. This usage survived in the Ottoman system to the extent that the regular infantry, including the Janissaries, artillerymen, and other lesser permanent corps, were regarded as in a particular and special sense the sultan's *kullar* (D'Ohsson, vii. 328; Djevad Bey, i. 15–18).

Institution, except the younger pages and the *Ajem-oghlans* who were as yet unfit, accompanied the master to war.[1] In fact, army and government were one. War was the external purpose, government the internal purpose, of one institution, composed of one body of men. On the military side, this institution carried on war abroad, repressed revolt at home, kept itself in power, and preserved sufficient order in the empire to allow a busy and varied economic and social activity. On the governmental side, it supplied itself with funds, regulated its own workings, — which was no small task, — kept the operations of the other institutions of the empire in order, and enforced the law. The high officials of government held high command in war. The generals of the army had extensive administrative duties in regard to the affairs of the troops under them, the management of departments of state, or the government of provinces.

The scope of the present treatise confines the discussion of the Ruling Institution as an army to those features which lie nearest the governmental aspect. The great majority of its members constituted the standing army of the empire, in the two great sections of Janissaries, or infantry, and *Spahis* of the Porte, or cavalry. Subordinate sections cared for the artillery and transport services, and for other necessary adjuncts to campaigning. Although the feudal *Spahis* did not receive pay from the sultan, and hence were not properly *kullar*, their officers were his slaves, even though many of them were supported during their term of service from fiefs. Besides these regular troops there were also attached to the Ottoman army certain irregular bodies of a lower order, — the *Akinji*, the *Azabs*, the Kurds, and so on.

THE JANISSARIES [2]

The body of regular infantry known as *Yenicheri*, or " new troops," a name which the West has changed to Janissaries,

---

[1] The *Bostanjis*, or gardeners, and other *Ajem-oghlans* of the palace service were not left behind: D'Ohsson, vii. 326; Djevad Bey, i. 7.

[2] Extended accounts of the Janissaries may be found in D'Ohsson, vii. 310 ff.; Hammer, *Staatsverwaltung*, 192 ff.; Zinkeisen, iii. 201 ff.; Djevad Bey, vol. i, book i.

comes near to standing in the Western imagination for the sultan's entire slave-family.[1] In the sixteenth century, however, it formed not more than a fourth of the whole number; nor does its importance seem to have been beyond its numerical proportion, except in one or two respects. Since its members were physically trained beyond comparison with their intellectual education, since they were kept in poverty and hence were comparatively irresponsible, and since a large portion of them were in comparative idleness in time of peace, they were liable to act as an organized and very dangerous mob. They might start a riot on short notice, or burn a section of the city in order to pillage the neighboring houses, or rifle the shops of the Jews, or plunder the grand vizier's establishment.[2] They could not easily be restrained from plundering cities which had capitulated or from violating terms of surrender.[3] They felt that the death of a sultan gave them an interregnum of license before the accession of a new sovereign.[4] They demanded donatives at the succession of a new ruler with such increasing rapacity as to embarrass the treasury;[5] and they needed to be braced at

[1] For an example of the persistence of this idea, see Bérard (1909), 12-13: " La Turquie désormais subsiste par le janissaire et doit vivre pour le janissaire d'abord. . . . depuis la prise de Rhodes (1522) jusqu'à l'apparition de la flotte russe aux Dardanelles (1770), tant vaut le janissaire et tant vaut l'empire." Professor A. C. Coolidge suggests that the hold which this remarkable organization had upon the imagination of fellow-countrymen as well as of foreigners was in part " due to the fact that in almost all Oriental history good infantrymen have been extremely rare, and the Janissaries were the only good infantrymen in the Ottoman Empire." It is also true that the Janissaries were that group within the Moslem fold which came least under the taming and subordinating influence of the system; they were a frontier province of Islamic society. When in the seventeenth century they ceased to be drawn directly from the Christian population and became a variety of military aristocracy, not only did they remain in part a fighting infantry, but their original freedom of spirit and action was by no means abandoned.

[2] D'Ohsson, vii. 359-360; Hammer, *Geschichte*, ii. 251, 361, iii. 45; Nicolay, 89.

[3] Rhodes was pillaged after capitulation (1521), and so were Ofen (1529), and Wychegrad (1544): Hammer, *Geschichte*, iii. 28, 83, 263.

[4] *Ibid*. ii. 252. Hence the death of a sultan was kept concealed until his successor had assumed power (*ibid*. 535; iii. 449).

[5] Mohammed II gave them ten purses of gold (1451), *ibid*. i. 504; Bayezid II gave them 2000 aspers each (1481), *ibid*. ii. 252; Selim I gave them 3000 aspers each (1512), *ibid*. 382; from Suleiman they asked 5000 aspers each, which he compounded by giving them one-third in cash and increased pay (1520), *ibid*. iii. 6.

critical moments by liberal presents.[1] In time of battle, however, they drew up an invincible line behind which the person of their sovereign was as safe as in an impregnable fortress. Their devotion to his person was the greater because they were in a special sense his *kullar*, and because he was one of them, being inscribed in one of their *odas* and receiving his pay regularly.[2] In small groups on garrison duty their severe training seems to have made of them an efficient police.[3] Yet their *esprit de corps*, resting on consciousness of power, made them feared at all times. They took an active part in determining the destinies of the empire in two ways, — by limiting conquests, and by influencing the succession to the throne.[4] They compelled the mighty Selim to turn back from both Persia and Egypt.[5] They murmured before Vienna, and without doubt hastened the raising of the siege.[6]

THE SUCCESSION TO THE THRONE

The Janissaries had no small influence in determining the succession to the throne.[7] There was no law fixing the succession, since neither the *Sheri* nor the *Kanuns* provided for such things;[8] but it was a matter of fundamental custom that a prince

---

[1] Before Vienna (1529), *ibid.* 88; on march toward Persia (1534), *ibid.* 148; at Tabriz (1535), *ibid.* 158.

[2] This usage dates from Suleiman; D'Ohsson, vii. 354.

[3] Busbecq, *Life and Letters*, i. 86: the Janissaries " are scattered through every part of the empire, either to garrison the forts against the enemy, or to protect the Christians and Jews from the violence of the mob. There is no district with any considerable amount of population, no borough or city, which has not a detachment of Janissaries to protect the Christians, Jews, and other helpless people from outrage and wrong." Janissaries might be detailed to attend on foreign ambassadors, or to escort foreign travelers within the empire (Knolles, ed. 1687, p. 985).

[4] Nicolay, 89, was perhaps the first to point out the likeness of the Janissaries to the Roman Pretorian Guard, and to see in them a great danger to the Ottoman Empire.

[5] Hammer, *Geschichte*, ii. 420, 520.

[6] *Ibid.* iii. 88.

[7] Trevisano, 129, says that they had sufficient authority on the death of a sultan to give the empire to which of his sons they pleased. Cf. J. Soranzo, 248; Morosini, 255; Garzoni, 432; Knolles (ed. 1687), 985 ("neither can any of the Turks Sultans account themselves fully invested in the Imperial Dignity, or assured of their Estate, until they be by them approved and proclaimed ").

[8] D'Ohsson, i. 278–284; Heidborn, 120.

of the house of Osman should rule, and it was almost as fundamental that a son of a sultan should succeed him. Not until 1617 was the present rule established, by which the oldest male of the royal house is heir apparent.[1] Before that, when a sultan had several sons, the eldest had no inherent right to succeed, as is the practice in Western Europe. The Turkish father naturally desired to choose which of his sons should follow him; and to this end, when he gave them provincial governments, he often placed the favorite nearest the capital. After Mohammed II had issued his famous *Kanun*, by which the son who reached the throne was legally authorized to execute his brothers,[2] a situation of unstable equilibrium arose as soon as the sons of a sultan began to grow up. Each knew that he must either obtain the throne or die soon after his father; hence revolt was almost forced upon a son who found himself placed farther from the capital than a favored brother. When Bayezid II grew old and feeble, his active and warlike son Selim opposed his wish to leave the empire to Achmet;[3] in the end Selim triumphed, and Bayezid, forced to abdicate, met a death that was believed by many not to have been natural.[4] The Janissaries turned the scale in this struggle, and henceforth they were felt to be a dangerous element whenever a sultan came to have more than one grown son. They had a great part in the death of both Mustapha and Bayezid, the ablest sons of Suleiman; indeed, their sympathy for the former was undoubtedly a chief reason in determining Suleiman to execute him, since only thus could his own safety be assured.[5] In the case of Bayezid, the fact that the Janissaries did not support him spelled his doom, even though his father, beyond all precedent, pardoned his first revolt,

---

[1] D'Ohsson, i. 284. This rule is sometimes stated erroneously as an old Turkish custom, a provision of Mohammedan law, or an old Ottoman law or custom.

[2] Hammer, *Staatsverfassung*, 98: " *Kanun* of the Security of the Throne: The majority of Legists (*Ulema*) have declared it allowable, that whoever among my illustrious children and grandchildren may come to the throne, should, for securing the peace of the world, order his brothers to be executed. Let them hereafter act accordingly."

[3] Hammer, *Geschichte*, ii. 352 ff.

[4] Menavino, 219; Trevisano, 129; Hammer, *Geschichte*, ii. 365.

[5] Hammer, *Geschichte*, iii. 314.

and though the influence of his mother Roxelana was strong in his favor.[1] Speculation is dangerous; but the Janissaries may have done Western Europe a great service on these occasions. Had either Mustapha or Bayezid come to the throne instead of the drunken and dissolute Selim II, the issue of Lepanto might have been different, a new expedition against Vienna led by a vigorous and idolized young monarch might have succeeded, the Ottoman power might have ruled more widely and permanently than it did, and the decay of the Ruling Institution might have been long postponed.[2]

The Janissaries in Suleiman's time numbered between twelve and fourteen thousand;[3] and this number probably did not include the garrison which supported the power of the empire in Egypt,[4] still less that which upheld the corsair rule in North Africa. Except in time of war many of the Janissaries were distributed in garrisons, so that probably not more than half resided in the capital.[5] Such of these as were married lived at home, and the others were lodged in two great barracks.[6] They were organized in messes of ten; ten messes constituted an *orta* or *oda*, of

[1] Busbecq, *Life and Letters*, i. 185–189.

[2] Postel, iii. 87, says, about 1537: Suleiman " has among others a son named Mustapha, marvelously well educated and prudent and of the age to reign; for he is 23 or 24 years old; and God grant that so great an atrocity may not come so near us (*Dieu ne permette qu'une Barbarie si grande vienne si pres de nous*)."

[3] 10,000 is the number according to Bragadino, 106. 12,000 is given by almost all contemporaries: Ramberti, below, p. 249; Junis Bey, below, p. 266; Giovio, *Commentarius*, 76; Geuffroy, 234; Navagero, 53; Trevisano, 128; Barbaro, 305; Postel, iii. 30; Busbecq, *Life and Letters*, i. 86; Nicolay, 88; Erizzo, 127. Navagero, 56, says some think that 15,500 or 16,000 were inscribed; and Garzoni, 416, says that there were 13,000 or 14,000. Djevad Bey, i. 90, gives 12,000 in 1523, and 13,599 in 1574. In 1564 D. Barbarigo, 33, gives a precise number, 13,502. D'Ohsson, vii. 330, says, without stating any authority and against the above contemporary evidence, that Suleiman raised the number to 40,000. Hammer (*Geschichte*, i. 95, and iii. 473) says, referring to D'Ohsson, that Suleiman had 20,000; but in his *Staatsverwaltung*, 195, he states that Suleiman had only 12,000 before Szigets. Knolles (ed. 1687, p. 990) says, about 1603, that the Janissaries numbered not over 12,000 to 14,000.

[4] Junis Bey, 272, and Ludovisi, 17, give the number of this garrison as 3000. Postel, 38, gives the number as 30,000; this must include the Mamelukes.

[5] Giovio, *Commentarius*, 77: about 6000 of the older of them stay about the Prince. Navagero, 55: 8000 to 10,000 are always ready.

[6] Ramberti, 249; Junis Bey, 267.

which there were one hundred and sixty-five in Suleiman's time.[1] Each *orta* had its officers, who had been promoted from its ranks; and above all the *ortas* was a graded set of officers, under the *Agha*, or general, of the Janissaries.[2] This official had never been a Janissary, but had come through the colleges of pages.[3] He not merely commanded the Janissaries, but was a sort of minister of war for them. Aided by his *Kiaya*, or lieutenant,[4] his chief *Yaziji*, or scribe, and a bureau of clerks, he directed their enrolment, the distribution of their pay, their promotions, their location, the purchase of their supplies and clothing, and all the other business of the corps. He was well paid and was of great authority, outranking all other generals, though on some occasions he was obliged to yield precedence to two of the generals of cavalry, whose corps were older than those of the Janissaries.[5]

The Janissaries had a regular ladder of promotion through the offices of their *odas* and above, as far as the position of *Segban-bashi*, which was the office next below that of *Agha*.[6] One hundred and fifty of their best bowmen were honored by being detailed to accompany the sultan on the march, as his *Solaks*.[7] They might also for distinguished ability or service be taken into the regular cavalry, and have all its opportunities open to them. No less than the rest of the army, they kept

---

[1] Hammer, *Staatsverwaltung*, 194; Ricaut, 365 (mentions 162 *odalar*); Djevad Bey, i. 28. In Chalcocondyles's time (1465), 97, the strength of each *oda* seems to have been of 50 men. In Suleiman's time it was less than 100. Later it became much larger.

[2] Nicolay, 96–97; D'Ohsson, vii. 313–320; Hammer, *Staatsverwaltung*, 201 ff.; Djevad Bey, i. 35, 45.

[3] D'Ohsson, vii. 314; Hammer, *Geschichte*, ii. 428. This was the case only from 1515 to 1582.

[4] *Kiaya* is a word which offered infinite difficulties of pronunciation and spelling; for example, gachaia, cacaia, checaya, quaia, queaya, caia, cahaia, chiccaia, chechessi. Some authors employ a different spelling each time they use the word. Trevisano, 118, gives chietcudasci. *Kiaya* represents the popular pronunciation. The more nearly correct form of the word, following the Turkish spelling, is *ketkhuda*.

[5] D'Ohsson, vii. 353.

[6] Djevad Bey, i. 35.

[7] Ramberti, below, p. 250; Junis Bey, below, p. 266.

marvellous order in camp, and, except at the crises above described, were completely obedient to their officers.[1] They were
punishable only by their own officers, not even the grand vizier
having direct jurisdiction over them.[2] They had a strong sense
of maintaining their privileges and what they considered to be
their rights. Busbecq, who gives illumination àt so many
points, shows how the grand vizier Rustem, and even Suleiman
himself, felt toward these men when they were all together and
their blood was hot. On one occasion Busbecq's servants
quarreled with some Janissaries, and he was disposed to back
his men up; whereupon Rustem sent a trusty messenger to
him with a verbal message, asking him " to remove every cause
of offence which might occasion a quarrel with those atrocious
scoundrels. Was I not aware," he asked, " that it was war
time, when they were masters, so that not even Solyman himself had control over them, and was actually himself afraid of
receiving violence at their hands ? "[3] Great care had to be
taken to keep the Janissaries under control, for they were capable
of wrecking the whole government. They were, to be sure,
constantly drained of their ablest men by promotion; but this
only left the others the more liable, like sheep, to follow a new
leader into evil. They could be repressed more or less by punishment: now and then an especially active promoter of trouble
was executed;[4] officers who offended were sometimes sent to
command distant garrisons, and sometimes they were stricken
from the roll.[5] Suleiman succeeded, on the whole, in keeping
the Janissaries in hand, and he was able to lead them farther
east than could his father Selim. They never revolted against
him,[6] and they supported him against Bayezid.

[1] Ludovisi (1534), 9, gives a pessimistic account of them; according to him,
they had not the order or the discipline or the astuteness which was found in the
Christian infantry. Postel, iii. 30, praises them greatly for order, frugality, and
temperance. Djevad Bey, i. 56–64, gives a favorable description; he says (p. 56)
that the first of their fundamental laws enjoined absolute obedience.

[2] Postel, iii. 31; D'Ohsson, vii. 353; Djevad Bey, i. 66, 69.

[3] Busbecq, Life and Letters, i. 296.

[4] D'Ohsson, vii. 351; Djevad Bey, i. 56–59.

[5] Ramberti, below, p. 249; Junis Bey, below, p. 267; D'Ohsson, vii. 352.

[6] Djevad Bey, i. 289.

THE SPAHIS OF THE PORTE [1]

The regular cavalry were all included under the general name of *Spahis*, or horsemen; but the name was also applied to one of the four divisions into which Osman's corps of daring riders had been organized after the model of the cavalry of the caliph Omar I.[2]   Their organization was older than that of the Janissaries; it had come down continuously from the early days.[3] The members were not organized into a single body, they had high pay, and they were in the presence of excellent opportunities to acquire wealth and to rise with rapidity.   Accordingly, they appear never to have caused Suleiman any special trouble.[4]

The four corps were the *Spahis* in the narrower sense, often called *Spahi-Oghlans;* the *Silihdars*, or weapon-bearers; the *Ulufajis*, or paid troops, in two divisions, the left and the right; and the *Ghurebas*, or Foreign Legion, also in two divisions, the left and the right.[5]   The *Spahis* were most honored and best paid, but each had to bring with him to war five or six armed slaves on horseback.   The *Silihdars* had less pay and furnished four or five horsemen.   The *Ulufajis* furnished two or three horsemen each.[6]   These three corps were recruited from the pages and the Janissaries, the *Ulufajis* receiving also occasional members by special promotions from the irregular troops.[7] The Foreign Legion had least pay of all, and its members came alone; not having begun as the sultan's *kullar*, and often not

---

[1] This name for the sultan's paid cavalry is that regularly employed by the Venetian writers of the sixteenth century: for example, Moro, 337; Bernardo, 330.

[2] Hammer, *Geschichte*, i. 95.

[3] D'Ohsson, vii. 353.

[4] For the great disturbance which they raised in 1593, see Zinkeisen, iii. 79.

[5] All of these names are spelled with an ingenious variety in contemporary writings: —

Spahi: spai, spachi, sipahi, sipah, spacoillain (spahi-oghlan).
Silihdar: selicter, sillictar, sulastrus, suluphtar.
Ulufagi: holofagi, allophase.
Ghureba: caripy, caripicus, ciarcagi, caripp (oglan), gharib (oglan), capi (oglan)
The word *Spahi* is of identical derivation with *Sepoy.*

[6] Ramberti, below, p. 250; Junis Bey, below, p. 267; Postel, iii. 34.   Giovio (*Commentarius*, 75) says that some *Spahis* brought as many as ten horsemen.

[7] Giovio, 75; Postel, iii. 35.

even as Ottomans, they enjoyed small honor.[1] Each of the first two corps, and each division of the last two corps of the *Spahis* of the Porte, was organized separately after the fashion of the Janissaries, with its own general, who supervised the administration of all its affairs.[2] The number of the *Spahis* of the Porte is given on two bases. In Suleiman's time the actual members of the four corps counted from ten to twelve thousand men, or a little less than the number of the Janissaries;[3] but, since most of them had each to bring from two to six additional horsemen, the total force which they assembled was from forty to fifty thousand.[4] Whether the entire number or only the actual members were regularly considered to be the sultan's *kullar*,

[1] They were called " poor youth " by Menavino, 152; Junis Bey, 267; Ramberti, 251; Trevisano, 126; Postel, iii. 36. Spandugino, 97, says that they were strangers from Asia, Egypt, and Africa. Giovio, 76, says that they were all Moslems from Persia, Turcomania, Syria, Africa, Arabia, Scythia, and even India; but he is wrong in confining them to Moslems in the sixteenth century. Trevisano, 126, asserts that they were renegades from every nation; and on this authority Zinkeisen falls into the opposite error of confining them to Christian renegades. Postel, iii. 36, says that they were chosen from the *Akinji*, Kurds, and *Azabs*. Menavino, 152, declares that they were not slaves of the great Turk, but that part were Turks, part Christian renegades, and part Arabs (*Mori*).

[2] The *Spahis* of the Porte are discussed at length in D'Ohsson, vii. 364 ff.; Hammer, *Staatsverwaltung*, 237 ff.; Zinkeisen, iii. 168 ff.

[3] Giovio (*Commentarius*, 75) mentions 2000 in each of the first two corps, and 1000 in each of the second two. Junis Bey (below, p. 267) puts 3000 in each of the first two corps, 2000 in each of the second two. Ramberti (below, p. 250) gives more than 3000 *Spahi-oghlans*, 3000 *Silihdars*, and 2000 in each of the other corps. Ludovisi, 15, puts 3000 in each of the first two, 2500 in the third, and 2000 in the fourth. Trevisano, 125, puts 2000 in each but the fourth, which contained 1500. D. Barbarigo, 33, mentions 7095 *Spahis*. Barbaro, 304, says that there were 15,000 *Spahis* of the Porte. There were under pay in 1660, after serious changes, 7203 *Spahis*, 6254 *Silihdars*, 976 *Ulufajis*, and 722 *Ghurebas:* Hammer, *Staatsverwaltung*, 175.

[4] A calculation based on Junis Bey's statements gives a total of between 41,000 and 49,000. Garzoni, 413, says distinctly that there were 40,000 *Spahis* of the Porte paid out of the sultan's treasury; that among these were 3000 *Spahi-oghlans*, 3000 *Silihdars*, 3000 *Ulufajis*, and 2000 *Ghurebas* (*ciarcagi*); and that the grand vizier had 1000 *Spahis* assigned to his retinue, and the other viziers each 500. D'Ohsson, vii. 364–365, states that the *Spahis* proper in the time of Mohammed II, numbered 10,000, and that Achmet III, raised their strength to 12,000; like figures for the *Silihdars* were 8000 and 12,000. This estimate must include the additional horsemen.

under his pay, does not appear clearly. Probably he did not pay the additional horsemen directly; for strictly speaking, they were *kullar* of his *kullar*. In time of battle all the regular troops, *Spahis* and Janissaries alike, were drawn up to protect the sultan, the Janissaries being aligned in front, the *Spahis* proper on the right, the *Silihdars* on the left, and the *Ulufajis* and *Ghurebas* in the rear.[1]

THE FEUDAL SPAHIS [2]

Outside the towns the greater part of the European dominions of the sultan, and a large part of Asia Minor, were granted in fief to Moslems who were for the most part not *kullar* of the sultan.[3] They deserve to be considered in a discussion of the government, however, not only because they collected the revenues and exercised seigniorial jurisdiction in their estates,[4] but also because they were officered by the sultan's *kullar*. The estates were of different sizes and were reckoned in three classes: *timars*, when the yearly revenue was under twenty thousand aspers; *ziamets*, when it was twenty thousand to one hundred thousand aspers; *khasses*, when it was over one hundred

---

[1] Hammer, *Geschichte*, iii. 57; Menavino, 148, 151.

[2] See above, pp. 47 (note 1), 91. The Ottoman feudal system is discussed at length in Hammer, *Staatsverfassung*, 337 ff.; D'Ohsson, vii. 372 ff.; Zinkeisen, iii. 145 ff.; Belin, *Du Régime des Fiefs Militaires en Turquie;* Tischendorf, *Moslemisches Lehnswesen.*

[3] Junis Bey (below, p. 271) says, shortly after describing the feudal *Spahis* of Europe, that " all the *Spahis* are slaves and sons of slaves of the Seigneur (*Tutti li spachi sono schiaui & figli de schiaui del Sig[nor]*); " but this statement is incomplete. Ramberti (below, p. 256) adds, " and sons of *Spahis*." The latter group undoubtedly contained the great majority of the feudal *Spahis*. Geuffroy 246, enlarges on the statement by saying that the 30,000 feudal *Spahis* of Europe were all *Ajem-oghlans* and slaves of the great Turk. No other writer terms them *kullar*. Garzoni, 412, calls them Turkish soldiers. The whole theory of the Ottoman feudal system made them such; the smaller fiefs were hereditary from of old, and gaps were filled from volunteers with the army, who must have been Moslems, since Christians were not allowed to bear arms: Hammer, *Staatsverfassung*, 349 ff. (" *Kanun-nameh* of the granting of *Timars* and *Ziamets* ").

[4] Junis Bey, p. 271 (they collect the income from the Christians, etc.); Moro, 339 (they are appointed by the king to administer justice); Hammer, *Geschichte*, iii. 478; D'Ohsson, vii. 373. Heidborn, 157, discusses their duties in some detail.

thousand aspers.[1] *Timars* might be united into a *ziamet*, but *ziamets* could not be divided.[2] Every fief-holder must appear in person when summoned to war. If the annual income of a *Timarji*, or Timariote, reached six thousand aspers, he must bring with him an armed horseman; and he must bring another for each additional three thousand aspers of his revenue. The holder of a larger fief must bring with him an armed horseman if his income amounted to ten thousand aspers, and another horseman for each additional five thousand aspers of income.[3] In the sixteenth century this service was strictly exacted, and the fief-holders were held to residence on their estates. The principle of heredity entered into the distribution of these estates, but under limitations. One son of the holder of a small fief had a right to the fief;[4] not more than three sons of the holder of a large fief were entitled to small fiefs.[5] The sons of *kullar* in high position might receive fiefs large in proportion to the rank of their father;[6] by this means they were honorably conveyed from the ruling Institution into the Moslem population. The *Zaims* and Timariotes, as the holders of the corresponding fiefs were named, were a class of country gentlemen, honest, sober, true to the Moslem faith and to the sultan, better in morals than the *kullar* if not so able of intellect, the substantial middle class of the empire, ancestors of those who today give hope that Turkey may become a modern nation. It was these who gave the first training to the *Ajem-oghlans*, starting them well on the road from Christianity to Islam, and preparing them to become members of the Ottoman nation.

1 Hammer, *Staatsverwaltung*, 275; Heidborn, 145.

2 Hammer, *Geschichte*, iii. 476.

3 Spandugino, 146, states that under Mohammed II, each fief-holder who had 5000 aspers of income was obliged to bring another with him to war; but in his time (under Bayezid II) this obligation was imposed upon those who had 3000 aspers, unless retired on account of age. Ramberti and Junis Bey (below, pp. 256–271) say that for each 100 ducats a *Spahi* must keep an armed horseman, and three or four servants, and a like number of horses; see also D'Ohsson, vii. 373. Heidborn, 145, states that holders of *timars* brought an additional warrior for each 3000 aspers of income, and holders of *ziamets* an additional one for each 5000 aspers; but in any case the first 3000 aspers was exempt.

4 D'Ohsson, vii. 374.

5 Hammer, *Staatsverfassung*, 352.   6 *Ibid.* 94.

In the time of Suleiman the system of fiefs had become greatly disarranged.[1] The distribution of them had been left to the local governors, and corruption had crept in; the frequent wars also had led to rapid changes and consequent confusion. Moreover, the army always contained a large number of *Gonnullu*, or volunteers, who came at their own expense, and fought with the hope, often realized, of receiving the fiefs of slain men as the reward of signally brave conduct.[2] It is said that during the course of a single bloody day one fief changed owners seven times. If fiefs might thus be granted in the midst of battle, it is not easy to see how a condition of reasonable order could have been preserved in the feudal system. Suleiman, therefore, by a *Kanun* of the year 1530, attached the granting of all fiefs above a certain size once more to the central government.[3] Each holder of such a fief must obtain a *teskereh*, or document, from Constantinople, in order to have good title.[4] The central treasury administered such estates during vacancies. Only those fief-holders who held by *teskereh* were entitled to be called *Spahis;*[5] the others were known as *Timarjis*, or Timariotes. The feudal *Spahis* of Anatolia were more under the authority of the governor than were those of Europe; they were not so well paid, did not have so much practice in fighting, and were not so highly esteemed as soldiers.[6]

Thus the country gentry were kept under good control; the accumulation of estates was prevented, any tendency toward independence could easily be thwarted, and the sultan obtained regularly the service for which the lands were granted. In addition, most of the subject Christian population was governed locally without any trouble to the sultan, and was held down well and uniformly by resident seigneurs. A great advantage

---

[1] Hammer (*ibid.* 143 ff.) describes Suleiman's legislation, giving translations of much of it.

[2] Ricaut, 343.

'[3] D'Ohsson, vii. 374; Hammer, *Staatsverfassung*, 352 ff.

[4] The limit differed according to region. In Rumelia a *teskereh* was required for all *timars* of 6000 aspers and over, and for all *ziamets:* Hammer, *Staatsverwaltung*, 275.

[5] Ramberti (below, p. 256) gives this limit as 100 ducats, or 5000 aspers.

[6] Garzoni, 413; Tanco, 209.

of the system was that, by the granting of new fiefs in newly-conquered lands, the territorial army was automatically increased in proportion to the increase of the empire.[1]

OFFICERS OF THE FEUDAL SPAHIS

Local government and the command of the feudal *Spahis* was cared for by officials who belonged to the sultan's great slave-family, and who brought with them to their posts a number, proportioned to their rank, of *Spahis* of the Porte, pages, *Ajem-oghlans*, and slaves of their own. The lowest of these officers were the *Subashis*, or captains, who were in time of peace governors of towns, with enough Janissaries and *Azabs*, or irregular infantry, to police the locality.[2] Next above these were the *Alai Beys*, or colonels, who in time of peace were ready with a company of from two hundred to five hundred troops to pass from place to place as there might be need.[3] Above these again were the *Sanjak Beys*, who governed important cities and held superior rule over a number of towns and the district in which they lay.[4] Finally, in the Balkan Peninsula and in Western Asia Minor there was from of old a *Beylerbey*, who had authority over all the *Beys* of his region. Incomes were provided by the assignment of fiefs proportioned in size to each officer's importance.[5] All of these officers of local government had a sufficient staff of lieutenants, treasurers, book-keepers and clerks.[6] The *Beylerbey* of Rumelia resided in time of peace at Constantinople. The *Beylerbey* of Anatolia seems to have spent much time in his

[1] Bernardo, 329; Knolles (ed. 1687), 983.

[2] Spandugino, 211; Zinkeisen, iii. 129. The feudal *Spahis* had lower officers who were not sent out from the capital, such as the *Cheri-bashis*.

[3] The name means " ensign bey," and was translated *flambole:* for example, Geuffroy, 246.

[4] Postel, iii. 44; Tiepolo, 138.

[5] Heidborn, 140, says that the *Subashis* had *ziamets*, the *Alai Beys* had small *khasses*, the *Sanjak Beys* had *khasses* of a million aspers or more, and the *Beylerbeys* much more. The amount which he assigns to the *Sanjak Beys* is too large for Suleiman's time. Ramberti (below, pp. 256-258) gives their income at from 4000 to 12,000 ducats, which would amount to from 200,000 to 600,000 aspers.

[6] Ramberti, below, p. 256; Junis Bey, below, p. 271.

dominions,[1] though undoubtedly he was often at the capital, since he had his regular place in the Divan.

In time of war this official scheme, detached from its function of local government, drew together the feudal *Spahis*, section by section, into a perfectly organized territorial army for each of the two regions. Notice of time and place was sent round, and within a month every man called had joined his proper standard.[2] After uniting with the sultan's regular army, the army of Rumelia under its *Beylerbey* had the right of the battle-line when fighting in Europe, and the army of Anatolia under its *Beylerbey* had the right of the line when fighting in Asia.[3] The enrolled feudal troops of Europe numbered about fifty thousand, and those of Asia, including Anatolia, Karamania, Amasia, and Avandole, thirty thousand.[4] In each case the number should be doubled or tripled to allow for the additional horsemen which all the *Spahis* were required to bring.[5] On the other hand, a considerable proportion of the feudal troops,

---

[1] Menavino, 186, 190, says that in his time the *Beylerbey* of Anatolia resided at Kutaia (Custage). Ramberti, 259, mentions the same place (Chiothachie) as the seat of his sanjakate. Knolles (ed. 1687, p. 986) says that all the *Beylerbeys* except the *Beylerbey* of Rumelia were supposed to reside within their dominions.

[2] *Tractatus*, ch. xi.   [3] Trevisano, 132.

[4] In Europe 30,000 *Spahis* and 20,000 *Timarjis;* in Anatolia 12,000 *Spahis;* in Karamania 7000, Amasia 4000, and Avandole 7000. This is the estimate of Junis Bey and Ramberti, which Geuffroy, 247, follows, and which Postel, iii. 37 ff., changes a little (Karamania 5000 instead of 7000, Amasia omitted). Ludovisi, 16, gives practically the same figures. Navagero, 41, gives 40,000 in Europe and 80,000 to 100,000 in Asia, the latter figure probably including the troops of Syria and Mesopotamia, and of Egypt, which was not provided with fiefs in the same way. Barbaro, 304, and Garzoni, 412, mention 80,000 in Europe and 50,000 in Asia. D. Barbarigo (1558), 33, speaks of a sum total of 160,000 feudal *Spahis.* Tiepolo (1576), 140, speaks of 60,000 *timars* in Europe which sent 80,000 *Spahis*, and 50,000 *Spahis* from Asia. The number may have increased about one-half during Suleiman's regin, but it is more likely that all the groups of figures are only estimates. Ricaut, 341, after careful inquiry, gives the number of *Zaims* in his time as 10,948, and of *Timarjis* as 72,436, for the whole empire except Egypt. He thinks that this estimate should be increased to 100,000. The total feudal contingent in the time of Achmet I, was by Turkish authority about the same (Tischendorf, 57 ff.). D'Ohsson, vii. 375, estimates the feudal troops at 200,000 in Suleiman's time; on p. 381, however, he speaks of more than 150,000 men. See below, p. 107, n. 1.

[5] Postel, iii. 38 (" triple pour le moins ").

sometimes estimated at one-half,[1] remained on duty at home in time of war to protect the provinces and prevent uprisings. The feudal troops, while brave, eager, and regardless of their lives, had not the physical strength nor the practice of fighting in squadrons which the regular troops had, and hence were not their equals.

The *Beylerbeys* of Rumelia and Anatolia were called out with their troops for every campaign. The eight other *Beylerbeys* of Suleiman's time, — those of Karamania, Amasia, Avandole, Syria, Mesopotamia, Egypt, Hungary,[2] and Temesvar,[3] — who had fewer feudal troops at command and more need of them at home, were summoned only when the war was in their region.

OTHER BODIES OF TROOPS

There were three principal bodies of irregular troops, the *Akinji* or cavalry, the *Azabs* or infantry, and the Kurds; besides various smaller groups, such as the descendants of the ancient corps of *Yayas* and *Mosellems*, who held fiefs of a sort in the oldest *sanjaks* of the empire, and the *Deli* or " crazy " company of scouts.[4] The *Akinji* numbered perhaps thirty thousand in time of peace and were mainly near the European frontier, where they made a living by raiding. They received no pay either in peace or in war, but gathered booty and slaves and hoped for promotion.[5] The *Azabs* numbered perhaps ten thousand in

---

[1] Chesneau, 46; D'Ohsson, vii. 381. Knolles (ed. 1687, p. 990) says that not over one-third could safely be called to arms.

[2] After the year 1541: Hammer, *Geschichte*, iii. 232.

[3] After the year 1552: Trevisano, 124. The number of the *Beylerbeys* was greatly increased in the last third of the sixteenth century. Knolles, 986–988, mentions five in Europe, 30 in Asia, and 4 in Africa, besides the *Beylerbey* of the Sea, whose office was created by Suleiman, but who is not mentioned above as having no part in the army.

[4] Spandugino, 153; Nicolay, 160.

[5] The name *akinji* is variously spelled: yachinji, alcanzi, alcangi, aconiziae, alengi, aquangi, achiar, aghiar. Spandugino, 150, says that the sultan can collect 200,000 of these for the war; Ramberti and Junis Bey (below, pp. 257, 271) mention 60,000 as inscribed; Giovio (*Commentarius*, 81) names 30,000; Garzoni, 414, says 25,000 or 30,000; Postel, iii. 26, says 50,000 or 60,000. Ramberti, 271, tells us that when in arms they were entitled to living expenses from the villages near which they passed.

peace and forty thousand in war.[1] Some of them served in the garrisons and some with the fleet.[2] The number of the *Akinjis* and *Azabs* was greatly augmented in time of war by the addition of volunteers, many of whom were criminals and ruffians.[3] The irregular troops were the terror of the invaded lands in war time; for the regular army was held under iron discipline, but these irresponsible creatures carried fire, rapine, and sword over wide areas of country. In time of siege and battle the *Azabs* were sent forward to break the charge of the enemy, or to aid in filling the moats by their own bodies.[4] Such as lived were rewarded generously; the rest were believed to pass at once by a martyr's death to heavenly reward.[5] The Kurds lay near the Persian frontier to the number of about thirty thousand. Individuals among the *Akinji, Azabs*, and Kurds might hope to become gentlemen through distinguished bravery, by being made *Ulufajis* among the *Spahis* of the Porte.[6]

Attached to the regular army there were also various auxiliary corps of armorers, cannoneers, men of transport service, musicians, commissaries, and the like, to the number of three or four thousand in all.[7] The Tartars of the Crimea, and the Moldavians and Wallachians, were also obliged to furnish contingents.[8] All told, the enrolled strength of the entire army was something more or less than two hundred thousand men. But, since the *Spahis* were required to bring other fighting men with them in proportion to their revenues, since numerous slaves and private servants accompanied the soldiers, and since the feudal and irregular troops were joined by great numbers of volunteers, both horse and foot, high and low, the complete

---

[1] Zinkeisen, iii. 203.
[2] Spandugino, 152. Junis Bey, 270, mentions 1000 with the fleet, and Postel, iii. 71, mentions 10,000.
[3] Postel, iii. 26.
[4] Chalcocondyles, 135; Giovio, *Commentarius*, 81, etc.
[5] Spandugino, 151.
[6] See above, p. 98.
[7] Junis Bey, below, p. 268. In addition were several thousand saddlers, etc., who were not reckoned as regular troops: the *Bostanjis*, older pages, body-guards, etc.
[8] Knolles (ed. 1687), 984.

army for the greatest expeditions probably numbered about three hundred thousand men.[1] At the close of Suleiman's reign the paid nucleus was about fifty thousand strong; the feudal *Spahis* for a European campaign numbered about sixty thousand, with perhaps a like number of helpers. The remaining troops were of no great value in battle, unless to break the first shock of the enemy's charge. They served chiefly to lay waste the hostile country and to gather booty and slaves.

[1] Several contemporary estimates of the complete army may be compared: Marini Sanuto, under date of October 26, 1529, gives an estimate of the Turkish army then before Vienna as containing 305,200 men. The same writer (*Diarii*, lvi) gives three or four estimates from the year 1532, when Suleiman went forth on the Güns campaign: on p. 768, Suleiman's army is said to contain 500,000 men; on p. 870 is found an account of Suleiman's entry into Belgrade, in which 170,300 men are mentioned, besides " adventurers " and " many others "; on the same page is estimated the number with which the Sultan was to leave Belgrade, which sums up 284,500, and does not seem to account fully for the territorial armies; on p. 894 he summarizes a despatch from Ratisbon, dated August 23, 1532, which relates the testimony of three Turkish prisoners to the effect that the Turkish army numbers over 300,000 persons, but that not over 80,000 are good fighting men. Postel, iii. 38, estimates the enrolled army at 218,000, and the whole at 500,000. He states elsewhere that Suleiman took 500,000 men with him on the Persian expedition of 1534–35. Chesneau's impression (pp. 106–108) of Suleiman's army, when he saw it near Aleppo in the spring of 1549, was that it occupied 80,000 to 100,000 tents, on a plain eight to ten miles long; that it contained 300,000 to 400,000 fighting men, of whom all but 10,000 or 12,000 Janissaries were on horse-back; and that the total number of persons assembled was about a million. Chesneau's chief, the ambassador D'Aramont, writing concerning the same expedition from Esdron (Erzerum ?) a few weeks later, speaks of " the mass of his (Suleiman's) army, which is by common estimate of 300,000 men, as may be judged from the extent of the camp, which extends ten or twelve miles in length, and contains at least 60,000 tents or more, with such order and obedience that, considering the great multitude, it is almost unbelievable " (Charrière, ii. 68). In the year 1558, A. Barbarigo, 150–151, estimated the cavalry alone at more than 300,000. Twenty-six years after Suleiman's death Bernardo, 331, says that the paid troops, in which he includes the sultan's household and the feudal army, amounted to 250,000 men. Zinkeisen, iii. 199, estimates the extreme total of the sultan's cavalry alone at 565,000. Knolles (ed. 1687, p. 984), writing about 1603, says that the sultan could always gather 150,000 Timariotes for a great expedition. He says that the Timariotes numbered in all 719,000 fighting men, of whom 257,000 were in Europe and 426,000 in Asia. The last two estimates are incredibly large.

DISCIPLINE AND ARDOR

Contemporary observers were strongly impressed with the wonderful discipline and intense zeal for fighting that was seen among the Turks. The silence, order, and cleanliness of the camps, the absolute obedience, enforced if need be by severe punishments and executions, the submissiveness to long marches, hard labor, and scanty food, the eagerness for battle, the joy in conflict, the recklessness of life, presented a perfection of discipline, self-control, and single-hearted purpose that seemed miraculous. A few of the many witnesses may be heard briefly:

" The Turks come together for war as though they had been invited to a wedding." [1]

" The Great Turk is the best obeyed by his subjects of all the lords that I know." [2]

" I think there is no prince in all the world who has his armies and camps in better order, both as regards the abundance of victuals and of all other necessities which are usually provided, and as regards the beautiful order and manner they use, in encamping without any confusion or embarrassment." [3]

" Their military discipline has such justice and severity as easily to surpass the ancient Greeks and Romans; the Turks surpass our soldiers for three reasons: they obey their commanders promptly; they never show the least concern for their lives in battle; they can live a long time without bread and wine, content with barley and water." [4]

" Peace and silence reign in a Turkish camp. . . . Such is the result produced by military discipline, and the stern laws bequeathed them by their ancestors." [5]

" It is marvellous how the force and rigor of justice increase in war. . . . If the soldiers rob or beat, the head comes off, or they are so beaten that they can never be well again." [6]

---

[1] *Tractatus*, ch. xi, marginal summary.

[2] La Broquière, 273.

[3] Chalcocondyles, 135.

[4] Giovio, *Commentarius*, 83 (condensed).

[5] Busbecq, *Life and Letters*, i. 293; on p. 221 he compares Turkish and Western soldiers most unfavorably for the latter.

[6] Postel, i. 126; see also Dandolo, 166. Georgevitz, 45, says that he accom-

" They keep the divinest order in the world." [1]

" In truth the discipline could not be better, nor the obedience greater." [2]

" For such as are acquainted with the Histories of the Turkish affaires, and doe aduisedly looke into the order and course of their proceedinges: doe well perceiue, that the chiefest cause of their sodaine and fearefull puissaunce, hath beene the excellencie of their Martial discipline joyned with a singular desire and resolution to aduaunce and enlarge both the bounds of their Empire and the profession of their Religion. The which was alwaies accompanied with such notable Policie and prudence, that the singularitie of their vertue and good gouernment, hath made their Armes alwaies fearefull and fortunate, and consequently, hath caused the greatnesse of their estate." [3]

THE SUPREME COMMAND

The sultan was commander-in-chief of the entire army, standing, feudal, and irregular. When the army was summoned for a great campaign, it gathered about him; on the march and in camp every body of troops had its place with reference to him; [4] in formation of battle, he was the central point about which the whole vast display was organized. When the army was assembled, and then only, the sultan stood fórth visibly and palpably as the head and center of the Ruling Institution and of the Ottoman nation upon which it rested. His *kullar* were gathered about him in devotion of body and soul; they were going forth under his leadership against the infidel or the heretic; they were manifesting the results of the long and careful training that he had given them; they marched, encamped, and fought under his eye and command; they formed an honored and privileged

panied the Turkish army on an expedition against Persia (probably 1533 to 1536): " I saw a *Spahi* decapitated together with his horse and servant, because the horse, having been left loose, entered some one's field."

[1] Postel, iii. 31, speaking particularly of the Janissaries.

[2] Morosini, 261.

[3] *The Policy of the Turkish Empire*, " To the Reader."

[4] Junis Bey (below, pp. 274, 275) gives the order of march; Postel, 29 ff., describes the encampment.

nucleus in the midst of a vast, loyal, and ambitious national army; they surrounded and served him as monarch with a splendor seen at no other time; [1] with complete apparatus of council, ministry, treasury, and chancery, they carried on his government from whatever city, valley, mountain, or plain he might be occupying. Here was the Ruling Institution in being, exhibiting in varying degrees all its aspects, revealing its essential unity, enforcing the despotic will of its master, commander-in-chief, and chief executive.

The very greatness and unity of the Ruling Institution as an army was not without serious disadvantages. The power could not wisely be delegated, and the army could not effectively be divided. At the opening of the campaign of 1529 Suleiman issued to Ibrahim a commission as *Seraskier*, or general of the army, which placed the Ruling Institution, the Moslem Institution, the Ottoman nation and all the subject nations under his command. The Sultan's order ran as follows: " My Viziers, *Beylerbeys*, Judges of the Army, Jurists, Judges, *Seids*, *Sheiks*, Dignitaries of the Court and Supports of the Empire, *Sanjak Beys*, Generals of Cavalry or of Infantry, *Alai Beys*, *Subashis*, *Cheribashis*, and all the victorious Soldiery great and small, high and low, the Officials and Appointees, all inhabitants of My kingdoms and lands, the people of city and country, rich and poor, distinguished and ordinary,' and all men are to recognize My above-named Grand Vizier as *Seraskier* . . . and to consider all that he says and desires as a command from My own mouth. . . ." [2] This was a delegation of the supreme command of the army and all the human military resources of the empire to Ibrahim. Since Suleiman himself went on this campaign, the supreme command was not then exercised apart from the sultan's presence. Four years later, however, Ibrahim, clothed with the same authority, was sent ahead to open the Persian campaign. On the return march he added the title of Sultan to that of *Seraskier* in issuing his daily orders.[3] Perhaps

[1] Chalcocondyles, 135, says that the Turks lodged more grandly in the field than in peace at home.
[2] Hammer, *Geschichte*, iii. 79.   [3] *Ibid.* 160.

he felt like Pepin the Short, that he who had the power of king should also bear the name. But Suleiman was no *roi fainéant;* Ibrahim had gone too far, the empire could have but one head, and Ibrahim suffered the bow-string.[1] Suleiman profited by the experience; he appointed no more *Seraskiers* with such exalted powers, but himself led the army when it was assembled as a whole. The campaign of Szigeth was the thirteenth which he directed in person.[2] The precedent of delegating the supreme command was, however, a fatal one; for Selim the Sot and all his successors were to use this method to avoid the exertion of campaigning, and from this step was to date the beginning of the empire's downfall.[3] " This so constituted organization had need of two things: it needed for its animation a man filled himself with a vivid spirit and free and mighty impulses, and to give it movement and activity it required continual campaigns and progressive conquests; in a word, war and a warlike chief." [4] When another than the sultan should become head of the Ruling Institution as visibly assembled, and yet be only an official removable at a cloistered monarch's caprice, the army would lose the keystone of its organization, and ere long victory would depart from its banners.

INDIVISIBILITY OF THE ARMY

The essential oneness of the army, based on the sultan's ownership of the standing body of cavalry and infantry and its attachment to his person,[5] and on the incapacity of the territorial armies to carry on great campaigns alone, was also a fact injurious to the Ottoman power. At the accession of Selim I, the empire had been nearly identical in territory with the Byzantine Empire

---

[1] Other reasons have been advanced to account for the fall of Ibrahim (cf. Postel, iii. 48 ff.). The fact that he had became a danger to the throne is sufficient.

[2] Hammer, *Geschichte*, iii. 438.

[3] Halil Ganem, i. 206.

[4] Ranke, 11.

[5] The *Spahis* of the Porte, and the Janissaries were not as a body put under a *Seraskier's* command until the time of Murad III: D'Ohsson, vii. 368; Djevad Bey, i. 16.

under the Macedonian dynasty.   No great power had marched
with it.   The conquests of Selim in the East and of Suleiman in
Hungary had pushed the frontiers to the borders of two great
powers: Persia on the east and Austria on the west remained
henceforth constantly hostile in feeling and often hostile in fact
to the Ottoman Empire.[1]   They were so far away from the Ottoman capital that the road to either was a journey of months for
the army, and relations with both were often disturbed at the
same time; but there was only one great army, and there could
be only one serious war.   If, while war was in progress on one
frontier, conditions became intolerable on the other, it was necessary to make peace on what terms could be had, and carry the
army to the other extremity of the empire.   Thus, Suleiman and
Ibrahim concluded the peace of 1533 with Charles and Ferdinand,
in order to be free to proceed against Persia at once;[2] and thus
Suleiman was obliged to arrange terms with Ferdinand in 1547,
in order to march against Persia in 1548.[3]   Had a Cardinal Ces-
arini absolved Charles and Ferdinand from either treaty, and
had they been able to act, they could have marched to Constantinople in 1534, 1535, or 1548 against practically no resistance.[4]
On the other hand, had the Ottoman standing army been divis-
ible, and separable from the person of the monarch, the Sultan
could have kept a steady pressure at both frontiers; and by
taking advantage of opportunities he might have conquered far
to the west and north, and realized his ambition of adding all
the heretical Persian dominions to his empire so as to reach

[1] Hammer, *Geschichte*, iii. 141.

[2] Final audience was given to the Austrian ambassadors on June 23 (*ibid.* 138),
and Ibrahim marched about September 21 (*ibid.* 143).

[3] *Ibid.* 277.

[4] Postel, iii. 54, speaking of Charles V in 1535-36, says: " The Emperor had
and lost during the war against the Sofi the fairest opportunity that ever Prince
had in this world, to recover Constantinople: for at every shaking of a leaf, all the
people trembled, and there was no guard in the city except the inhabitants and ten
thousand *Ajem-oghlans*" [these from the time of Mohammed II had been commissioned to guard the capital during the army's absence: D'Ohsson, vii. 348].
Erizzo, 131, also discusses this danger, emphasizing the valor of the Persians and
the readiness of Asia Minor to revolt.   The Turks in Constantinople in 1535
feared that the expedition which Charles V was preparing against Tunis was
intended for an attack upon their city (*Revue Africaine*, xix. 352).

the Chinese frontier, and of sending the horsetail standards to the Atlantic shore of North Africa.[1] Or he might have carried out the intention expressed through Ibrahim in 1533 — which was quite in keeping with his character — of aiding the Emperor Charles V to enforce unity of religious belief upon the Protestants and the pope.[2] It is interesting to notice that Austria possessed two great advantages over Persia in the wars with Turkey. The Ottomans did not wish to pass the winter in the cold north, but they did not object seriously to staying in Aleppo or Bagdad. This attitude probably saved Vienna for Austria and lost Bagdad for Persia. Again, since the journey from Vienna to Constantinople was much easier than that from Tabriz to Constantinople, the Austrians could have reached Constantinople while the Ottoman army was in the East, whereas the Persians could not have reached Constantinople while the Ottomans were in Austria. This advantage remained theoretical, however, in Suleiman's time, since neither Austria nor Persia was ever able to attempt invasion.

Thus the inherent character of the Ottoman Ruling Institution, as a single magnificent army united under the supreme command of the sultan, made the institution incapable of adaptation to an indefinitely expanding empire, and so set bounds, certain as those of fate, to Ottoman conquest. The sultan had but one arm; it was a long arm and a strong one, yet it could reach only a fixed distance, and it could strike but one blow.

[1] Suleiman in his letter to Ferdinand, November 27, 1562, says, " I, Lord of the Orient from the land of Tsin to the extremity of Africa ": Busbecq, *De Re Militari*, 272.

[2] Ibrahim said, " I, if I now wished it, could place Luther on one side and the Pope on the other, and compel them to hold a council; what Charles ought to have done, the Sultan and I will now do ": Hammer, *Geschichte*, iii. 134.

CHAPTER V

THE RULING INSTITUTION: AS A NOBILITY AND A COURT

I. PRIVILEGES OF THE KULLAR

No disgrace was attached to the condition of being the sultan's slave; on the contrary, the title of *kul* was felt to be an honor. Boys longed to bear it.[1] No one who had it desired to be rid of it. It carried marked distinction and secured deference everywhere. Those who revealed by their costume, bearing, or assertion that they were the sultan's property were treated with the consideration always granted in monarchies to property and persons closely related to the sovereign.

This honor shown to the *kullar* rested, however, on no mere servile attachment to the sultan and on no mere fear of an Oriental despot. The sultan's slaves from lowest to highest were set off from his subjects by a distinct set of privileges which in Western minds were associated only with nobility. Besides a general protection over them all by means of careful registration and watchful organization, the sultan bestowed upon all his *kullar* the personal rights of immunity from taxation,[2] and responsibility to none but their own officials and courts and to him.[3] At the same time he freed them all from anxiety about the necessities of life, and enabled most of them to enjoy its luxuries, by regular pay from his treasury, or, in the case of some high officials, by revenues from ample estates. In return for these privileges they were all sternly required to render him honorable service, usually of a military character. This service was not always of a character that the West considered honorable. The labors of the *Ajem-oghlans*, and the foot service of the Janissaries and auxiliary corps were not noble in Christian feudalism,

---

[1] Gerlach, 257, quoted in Zinkeisen, iii. 222.
[2] Postel, iii. 19.
[3] Spandugino, 218; Postel, i. 126.

which knew no implements but sword and spear and fought from the back of a horse. But these humble slaves of the sultan possessed the same privileges as the highest, and any service was honorable which would make their muscles stronger for fighting and teach them to contribute to the sultan's military undertakings on sea and land. All members of the sultan's family were supposed to use their income in strengthening his military forces. Janissaries had pay for themselves alone. *Ghurebas* had only enough to keep themselves and one horse for each man. Other *Spahis* of the Porte brought additional horsemen in accordance with their pay. Higher officials were expected to support armed households large in proportion to their revenues. After the model of the sultan's household, every *kul* according to his means built up a military establishment which followed him and his master to war.

Immunity from taxation grew naturally out of the slave status. There would be no advantage to the sultan in exacting taxes from persons whom he supported and who were supposed to devote all their energies to his service and use all their income for him. As long as the Ruling Institution was kept firmly to its purpose, pressure was applied, not so that successful *kullar* would surrender part of their income to the master, but so that they would bring as large a contingent as possible to fight his battles. Suleiman's grand vizier, Rustem, following a long-disused precedent of the time of Bayezid I,[1] — a reign which had in various ways fore-shadowed later evils, — established a tax upon the greater offices of the empire;[2] but, since the sultan did not receive the whole of such charges, the custom amounted to the sale of offices. Not only was such a practice out of harmony with the theory of the Ruling Institution, but it proved very injurious in operation, and was rightly accounted one of the causes of the decay of the empire. The sultan took pay at the granting of an office, and so presently did every official from the men under him; until in time the practice became so sys-

---

[1] D'Ohsson, vii. 202.

[2] Suleiman permitted this because of the increase it produced in his income: Busbecq, *Life and Letters*, i. 114; Halil Ganem, i. 197.

tematized that a regular tariff was arranged and brought into use on the occasion of every appointment.[1] Those who thus were put to great expense on coming into office felt the necessity of recouping themselves by whatever means lay in their power.[2] Hence arose not merely oppression of the sultan's subjects, both Christian and Moslem, but also a partial recovery of losses at the expense of the sultan himself. His servants were forced to devote to personal affairs a large part of the attention that should have been all his, and to curtail by various devices the contingent which they furnished for his military service. When the members of the Ruling Institution began to prey upon each other, the grand vizier, on behalf of the sultan, taking the lead, the solidarity of the institution began to be broken. It may be true that in the West, as Montesquieu said, the honor of a monarchy was not inconsistent with the sale of office;[3] but in the Ottoman Empire it opened the door to fatal corruption.

The members of the Ruling Institution had not always had their own system of justice; they had long been under the jurisdiction of the ordinary Moslem courts. This had led to an essential difficulty; the ordinary courts were part of another institution and were recruited in a wholly different way; their judges had risen through a rival system of education, and were men of letters rather than men of war; the favored *kullar* of the sultan had, therefore, come to feel averse to obeying them.[4] Accordingly, Bayezid II had ordered that the members of his family should be judged by their own officers.[5] This was a radical change; for it brought into prominence the distinction between the two institutions, and had the further effect of setting off the *kullar* from all the rest of the population of the empire, and of constituting them almost a separate nationality. Their

[1] D'Ohsson, vii. 182, 202.

[2] Ricaut, 140; D'Ohsson, vii. 287.

[3] Montesquieu, livre v, ch. xix.

[4] Postel, i. 126: "les gents de la court, qui ont leurs chefs *Aga & Bassi* pour Iuges," etc.

[5] Spandugino, 214 ff., relates how this came about, and says (p. 218), "No *Cadi* can have power and authority over the slaves who receive pay from the Seigneur."

position became one greatly to be desired. The Moslem-born population came to feel that somewhere there was a great injustice. They whose ancestors had shed their blood for the faith were, in the lands which their fathers had conquered, denied admittance to the class which not only filled most of the offices of army and state but enjoyed high privileges. Sons of the conquered inhabitants, infidel-born, might alone become nobles, paid by the state rather than contributing to its expenses, not subject to the judges trained from boyhood in the Sacred Law; while their own Moslem sons were rigidly excluded from the honored class, were obliged to bear a part in the burdens of the state with small hope of sharing its glory, and were expected to take their chances before the same courts to which Christians and Jews were brought for civil and criminal cases. The very extent of the privileges of the *kullar* made toward the break-down of the system.

NOBILITY NOT HEREDITARY

The privileges of the sultan's *kullar* fell short of those of Western nobility in one very important respect, namely, that they could not normally be handed on to the descendants and heirs of those privileged. This exception is so important that various Western writers have affirmed that the Turks had no nobles.[1] As the word is used in this treatise, heredity is not regarded as of the essence of nobility; the latter is considered to lie in the possession of special personal privilege, recognized in the structure of the state.

In the early Ottoman days, several of the high offices of state became the appanages of particular families. The family of Kara Khalil Chendereli held the office of grand vizier continuously for a century, and furnished an occupant of the office at a later date.[2] The descendants of Michael of the Pointed Beard led the *Akinjis* until the time of the first siege of Vienna.[3]

---

[1] Zane, 407; Robertson, i. 249.

[2] Hammer, *Geschichte*, i. 176, 684; ii. 674.

[3] *Ibid.* i. 96. The descendants of Michael have been among the very few families who were constituted landed nobles in the Ottoman Empire. Seven " endowments of the Conquerors " still exist, one of which benefits his line: Heidborn, 314.

The family of Samsamat Chaush held the office of master of ceremonies for generations.[1] A descendant of the thirteenth-century poet Jelal ad-din Rumi held office under Suleiman.[2] Some writers of the early sixteenth century said that, whereas Osman had been aided in winning his dominions by two Greek renegades, Michael of the Pointed Beard, and Malco, and by Aurami or Eurcasi, a Turk, he had promised that he would "never put hand in their blood or fail to give them a magistracy."[3] The promise had been kept, and in 1537 one of the Michaloglou was *Sanjak* in Bosnia and one of the Malcosoglou was *Sanjak* in Greece. The other family was then extinct. It is said that these were considered to be of royal blood, and that in case of failure in the line of Osman the succession to the throne would fall to them.

Apart from these few exceptions, the principle of heredity in office had been excluded from the Ottoman system by the time of Suleiman. The Ottomans, by old Turkish rule probably derived from the Chinese, knew no nobility apart from office and public service. An exception was introduced by Islam in the case of *Seids*, or *Emirs*, descendants of the Prophet; but this modification the Ottomans did not wholly respect.[4] Accordingly, Ottoman nobility became official,[5] personal, and without hereditary quality. It was, in fact, the reverse of hereditary, since nobility in the father was an actual hindrance to the son and to all his descendants. But the *kullar* were not the only class in the Ottoman Empire which enjoyed official, personal nobility. The members of the Moslem Institution were also exempt from

[1] Hammer, *Geschichte*, i. 96.

[2] *Ibid*. iii. 18.

[3] Spandugino, 13; Ramberti, below, p. 242; Junis Bey, below, p. 273. D. Barbarigo, 19, names eight great families among whom the succession might fall (he says that some thought it should pass through the female line): in Rumelia four, — Micali, Ersecli, Eurenesli, Egiachiali; in Anatolia, four, — Cheselamath, Diercauli, Durcadurli, Ramadanli, formerly called Spendial. Ricaut, 107, says that in his time there existed an "ancient compact" by which, in default of heirs male in the Ottoman line, the empire was to descend to the Crimean Tartars.

[4] Ricaut, 211.

[5] *Ibid*. 129: "A Turk is never reverenced but for his Office, that is made the sole measure and rule of his greatness and honour, without other considerations of Vertue or Nobility."

taxation, were supported out of public revenues, and were left in enjoyment of their own government as a part of their general jurisdiction in the empire. They had an advantage over the *kullar* in that their property was not subject to confiscation. Their position will be discussed later.[1]

In the program of the Ruling Institution the policy of avoiding heredity of nobility fitted in exactly with the slave system, the educational scheme, and the army arrangements; for the knowledge that every man was considered to be " his own ancestry," and that increased honor and privilege depended on achievement alone, made every ambitious member a devoted slave, an indefatigable learner, and a dauntless warrior. The reasons for this policy, the method of applying it by advancement through merit, and the vivid impression which it made on thoughtful Western observers have been described already;[2] but for its observance an additional reason of great weight may be mentioned. Not only did it prevent the accumulation of property and power in the hands of the members of one family, but it allowed no influence to become intrenched in the offices of central and local government. No *Beylerbey* or *Sanjak Bey* could hope to rebel successfully. All were " but strangers and foreigners in the countries they ruled,"[3] and held their positions by the most insecure tenure. The Ottoman Empire was not destined to go the way of that of Charlemagne or of the Seljuk Turks. Whatever decay it might undergo, it could not break up into small independent states under officials who had converted their governorships into sovereignties, so long as its two great institutions were maintained consistently.[4]

---

[1] Below, ch. vii.
[2] Above, ch. iii, under heads " Other Motives for Incorporating Christians," " Advancement Based on Merit."
[3] Ricaut, 129.
[4] About the year 1800, when the two institutions, and particularly the Ruling Institution, had reached an extreme state of decay, and before new institutions after Western models had yet been introduced, the Ottoman Empire was to come very near to such a breaking-up. It seems actually to have been saved by the lingering of the tradition against heredity in office; for, though life-tenure of purchased governorships had become regular, no Pasha except the North African corsairs of the seventeenth century, and Ibrahim in Egypt in the early nineteenth century,

Against this policy two main tendencies conspired, both based on " human nature," the strife of favor against merit, and the desire of the excluded to share in privilege. The first was liable to disturb the order of promotion, the second to open the system to the sons and descendants of the officials and to other Moslems. No one but Selim the Grim was fitted to maintain the policy rigidly against such pressure. Suleiman yielded a little on the first point, in such matters as the promotion of Ibrahim and Rustem; [1] and the second began in his time to gain ground at the bottom, by the admission of sons of Janissaries to the ranks of the *Ajem-oghlans.* Within a generation after his death, however, the flood-gates were to be opened. [2] The body of Janissaries and the body of *Spahis* of the Porte were gradually but swiftly to be made Moslem and so cut off from the Ruling Institution; the age at which the pages passed out of the palace was to be postponed; and in time the divided Ruling Institution was to cease to be the admiration of the West and was to become its laughing-stock. But Suleiman was spared the sight of such a decadence. Near the end of his reign, after Rustem and Roxelana had ceased to disturb, the system brought to the top one of the greatest of Ottoman statesmen, Mohammed Sokolli. At about the same time the Moslem Institution also raised up a great legist, Ebu su'ud. [3] These two upheld the institutions and the empire at the height of their glory for nearly thirty years, of which fifteen lay after the death of Suleiman.

II. Character of the Sultan's Court

In the early stages of all monarchies the household of the prince and the government of the state have probably been identical. [4] After the period of establishment has come to an end and settled institutions have been organized, the household and the government have tended to draw apart into separate and distinct systems under different officials. Which of the two

succeeded in founding a dynasty upon Ottoman soil. For the disorders about 1800, see Heidborn, 144.

[1] Hammer, *Geschichte*, iii. 490–491, quoting Kochi Bey.

[2] See above, p. 69, note 3.

[3] Hammer, *Geschichte*, iii. 278.   [4] Hammer, *Staatsverwaltung*, 6.

has become of the greater importance in the eyes of the sovereign and in influence upon the policy and destiny of the nation has depended on circumstances, and particularly on the character of individual monarchs. While such a state has been in a period of increase of power and influence, the government has regularly been the more prominent: men of practical experience in affairs and in the field have overshadowed the palace servants. When decay and decline have set in, the household, partly by way of cause and partly by way of effect, has risen to supremacy: individuals of more or less secluded life, but possessing opportunities for personal intercourse with the monarch, — favorites, body-servants, women, and eunuchs, — have made the men of affairs and of war dependent upon them for place and authority. The Ottoman Empire came clearly into the stage of differentiation between household and government after the conquest of Constantinople in the reign of Mohammed II. In the time of Suleiman the empire was still in the period when government was greater than household; but clear signs were appearing that a less active and more plastic sovereign would turn the scale.

The household of the Ottoman sultan was curiously divided and limited. An essential difference between the courts of Christian and Moslem monarchs was created by the seclusion of women in Mohammedan society. In the West, women appeared with the men of the court not only on occasions of amusement and diversion, but also in public parades and ceremonies of less and greater importance, and the ladies of the royal family led the fashionable society of the land. In the East, on the other hand, the visible court and retinue of the monarch was wholly ungraced by the presence of the fair sex; all the great ceremonies and cavalcades were participated in by men alone. It seems to be a fact that, before the middle of the reign of Suleiman, no woman resided in the entire vast palace where the sultan spent most of his time.[1] The women of his family were

[1] Postel, i. 31, says that Suleiman occasionally sent for one of his women to visit him in the principal palace. Nicolay, 62, reports that about 1551 Roxelana was residing within the palace grounds. By 1585 the principal ladies of the

elsewhere, carefully guarded behind walls which with very few exceptions no man but himself might pass.[1]   The men and the women who were associated with the sultan constituted two separate worlds, between which the only bond was himself.

The sultan's household was divided in another way.   By the maxims of despotic government it is forbidden that the ruler should associate on terms of intimate friendship with those who are his high officials of state.   In order to avoid this regulation and yet provide his master with intelligent and amusing companionship, the *Nizam-al-mulk* advised the Seljuk sultan Melik Shah to choose as boon companions a band of courtiers who would be allowed to have no share whatever in the conduct of affairs.[2]   This resource was hardly open to the Ottoman sultans, first because the dignity and independence of Moslem-born Ottoman Turks deprived them of the pliancy which is expected from courtiers, and second because the sultan's Christian-born slaves, who had been led onward by ambition ever since they had entered his service, and at the end of their education were ready to become men of affairs, were not fitted to be mere courtiers. The difficulty became greater after Mohammed II, filled with the Byzantine notion of imperial sacredness, ordered that no one should sit with him at table.[3]   A sultan was thus practically forced by a combination of principles and circumstances to spend his leisure hours with boys, eunuchs, and women.[4]   The only mature men with whom he could converse freely were a small and select group of religious advisers, astrologers, and physicians; all the other men of his household met him only formally and for

harem had been transferred to the new palace, leaving the old palace to the function of a training-school for recruits.   These steps illustrate the rapid increase of the importance of the harem in the Ottoman scheme.

[1] Exceptions were made in case of the old *Hojas*, or teachers of the young princes, the religious advisers of the queen mother, and physicians.   See Postel, i. 35; Ricaut, 68; D'Ohsson, vii.   11; Hammer, *Staatsverwaltung*, 73.

[2] *Siasset Naméh*, 121, 123, 163.

[3] " *Kanun* of the Imperial Table," printed in Hammer's *Staatsverfassung*, 98: " It is not my *Kanun* that any one should dine with my Imperial Majesty;   it might be some one not of Imperial blood."   Suleiman did not always observe this *Kanun* (cf. Hammer, *Geschichte*, iii. 99).

[4] Erizzo, 138; Morosini, 281.

the transaction of business. So great limitations on his companionship could not fail to influence his character, and in the course of a few generations to tend greatly toward the predominance of household over government.

To confine the consideration of Suleiman's court to his immediate household would be to narrow the discussion too much. The chief officers of government formed a part of his retinue on all ceremonial occasions, and had not ceased to be counted as his personal followers. In fact, all the members of the Ruling Institution, except the *Ajem-oghlans* and young pages, may be regarded as belonging to the sultan's court in that large sense of the term which includes all those individuals who are attached to the person of the monarch as his daily associates, his councillors, the officers and members of his household, his body-guard and palace-guard, and his retinue on ceremonial occasions and in camp. The splendid court of Suleiman the Magnificent is worthy of separate and special treatment for which there is no room here; in describing it, as in describing his army, only those aspects which are of a governmental nature can be considered. The topics that will claim attention are the subdivisions of his household and the main features of its organization, the importance given to personal and public ceremony, the splendor of the court, and the influence of the court on the destiny of the empire.

ORGANIZATION OF THE HOUSEHOLD [1]

The sultan's household may be considered in three principal subdivisions, each of them composed of a number of parts: the outside service of the palace, the inside service of the palace, and the harem. The outside service was composed of men and *Ajem-oghlans*, the inside service of white eunuchs and pages, the harem of black eunuchs and women. The first two subdivisions were, in time of peace, in attendance at the principal palace which had been built by Mohammed II on the site of the

[1] Extended descriptions of the household are found in D'Ohsson, vii and Hammer's *Staatsverwaltung*. Lane-Poole, in his *Story of Turkey*, ch. xiv, gives a good, clear summary of D'Ohsson. References to these authorities are here omitted except in a few instances of special interest.

acropolis of ancient Byzantium. The grounds of this palace were extensive: within the first gate was a large open space used on state occasions as a parade ground; within the second gate were the buildings of the palace proper, a beautiful garden, and an exercise ground for the pages. The members of the outside service, except the gardeners, did not ordinarily pass beyond the second gate of this palace. The harem was permanently located some distance away in the center of the city, in the first palace occupied after the conquest, known in the sixteenth century as the Old Palace.[1] In time of war, practically the entire outside service, and the principal officers and personal attendants from the inside service, accompanied the sultan. None of the women of the harem were taken with the army, as this was against the Ottoman custom, though permitted by the Sacred Law.[2] In excursions during time of peace some of the ladies might accompany their lord.[3] The three subdivisions of the household will be considered in the reverse order.

THE HAREM

The harem was so distinct in Suleiman's time from the rest of his household, so little seen and known, so much his personal affair, that it would seem scarcely to demand attention in a consideration of his court. The importance of its officials and personages was small as compared with later times, after the harem had been removed to the principal palace and the sultans had begun to spend a much larger portion of their time in its society. Yet the influence of two of its ladies upon Suleiman was so great as to give them a place in history and a relation to the destiny of the nation. Accordingly, the harem cannot be passed over without mention. Its organization has already been sketched so far as regards the recruiting, conversion, and education of the women;[4] its groupings and principal personages remain to be described.

---

[1] Hammer, *Staatsverwaltung*, 71; Menavino, 179. The *Eski Serai* of the sixteenth century stood where the *Seraskierat*, or War Office, now stands.

[2] D'Ohsson, v. 52.   [3] Postel, i. 32.

[4] See above, pp. 56, 57, 78, 79.

The guard and order of the palace of the harem was committed to forty or more black eunuchs,[1] under an official known as the *Kizlar Aghasi*, or, literally, the " general of the girls." This *Agha* was held in great honor, and was made administrator of many religious endowments for the benefit of various mosques, and particularly of the *vakfs* of the Holy Cities of Mecca and Medina. His importance in Suleiman's time bears no comparison with what it became later. Other black eunuchs held official positions in the service of the principal ladies, and had the oversight of the education of the young princes.[2]

The greatest lady of the harem, while life was spared to her, was the sultan's mother, the *Sultana Valideh*. Not only did she receive great respect and deference from her son, but she had a general oversight and authority over all his women. The next lady in importance was the mother of the sultan's first son; and after her came the mothers of other sons. Mothers of daughters enjoyed much less consideration. Each of these favored ladies had her own suite of apartments, her business staff under a woman known as her *Kiaya*, which may here be translated as steward or housekeeper, and her group of personal and domestic servants. The *Kiaya* of the queen mother enjoyed great importance. The group of slave girls who were the sultan's personal and domestic servants when he visited the harem were also under a *Kiaya* with assistants. Sons of the sultan lived with their mothers during their tender years. They were carefully educated in letters and arms, much as were the pages, but with greater deference.[3] At a suitable age they were sent out, with carefully selected little courts, to the governorship of provinces. Daughters were married at an early age to high officials of the sultan.[4] In later generations infant sons who might be born to them were not allowed to live, lest they might become a menace to the throne. This seems not to have been the case in the time

---

[1] Junis Bey (below, p. 269) says twenty, a number scarcely sufficient. Twenty years earlier Menavino, 180, speaks of about forty.
[2] Ricaut, 67–68, mentions several of these.
[3] Postel, i. 35.
[4] Ricaut, 73.

of Suleiman, who avoided danger by excluding them carefully from office.[1]

Information about Suleiman's harem and family comes guarded with explanations of the difficulty found in obtaining trustworthy reports. Some facts are known, and probabilities exist as to others. Suleiman's mother lived until far along in his reign. The mother of his eldest son, Mustapha, held, according to custom, the next place in his harem. After the year 1534 she divided her time between the palace at Magnesia, where her son was *Sanjak Bey*, and the harem palace in Constantinople.[2] Khurrem, usually called Roxelana, had supplanted her in favor at some previous date, and, being legal wife of the Sultan, held a position superior to hers in some respects. Suleiman seems not to have visited his harem very often.[3] Mihrmah, his daughter by Roxelana, who became the wife of Rustem, was very dear to him.

THE INSIDE SERVICE

The five chambers of pages, under the control of white eunuchs, and the doorkeepers supplied the inside service of the principal palace. The head of this service was the *Kapu Aghasi*, or " general of the gate," a white eunuch, who was also charged with the management of many religious endowments. He had the right to speak to the sultan when he wished,[4] and hence was very highly regarded. The *Kapuji-bashi*, or head doorkeeper, was also a white eunuch, who had charge constantly of the second gate of the principal palace, with a company of twenty or more white eunuchs who were guards under him.[5] The pages have already received attention from the educational point of view. Nearest the person of the sultan were the pages of the *Khas Oda*, or Inner Chamber, of whom there were probably thirty-

---

[1] Hammer (*Geschichte*, ii. 222) says that the custom of accomplishing the death of sons of daughters of sultans (by neglecting to tie the navel cord) dates from Mohammed II; but no contemporary authority appears to mention such a custom. D'Ohsson, vii. 93, says that it was instituted in the time of Achmet I. The son of a sister of Selim I was *Beylerbey* of Aleppo about 1550 (Alberi, *Anonimo* of 1553, 228).

[2] Ludovisi, 29; Postel, i. 31. See p. 141, note 2.   [4] Spandugino, 64.

[3] Postel, i. 31.   [5] Menavino, 137.

nine, the sultan himself being reckoned the fortieth.[1]   A number of these pages later bore the title of *Agha*, but they seem not to have done so in Suleiman's time.   Their chief officer was the *Khas Oda-bashi*, or head of the Inner Chamber, one of the pages in Suleiman's day, but in later times a white eunuch.   The pages of highest rank were the *Silihdar*, who outside the palace carried the sultan's weapons, the *Chokadar*, who carried his garments, and the *Sharabdar*, or cup-bearer.[2]   The others took care of his apartments and his wardrobe, and brought his food to him.   The second group of pages constituted the *Khazineh Odassi*, or treasury, under a well-paid white eunuch, the inside *Khazinehdar-bashi*.   These, to the number of sixty or seventy, cared for all the treasures in the sultan's palace, made all payments, and kept all accounts.[3]   Another *Khazinehdar-bashi* took care of all the financial affairs of the inside service which needed attention outside the palace walls.   The *Kiler Odassi*, or pantry, under a white eunuch called the *Kilerji-bashi*, cared for the bread, pastry, and game of the sultan; their chief controlled also the kitchen service of the palace.   The pages of this chamber seem not yet to have finished their education.[4]   They, together with the pages of the Inner Chamber, rode with the sultan whenever he left the palace.   The remaining two chambers, the Large and the Small, or the Old and the New, were concerned wholly with the education of the pages.[5]   They were under the

[1] D'Ohsson, vii. 34.   Whether this number was fixed in Suleiman's time does not appear from the records.   Mohammed II had 32 officers of the *Khas Oda* (Hammer, *Staatsverfassung*, 96).   Menavino, 121–123, names three special officers, 15 of second grade, and 35 of third grade, before mentioning the treasury. Ramberti and Junis Bey (below, pp. 243, 263) name 6 principal officers, but do not distinguish the *odalar* further.   Chesneau, 39, says that 25 of the pages were Suleiman's personal servants, and that 5 served him specially.   Navagero, 45, speaks of 25 or 30 in the *Khas Oda*.   Ricaut, 52, speaks of 40.

[2] Ramberti and Junis Bey, as above; Postel, iii. 4; Navagero, 45.

[3] Navagero, 44.

[4] The number of pages in the *Kiler Odassi* is given by Menavino, 125, as 25, all between 20 and 22 years of age.   Navagero, 44, says that they numbered 300 or 400; but this is incredible.   He gives no numbers for the purely educational *odalar*, and evidently has counted them all in the *Kiler Odassi*.

[5] Hammer (*Staatsverwaltung*, 30) erroneously says that the pages of these *odalar* attended to the lowest duties of the palace, and were recruited from three palace schools outside.   Navagero, 44, disproves this.

general direction of the *Ikinji-Kapu-oghlan*, or eunuch of the second gate.[1] The entire personnel of the inside service amounted to from six to eight hundred persons. The eunuch officers maintained severe discipline, exact obedience, and perfect order among them all.[2] The groups of eunuchs who had charge of the colleges of pages in Pera and Adrianople may also be reckoned in the inside service. It would seem that the accounts of all these palaces were kept as one, and that therefore the chief officers of the principal palace must have supervised the officers of the others.[3]

THE OUTSIDE SERVICE

The members of the household who were not held within the inner regions of the palace or near the person of the sultan were far more numerous. Many stood in close relations to the members of the inner service, either being under their authority or having regular dealings with them. All, of course, served the sultan, either directly or nearly so, through the mediation of one or more officers. To describe at length their subdivisions, duties, and officers would be to repeat an account which has been given often by others. Only a general sketch will be attempted here, by way of distinguishing the various groups of the service. Beginning with those in closest relations to the sultan, they were the learned associates of the master, the kitchen service, the body-guard, the palace-guards, the gardeners, the stable service, the tent-pitchers, the masters of the hunt, and the intendants.

The learned associates of the sultan belonged chiefly to the corps of the *Ulema*. They therefore represented the Moslem Institution near the person of the monarch. Chief among them was the sultan's *Hoja*, or teacher, a confessor or adviser in religious matters, who was held in very great esteem and was often

---

[1] An additional chamber, the *Seferli Odassi*, or Chamber of Campaign, was instituted by Murad IV to attend to his laundry work and other special duties in time of war. The membership was chosen out of the educational *odalar*, and it ranked next after the *Kiler Odassi*. See Hammer, *Staatsverwaltung*, 28.

[2] Ricaut, 47.

[3] Ramberti, below, p. 255.

advanced to high judicial office. Next came two *Imâms*, or preachers to the sultan, associated with whom were a number of muezzins, or chanters. After these ranked the *Hekim-bashi*, or chief physician, who had ten or more associates; the *Munejim-bashi*, or chief astrologer, whose services were believed to have a very real value; and the *Jerrah-bashi*, or chief surgeon, with ten or more helpers.

The kitchen service under the oversight of the *Kilerji-bashi* comprised bakers, scullions, cooks, confectioners, tasters, and musicians, each to the number of from fifty to one hundred.[1] Allied to these were the companies of tailors, shoemakers, furriers, goldsmiths, and the like, who were employed exclusively in the palace service.[2] Each group had its responsible head and was subject to a thorough oversight, since even such remote affairs, when under the care of the Ottoman Ruling Institution, were regulated and ordered with great precision. A number of these servants, such as the scullions, wood-cutters, and water-carriers, were *Ajem-oghlans*.

The body-guards were three, the *Muteferrika*, the *Solaks*, and the *Peiks*. The *Muteferrika*, or Noble Guard, consisted of from one to two hundred of the choicest graduates from the page schools and of sons of high officials.[3] Among them, in 1575, were brothers of the *Voivodes* of Wallachia and Moldavia. The *Muteferrika* followed immediately after the sultan on horseback, and in time of battle were ready to defend him to the end. The *Solaks* were veteran Janissary archers, to the number of

[1] Ramberti and Junis Bey, below, pp. 245, 264.
[2] Menavino, 160 ff.
[3] Zinkeisen, iii. 181, states erroneously on the authority of Trevisano, 125 (meaning p. 128), that these were all Turks and of noble blood. The fact that Menavino, 146, calls them "schiaui" is sufficient disproof. Zinkeisen also quotes Spandugino, 114, to the effect that the *Muteferrika* were all lords, or sons of princes or of lords; but Spandugino, 62, says that pages pass to the office of *Muteferrika* from the highest four offices at least. Trevisano, 127, says, "Li quali sono giovani nati Turchi, e figliuoli d'uomini di autorità" (italics not in original); but "men of authority" were practically all renegades. Moro, 341, calls them, in 1590, sons of the principal Turks. The fact seems to be that most of the *Muteferrika* were Ottomans of the second generation (*i. e.*, sons of renegades) and that the rest were regarded as ennobled by passage through the high offices of the *Khas Oda*.

about one hundred and fifty, who marched on foot beside the sultan wherever he went, with bows and arrows ready for instant use. The *Peiks* were a picturesque company of halberdiers of about one hundred men,[1] which had been taken over, arms, costumes, and all, from the Byzantine emperors. They ran in front of the sultan when he rode, and were always ready to be sent on missions.

The palace-guards were the *Kapujis*, the *Chaushes*, and the *Bostanjis*. The *Kapujis*, or gatekeepers, were *Ajem-oghlans* who, to the number of three or four hundred,[2] watched the outside gates of the principal palace and of the palace of the harem. Like all the other guards, they accompanied the sultan to war, where they were the guards of his tent. The *Chaushes*, who numbered about one hundred,[3] were ushers who acted as marshals on the days of Divan and of state ceremony, and who in time of war dressed the ranks of the troops.[4] They also acted as messengers of state within the empire. When a distant officer had been condemned to death, a *Chaush* was sent to execute the sentence and bring back the offender's head.[5] Since among the *Chaushes* there were many renegades who knew various European languages, they were useful as interpreters and were sometimes sent as envoys on important missions.[6] The *Bostanjis*, or gardeners, were *Ajem-oghlans*, and as such have been mentioned already. To the number of about four hundred,[7] they cared for the garden and grounds of the principal palace, and rowed the sultan's caiques when he wished to enjoy the matchless scenery of the Bosphorus. Their chief, the *Bostanji-bashi*, who had risen from their ranks, seems to have

---

[1] Menavino, 155 (he says they were Persians); Nicolay, 98; Ramberti, below, p. 251.

[2] Spandugino, 116, gives the number 300, and says that they became Janissaries. Menavino, 140, mentions 500. Ramberti (pp. 246, 253) mentions 250 at the principal palace and 100 at the palace of the harem; the latter he calls Janissaries.

[3] Junis Bey, below, p. 265.

[4] Spandugino, 125.

[5] Postel, iii. 9.

[6] Ricaut, 373. In his time they numbered 500 or 600.

[7] Junis Bey, 263. Ramberti, 245, speaks of 35, which is clearly too few.

been the only adult man besides the sultan who resided within the inner regions of the palace.[1] His general charge over all the sultan's gardens, wherever they might be, included oversight of the banks and shores of the Bosphorus, the Sea of Marmora, and the Dardanelles.[2] This gave him great power, and his favor was much courted.

The stable service was exceedingly important in a nation which relied so much upon cavalry, and which was still under the influence of the tradition of the steppe lands. The sultan for his own use kept a stable of two hundred horses tended by a hundred men, and for the use of his retinue four thousand horses tended by two thousand men.[3] Besides these, a thousand or more Bulgarian Christians known as Voinaks tended herds of horses on the great domanial pastures.[4] All these followed the army to war as grooms. They were under the control of a very great official, the *Emir-al-Akhor*,[5] or grand equerry, who, with the second equerry, also had oversight of the numerous saddlers, camel-drivers, and muleteers of the imperial service, and control of all the domanial pastures and forests of the empire.[6]

The head gardener, the head gatekeeper, the grand equerry, the second equerry, and the *Mir-Alem*,[7] or standard-bearer, constituted the special group of officers known as the *Rekiab-Aghalari*, or " generals of the [imperial] stirrup." The *Mir-Alem* had charge of the imperial standards and the six horsetails which were borne before the sultan. He distributed standards and horsetails to *Beylerbeys* and *Sanjak Beys*, who thus in a way

---

[1] Postel, iii. 11.

[2] Menavino, 129. In D'Ohsson's time (vii. 15) this official was also the jailer and presiding executioner of the palace, inspector of the water supply and forests near the capital, and overseer of hunting and fishing and of the trade in wine and lime. How many of these functions he exercised under Suleiman seems not to have been recorded. In Spandugino's time (p. 118) the chief *Kapuji* was presiding executioner.

[3] Ramberti, 251; Junis Bey, 268.

[4] Menavino, 150. They were not *kullar*. Cf. the *Zainogiler*, below, pp. 252, 268.

[5] Shortened in use to *Miri-akhor, Imrakhor, Imbrahor, Imbroor, Imror*, etc.

[6] D'Ohsson, vii. 17; Menavino, 148–150.

[7] A short form of *Emir-Alem*.

received investiture at his hands.[1] As a consequence he ranked first among the officers of the household as related to the government. He also had superior control over the gatekeepers, and he commanded the military music.

The tent-pitchers, under a *Mihter-bashi*, cared for the sultan's tents in peace and war. Similar groups were the *Veznedars* (who weighed the money received by the sultan), the guards of the outside treasury, the purchasing agents of cloth and muslins for the palace, and the guardians of presents.[2]

The masters of the hunt were important officials in the time of Suleiman, who practised the ancient royal custom of going with great state and numerous attendants to hunt over a large region.[3] Heads of the dog-keepers, falconers, vulturers, gerfalconers, and hawkers held honorable position. A number of the pages of the higher *odalar* had subsidiary duties as falconers;[4] Ibrahim was chief falconer at the time of his promotion to the position of grand vizier. A part of the regular army aided in the hunts. The Janissaries show by the names of some of their chief officers that their corps grew in part out of the hunting organization of the early sultans.[5]

The intendants, or *Umena*, had charge of various departments of supply and administration. They were the *Shehr-emini*, or intendant of imperial buildings; the *Zarabkhaneh-emini*, or intendant of mints and mines; the *Mutbakh-emini*, or intendant of the kitchen and pantry; the *Arpa-emini*, or intendant of forage for the stables of the palace; and the *Masraf-shehriyari*, or substitute for the intendant of the kitchens.

This rapid survey, though by no means complete, shows something of the complicated organization, the numerous personnel, and the various functions of the groups of the imperial

[1] Menavino, 145.

[2] D'Ohsson, vii. 21. In his time these were under the " Chief of the Black Eunuchs." It does not appear who controlled them under Suleiman.

[3] Postel, iii. 12; Hammer, *Geschichte*, iii. 44.

[4] Hammer, *Staatsverwaltung*, 37.

[5] Spandugino, 127–128, describes the hunting organization under Bayezid II. Ramberti and Junis Bey (below, pp. 249, 266) state that 2700 or 900 Janissaries served under the *Segban-bashi* and *Zagarji-bashi* in the care of the dogs.

household. The number of individuals connected with it may be estimated to have been between ten and fifteen thousand, many of whom were not the sultan's slaves, but his servants and employees in various capacities. All, however, except the few members of the *Ulema*, were under the complete control and command of members of the Ruling Institution. No confusion resulted from such great complexity, for each group of servants had its definite duties, and knew exactly from whom to receive orders and to whom to report accomplishment.

It is clear that the functions of many of the officials of the household, especially those of the head gardener, the grand equerry, and the standard-bearer, intrenched upon the province of government. The chief black eunuch and the chief white eunuch collected and administered the revenues of many parcels of land which were devoted to special purposes. The *Umena* were so clearly recognized as exercising governmental functions that they were regarded as chancellors, — an exception, made for the sake of convenience, to the rule of separating household and governmental officials. It resulted, therefore, that, while order was maintained with comparative ease within the mechanism of the household and, as will be seen, of the government, difficulty and confusion accumulated in the relations of the Ruling Institution to the rest of the empire. The splendid organization worked admirably down a certain distance from the top; but, as the energy of the single will became mediated by many officials, and as the multiplex land-ownership and varied population of the empire was approached, disorder to the extent of unworkability was so constantly threatened that only more or less convulsive readjustments, resorted to from time to time, enabled the institutions of the empire to remain in being.

THE CEREMONIES OF THE COURT

The Sacred Law, based on the practice of Mohammed and the four early caliphs, discouraged display of every sort;[1] nor did the Seljuk Turks take readily to the magnificence which under Persian influence had prevailed at the court of the Bagdad

[1] D'Ohsson, iv. 98 ff.

caliphate.[1]   So, too, the early Ottoman sovereigns appear to have maintained simplicity of life down to the time of Murad II. A contemporary observer said: " The very Magnates and Princes òbserve such simplicity in all things, that they cannot be distinguished from others.   I saw the King going a long distance from his palace to Church accompanied by two youths. . . . I saw him also praying in Church, not in a chair (*cathedra*) or royal throne, but seated like the rest on a rug spread on the ground; nor was there about him any ornament, either suspended or exhibited or displayed.   He used no singularity in regard to his garments or his horse, by which he could be distinguished from others.   I saw him at the funeral of his mother, and I could not possibly have recognized him, had he not been pointed out to me." [2]

In the understanding of Mohammed II, however, the capture of the imperial city seems to have included the appropriation of imperial forms and ceremonies; for no small number of his *Kanuns* dealt with matters of rank and ceremony.[3]   By the time of Suleiman the *Kanuni Teshrifat*, or Law of Ceremonies, had become a collection of considerable magnitude.[4]   It is significant that the regulations concerning such matters as the color and shape and material of robes and turbans, the order of precedence on small as well as great occasions, and the observances proper to each such occasion were made a matter of law.   On the one hand, a body of practice was set up which, though not distinctly forbidden by the Sacred Law, was contrary to its essential spirit. On the other hand, to rules of court etiquette, which in the West are often unwritten and certainly have not similar standing with acts of legislation, were given the rank and authority of imperial laws.   The Law of Ceremonies stood on a par with the Law of Subjects, the Law of Fiefs, the Law of Egypt, and the Law of Fines and Punishments.   In fact, this law was observed even more carefully than the others, since the matters which it covered usually came under the eye of the sultan himself. It was as much the duty of an officer to wear the proper costume,

---

[1] *Siasset Namèh*, 161.   [3] Hammer, *Staatsverfassung*, 88 ff.
[2] *Tractatus*, ch. ix.   [4] *Ibid.*, 434 ff.

and to appear in the right place and at the right time at public ceremonies, as to attend to the business connected with his position.

All the classes of members of the sultan's household, all the high officers of government, and all the separate bodies of troops in the standing army were clearly distinguished from each other by costume or head-dress or by both. Each group and every officer in each group had his exact place in every ceremonial assembly and his exact rank in every procession. Each great official, beginning with the sultan, had his title for use in public documents, a designation which, though not exactly fixed, varied little from time to time.[1]

Ceremonial occasions were numerous and splendid. All were participated in by representatives from each division of the Ruling Institution, and on the greatest occasions practically its whole membership was present. The ceremonies may be grouped as simple occasions, religious festivals, and extraordinary ceremonies. Among the simpler ceremonial occasions were the regular meetings of the Divan, which in time of peace took place four times a week, on Saturday, Sunday, Monday, and Tuesday. On Fridays the sultan rode forth to mosque in magnificent state.[2] On other days some of the officials made visits of state to their superiors. Every three months the Janissaries were paid with much ceremony in the parade-ground between the first and second gates of the palace. For the sake of giving an impression of wealth and magnificence, such occasions were frequently chosen for the reception of ambassadors.[3]

The great religious festivals of Islam, in which all the Moslems of the empire participated, were celebrated by the court with great pomp. These were the two feasts of Bairam, one of which comes at the close of the fast of the month of Ramazan, and the

---

[1] The statements of this paragraph are based upon the *Kanuni Teshrifat* as given in Hammer, *Staatsverfassung*, 434 ff. See Della Valle, i. 45: "Tutti gli uffici, e tutti gli ordini, tanto della militia, quanto della Corte, e d'ogni altra sorte di persone, hanno qui il loro habito proprio, and in particolare al portamento della testa, si cognosce ciascuno che cosa è."

[2] Postel, iii. 13; Hammer, *Geschichte*, iii. 18.

[3] Ricaut, 156.

other and greater seventy days later.[1] On the great day of Bairam the ceremony of kissing the hand of the sultan was performed by all the officials of the household and government. The principal extraordinary ceremonies were those in celebration of the birth of sons or daughters to the sultan, of the circumcision of princes and the marriage of princesses, the accession to the throne, and the going forth of the sultan to war. The greatest of all Suleiman's celebrations was probably that of the circumcision of his sons, Mustapha, Mohammed, and Selim, in 1530. Twenty-one successive days of display, feasting, games, and formal presentation of gifts contributed to the unparalleled grandeur of the occasion.[2]

It is not impossible to obtain an idea of the appearance of the sultan's court and retinue at this time of the empire's greatest splendor. One observer, often quoted already, who was gifted with superb powers of expression, has left a clear record. Seer and seen alike vanished from the earth more than three centuries ago; yet through the keen eyes of Ogier Ghiselin de Busbecq the world has ever since looked upon the great Suleiman as he sat and rode in state. Busbecq, ambassador to the Ottoman court from Emperor Charles the Fifth and his brother Ferdinand, describes his first audience with Suleiman in camp at Amasia in 1555, also the train that attended the sultan as he went forth from Constantinople to war against his son Bayezid in 1559, and a Bairam ceremony in camp near Scutari a few weeks after the latter event. Some quotations from these descriptions will give a better idea of Suleiman's court than any number of statistics. The first describes the audience at Amasia: —

" The Sultan was seated on a very low ottoman, not more than a foot from the ground, which was covered with a quantity of costly rugs and cushions of exquisite workmanship; near him lay his bow and arrows. . . .

---

[1] The festival of the Birth of the Prophet was not instituted until the reign of Murad III (Hammer, *Staatsverfassung*, 469). The sultan's annual visit to the relics of the Prophet also became a great ceremony.

[2] Hammer, *Geschichte*, iii. 96–101. Only less splendid was the marriage of Ibrahim to Suleiman's sister in 1524 (*ibid.* 38).

" On entering we were separately conducted into the royal presence by the chamberlains, who grasped our arms. This has been the Turkish fashion of admitting people to the Sovereign ever since a Croat, in order to avenge the death of his master, Marcus, Despot of Servia, asked Amurath for an audience, and took advantage of it to slay him. After having gone through a pretence of kissing his hand, we were conducted backwards to the wall opposite his seat, care being taken that we should never turn our backs on him. . . .

" The Sultan's hall was crowded with people, among whom were several officers of high rank. Besides these there were all the troopers of the Imperial guard, Spàhis, Ghourebas, Ouloufedgis, and a large force of Janissaries. . . . Take your stand by my side, and look at the sea of turbaned heads, each wrapped in twisted folds of the whitest silk; look at those marvellously handsome dresses of every kind and every colour; time would fail me to tell how all around is glittering with gold, with silver, with purple, with silk, and with velvet; words cannot convey an adequate idea of that strange and wondrous sight: it was the most beautiful spectacle I ever saw.

" With all this luxury great simplicity and economy are combined; every man's dress, whatever his position may be, is of the same pattern; no fringes or useless points are sewn on, as is the case with us, appendages which cost a great deal of money, and are worn out in three days. In Turkey the tailor's bill for a silk or velvet dress, even though it be richly embroidered, as most of them are, is only a ducat. They were quite as much surprised at our manner of dressing as we were at theirs. They use long robes reaching down to the ankles, which have a stately effect and add to the wearer's height, while our dress is so short and scanty that it leaves exposed to view more than is comely of the human shape; besides, somehow or other, our fashion of dress seems to take from the wearer's height, and make him look shorter than he really is.

" I was greatly struck with the silence and order that prevailed in this great crowd. There were no cries, no hum of voices, the usual accompaniments of a motley gathering, neither was there any jostling; without the slightest disturbance each man took his proper place according to his rank. The Agas, as they call their chiefs, were seated, to wit, generals, colonels (bimbaschi), and captains (soubaschi). Men of a lower position stood. The most interesting sight in this assembly was a body of several thousand Janissaries, who were drawn up in a long line apart from the rest; their array was so steady and motionless that, being at a little distance, it was some time before I could make up my mind as to whether they were human beings or statues; at last I received a hint to salute them, and saw all their heads bending at the same moment to return my bow.[1] On leaving the assembly we had a fresh treat in the sight of the household cavalry returning to their quarters; the men were mounted on splendid horses, excellently groomed, and gorgeously accoutred. And so we left the royal presence." [2]

On the second occasion, when Suleiman was going forth to war, Busbecq obtained a place at a window: —

" From this I had the pleasure of seeing the magnificent column which was marching out. The Ghourebas and Ouloufedgis rode in double, and the Silihdars and Spahis in single file. The cavalry of the Imperial guard consists of these regiments, each of which forms a distinct body, and has separate quarters. They are believed to amount to about 6000 men, more or less. Besides these, I saw a large force, consisting of the household slaves belonging to the sultan himself, the Pashas, and the other court dignitaries. The spectacle presented by a Turkish horseman is indeed magnificent. His high-bred steed generally comes from Cappadocia or Syria, and its trappings and saddle sparkle with gold and jewels in silver settings. The rider himself is resplendent in a dress of cloth of gold or silver, or else of silk or velvet. The very lowest of them is clothed in scarlet, violet, or blue robes of the finest cloth. Right and left hang two handsome cases, one of which holds his bow, and the other is full of

---

[1] Compare Gritti, 27: the Janissaries at the reception of ambassadors "stand in such quiet and order as for war that it is a marvellous thing and not to be believed by those who have not seen it with their own eyes."

[2] Busbecq, *Life and Letters*, i. 152 ff.

painted arrows. Both of these cases are curiously wrought, and come from Babylon,[1] as does also the targe, which is fitted to the left arm, and is proof only against arrows or the blows of a mace or sword. In the right hand, unless he prefers to keep it disengaged, is a light spear, which is generally painted green. Round his waist is girt a jewelled scimitar, while a mace of steel hangs from his saddle-bow. . . . The covering they wear on the head is made of the whitest and lightest cotton-cloth, in the middle of which rises a fluted peak of fine purple silk. It is a favorite fashion to ornament this head-dress with black plumes.

" When the cavalry had ridden past, they were followed by a long procession of Janissaries, but few of whom carried any arms except their regular weapon, the musket. They were dressed in uniforms of almost the same shape and colour, so that you might recognize them to be the slaves, and as it were the household, of the same master. Among them no extraordinary or startling dress was to be seen, and nothing slashed or pierced. They say their clothes wear out quite fast enough without their tearing them themselves. There is only one thing in which they are extravagant, viz., plumes, head-dresses, etc., and the veterans who formed the rear guard were specially distinguished by ornaments of this kind. The plumes which they insert in their frontlets might well be mistaken for a walking forest.[2] Then followed on horseback their captains and colonels, distinguished by the badges of their rank. Last of all, rode their Aga by himself. Then succeeded the chief dignitaries of the Court, and among them the Pashas, and then the royal bodyguard, consisting of infantry, who wore a special uniform and carried bows ready strung, all of them being archers.[3] Next came the Sultan's grooms leading a number of fine horses with handsome trappings for their master's use. He was mounted himself on a noble steed; his look was stern, and there was a

[1] A name for Cairo, used much from the time of the crusades onward.

[2] Nicolay, 88–89, explains that the wearing of ostrich plumes, attached in a tube of jeweled gold to the front of the turban, and curving over the head and down the back, was a highly-valued privilege accorded only to such Janissaries as had distinguished themselves in action.

[3] The *Solaks*.

frown on his brow; it was easy to see that his anger had been aroused. Behind him came three pages, one of whom carried a flask of water, another a cloak, and the third a box.[1] These were followed by some eunuchs of the bed-chamber, and the procession was closed by a squadron of horse about two hundred strong [the Muteferrika]." [2]

Busbecq spent three months in Suleiman's camp near Scutari: —

" I should have returned to Constantinople on the day before the Bairam, had I not been detained by my wish to see that day's ceremonies. The Turks were about to celebrate the rites of the festival on an open and level plain before the tents of Solyman; and I could hardly hope that such an occasion of seeing them would ever present itself again. I gave my servants orders to promise a soldier some money and so get me a place in his tent, on a mound which commanded a good view of Solyman's pavilions. Thither I repaired at sunrise. I saw assembled on the plain a mighty multitude of turbaned heads, attentively following, in the most profound silence, the words of the priest who was leading their devotions. They kept their ranks, each in his proper position; the lines of troops looked like so many hedges or walls parting out the wide plain, on which they were drawn up. According to its rank in the service each corps was posted nearer to, or farther from, the place where the Sultan stood. The troops were dressed in brilliant uniforms, their head-dresses rivalling snow in whiteness. The scene which met my eyes was charming, the different colours having a most pleasing effect. The men were so motionless that they seemed rooted to the ground on which they stood. There was no coughing, no clearing the throat, and no voice to be heard, and no one looked behind him or moved his head. When the priest pronounced the name of Mahommet all alike bowed their heads to their knees at the same moment, and when he uttered the name of God they fell on their faces in worship and kissed the ground. . . . When prayers were finished, the serried ranks

---

[1] The *Sharabdar*, the *Chokadar*, and the *Silihdar*.
[2] Busbecq, *Life and Letters*, i. 283 ff.

broke up, and the whole plain was gradually covered with their surging masses. Presently the Sultan's servants appeared bringing their master's dinner, when, lo and behold! the Janissaries laid their hands on the dishes, seized their contents and devoured them, amid much merriment. This licence is allowed by ancient custom as part of that day's festivity, and the Sultan's wants are otherwise provided for. I returned to Constantinople full of the brilliant spectacle, which I had thoroughly enjoyed." [1]

INFLUENCE OF THE COURT

The influence of the Ottoman court may be looked at in three ways, — as affecting the sultan, the Ruling Institution, and the destiny of the empire; but all three ultimately reduce to the last. The sultan was influenced by his personal relationships with the different individuals or groups which came into closest contact with him. Reference has already been made to Roxelana. Undoubtedly she had much influence over her imperial husband, but to what extent she pushed him toward particular decisions and actions cannot be known. It is improbable that she had anything of consequence to do with the death of Ibrahim, since the favorite's own actions had brought matters to such a pass that he was a menace to the throne; moreover, her influence in public affairs seems not yet to have become great. Some writers of that date do not mention her at all, though she had already won the supreme affection of Suleiman, and had, so to speak, passed round the superior position of the mother of the first-born son by being made a legal wife. [2] Seventeen years

---

[1] *Ibid.*, 302 ff. These quotations may profitably be compared with those from the *Tractatus* in regard to the simplicity of Murad II (above, p. 134). Not a few descriptions of court and camp ceremonies in the century following the accession of Suleiman have been handed down. For example: Suleiman's entry into Belgrade in 1532 (Marini Sanuto, lvi. 870); Suleiman's entry into Aleppo, 1548 (anonymous report, in Alberi, 3d series, i. 224 ff.); Suleiman's reception of Captain Pinon in 1544 (Maurand, 207–225); Selim II's reception of De Noailles in 1573 (Du Fresne-Canaye, 59–72); Ahmed I's going to mosque, 1614 (Della Valle, 68–71); Ahmed I's reception of the Venetian *Bailo*, 1615 (*ibid.* 98 ff.).

[2] Postel, i. 31, speaks of the mother of Mustapha as having superior authority about 1537, though residing much at Magnesia; and he does not speak of Roxelana. But Ludovisi, 29, shows that Roxelana was in 1534 the wife of Suleiman, and that

later the situation was clear: Roxelana had triumphed completely over the mother of Mustapha; her son-in-law Rustem, married to Suleiman's well-beloved daughter Mihrmah, had held the supreme office of grand vizier for nine years; her hump-backed son Jehangir was Suleiman's favorite child. Nevertheless, as late as the beginning of 1553 Suleiman seems to have intended still that Mustapha should occupy the throne.[1]

Mustapha became a victim less of Roxelana and Rustem than of the indeterminate and dangerous condition of the rules of succession to the throne.[2]   Had primogeniture been the established order, Mustapha need only have been on his guard against poison; he would have lacked motive for rebellion, and his father would not have been in fear of deposition.   Had not Mohammed II established the terrible *Kanun* which ordered the execution of the brothers of a sultan at his accession, Roxelana need not have feared for the lives of her own sons.   Had not the Janissaries helped Selim to the throne ahead of time and against the wishes of his father, their favor toward Mustapha would not have forced a crisis.   If Suleiman really desired Mustapha to succeed him, he made a great mistake in sending him far away to the governorship of Amasia.   Bayezid, the ablest living son of Roxelana, was in Karamania; and Selim, the least promising of Roxelana's children, but apparently her favorite, was assigned to the governorship at Magnesia.   Selim was thus removed from the capital by a journey of only five or six days, Bayezid by a somewhat greater distance, and Mustapha by a journey of twenty-six days.[3]   Suleiman may have meant by these appointments only to promote his sons to more distant governorships as they grew in experience and could be entrusted with greater responsibilities; they, on the other hand, could hardly fail to suspect that he had different intentions.   Without further discussion, suffice it to say that, with custom and law as it was,

the mother of Mustapha then resided with her son at Magnesia. For the decisive quarrel between Roxelana and the mother of Mustapha, see Navagero, 75.
    [1] Navagero, 79.
    [2] Described above, pp. 93–95.
    [3] Navagero, 76–77.

the situation was untenable. First Mustapha, and later Roxelana's own son Bayezid, became the victims of inexorable circumstances in which she undoubtedly played some part, though
exactly what it was cannot be known.[1] In so far as she contributed to the fatal outcome, she hastened the fall of the empire.
If ever a government demanded a strong man to keep it in operation, the Ottoman government needed one to maintain its
Ruling Institution. From the beginning there had been as yet
no failure; but after Suleiman the Magnificent, the Legislator,
was to come Selim the Sot, the Debauché!

Nor was the beloved and pious Mihrmah without her influence
on the fate of the empire, if it be true that she urged her father
on to the great expedition against Malta.[2] His reign had opened
with two great triumphs: the fortresses that had defied the
great Conqueror, Belgrade and Rhodes, had fallen before his
troops. He had failed before Vienna, it is true; but in the
thirty-five succeeding years he had made large conquests, he had
strengthened his power, and his prestige had grown steadily.
Now, near the close of his life, his mailed fist was broken upon a
rocky isle in the Mediterranean. What but the confidence
gained by that successful resistance gathered and nerved the
Christian fleet that won the day at Lepanto ? The influence
of Roxelana and Mihrmah foreshadowed the power exerted
in later reigns by far inferior and far worse women.

The influence of Ibrahim, for whose promotion Suleiman
violated the rules of advancement in the government service,
and of Rustem, for whom he broke the rule of giving no high
place to relatives of the imperial family, has been discussed
already.[3] In his late years the Sultan came greatly under the
influence of the Ulema, who had readier access to him than had
any other outside force,[4] and whose power over him has been
thought by some to have been unfavorable. Just what ills it

---

[1] The unfortunate Jehangir also was thought to have come to his death from
shock at the death of Mustapha and fear of a similar fate for himself. See
Busbecq, Life and Letters, i. 178; Navagero, 77. But see Alberi, Anonimo of 1553,
216, for another and more credible account.

[2] Hammer, Geschichte, iii. 425.   [3] See above, pp. 78, 120.

[4] Busbecq, Life and Letters, i. 331; Halil Ganem, i. 199.

brought about in his own time, however, are not easily to be discovered.

The Ruling Institution was affected strongly by the splendor and luxury of the court of Suleiman. The Sultan had so enormous an establishment, and was so fond of display and ceremony, that a similar spirit developed in all his *kullar*. Each officer of position became inordinately ambitious to have a large household, many horses, much portable wealth, and superb equipment for his horses and servants on state occasions and in time of war. Just as Suleiman's splendor embarrassed his finances, so that he was willing that Rustem should require payment for office from newly-appointed great officials, so most of his *kullar*, in order to keep up display, were led to undignified and extortionate procedures. In the time of Suleiman's grandfather the Ottomans of high position had already been excessively grasping. " And to tell the truth," writes Spandugino, " in that country they are more eager after money than devils after souls. And one cannot accomplish anything with the princes or lords except by the power of money. In general, as well the emperor as his princes and lords have mouths only for eating, for if you go to them without giving them some present you will accomplish nothing." [1]

That eagerness for wealth with which Spandugino reproached the Turks became only worse under the Magnificent sultan's example. The members of the Ruling Institution might prey on each other to a certain extent by the sale of offices; but the ultimate evil effect fell upon the subjects outside. They in the end must pay for all the luxury and splendor of the great court and the little courts. The pressure upon them tended to become worse and worse. Lands began to grow less productive and to pass out of cultivation. That dead blight began to descend upon agriculture and trade which persists in Turkey to the present day.[2] Yet in the time of Suleiman this weakness hardly appeared.

[1] Spandugino, 185. A generation earlier still La Broquière, 186, said: " No one speaks to them [the pashas] unless he brings them a present, as well as one for each of the slaves who guard their gate."

[2] Spandugino, 145, relates how in his time the peasants were eaten, as it were, all the year by tithes, compulsory presents, land-tax, and extortion. The earlier

Although his best two sons had come to cruel deaths, although twenty thousand of his troops had lately died in vain at Malta, he went forth to his last campaign with a train which surpassed in pomp and splendor all that he had led before.[1]

sixteenth-century writers seem not to have observed that the sultan's subjects were especially miserable. Morosini (1585), 272, remarks vigorously upon the tyranny and oppression which were causing depopulation and destroying the incentive of the farm-dwellers to produce more than a bare sustenance. Zane (1595), 395, 415, writes in a similar vein. Gerlach, 52 (quoted in Zinkeisen, iii. 361), found those who lived at a distance from Constantinople in a wretched state of oppression. Knolles (ed. 1687, p. 982), writing about 1603, speaks of the desolate condition of the empire, especially in those regions through which the army was accustomed to pass. In Ricaut's time (pp. 124, 145, 323) agricultural decline, accompanied by misery and depopulation, was apparent.

[1] Hammer, *Geschichte*, iii. 438.

CHAPTER VI

THE RULING INSTITUTION: AS GOVERNMENT

SUMMARY

THE Ottoman Ruling Institution has now been considered in all but the last of its aspects. The recruiting of its members from Christian subjects and enemies, their conversion to Mohammedanism, and their training for the duties of war and government were first explained; then the military duties and organization of the sultan's *kullar*, their privileged and noble status, and their organization and activity as a household and court were described. Of the seven aspects in which the Ruling Institution may be considered only one remains, that of government in the narrow sense.

With certain exceptions, the Ruling Institution constituted the government of the Ottoman Empire. According to the Sacred Law, the rendering of justice belonged to the Moslem Institution, and many internal matters were left to be regulated by the subject nationalities, which were organized as churches, and by the foreign colonies, which remained under their own laws; but even over these bodies the Ruling Institution held the sword, and in the case of the Moslem Institution it held the purse-strings also. Aside from such exceptions, it attended to all the functions of government that were performed within the empire. These, however, as will appear, were by no means so numerous and extensive as are the activities of a progressive twentieth-century state.

Some of the functions of government cared for by the Ruling Institution have already been described in the previous chapters. The guidance of the educational system, the management of the army of the empire, the conduct of local government, the oversight of the household, the care of the sultan's gardens, pastures, and forests, the regulation of ceremonies at his court, may be all be regarded as tasks of government. To some of them it will be necessary to refer again briefly; but the fact that they have been described already simplifies the problem of setting forth the plan of the government in its narrower sense.

FUNCTIONS OF THE OTTOMAN GOVERNMENT

All governments must in some fashion maintain themselves in place and in operation; they must obtain means to meet expenses, and they must keep some kind of record of their receipts and expenditures and of their acts. They must alter and expand the unwritten and the written rules under which they operate, at least enough to keep their system workable. They must protect their subjects sufficiently to enable them to earn a living and the means to meet taxation. They must meet the efforts of other governments of both a diplomatic and a military character. All these things the Ottoman government did in its own way. In addition, it remained in the sixteenth century strongly under the ancient impulse to increase its bounds and the number of its subjects, particularly at the expense of Christians and Shiites and in the interest of Sunnite Islam.

The Ottoman government did not include among its functions the building and maintenance of systems of roads, bridges, and ferries, the conduct of a public postal service, the promotion of agriculture, industry, and commerce, the organization of a system of public and universal education, the adjustment of taxation and customs duties in the interest of the welfare of its subjects, or an extension of the activities and liberties of its subjects. Benevolence toward the common people had hardly emerged into the consciousness of any sixteenth-century state. Self-maintenance in power by the most available means, which were usually military force; increase of power, authority, and territory, by similar means; and, incidentally, an assurance of the well-being of all the privileged persons who were connected with the government, in proportion to their importance: these were the chief objects aimed at by the governments of that day, whether in the West or in the East.

Accordingly, the chief energies of the Ottoman Ruling Institution in its capacity as government were directed toward the smooth running of the machine. For this object the best and most devoted men were obtained and trained. They, with as many other members of the Ottoman nationality as possible, were organized into a magnificent army, which first of all defended and maintained the government against enemies at home and abroad, and then increased its dominions and greatness by victorious campaigns in the " land of war." The religious motive entered strongly here, since the power and conquests of the Ottoman nation were felt to be the power and conquests of Islam. The welfare and contentment of the members of the government, beginning with the sovereign, were assured by exclusive privileges, elaborate organization of personal service, and ceremonies in which they could be flattered by opportunities for display and by gradations of honor.

There remained as the special functions of government, first, the careful elaboration and watchful improvement of the regulations under which the Ruling Institution and the state were organized; second, the keeping of every part of the administrative machinery in the best possible order and condition; third, the acquisition of enough money and means to carry out the purposes of the government, and the supplying of this money and means in suitable quantity at the time and place needed and to the proper persons; and, fourth, the preparing and recording of all written acts necessary to the transaction of the business of the government. A fifth function was the adjustment of disputes between subjects of the empire who were not connected with the government; this was attended to largely by another institution, though supported and executed by the members of the government itself. The first of these functions, that of legislation, was cared for chiefly by the sultan himself; the second, of administration, was controlled by his viziers; the third, of finance, was managed by the *Defterdars* through twenty-five departments; the fourth, of chancery, was under the power of the *Nishanjis;* the fifth, of justice between the subjects, was, in matters controlled by the Sacred Law, administered by the *Ulema*, the learned men of the Moslem Institution, under the headship of the *Kaziaskers*. These five functions were by no means so clearly separated as were the groups of officials concerned with them. A logical classification of duties would have necessitated much readjustment.

The striking way in which the Ottoman Ruling Institution, when regarded as a government, limited its operations almost exclusively to its own affairs seems to have resulted from its character as a single slave-family. Although its essential character is somewhat obscured by the facts that it was by far the largest slave-family in the empire, that it had ruling authority, and that some of its members exercised general governmental functions, it is nevertheless true that the legislation of the sultans and of Suleiman himself was largely directed to the regulation of the institution itself, most laws of wider and deeper import being included in the almost unchangeable Sacred Law. The business of the viziers was also largely that of the institution, aside from the fact that the grand vizier, as representative of the sultan, headed also the justice of the empire. The imperial treasury, again, was concerned, in the first place, with obtaining the revenues due to the sultan, such of them as did not come from his personal rights as the owner of domain lands being farmed out, so that the government did not even here touch the people directly. In the second place, the revenues were paid out to the members of the institution as soldiers, servants, officials, and members of the royal family. All who followed the sultan to war without belonging to his great household provided their own support. Even the officers of local government, though appointed from his *kullar*, were supported by the assignment of lands which they administered themselves by means of the Ruling Institution. The sultan's chancery was similarly confined in its operations to the preparation and registration of acts, decrees, commissions, and the like, most of which were concerned with the adjustment and operation of the Ruling Institution. Finally, the officers of the army and the government rendered and administered justice to all the *kullar*, besides deciding many law cases under imperial laws. To a very great extent, then, the sultan's government was that of a large slave-family, which secured its own interests and managed to the best advantage its own affairs, which cared little for the welfare of the great majority of the people of the empire, and which had dealings with them and attended to their affairs only when obliged to do so by the pursuit of its own aims.

THE SULTAN AS HEAD OF THE STATE AND OF THE GOVERNMENT

Suleiman's authority rested actually and immediately upon the military might which he controlled. Psychologically, it was strongly supported by the ancient Turkish tradition of absolute obedience to the ruler who led and fed his people, and by the undying allegiance of the population of wide areas to the Caesar of New Rome, to whose seat and splendor Suleiman had succeeded. Theoretically, and, if a modern expression may be used, constitutionally, Suleiman's power was that of the ancient caliphs of Islam. It is true that he suffered under one apparently complete disqualification. A tradition of high order asserted that the *Imâms* must be of the Prophet's tribe, the Koreish;[1] but by an extension of the principle of agreement (*ijma*) by which the consensus of the Islamic doctors of the law of any period may establish an interpretation of some passage of the Sacred Law, Suleiman's father, after the acquisition of the Holy Cities and the resignation of the last Abbassid caliph at Cairo, had come into full rights as caliph. The title itself seems to have been known by none of the Western writers of the sixteenth century, nor was it commonly used by Suleiman in public documents.

In his capacity as caliph, Suleiman was head of the Islamic state, defender, executor, and interpreter of the Sacred Law, and defender of the faith. He was under obligation to punish heretics and unsubmissive infidels, to protect true believers, and to extend the area of his divinely-appointed rule. To him, after Allah and the Prophet, was due the absolute obedience of all good Moslems within his dominions. As for his Christian sub-

---

[1] D'Ohsson, i. 268; Heidborn, 112, note 11. Heidborn, 106–121, treats fully the constitutional position of the sultan.

jects, they also regarded him as their lawful sovereign, given by God as a punishment for their sins. The Sacred Law recognized no power of legislation in the head of the state, since God through Mohammed had legislated once for all; but it entrusted to him the functions of administration and justice, to be exercised to the fullest possible extent, subject always to the prescriptions of the Law. The sultan being thus supreme, all the great institutions of the Ottoman Empire are to be thought of, not as built upward from a basis in the popular will, but as extended downward from the divinely-appointed sovereign at the top. To what extent the Ruling Institution held this relationship has been indicated already. Central and local government, household and court, standing, feudal, and irregular army, all depended upon the sultan. The Moslem Institution recognized him as its head, and the highest officials of the judiciary, chosen out of its membership, were appointed by him and removable at his will.[1] So also the *Mufti*, the chief of the jurists, was appointed by the sultan.[2] Even the ecclesiastical organizations of the subject Christians and Jews were likewise extended downward from his authority, since at the capture of Constantinople the Conqueror had at once assumed that temporal headship of the Christian churches which had been held by the Byzantine emperors.[3] The Greek Patriarch received from the sultan appointment and investiture, including a command to bishops, clergy, and people of his faith to render obedience to him in matters within his province; the other Christian groups and the Jews were likewise dependent. Finally, the privileges enjoyed by the foreign settlements all depended upon grants from the sultan or upon treaties made with him in his sovereign capacity.[4] As for the officials of the Ruling Institution, they were all either directly or indirectly the sultan's appointees. Grand vizier, viziers, treasurers, chancellor, generals of the inside service, generals of the outside service and the army, *Beylerbeys* and *Sanjak Beys*, all took their places at a word from him, and at a second word all left them without a murmur.

---

[1] Hammer, *Geschichte*, ii. 226.
[2] D'Ohsson, iv. 482 ff.
[3] Hammer, *Geschichte*, ii. 1–3.
[4] *Ibid.* i. 557, iii. 159, etc.

The Sultan as Legislator

So far as legislation was possible under the Ottoman system, the sole power to issue it rested in the sultan. The law which demanded obedience within the Ottoman Empire was fourfold: the *Sheri*, or Sacred Law of Islam; the *Kanuns*, or written decrees of the sultans; the *Adet*, or established custom; and the *Urf*, or sovereign will of the reigning sultan.[1] The *Sheri* was above the sultan and unchangeable by him; the *Kanuns* and the *Adet* were subordinate to the *Urf;* the *Urf*, when expressed and written, became *Kanun.* and annulled all contradictory *Kanuns* and *Adet*.

The *Sheri* was the whole body of Islamic law as accepted by the Ottoman nation. Its long history cannot be detailed here. Based originally on the Koran, supplemented by traditions of Mohammed's legal decisions and sayings, and by the decisions of the early caliphs and the interpretations of early judges,[2] it was first formulated by Abu Hanifa, who was the earliest of the four great orthodox Moslem doctors, and who became the accepted teacher of all Turkish peoples.[3] His code was worked over again and again in the course of six centuries, as new decisions of judges and interpretations of jurists accumulated. Mohammed II found it necessary to have a new code prepared, a task for which he chose Khosrew Pasha, who, singularly enough, was a Christian renegade, seemingly almost the only one who rose high in the Moslem Institution.[4] This work, finished in 1470,[5] was not sufficient in the days of Suleiman. At the time of its preparation the Ottoman Empire had been still wholly within territory that had remained Christian during all the early brilliant period of Islam; but since then the sultans had conquered three seats of the later caliphate, Damascus, Bagdad, and Cairo, and

---

[1] Hammer, *Staatsverfassung*, 29. This use of the word *Urf* in Turkish is not the same as that of its Arabic original (see Redhouse, 1294; Youssouf Fehmi, 237). Heidborn, 37 ff., discusses the sources of Ottoman law, giving an especially thorough and excellent treatment to the Sacred Law.

[2] Macdonald, 71; D'Ohsson, i. 5 ff.

[3] Macdonald, 94, 115; Hammer, *Staatsverfassung*, 4; D'Ohsson, i. 11 ff.

[4] Hammer, *Staatsverfassung*, 9.

[5] D'Ohsson, 21.

had come to hold the protectorate of the Holy Cities, where Mohammed and the early caliphs had ruled. A new code of law, therefore, better adapted to the more widely Moslem character which the empire had assumed, was demanded. Suleiman charged Sheik Ibrahim Halebi (of Aleppo) with the task of preparing such a code; and the result, prepared before 1549, was the *Multeka ol-ebhar*, the " Confluence of the Seas," which remained the foundation of Ottoman law until the reforms of the nineteenth century.[1] The *Multeka* did not, however, entirely replace the previous codes and collections of *fetvas*, or authoritative juristic opinions, which continued to be used as law books of less weight.

Early in the process of formulation, the Sacred Law was separated logically into two great divisions, — matters of faith and morals, and practical regulations, groups corresponding more or less closely to the Western conceptions of theology and law. The Moslems never made an actual separation of these two divisions of the Sacred Law; both in education and in practice they regarded them as parts of one great unity of advice, precept, and command, divinely sanctioned and binding upon all true believers. The practical regulations, or the Law proper, went by the Arabic name of *fikh;* it included both jurisprudence and positive law.[2]

A group of Dutch and German thinkers, led by Dr. Snouck Hurgronje, has been so strongly impressed by the jurisprudential side of the *Sheri* as almost to deny that it has or has ever had an important practical side;[3] but a careful consideration of the early history of the Ottoman Empire suggests that their view in its entirety is not supported by the facts. Dr. Goldziher says: " In later days, historical consideration has proved that only

[1] Hammer, *Staatsverfassung*, 10; D'Ohsson, i. 22–24. The *Multeka* is the basis of D'Ohsson's excellent work, which consists of a translation of the code with its comments, to which he has added observations of great value based on historical studies and on his own investigations during many years' residence in Turkey. Heidborn, 44–69, gives a detailed account of the development of the Sacred Law. He also (pp. 85–89) describes the *Multeka* and gives a table of its contents.

[2] Heidborn, 40–41. This writer uses the form *fykyh*.

[3] Snouck Hurgronje, in *Revue de l'Histoire des Religions*, xxvii. 1 ff., 74 ff.

a small part of this system, connected with religious and family life, has a practical effect as of old, while in many parts of merely juristic character this theological law is entirely put aside in actual jurisdiction. . . . Snouck Hurgronje was really the first who set forth with great acuteness and sure judgment the historical truth, namely, that what we call Muhammedan law is nothing but an *ideal* law, a theoretical system; in a word, a learned *school-law*, which reflects the thoughts of pious theologians about the arrangement of Islamic society, whose sphere of influence was willingly extended by pious rulers — as far as possible — but which as a whole could hardly ever have been the real practical standard of public life. He finds there rather *a doctrine of duties* (*Pflichtenlehre*) of quite an ideal and theological character, traced out by generations of religious scholars, who wished to rule life by the scale of an age which in their idea was the golden period, and whose traditions they wished to maintain, propagate, and develop. Even the penalties for offenses against religious laws are often nothing else but ideal claims of the pious, dead letters conceived in studies and fostered in the hearts of God-fearing scholars, but neglected and suppressed in life where other rules become prevailing. We find even in the oldest literature of Islam many complaints about the negligence of the religious law by *Ulema* in their struggle against the practical judges, that is to say against the executors of actual law." [1]

The last sentence quoted contains by implication a genuine distinction between the " religious law," which may be called jurisprudence, and the " actual law." It is true that at the present time " actual law " in all Mohammedan lands consists only in a comparatively small proportion of precepts drawn from the *Sheri;* yet a body of precepts which today requires an elaborate system of courts for its enforcement, and which offers a career to many thousands of living men as teachers, advisers, and judges, can hardly be adjudged a mere " doctrine of duties." [2]

[1] Goldziher, in *Zeitschrift für Vergleichende Rechtswissenschaft*, viii. 406 ff.; Kohler, *ibid.* 424 ff.; Juynboll, 8, 310.
[2] In Turkey at the present day the courts of the Sacred Law (*Sheriyeh*) have sole cognizance of the following classes of cases: " in civil law, questions concerning

Undoubtedly the *Sheri* has suffered a gradual shifting of emphasis from its practical to its jurisprudential side; undoubtedly it has suffered progressive encroachment upon the area of its practical application, beginning in very early times and leading up to an invasion in force in the nineteenth century by the principles, practice, and procedure of Western Europe. But in the Ottoman Empire of the sixteenth century the *Sheri* had no such inferior place. Even then, to be sure, it occupied by no means the whole field of practical law; but an examination of the quotations from the Venetian reports which were presented in an earlier chapter is of itself sufficient to show that at that time the *Sheri* held the place of overwhelming preëminence in legal matters, in point of usefulness as well as of honor; that its practical precepts to the full extent of their formulated scope were the private law of the land; that its judges were of equal or greater authority and repute than were the high officers of government; that the latter were in most cases obliged to execute decisions of the former, their independent jurisdiction being confined to a limited class of persons, and to the decision of administrative cases according to *Kanuns* outside the field of the Sacred Law.[1]

marriage, alimony, education of children, liberty, slavery, inheritance, wills, absence, and disappearance; in criminal law, suits concerning retaliation, the price of blood, the price of laming a limb, the price of causing an abortion, damages for disfigurements, the division of the price of blood " (Heidborn, 255). The *Nizamiyeh*, or secular courts, have sole cognizance of commercial and penal cases, and a few other groups. All other causes are taken before the *Sheriyeh* courts if the parties agree; otherwise before the *Nizamiyeh* courts. Thus the courts of the Sacred Law still retain a great deal of importance in Turkey.

[1] See, in particular, above, pp. 40, 41, 42. See also Postel, i. 116 ff., 124 ff.; Ricaut, 200 ff. Heidborn, 43, comments on this state of affairs, and explains the comparatively recent further legal developments in Turkey as follows: —

" Durant de longs siècles le fykyh, tout pétrifié qu'il était, put suffire aux besoins de la société islamique et son manque de souplesse fut d'autant moins ressenti, que l'évolution de cette société elle-même a été à peu près nulle. Assoupie dans une léthargie profonde, elle semble se recueillir de son immense effort de jeunesse et contempler en spectatrice indifférente ou dédaigneuse les progrès réalisés, depuis, par l'Occident. En Turquie seulement, à mesure que se resserraient ses liens avec l'Europe, fut comprise l'impérieuse nécessité de sortir de cet isolement et d'emprunter à la culture occidentale certaines méthodes susceptibles de rajeunir le corps vielli de l'empire. Par suite de cette orientation récente, le fykyh a subi, en Turquie, d'importantes abrogations de fait sinon de droit, qui atteignent

The Sacred Law reached out far beyond the conception of law in the West. It was originally supposed to be sufficient for the entire government of the Islamic state (of which there was believed to be but one upon the earth),[1] as well as for the minute regulation of the social, ethical, and religious life of all its members.[2] From two circumstances, however, it rapidly became inadequate as a political constitution: first, from the expansion of the original simple Islamic society into a great world-power, with interests and relationships far more complex than had been dreamed of by the founders; and, second, from the fact that the Law, believed to be of divine origin,[3] was proclaimed unchangeable by its own provisions, and hence could not, except with extreme difficulty, be adapted to new responsibilities and times. Judges and jurists labored manfully to provide elasticity by interpretation, but the task was too great to be completely successful. It became necessary, therefore, for princes to supplement the Sacred Law by decrees of their own, a course in which they could not transgress the positive commands of the Sacred Law. But even within the Law itself the jurists had allowed them considerable latitude, by classifying its provisions under different heads as of various degrees of obligation: some acts were forbidden, some were advised against, some were considered indifferent, some were recommended, and some were rigidly prescribed.[4] Princes were compelled to keep hands off all matters that were forbidden or prescribed; but in the wide intervening field there was much that they might do, and an even larger field was left open in matters that were not touched at all by the Sacred Law because they had lain outside the experience of the fathers of Islam or had developed since their

cependant plutôt le domaine du droit public que celui du droit privé. Celui-ci subsiste, dans une large mesure, malgré ses imperfections et son absence de plan et de clarté. On s'est contenté de combler ses lacunes les plus apparentes par des lois empruntées à la législation occidentale, sans se soucier de la complète disparate créée par la réunion d'éléments aussi hétérogènes."

[1] D'Ohsson, i. 261, v. 11.
[2] Macdonald, 66; Hammer, *Staatsverfassung*, 12.
[3] Heidborn, 69.
[4] Hammer, *Staatsverfassung*, 14; Heidborn, 71.

time. In case of undoubted transgression of the Sacred Law, the Moslem society, led by the *Ulema*, was considered absolved from allegiance to the sovereign and justified in exercising the right of revolution.[1] The *Sheri* was thus a written constitution for the Ottoman Empire, not subject to amendment, but capable of some slight modification by judicial and juristic decision and interpretation.[2] The sultan had no power over it except as guardian, interpreter, and executor. The popular consent which allowed him to remain in authority did not recognize in him any right to amend or abolish any part of the Sacred Law.

The Ottoman sovereigns at first issued their new legislation as *firmans*, or ordinances,[3] but in the course of time they adopted from the Greek word κανών, or rule, the word *kanun*, which they applied to every general law. This Greek word as applied to law thus came to be used in contrary senses in the East and the West. To the canon law of the West corresponded the *Sheri*, and to the civil or rather the national law of the West, the *Kanuns*. It is to be noted, however, that the *Sheri* had wider sway in Turkey in the sixteenth century than the canon law ever had in the West. Not only did it deal with a far larger field, but its judges seem sometimes to have administered the *Kanuns* also; they had, further, the support of the national government, whereas the rival courts of the great officials had ordinarily a very limited jurisdiction. The position of the ecclesiastical courts of the Christian subjects was much more like that of similar courts in the West.[4]

The *Kanuns* were issued in accordance with a general formula of the Sacred Law. " The *Imâm*," quotes Von Hammer, " has the right to make all civil and political regulations which are demanded by prudence, the circumstances, and the public

---

[1] Hammer, *Staatsverfassung*, 32; D'Ohsson, i. 291.

[2] Ricaut, 202; Steen de Jehay, 13 ff.

[3] Hammer, *Staatsverfassung*, 31.

[4] In the course of time the development of civil courts in the Ottoman Empire has relegated the former judicial system to the position of ecclesiastical courts with jurisdiction similar to that of Christian church courts of the Middle Ages. See Macdonald, 113; and above, p. 154, note 2.

welfare of the administration and the highest executive power." [1] The *Kanuns* of previous sultans were not binding upon a reigning sultan, except so far as he chose to put them in force; [2] but the necessity of preserving a continuous administration led ordinarily to the carrying over to a new reign of all *Kanuns* that were actually in use. Reforms or readjustments were often accomplished by the revival, with modifications, of old *Kanuns*, rather than by wholly new legislation. [3]

The *Kanuns* dealt with matters of military, financial, feudal, criminal, and police law, and with the law of ceremonies. [4] All these were also covered in a measure by the Sacred Law, with two exceptions, — the feudal law and the law of ceremonies, which had to do with matters non-existent in the early Islamic state. [5] Within these two fields the sultans had a free hand; in all others their *Kanuns* were strictly supplementary and administrative. [6]

The *Kanuns* were issued separately to meet special circumstances. A number of them, when collected according to subject-matter or under the name of the sultan who issued them, constituted a *Kanun-nameh*, or book of laws. Each department of the government had its own *Kanun-nameh*, and the laws of taxation for each *sanjak* were collected into a separate group. [7] It is incorrect to think of a *Kanun-nameh* of Mohammed II or of Suleiman as bearing any resemblance to the codes of Theodosius or Justinian. Not in magnitude, scope, character of contents, authorized unification, or prevailing authority can any comparison be made. The *Kanun-nameh* of Mohammed II seems from its opening words to have had his sanction as a collected body: " This is the *Kanun* of my fathers and ancestors, according to which my successors shall act from generation to generation." [8] These words themselves show, however, that the contents were not a unified body, but a collection of *Kanuns*

---

[1] Hammer, *Staatsverfassung*, 30.   [2] *Ibid*. 31.
[3] For an example of this practice, see *ibid*. 343.
[4] *Ibid*. 2.   [5] *Ibid*. 29.   [6] Heidborn, 90.
[7] Hammer, *Staatsverfassung*, 31; in pages 219–327 are found the *Kanun-namehs* of all the *sanjaks*.
[8] *Ibid*. 87–101.

issued at different times by former sultans as well as by the one who was reigning; and an examination of the contents bears out the statement. Nor does the collection possess completeness in any sense. The first of the three parts deals mainly with the relative rank of officials, the second with a miscellaneous lot of usages, chiefly ceremonial, the third with fines for some serious offenses and with the salaries of some great officials. The whole code is brief and shows great economy of legislation.

THE LEGISLATION OF SULEIMAN

Suleiman's laws are not contained in a single *Kanun-nameh*. He is rightly named the Legislator by comparison with preceding Ottoman sultans, who were men of the sword and not of the pen; who, saying little, but doing much, had built up a great empire. With the empire, institutions which started from small beginnings had also grown great; but, resting as they did on few written laws or ordinances, they had tended to reach a confused and complicated condition. The Ruling Institution itself, gathered closely about the sultans and constantly amended by them, was kept in excellent order; it needed no *Kanun-nameh*, and as a whole never had one, though many *Kanuns* of rank, ceremony, salary, and inheritance had reference to it. More remote matters, however, could not have so much attention. By the time of Suleiman's accession, for example, the feudal system, and the bearing of the various forms of taxation and land tenure on the subject population, had come into great disorder; criminal law also needed further development, and the market and gild regulations of the cities of the empire demanded attention. Egyptian affairs were likewise in wild confusion. Already disordered under the last Mameluke sultans,[1] they were now, by reason of the many deaths and confiscations in the war of conquest and the setting-up of a new governing authority, imperatively demanding settlement. In accordance with the needs of the time, therefore, Suleiman issued a large number of *Kanuns*, dealing especially with *timars* or fiefs, *rayahs* or subjects, cere-

---

[1] Hammer, *Geschichte*, iii. 480.

monies, and criminal and market regulations, and comprising a constitution for Egypt, the *Kanun-nameh Misr*.[1] The latter appears to be the only body of *Kanuns* which the Legislator published as a whole, and which formed a complete system; issued in 1532,[2] it was probably inspired by Ibrahim, following up his visit to Egypt in 1524.[3] The collection of the great *Mufti Ebu su'ud*, which is called the *Kanun-nameh* of Suleiman, contains chiefly his ordinances in regard to the land tenure and taxes of the subject Christians, together with a number of laws designed to regulate the feudal system, and a few relating to judges and legal processes.[4] Suleiman was great as a legislator only by comparison with his predecessors. He set nothing in final order; and the ground had to be gone over again within fifty years after his death, in the reign of Achmet I.[5] His legislation was doubly hindered: first, by the conservatism of his people and his religion, which alike believed that the old ways were the best, and which made radical departures practically impossible; and, second, by the weakness inherent in despotic legislation, in which the distance of the law-giver from the subjects affected makes true adaptation to circumstances and complete enforcement impossible of attainment. Because of the first hindrance, most of Suleiman's laws professed an attempt to restore a former better state of affairs. As a matter of fact,

[1] Hammer, *Staatsverfassung:* 101–143, the *Kanun-nameh Misr;* 143–162, police and market laws of Suleiman; 187–211, *Kanuni Rayah;* 337–434, *Kanuni Timar.* Hammer does not make it clear where he found particular *Kanuns*, or how completely he has presented the originals; nor has he attempted to distinguish *Kanuns* of Suleiman from those of earlier and later sultans. The *Kanuni Rayah* was not made into a formal *Kanun-nameh* till 1614 (*ibid.* 211). See Heidborn, 91–92.

[2] Hammer, *Staatsverfassung,* 142.

[3] Hammer, *Geschichte,* iii. 39.

[4] A translation of a portion of the table of contents of this collection, as found in the manuscript Fluegel No. 1816, in the Imperial Library at Vienna, is given in Appendix iii, below. This shows by comparison with the headings in Hammer's *Staatsverfassung,* 396–424, that Hammer has there translated at least one-half of the manuscript, though he appears to attribute these sections to the *Kanun-nameh* of Achmet I (*ibid.* 384). The table of contents of the latter collection of laws is very different (see next note).

[5] The *Kanun-nameh* of Achmet I, issued in 1619, contained collections of (1) feudal laws; (2) laws of the army, the navy, the outer and the inner service; (3) laws of police, finance, and fiefs. See Hammer, *Staatsverfassung,* pp. xviii, xix.

they probably did not contain much more than a statement in black and white, with necessary simplifications, of a confused body of practice that had grown up gradually, formulated in parts by the ordinances of his predecessors. Because of the second hindrance to his legislation, Suleiman was not able to put into satisfactory and enduring order matters of such vital interest to the people as the feudal and financial systems. Conferring only with a few religious men and a limited number of high officials, aside from the shut-in members of his inner service, he could not possibly know how his regulations would bear upon the holders of small fiefs and the Christian tenants and tax-payers in remote parts of the empire. The officials who formulated the *Kanuns* for him were only a little better able than he to judge of such matters; and the persons chiefly affected by the laws were not consulted at all. Moreover, after issuing his laws the sultan could not follow them up to see to their execution. In later times, orders to readjust land titles were sometimes given, but with little further result than to enrich officials by the bribes which they accepted for declaring titles good, or by their confiscations of property on which the owners could not pay enough.[1] Although official corruption was undoubtedly not so bad under Suleiman as it became later, the suspiciously great wealth of high officials like Ibrahim and Rustem and the fact that fiefs and finances were in worse disorder than ever, after no great time had elapsed, gives evidence that his laws were not faithfully enforced.[2]

Not much need be said about *Adet* and *Urf*. *Adet*, or custom, corresponds primarily to the body of unwritten regulations under which the Turks of the steppe lands lived. As in most semi-civilized societies, it was at once far wider in scope, more rigid, and more binding, as enforced by popular opinion, than written laws in more advanced societies usually are. Something of these primitive characteristics were carried over into the Ottoman nation, with all its acquisition of new membership and

---

[1] This statement is based on information obtained from a gentleman long resident in Turkey.

[2] Zinkeisen, iii. 161 ff.

incorporation of useful ideas. The conservative character of Islam strengthened the tendency to perpetuate established custom. It has been remarked of the caliphate that in no other state have little causes near the beginning produced such great effects, because of the tendency to follow precedent minutely.[1] A very similar observation has been made in regard to the Ottoman state: " The changeless perpetuity of a primitive institution appears at every step in Ottoman history." [2]   What has been shall be, was a precept observed by the Ottomans in matters small and great. The principles of the Sacred Law, the accepted *Kanuns*, and the local *Adet* of towns, districts, and manors had almost equally binding force. In fact, to the unlettered citizen they probably formed one indistinguishable whole, which seemed almost a feature of the ordering of nature. Although such sentiments tended strongly toward stability, they were a great hindrance to improvement. The early Ottomans had adopted new ideas and institutions with great readiness; but, since they held to them with equal tenacity, in the course of time they had no room left for the admission of more novelties. As fusion and combination were processes little understood, the tendency was thus toward stagnation, interrupted violently and for short periods when evils became too great to be endured. But, while the disposition to adhere to the established order was exceedingly strong among the Ottomans, *Urf*, the will of the sovereign was recognized to be superior to *Adet*, much as the Creator was held to be superior to the ordinary operations of nature. The sultan's will, however, penetrated but seldom so far as to the masses of the people.

Adet supplemented the Sacred Law and the *Kanuns* in matters which they did not cover.[3]   It differed from district to district, as it does in the West. *Urf* was the sovereign will of the reigning sultan; it was the seat and organ of sovereignty, being absolute to the full extent in which, according to the Sacred Law, God has delegated the right of legislation and rule to human beings.[4] The will of a past sultan could prevail only if it had been expressed

---

[1] Macdonald, 10.
[2] Hammer, *Geschichte*, i. 96.
[3] Hammer, *Staatsverfassung*, 32.
[4] D'Ohsson, i. 258 ff.

in a *Kanun* and was enforced by the reigning sovereign. It was by the expression of *Urf* that *Kanuns* were issued or annulled and that *Adet* was replaced by *Kanun*. So long as the Sacred Law was untouched, *Urf* might be exercised oppressively, cruelly, or unworthily, without giving any one the right to resist.[1] Against the *Sheri*, however, it had no force; any attempt to exercise it thus was an invitation to disaster.[2]

Suleiman was never in danger from transgression of the Sacred Law. A devout Moslem, whose piety increased in old age, he took seriously his duty of enforcing its provisions, not even hesitating at such as were unpopular, like the prohibition of wine-drinking,[3] or at such as demanded self-sacrifice on his part, like the disapproval of musical instruments and silver plate.[4] If he did not enact measures directly to increase the welfare of the common people, his attempts to regulate the tax and tenancy systems tended to lighten their condition. Moreover, he used severe measures to put down extortion; and he strove by his market and police regulations to maintain justice, fairness, and order.[5]

THE VIZIERS

Ottoman writers represented their government under the figure of a tent supported by four lofty pillars,[6] — the Viziers, the *Kaziaskers*, the *Defterdars*, and the *Nishanjis*. It is not safe to press comparisons too far, however; for, as a matter of fact, the pillars did not bear equal weight. All four groups of officials were necessary, but they were not of like importance: the

---

[1] " The dignity of the Imâmate does not absolutely demand that the Imâm be just, virtuous, or irreproachable, or that he be the most eminent and the most excellent of the human beings of his time " (from the *Multeka*, quoted by D'Ohsson, i. 271); " Vices or tyranny in an Imâm do not demand his deposition " (*ibid.* 288). This is the doctrine of orthodox Islam, as the outcome of the early Kharijite schisms. The Shiites are more critical as regards their sovereigns, who are not regarded as *Imâms*.

[2] Hammer, *Staatsverfassung*, 32; D'Ohsson, i. 291.

[3] Busbecq, *Life and Letters*, i. 331–333; D'Ohsson, iv. 50 ff.

[4] Busbecq, i. 331; D'Ohsson, iv. 103, 280.

[5] Hammer, *Geschichte*, iii. 71, 486.

[6] *Ibid.* ii. 216–217, 223.

Nishanjis were far less esteemed than the others; the grand vizier, on the other hand, carried, from the time of Suleiman, so much greater a burden than any one else that he might be compared to a central pillar which supported the entire tent.

The viziers were the chief councillors of the sultan for peace and war, administration and justice; and they deliberated all important questions in the meetings of the Divan, which will be described later. The word vizier means burden-bearer, the idea being that an official so designated lifted from the shoulders of the sovereign the burden of state, and bore it upon his own shoulders. The number of viziers was not rigidly fixed, but in the reign of Suleiman, there were ordinarily four, that being a sacred number with both Turks and Moslems.[1] All bore the title pasha, which was sparingly used in the sixteenth century. Ordinary viziers had no regular responsibilities besides their function as councillors; they had great incomes from both regular and irregular sources, and kept large establishments modeled on that of their master.[2]

In the time of Suleiman, the office of grand vizier reached the climax of a noteworthy development. Whereas formerly this official had been the senior member of the sultan's board of advisers, *primus inter pares*, he now became a personage far above his fellow-viziers. His position came to differ from theirs not merely in degree, but in kind, a difference typified by the fact that, in reporting to Suleiman after the meetings of the Divan, none spoke but the grand vizier.[3] This development of the office seems to have resulted from Suleiman's willingness to entrust much power to a chosen instrument, who would thus relieve him of many of the immense cares of empire. Ibrahim first held his master's confidence for many years. Later Rustem came to full power, supported by the wife and the favorite daughter of the monarch. In Suleiman's last years he left well-nigh everything to Ali and to Mohammed Sokolli.[4]

[1] *Ibid.* i. 565, ii. 223.   [2] See above, pp. 58, 59.
[3] A. Barbarigo, 155; D. Barbarigo, 26; Bernardo, 326; Erizzo, 136. See also Chesneau, 41.
[4] Barbaro, 319.

The grand vizier thus came practically to wield the sovereign power of the Ottoman state: the sultan might almost discharge his mind of public care. That is why it became easy for Selim II and his successors to withdraw into the harem, and devote most of their energies to carousing and debauchery. Had the position of the grand vizier been more secure, this change might have been for the good of the Ottoman state, as affording a means of supplementing the scanty abilities of weak sultans by those of the ablest men of the empire. In the case of Mohammed Sokolli, and of the Kiuprilis three generations later, such was to be the fact. More often, however, the place of grand vizier was to be so thoroughly at the mercy of harem intrigue that only a master of this art could retain his precarious position by immense efforts, such as would leave a mere remnant of his energies free for the service of the state. The increase under Suleiman of the relative power of the grand vizier was thus a dangerous and eventually a disastrous development.

It is clear that the grand vizier fully deserved the name of burden-bearer. Whereas even so earnest a sovereign as Suleiman appears to have had a sufficiently leisurely life in time of peace, in spite of his great responsibilities as head of a despotic government,[1] his grand viziers must have been kept fully occupied. He that has been called the greatest of all viziers, the *Nizam al-mulk*, spoke out of his experience when he said: " It is necessary that the sovereign consider with his vizier affairs of state and all that concerns the army, the finances and general prosperity. He must needs give attention to the measures which should be taken against the enemies of the empire and everything that relates to the subject. All these matters give rise to a great many annoyances and preoccupations and put the spirit to torture, for they do not leave a single instant of repose." [2]

The grand vizier represented the sultan as head of the civil and military administration and as supreme judge.[3] He ap-

---

[1] Postel, iii. *passim*, gives various glimpses of his life.

[2] *Siasset Namèh*, 163.

[3] The position and duties of the grand vizier at a later date are described at length by Hammer, *Staatsverwaltung*, 79–101, and by D'Ohsson, vii. 177–189.

pointed the highest officials in these departments. He presided over long sessions of the Divan four days in the week. Some of his other duties, cares, and obligatory ceremonies appear in the catalogue of his ten special prerogatives: [1] —

1. He had the care of the imperial seal, with which, on the days of the Divan, the doors of the treasury and chancery were sealed. The delivery of the seal was the symbol of investiture with the office of grand vizier.

2. He might hold a Divan of his own at his palace in the afternoon. This was an important session of court at which many cases, both great and small, were decided.[2]

3. He had the right to be escorted by the *Chaush-bashi* and all the *Chaushes* from his palace to and from the sultan's palace.

4. He received visits of state from the *Kaziaskers* and *Defterdars* every Wednesday.

5. He was honored by the appearance of the officers of the imperial stirrup every Monday in the Divan.

6. He went in solemn procession on Friday to the mosque, escorted by the *Chaushes*, the *Muteferrika*, and others of the outside service in turbans of ceremony.

7. He received a weekly visit from the *Agha* of the Janissaries, and a monthly visit from the other viziers.

8. He inspected the city of Constantinople and its markets, escorted by the judge of Constantinople, the *Agha* of the Janissaries, the provost of the markets, and the prefect of the city.

9. He received a weekly visit of state from various magistrates and *Sanjak Beys*.

10. He was honored at the two Bairams with official felicitations from the other viziers, the *Defterdars*, the *Beys*, the magistrates, and the generals of the army.

Customary ceremonies alone were evidently enough to absorb a very large part of the grand vizier's time; but they were a mere incident to the vast amount of administrative and judicial business that demanded his attention. It is not to be wondered

---

[1] Hammer, *Geschichte*, ii. 226; taken from the Turkish historian Aali and referring to the time of Mohammed II.

[2] Postel, i. 123.

at that the period of service in this office was short, on the average. The post was a dangerous one; for the possessor, with all his greatness, was the sultan's *kul*, and liable to summary execution if he failed to give satisfaction. Of some two hundred men who served as grand viziers in the course of five hundred years, about twenty were executed at the time of their deposition.[1]

Suleiman's grand viziers held office for comparatively long periods.[2] Seven, taken together, served him forty years; Mohammed Piri Pasha, whom he found in office at his accession, served in all six years, and Mohammed Sokolli, whom he left in office at his death, served fifteen years. Thus in sixty-two years there were only nine in all. Three of them deserve to be called great, — Ibrahim for his splendor, his breadth of mind, and his continuance in favor, Rustem for his financial shrewdness, and Mohammed Sokolli for his statesmanship. These three also served the longest, — Ibrahim thirteen years, Rustem fifteen years in two periods, and Mohammed Sokolli fifteen years without a break. Four of the nine ended their service at death, two were deposed and executed, three were simply deposed. All except Mohammed Piri Pasha were Christian renegades, who had risen as slaves to the highest honor of the empire.

The *Kaziaskers* were, under the sultan and the grand vizier, the heads of the judiciary of the empire. They sat in the Divan, where they ranked next to the grand vizier. Since they belonged to the Moslem Institution, discussion of their duties will be postponed to the next chapter.

THE DEFTERDARS, OR TREASURERS [3]

The great labor of accounting for the receipts and expenditures of the Ruling Institution in practically all its capacities

[1] Hammer, *Geschichte*, ii. 5.

[2] *Ibid.* iii. 793.

[3] The position of the *Defterdars* about the year 1800 is discussed in D'Ohsson, vii. 261 ff., and in Hammer, *Staatsverwaltung*, 137 ff. Contemporary accounts are found in Menavino, 168; Ramberti, below, p. 247; Junis Bey, below, p. 265; Postel, iii. 66–70.

was under the care of the two principal *Defterdars*, or treasurers, one for Rumelia and one for Anatolia, aided by two of lower rank, one for Aleppo and the southwest and one for the Danubian countries.[1] The principal *Defterdars* were men of great position, with large incomes and households, and possessing the right of audience with the sultan in regard to matters of revenue.[2] Under them were twenty-five departments or bureaus, as instituted by the Conqueror, each with a chief, or *Khojagan*, who directed a number of clerks of different grades. Between these and the *Defterdars* were several intermediate officials, of whom the most important were the two *Rusnamehjis*, or book-keepers. The total personnel of the treasury department numbered more than eight hundred.[3]

A list of the twenty-five bureaus, or *kalems*, with a statement of the provinces of each, will give an excellent idea of the complicated financial arrangements of the Ottoman government.[4] Taken as a whole, they show in outline the economic substructure of the Ruling Institution, as well as that of the Moslem Institution, with exception of the sultan's private treasury, out of which most of the inner service of the court was paid, and of the provisions for the officers and judges of local government: —

1. The *Buyuk Rusnameh Kalemi*, or greater book-keeping bureau, was the central office to which all the accounts were brought from the other bureaus. Once or twice a year it drew

---

[1] The word means primarily "book-keeper." It is derived either from the Greek word διφθέρα or from a similar Persian word (Hammer, *Geschichte*, ii. 228). Ramberti (below, p. 247) mentions but two *Defterdars*, one who took care of the revenue from all the Asiatic provinces, Egypt, and the Danubian countries, and received ten thousand ducats a year, and perquisites, the other who took care of the revenue from the rest of the European dominions, received six thousand ducats and perquisites, and was governor of Constantinople in the sultan's absence.

[2] Spandugino, 98.

[3] Junis Bey (below, p. 265) says that the *Defterdars* had 200 slaves each for their courts. Then he speaks of 50 scribes, each with 15 or 20 slaves, and of 25 secretaries who must have been the heads of the bureaus, and who had slaves. Next he mentions the two *Rusnamehjis*, who had 20 or 25 companions under them. Ramberti, 247, says that the first *Defterdar* had 1000 slaves in his household, and the second 500. Postel, iii. 69, mentions only one *Rusnamehji*, but clearly states that he is over the chiefs of the twenty-five bureaus.

[4] D'Ohsson, vii. 264–273; Hammer, *Staatsverwaltung*, 145–170.

up a statement of the finances of the government. The income of this bureau seems to have been the greatest of all.[1]

2. The *Bash Muhasebeh Kalemi*, or head bureau of accounts, was the largest of all in numerical strength, and the second in income. It kept account of tithes and taxes from the *sanjaks*, of munitions of war of all kinds, of the pay of the garrisons of Rumelia and Anatolia, of the receipts and expenses of the intendants of buildings, the admiralty, the kitchen, forage,[2] the mint, the three powder factories at Constantinople, Salonika, and Gallipoli, and of the inspector of artillery. This bureau received copies of all contracts made in the public service, and it registered and countersigned the entire vast number of orders on the treasury.

3. The *Anatoli Muhasebesi Kalemi*, or bureau of accounts for Anatolia (though it was by no means confined to Anatolia in its scope), kept accounts for certain domanial lands, for the garrisons in the Aegean Islands, and for the pensions of veteran soldiers.

4. The *Suvari Mukabelesi Kalemi*, or bureau of control for the cavalry, kept account of the salaries of officials of the inner service, of the *Kapujis*, of the imperial stables, and of all the *Spahis* of the Porte.

5. The *Sipahi Kalemi*, or bureau of the *Spahis*, issued orders for the pay of the *Spahis* proper, which required to be countersigned by the head of the fourth bureau.

6. The *Silihdar Kalemi*, or bureau of *Silihdars*, was similar to the fifth bureau, except that it was concerned with the *Silihdars*.

7. The *Haremein Muhasebeh Kalemi*, or bureau of accounts of the Holy Cities of Mecca and Medina, kept the books of the religious endowments or *vakfs* of the imperial mosques, of the salaries of all persons connected with these mosques, of all other religious endowments in Constantinople and elsewhere in Rumelia, and of all Rumelian property dedicated to the Holy Cities. All certificates of nomination to service in connection with

---

[1] It certainly was in 1660. Cf. Hammer, *Staatsverwaltung*, 170.
[2] D'Ohsson, vii. 265, omits the intendants of buildings and forage.

mosques in Rumelia were prepared here, to be presented to the tenth bureau for the issuance of diplomas.

8. The *Jizyeh Muhasebesi Kalemi*, or bureau of accounts for the capitation tax, issued orders yearly for the payment of this tax according to the estimated number of adult male subject Christians. A specified number of these orders was sent to each district, which was held responsible for a corresponding revenue.[1] The income of this bureau was only a little less than that of the second bureau.

9. The *Mevkufat Kalemi*, or bureau of tributes, kept account of taxes paid in kind, of the quantity of grain in the public storehouses of Constantinople and the border fortresses, and of the grants of supplies from these stores to the several army corps and to the households of military and civil *kullar* who were required to follow the army.

10. The *Maliyeh Kalemi*, or chancery bureau of the treasury department, issued diplomas to all employees of mosques who brought certificates of nomination from the seventh and twentieth bureaus, and to all administrators of religious endowments and pensioners upon such funds; and it drew up for the approval of the sultan and the countersignature of the *Defterdars* all *firmans*, or administrative orders, that concerned the treasury department.

11. The *Kuchuk Rusnameh Kalemi*, or lesser book-keeping bureau, kept the accounts of the head *Kapujis*, the stewards, and the marine.

12. The *Piadeh Mukabelesi Kalemi*, or bureau of control for the infantry, kept the books of the Janissaries and the auxiliary corps of the standing army.

13. The *Kuchuk Evkaf Muhasebesi Kalemi*, or lesser bureau of accounts of religious endowments, kept the accounts of all pensioners and attendants of the endowed public hospitals, soup-kitchens, insane asylums, and the like.

14. The *Buyuk Kalaa Kalemi*, or greater bureau of fortresses, kept record of the garrisons and of the militia who were liable for the service of the fortresses of the Danube regions.

---

[1] D'Ohsson, vii. 236.

15. The *Kuchuk Kalaa Kalemi*, or lesser bureau of fortresses, kept like records for fortresses in Albania and the Morea.

16. The *Maaden Mukataasi Kalemi*, or bureau of mine leases, kept account of the tribute required from gipsies, of the receipts from gold and silver mines in Europe and Asia, of the tributes from Moldavia and Wallachia, and of the customs duties of Constantinople, Adrianople, Smyrna, Gallipoli, Chios, and other places.[1]

17. The *Saliyaneh Mukataasi Kalemi*, or bureau of salaries, arranged the yearly pay of the captains of the fleet, and of the Khan of the Crimea and some of his officials.

18. The *Khaslar Mukataasi Kalemi*, or bureau of domanial leases, kept the books of the domain lands whose revenues were assigned to the chief ladies of the harem, including the *Sultana Valideh* and the sultan's daughters, and to the high officials of the government.[2]

19. The *Bash Mukataasi Kalemi*, or head bureau of leases, cared for the revenues from the domains in some lower Danubian lands, from the rice fields of Eastern Rumelia, from various salt works, from the fisheries of the Aegean and Black seas, and from the forests.

20. The *Haremein Mukataasi Kalemi*, or bureau of leases of the Holy Cities, was charged with regard to Anatolia, as was the seventh bureau with regard to Rumelia.

21. The *Istambol Mukataasi Kalemi*, or bureau of leases for Constantinople, kept account of the domanial leases of Salonika, Tirhala, and Brusa, the market dues of Constantinople and Adrianople, the revenues from silk and from the manufacture of articles in gold and silver.

22. The *Brusa Mukataasi Kalemi*, or bureau of the leases of Brusa, kept account of the domanial leases in the neighborhood of that city.

[1] Charges for the right to plant and transport tobacco were later assigned to the care of this bureau. See Hammer, *Staatsverwaltung*, 156.

[2] At a later date, when the expenses of the harem became greater, the customs duties of certain regions, the tobacco revenue from Syria and Arabia, and the tax on wool and yarn were also assigned to this bureau (*ibid.* 158).

23. The *Avlonia Mukataasi Kalemi*, kept similar accounts for the island of Euboea, or Negropont.

24. The *Kaffa Mukataasi Kalemi* kept similar accounts for Kaffa and certain domain lands of Anatolia.

25. The *Tarishji Kalemi*, or bureau of dates, dated all public documents that came from the other bureaus, and, at least in later times, prepared assignments on the public revenues on behalf of creditors of the government.

Supplementary bureaus, attached to some of the others, were the bureau of confiscations and escheats to the crown, the bureau of the tax on animals, and the bureau of the Christian churches and monasteries. An additional office of great importance, called the *Oda* of the treasury department, attended to the correspondance of the *Defterdars*, to their reports to the grand vizier and the sultan, and to the forwarding of leases for sections of the crown lands. Attached to the treasury department was a special court under a judge appointed by the *Kaziasker* of Rumelia, which was designed to adjust disputes between the department and private citizens.

A *Defter-emini*, or book-keeper intendant, kept the records of the fief-holders and administered their estates during vacancies. He was well paid, and had a staff of clerks.[1] He appears to have been independent of the *Defterdars*. Two household treasurers were in charge of the sultan's personal funds: the eunuch *Khazinehdar-bashi*, already mentioned as chief of the treasury chamber of pages, guarded the treasure stored there, and paid the members of the inner service; a second official, under the authority of the former and apparently called by the same name, attended to the business of the sultan's private purse outside the palace.[2] The sultan had in the castle of the Seven Towers, or *Yedi-kuleh*, another deposit of treasure which was supposed to be very large.[3]

---

[1] Junis Bey (below, p. 266) and Postel, iii. 70, call this official *Defterdar-emini*. His department, in three bureaus, became a record office of land titles (D'Ohsson, vii. 193). It may have had this wider function in the sixteenth century.

[2] Spandugino, 65, 119; Ramberti, below, pp. 244, 248.

[3] Menavino, 182; Postel, iii. 70.

The characteristics of the treasury scheme give evidence that it developed by a gradual growth without systematic revision at any time. As new occasions for expenditure arose, they were put in charge of various bureaus; as new provinces or other sources of fresh income appeared, they were either assigned to existing bureaus or given to new ones created for the purpose. The bureaus of Istambol, Avlona, and Kaffa evidently date from the time of the Conqueror; most of the others must have been older. That the conquests of Selim and Suleiman were not administered from Constantinople is evident from a study of the bureaus, and from the separate listing of the revenues from Syria, Mesopotamia, and Egypt in contemporary estimates. Since the authorities give no source of revenue for the first bureau, which nevertheless seems to have had the greatest income of all, it is probable that the tribute from the later conquests was paid into that department, and by it apportioned to bureaus of expenditure, such as the fourth, the eleventh, and the twelfth. It is worthy of notice to what an extent the sources of revenue were ear-marked for expenditure. The second bureau received the tithes and taxes of the *sanjaks*, and paid them out for munitions of war, the maintenance of garrisons, and the expenses of the intendants of the outside service of the court. The third bureau received the revenue from certain domanial lands, and supported the garrisons of the Aegean Islands and soldiers who had been pensioned. The eighteenth bureau administered domanial lands for the support of the harem and high officials. The ninth bureau received and delivered to the army taxes paid in kind. The seventh, thirteenth, and twentieth bureaus took revenues from lands assigned by religious endowment for the support of the Moslem Institution and certain beneficiaries, and paid them out as stipulated by the givers.

Instead of one treasury, into which all revenues should come and out of which all disbursements should be made, there were fifteen or more bureaus which received, and as many which spent; and some of those which both received and spent were, except for the oversight of the first bureau, practically independent institutions. A distinct tendency toward decentralization of management is manifest. Whatever could be set off by itself was made as nearly independent as possible, subject only to inspection and supervision. This policy undoubtedly resulted from the despotic character of the government. Since one man, the founder of a despotic state, can attend to only a limited number of duties, he is forced, as his power develops, to assign more and more responsibilities to subordinates. The method which most relieves the central management is to entrust definite duties to definite groups of men, to support these with sufficient revenues, and then to leave them to themselves. If things go wrong in any department, the central authority intervenes, punishes severely those who were responsible, sets things to rights forcibly, and again leaves the department to itself. The system is very dangerous unless the central management can be kept constantly strong and able to assume full control promptly and effectively. This was the case in the Ottoman Empire until after the time of Suleiman.

A yet stronger tendency toward decentralization appeared in connection with local government. Each *Beylerbey* had his own *mufti, reis effendi,* and *defterdar,* with a considerable body of clerks, who advised him, recorded his decisions, attended to the revenues from the estates assigned for the support of his household, and kept account of the fief-holders in his dominion.[1] Each *Sanjak Bey* again had his group of assistants, with similar duties on a lesser scale.[2] Some generations later the extension of this decentralization was to become a great evil.

The duties of the bureaus of the treasury department reveal clearly the limited purposes and activities of the Ottoman government. The support of the Ruling Institution as standing army, court, and government was provided for; the revenues assigned by former sultans and by private individuals to the support of the Moslem Institution in its religious and charitable aspects were supervised; the navy was provided for; and the

---

[1] Ricaut, 103, Ramberti and Junis Bey (below, pp. 256, 271) say that the *Beylerbey* of Rumelia had 100 scribes.

[2] Spandugino, 148; Postel, iii. 63.

Khan of the Crimea was pensioned. But nothing was done for the great mass of the population. They were expected to furnish the means for these activities; and the duty of the most conscientious sovereign was fully performed if he provided that they should labor unmolested, and should not be burdened with taxation beyond their ability to pay. Under a strong ruling hand the Ottoman system easily maintained order through the standing and feudal armies, but it did not so easily regulate the burden of taxation. This subject deserves special consideration.

TAXATION IN THE OTTOMAN EMPIRE [1]

A distinction was drawn between taxes authorized by the Sacred Law, which were called legal, and all others, which were called arbitrary as depending on the will of the sovereign. The early Islamic system of taxation, taken over, it would seem, from the Sassanian Persian Empire,[2] was extremely simple. No taxes were laid except on land and on persons. The lands of Arabia and Bosra were charged with a tithe, or *'ushr*, of their produce. Other conquered lands were more heavily burdened, being assessed with a *kharâj*, or tax payable in money, and with a share of the produce, which might be from the tenth to the half according to the fertility of the land. The tax on persons, the *jizyeh*, was limited to a poll or capitation tax on adult male subjects who were not Moslems. The *'ushr*, the *kharâj*, and the *jizyeh* were the only taxes recognized by the Sacred Law. Other methods of taxation were utilized almost from the beginning. When, with the conquest of Syria and Egypt, the Byzantine Empire was entered, it did not seem best to sweep away the customs, tolls, and other impositions which drew revenue from trade. As such taxes did not rest on a constitutional foundation, they were discouraged by some legists; but they became more and more necessary as a worldly government developed, and as the revenues from a large part of the land were set aside for religious foundations.

---

[1] This subject is treated in Hammer, *Geschichte*, iii. 478–483, and *Staatsverfassung*, 180–337; D'Ohsson, v. 15–37; and, as concerns the legal taxes, in Belin, *La Propriété Foncière*.

[2] Hammer, *Staatsverfassung*, 37 ff.

The early Islamic state also had a vast source of revenue in booty.. Four-fifths of this went to the generals and soldiers actually concerned in conquest; the remaining fifth was sent to Medina. After the capital had been removed from Arabia, the " Prophet's fifth " was still claimed for the support of legists and judges.

The Islamic system, with its distinction of legal and arbitrary taxes, its rules regulating the distribution of booty, and its custom of devoting revenues to religious foundations, was taken up by the Ottoman state. At the same time the feudal system, based upon both Seljuk and Byzantine example, was applied to a large part of the lands conquered from Christians, an arrangement which yielded considerable revenue for the support of individuals; and a host of Seljuk and Byzantine imposts lengthened the list of arbitrary taxes. Much land was retained as imperial domain, perhaps in many cases land that was already domain of the Byzantine emperors and other rulers whom the Ottomans dispossessed. The conquests in Cilicia, Syria, Mesopotamia, and Egypt were left under the old regulations, with some clearing away of arbitrary taxes, and preparing of cadasters in the Turkish language.[1] Hungary was carefully cadastered, to be administered thus during a century and a half.[2] Special arrangements and exemptions were made for the foreign colonists, of a character similar to old Byzantine and Saracen treaties and agreements.

As a result of all this, the system of taxation in the Ottoman Empire was very complex. It contained a great variety of taxes, — on persons, land, trade, animals, produce, mines, markets, and the like, — differing from *sanjak* to *sanjak* and from town to town; and it collected its income by various methods and through various agencies. The details of the system cannot be considered here, but a few general observations may be made.

[1] Hammer, *Geschichte*, ii. 523, iii. 65.

[2] *Ibid*. iii. 266. According to Heidborn, 339, the registering of the lands of the different regions of the Ottoman Empire, begun in 1548 by Suleiman's order and completed after some 55 years, remains to the present time the basis of land titles in Turkey.

Until the time of Mohammed II the revenues were administered directly by the treasury department, but this method led to so many malversations at the cost of the government that he changed the system to one of tax-farming. By this means the government became sure of its money. The malversations did not stop, however, but went on now at the cost of the tax-payers.[1] The taxes of regions of large size were sold by the treasury, usually to high officers among the *kullar*, who did not intend to collect the taxes themselves, but sold them again by sections. This process might be repeated several times, till in the end it would probably be, not Ottomans, but Christians and Jews who applied the screws to the unfortunate subjects.[2] The amount wrung from them might easily be double what the government received.

The strongly conservative tendency of the Ottoman people showed markedly in regard to taxation. The taxes that had been agreed upon of old were paid, but a general revision of the system in the direction of uniformity was never thought of. The revenues of the empire were thus extremely inelastic.[3] A special war contribution might be laid, as was done by Suleiman before Mohacs,[4] and requisitions might be made upon the inhabitants of a region through which the army passed; but a permanent increase of revenue was practically impossible. The tendency was in the other direction. As the value of money declined, not without assistance from the sultans,[5] all revenues payable in agreed sums declined likewise. Payments in kind from agricultural products may have increased for a time under local peace and security, but in the end they were to diminish also. Treaties with Western nations were so favorable to the latter commercially as to prevent the receipt of extensive rev-

[1] D'Ohsson, vii. 242.

[2] Spandugino, 144. Postel, iii. 65, says that the tithes (apparently those revenues not sold in the lump or left for individual collection) were collected by Christian receivers (*tous Chrestiens*), who delivered them to the *Kadis*, and these to the *Sanjak*, he to the *Beylerbey*, and the *Beylerbey* to the *Defterdars*.

[3] D'Ohsson, vii. 258.

[4] Hammer, *Geschichte*, iii. 471. It was a poll-tax of 15 aspers on each male inhabitant.

[5] Spandugino, 57.

enues from foreign customs duties; and such trade must have increased with the growth of the empire and the increasing luxury of the court. But on the whole the sultan's receipts from taxation, aside from the effect of new conquests, and allowing for the fluctuations in tithes due to good and bad harvests, were probably not far from stationary.

The receipts from the sultan's fifth of booty taken in war, which included slaves, must have been considerable up to the end of Suleiman's reign. They were all devoted, however, to the support of the Moslem Institution.[1] Tribute came in from several countries, as Moldavia, Wallachia, Transylvania, Ragusa, from Venice for Cyprus, and after 1547 from Austria for Hungary. This was forced up whenever possible as punishment for unrest, and was shared by the sultan with high officials.[2] Confiscations of the property of executed persons brought several great sums to Suleiman. The estates of *kullar* who died without children, and the tithes of the estates of those who left children, constituted a valuable though irregular revenue.[3] The great treasure of the prince of Gujarat came to Suleiman after the prince's death.[4] Something was realized from the administration of the estates of fief-holders who died without sons; but the lands of these had to be granted again before long in order to keep up the strength of the feudal army.[5] Fees connected with the administration of justice went directly to the support of the judges and other officials concerned.[6] With regular taxation nearly stationary, the increase from extraordinary sources did not keep pace with advancing expenditures.[7]

Suleiman's expenses grew particularly in regard to the fleet and the household. Some Western writers remarked that the sultan was put to no expense by war, since his standing army required to be paid in peace as well as in war, and since the

[1] Hammer, *Geschichte*, i. 167, 592.
[2] By *Kanun* of Mohammed II: Hammer, *Staatsverfassung*, 99.
[3] Postel, iii. 68.
[4] Hammer, *Geschichte*, iii. 472.   [6] Hammer, *Geschichte*, i. 236.
[5] Postel, iii. 70.   [7] *Ibid*. iii. 471.

remainder of his troops came at their own expense.[1] It is true that his additional expenditure was small as compared with that for a contemporary Western army, built from a small permanent nucleus by the hiring of mercenaries and the levy of national troops which had to be supported by the treasury; but the sultan had to replace large quantities of munitions of war that were used up or destroyed, and great numbers of animals of transport. Moreover, the Janissaries and *Spahis* had to be placated at times by presents, and it was more expensive to feed the army in the field than in the barracks. But the fleet was a great and growing expense, despite the extent to which it was supported by raiding and by revenues from North Africa;[2] and the luxury and splendor of the Magnificent Sultan's court grew apace. In spite of fresh conquests and large confiscations, therefore, Suleiman learned to feel the need of money. He found it necessary to compel his great officials to help him, by exacting sums of money from them at the time of their appointment.[3] These sums were moderate, but, as already pointed out, they set a fatal example.[4]

SULEIMAN'S INCOME

Suleiman's revenues have been variously estimated. The lowest, and probably the most accurate for the field which it covers, during the years between 1530 and 1537, is that given by Junis Bey, chief interpreter of the Ottoman court, and Alvise Gritti, natural son of the Doge of Venice, and business partner of the grand vizier Ibrahim.[5] Junis Bey says: " The income of the Great Turk from *kharâj* or tribute amounts to 1,300,000 ducats from Anatolia and Greece, and 1,600,000 ducats from Egypt, and 700,000 ducats from Syria and 150,000 ducats from Mesopotamia and 250,000 ducats from his farms, the islands which are under him, and the customs of Constantinople and Pera. Signor Alvise Gritti says that the income is rather more than less than I have stated, and I think that the expenses of the

---

[1] La Broquière, 182; Ricaut, 404.
[2] Ricaut, 404.
[3] Hammer, *Geschichte*, iii. 472.
[4] See above, pp. 115, 116.
[5] Postel, iii. 49.

Porte or of the Seigneur's court consume the entire income or a little less." [1]

The total regular revenue of Suleiman would thus have been about four million ducats.[2] Two estimates made twenty-five or thirty years later differ notably, however. They indicate about half as much revenue from Syria and Egypt, allow several times as much from the farms and the customs duties, and introduce taxes on mines and salt works, tithes paid in kind, the animal tax, tributes, escheats, and document fees.[3] Accord-

[1] Below, p. 273.

[2] La Broquière, 182, estimated the sultan's revenue in 1433 at 2,500,000 ducats. Chalcocondyles, 171, overestimated it at 8,000,000 ducats about the year 1465. Alvise Sagudino (quoted in Schéfer's edition of Spandugino, p. lv) reckoned it in 1496 at 3,300,000 ducats; Andrea Gritti, father of Alvise, made it 5,000,000 in 1503 (ibid. lviii); Spandugino's estimate, under Bayezid, was 3,600,000 (ibid. 132). Mocenigo, 54, set Selim I's income at 3,130,000, besides 800,000 from the Persian conquests, all spent in Persia. Minio (1522), 71, estimated the revenue as 3,000,000. Zeno (1524), 95, called it 4,500,000, and the expenses 3,000,000. Bragadin (1526), 106, says that the treasury had an income of 12,000,000, of which the sultan took 4,500,000 (the larger amount would no doubt include the feudal income). Minio (1527), 115, states the income as 7,000,000. Zeno (1530), 121, gives 6,000,000 or more for the income, 4,000,000 for the expenses. Giovio (Commentaries, 73) sets the revenue at 6,000,000, and the expenses at 4,000,000 or 5,000,000, Postel, iii. 68, gives 4,000,000 on Alvise Gritti's authority, though he apportions it differently from Junis Bey. D'Ohsson, vii. 258, says that Suleiman's revenues rose to 26,000,000 piasters. At 40 aspers to the piaster and 50 aspers to the ducat, this gives about 20,000,000 ducats, which is far too much.

[3] Navagero (1553), 37–39, estimates 7,166,000 ducats; Trevisano (1554), 149–150, says 8,196,000 ducats. Navagero seems to overestimate the mines (1,500,000 ducats) and the duties (1,200,000); Trevisano's estimate of 2,000,000 from the animal tax seems unwarranted. Erizzo (1557), 130, claims to give an authentic statement of the sultan's income and expenditure; the former he sets at 4,600,000 ducats and the latter at 3,600,000. A. Barbarigo (1558), 150, gives 7,740,000 ducats as income and 4,100,000 as expenditure. Donini, 190, says that after great efforts he knows most certainly that the income of the treasury for 1561 was 216,519,826 aspers, or 4,330,396 ducats and 26 soldi, and the expenditure 206,581,957 aspers, or 4,131,639 ducats and 7 soldi. He states that this income is less by 400,000 ducats than usual, because of the prohibition of wine. Erizzo does not include the tax on mines and salt works, and the income from Mesopotamia and the domain lands, in his list of sources of revenue; and Donini does not specify the sources. Bernardo, 347, says that the income in his time of service (1584–87) was 9,000,000 ducats, and that by 1592 it was 10,000,000. Knolles (ed. 1687, p. 982) estimates the sultan's ordinary revenues about 1603 as 8,000,000. This does not, however, include confiscations, fines, tribute, customs, booty, etc., which

ing to their estimated total of seven or eight million ducats, it would seem that a million ducats ought to be added to Junis Bey's estimate for the mines, salt works, and tributes, and a million for the other revenues mentioned. This would give an estimate of six million ducats for Suleiman's revenues in the early part of his reign. Toward the close of his reign, after large territories in Europe and Asia had been incorporated, and after Rustem had made new arrangements, the total amount was probably seven or eight million ducats.[1] The bullion value of six million ducats is less than fourteen million dollars. If, then, the purchasing power of money be estimated at five times what it is now, the regular revenue of Suleiman's government was equivalent to less than seventy million dollars nowadays, no large sum for so great an empire. It is necessary to remember, however, that this by no means covers all the expenses for public purposes within the empire. It probably includes none of the revenues devoted to the Moslem Institution, nor those specifically assigned by feudal grant to the officers of local government; certainly it does not include those gathered by the permanent fief-holders and used for their own support, which probably amounted to about twice as much more.[2] Allowing for all this,

Knolles (p. 983) believed to exceed the ordinary revenue. Hammer, *Staatsverwaltung*, 170, gives official figures for a hundred years later (1660): the income of the treasury then was 600,000,000 aspers, or 11,000,000 to 12,000,000 ducats at sixteenth-century valuations; capitation was nearly 2,000,000, land tax about as much, mines 1,000,000, etc.

[1] The extensive notes given above show clearly that from 1433 to 1660 there was a progressive increase in the sultan's income, as measured in aspers or ducats. Brosch (in *Cambridge Modern History*, iii. 130) accuses Suleiman of raising by taxation double the amount exacted by Mohammed II, and thus bringing undue pressure to bear. This statement fails to take account of the fact that Suleiman's empire was about double that of Mohammed II's in area, population, and wealth. Also it seems to have been the case that the value of gold and silver fell greatly after the discovery of the American mines (Day, 135). If these effects were felt promptly in the Levant, Suleiman's income in the last years of his life may have had little more purchasing power than Mohammed II's. Distributed over a wider area, the pressure of taxation in his time may easily have been lighter than it was three generations before.

[2] Postel, iii. 67, says that it does not include the *timars*. He says (iii. 168) that some call the total revenue 12,000,000 ducats, in which they must include the income of the fief-holders. Bragadin, 106, says that the income is 12,000,000.

the sum total, the equivalent of perhaps two hundred million dollars, for all the expenses of central and local government was small in proportion to population, according to modern standards. Had there been no extortion, the people of the empire would not have been burdened heavily. Even with it, as indicated already, they probably did not suffer greatly in Suleiman's time.[1]

THE NISHANJI OR CHANCELLOR

The chancery department of the Ottoman government seems not to have reached such a stage of development in the sixteenth century as had the treasury department; certainly it was not so conspicuous. Contemporary writers give so little information about it that it is hard to draw a reasonably complete picture of it. They mention several of the officials who were prominent in the department in later times; but evidently those of the earlier period were not under the same relationships to each other as were later ones who bore the same titles. The *Nishanji-bashi*, often called simply the *Nishanji*, was clearly the chief, but other details are not easily to be ascertained. It seems necessary, therefore, to describe the Ottoman chancery as it was two centuries after Suleiman's death, and then to endeavor to conjecture what it was in his time.[2]

In the latter part of the eighteenth century the Ottoman government had three ministers of state and six under-secretaries of state. The three ministers were the *Kiaya-bey*, the *Chaush-bashi*, and the *Reis Effendi*, the last named being by far the most important. The *Kiaya-bey* was the substitute or

Ramberti (below, p. 261) estimates it at 15,000,000, of which 5,000,000 goes into the treasury and 10,000,000 remains for the " servants of war."

[1] Hammer, *Geschichte*, iii. 472; and see above, p. 144 and note 2.

[2] Accounts are given in D'Ohsson, vii. 159–172, and in Hammer, *Staatsverwaltung*, 101–137. References to the *Nishanji* are found in Spandugino, 99; Menavino, 168; Ramberti, below, p. 248; Ludovisi, 14; Navagero, 94; Trevisano, 118; Garzoni, 430; Junis Bey (below, p. 266) and Postel, iii. 63, speak of a *Teskerejibashi*, giving a description which applies exactly to the *Nishanji* as represented by contemporaries. Since the word means merely " chief of document-writers," it refers without doubt to the *Nishanji*.

lieutenant of the grand vizier, and attended especially to affairs of the interior and of war; under him were a number of officials who formed connecting links between the grand vizier and the various groups of *kullar* in the household and the army. The *Chaush-bashi* was at the same time second official in the grand vizier's court of justice, minister of police, introducer of ambassadors, grand marshal of the court, and chief of the *Chaushes*. To assist him in the execution of these varied functions, he had a large number of under officers and clerks. The *Reis Effendi*, whose full title was *Reis ul-Khuttab*, " Chief of the Men of the Pen," was minister of foreign affairs, secretary of state, and chancellor. In the first capacity he was prominent in international relations; in the second he was responsible for the preparation of the addresses and reports which the grand vizier made to the sultan; in the third, he was head of the three bureaus of the chancery. In charge of these under him were a *Beylikji*, or general director of the three bureaus, a *Terjuman Divani Humayun*, or chief interpreter, and an *Ameji*, who drew up the grand vizier's reports to the sultan for the inspection of the *Reis Effendi*.

Of the three bureaus, the *Beylik Kalemi* prepared, recorded, or transmitted, as was proper in each case, *Kanuns*, treaties, and all *firmans* that did not concern the treasury department. The *Tahvil Kalemi* prepared the diplomas of governors, of judges of large towns, and of fief-holders. The *Ruus Kalemi* made out certificates for the clerks of all bureaus, for *Kapuji-bashis*, professors in endowed colleges, administrators of religious endowments, pensioners on the treasury or on religious benefactions, and soldiers of the auxiliary corps of the regular army. Together the three bureaus kept employed about one hundred and fifty clerks of three grades, provided for by fiefs. The *Nishanji's* sole duty was to authenticate *firmans* sent to the provinces, by tracing at the head of each document the sultan's *tughra*, or official signature. He had no influence on the conduct of business, but, as evidence of past greatness, he ranked above even the *Reis Effendi* on ceremonial occasions.[1]

[1] Hammer, *Staatsverwaltung*, 133.

The under-secretaries were attached by pairs to the ministers. The *Teshrifatji*, or master of ceremonies, and the *Kiaya Katibi*, or private secretary, of the *Kiaya-bey* were attached to the *Kiaya-bey*. The greater and lesser *Teskerejis*, or masters of petitions, were attached to the *Chaush-bashi*. The *Beylikji*, mentioned above as head of the three bureaus of the chancery, and the *Mektubji*, or private secretary of the grand vizier, in which office he was assisted by a bureau of thirty clerks, were attached to the *Reis Effendi*.

It is evident that all the functions of the officials and bureaus described above must have been performed in some fashion in the time of Suleiman. The conservative character of Turkish institutions simplifies the problem of determining how they were performed. It has been seen, partly by external and partly by internal evidence, that the bureaus of the treasury department persisted from the time of Mohammed II to the end of the eighteenth century with few changes. Accordingly, the inference may fairly be made that the same was true of the chancery department. Moreover, the chief officials of the later date are mentioned in sixteenth-century writings, among them the *Kiaya* of the grand vizier, the *Chaush-bashi*, and the *Reis Effendi;* Junis Bey held the position of chief interpreter;[1] and the duties of Suleiman's master of ceremonies must have been important. The great change in the chancery in the interval was the decline of the *Nishanji* from the highest place in the department to one of little importance, and the rise of the *Reis Effendi* from a subordinate place to the top. From of old the *Nishanji* had had the duty of affixing the sultan's signature to documents; but in early Ottoman days, when the pen was of very little consequence in comparison with the sword, he had been held in small esteem. He was responsible, however, for the accurate and legal formulation of the papers which he signed; and as the nation grew his importance increased, till by the sixteenth century he had become a great official, clearly the head of the chancery department, and the recipient of a large salary. A description of about the year 1537 says of the *Nishanji*: " There is a *Teskereji-*

[1] Hammer, *Geschichte*, iii. 54.

bashi, who has the duty of engrossing the ordinances and commands of the prince and the court, when it has transmitted them to him, and is like a general secretary of the commands, or recorder of the documents of the prince, which are called *Teskereh;* and it is also his duty, in consultation with the pashas, to revise the writings and take care that they contain no ambiguous expressions, as though he were a keeper of the seals. The present occupant of the office has seven thousand ducats of revenue from fiefs, and a large number of slaves, and other lesser recorders who also prepare commands, licenses, safe-conducts, and other letters as there may be need. These are paid here for their trouble, and they may receive three or four hundred livres. It is said that the present [*Nishanji*] is so just a man, that he has never in his life received a *sou* from any one with whom he has transacted business." [1]

The *Reis Effendi* was at that time, it would seem, little more than recording secretary of the Divan. [2] The reasons for the later change in the relative importance of these two officials probably lay in the withdrawal of the sultan into his inner palace, and the development of foreign relations. As the sultan became more sequestered, the *Nishanji's* personal relation to him was gradually cut off; for the same reason the grand vizier came to be more heavily burdened, and left more responsibility on the *Reis Effendi.* Beginning with Suleiman's reign, relations with the Western European nations became ever closer and more complicated. Cared for in his time by the grand viziers Ibrahim, Rustem, and Ali, [3] they were entrusted in later reigns to the *Reis Effendi.* Presently, then, this official displaced the *Nishanji* at the head of the chancery, and the latter was gradually reduced almost to the functions of a name-stamp. Aside from this important difference, and the general fact that the business of the chancery was not so extensive in Suleiman's time as it became

[1] Postel, iii. 63. See also Ramberti, below, p. 248.

[2] Hammer, *Geschichte,* ii. 229, iii. 796. The first *Reis Effendi* whose name is known was Haider Effendi, executed in 1525 on the charge of promoting an uprising of the Janissaries. The office is mentioned in the *Kanun-nameh* of Mohammed II (Hammer, *Staatsverfassung,* 90).

[3] Hammer, *Geschichte,* iii. 126 ff.; Busbecq, *Life and Letters, passim.*

later, and that the functions of separate officials had not come to be so rigidly defined, the inference may be made that the description of the late eighteenth century holds good generally of the Ottoman chancery of the sixteenth century.

Little evidence appears as to the status of the personnel of the treasury and chancery departments. The upper officials were drawn from the quieter and more studious members of the school of pages;[1] in the time of Mohammed II the *Nishanji* might be drawn from the ranks of the *Ulema*.[2] Junis Bey refers to the employees of the bureaus sometimes as slaves and sometimes as companions or scribes. They were paid not in money but by fiefs. Near the close of Suleiman's reign, it is said, the chancery clerks were Turks, whereas they had been Christians and Greeks not long before, and had written their documents in Greek.[3] Whether or not this be true, the books of the treasury department had been kept in Turkish from the first;[4] but it does not follow, of course, that the clerks of this department had always been Ottomans, or that, if they were, they had been regularly either Moslem-born or renegades. The general reasons which led the sultan to build the Ruling Institution out of slaves in its other aspects would tend to operate here also; on the other hand, the nature of the work demanded persons of quiet tastes and, for many positions, those of considerable learning in language and law, and such persons were more easily to be found in the Moslem-born population than among the Christian subjects or renegades. It would seem that in Suleiman's time, or shortly before, the personnel of the chancery changed from Christian-born to Moslem-born. Naturally, then, the personnel of the treasury would have been likely to undergo a similar transformation at the same time.

It has been said that when Turks dismount from their horses, they become bureaucrats and paper-scribblers.[5] Undoubtedly

---

[1] Ricaut, 57.   [2] Hammer, *Staatsverfassung*, 90.

[3] Trevisano (1554), 118. Morosini (1585), 266, says that the employees of the chancery were then native Turks.

[4] Hammer, *Geschichte*, i. 35.

[5] Cahun, *Introduction*, 82, speaking of Turks of the steppe lands: " Dès qu'ils descendaient de cheval, c'étaient des barbares bureaucrates et paperassiers."

the Ottoman government gave evidence of the truth of this statement. The twenty-five bureaus of the treasury and the appended bureaus, the three bureaus of the chancery, the treasuries and chanceries of *Beylerbeys* and *Sanjak Beys*, the offices of the generals of cavalry and infantry, and of the *Umena* and other household officials without and within, contained some thousands of men whose whole time was occupied in writing, recording, and transmitting laws, ordinances, diplomas, nominations, projects, deeds, grants, orders for pay, receipts, reports, addresses, petitions, answers, and the like. The existence of so many component institutions, connected only at the top and paralleling each other's activities both near and far, together with the custom of verifying, authenticating, and recording many papers in different bureaus and by different officials, created a vast and growing amount of red tape that in time was greatly to hinder all government business. Even in Suleiman's day it seems to have been the practice on the part of clerks and officials to demand a private fee for each act of writing or signing or stamping or recording or approving or inspecting.[1] In the time of prosperity, however, this practice can hardly have been so vexatious and dilatory as it became later. The bureaucratic tendency was no doubt based on a desire to keep everything in order by checks and cross-recording; but in the end it defeated its object by employing such a multiplicity of devices that order was lost in confusion.

THE DIVAN OR COUNCIL [2]

In a land where the law was nearly fixed, and where whatever power of legislation was allowed was definitely lodged in one man, the only deliberation possible was on administrative and judicial subjects. The oversight of these matters was given in charge to a council, the Divan, which held long sessions four

---

[1] Spandugino, 185.

[2] The Divan, as it was about 1800, is described in D'Ohsson, vii. 211–232; and in Hammer, *Staatsverwaltung*, 412–436. Contemporary references are Menavino, 169; Postel, i. 122; Navagero, 93; Trevisano, 117; Garzoni, 430. Zinkeisen, iii. 117–125, has pictured the Divan in the sixteenth century.

times each week throughout the year in time of peace, unless perhaps in the month of fasting. This council was composed of *ex officio* members who represented (when those who came only on special days are added to those who came each day) all the great component parts of the Ruling Institution. The Moslem Institution also was represented in the two *Kaziaskers;* for the grand vizier and the Divan constituted not only the supreme council of administration but the supreme court of the empire. It was thus not strictly a part of the Ruling Institution, but rather the cap-stone of both institutions, the body that gave final unity, immediately under the sultan, to the organization of the empire.

In former times the sultan had presided at the Divan. Suleiman did not, and he has been greatly blamed for discontinuing the custom.[1] It is not impossible to sympathize with him, however, for he thus freed himself from a great burden; to spend several hours in deliberation on four days of each week during a lifetime is a prospect from which any man would shrink. Nevertheless, it was a serious rift in both of the great institutions of the empire at the most dangerous place, and its effect was decidedly to hasten their disintegration. Suleiman kept the Divan under control by means of a grated window in the wall of the room where it met.[2] Not knowing when he might be listening there, his councillors had always to speak as if he were present with them.

The arrival of the councillors at the hall of the Divan, their entry, their places for sitting or standing, their rank at the simple meal of which they partook while there, the order of their going in to audience with the sultan afterward, and the manner of their departure, were all according to *Kanun* or equally rigid custom. At a later time the details of these ceremonies were all minutely specified.[3] Probably they were not so elaborate in the time of

[1] Hammer, *Geschichte*, iii. 489. This is the first of the reasons given by Kochi Bey for the decline of the empire after Suleiman.

[2] Postel, i. 123; Trevisano, 119; Garzoni, 431. D. Barbarigo, 32, gives an instance in which Suleiman made use of this means of information, and in consequence ordered the execution of the grand vizier Achmet.

[3] Hammer (*Staatsverwaltung*, 412–436) gives them with great exactness.

Suleiman, but contemporary writings show them already considerably developed.

The sessions of the Divan have been described so often that it is not necessary to go into detail here. Soon after sunrise on Saturday, Sunday, Monday, and Tuesday the officials who were to participate came to the palace, accompanied by their secretaries, ushers, body-guards, and other attendants. They passed the second gate of the palace in the inverse order of rank, and waited at their prescribed places in the hall of the Divan until the grand vizier approached, accompanied by his retinue, when all came out and took places according to rank in two lines, between which the grand vizier entered. Those who had the right then followed him in by pairs, and once more took their places.[1] Officials who might be summoned waited in antechambers near; and attendants, guards, and soldiers, stood at suitable distances.

The grand vizier sat Turkish fashion in the middle of a long sofa which extended round three sides of the hall. On his right sat the other viziers (unless one or more happened to be absent on a special mission), and beyond them, on the sofa at the end of the room, the *Nishanji*. On the grand vizier's left were the two *Kaziaskers*, and beyond them the *Defterdars*.[2] The *Beylerbeys* of Anatolia and Greece, and, after Barbarossa's appointment, the *Kapudan Pasha*, sat beyond the viziers on the right. The *Agha* of the Janissaries also had a place, and the chief interpreter was often needed. Other generals and high officials might be summoned; heads, officials, and clerks of bureaus were at hand; and *Chaushes*, *Kapuji-bashis*, and *Kapujis* were in readiness to be sent on errands and missions. Before the grand vizier, when judicial business was being considered, stood

---

[1] In the time of Mohammed II a procession was formed by the members of the Divan, the men of the lowest rank in front, and the grand vizier last. On reaching the door of the hall, the lesser officials stopped and separated into two lines, between which the grand vizier advanced. The greater officials followed, so that the hall was entered in the order of rank. See Hammer, *Geschichte*, ii. 225.

[2] From the *Kanun* of Mohammed II: Hammer, *Staatsverfassung*, 89. Aali (used by Hammer, *Geschichte*, ii. 225) gives a different arrangement, which can hardly have been correct.

the *Teskerejis*, or masters of petitions. On the floor at his left sat the *Reis Effendi*. The *Kapujilar-kiayasi*, or grand chamberlain of the household, was present; and the *Chaush-bashi*, as grand marshal of the court, here bearing the additional title of *Bey* of the Divan, saw that all went according to rule. After greetings and other formalities the business was taken up in order of importance.[1] Great questions, like proposals of ambassadors, the condition of the provinces, and the possibility or desirability of war were discussed briefly by the viziers, the others present being called upon to speak if their views were desired. The grand vizier either declared the decision on such matters, subject to the sultan's approval, or reserved the decision for the master.[2] Lesser matters were decided by the viziers individually, or were referred by them to the other great officials present, or to an official in attendance outside. Much of the time there was no general deliberation, but several affairs might be considered by different members of the Divan simultaneously. Lawsuits were presented to the grand vizier by the masters of petitions, and the parties might appear to plead their own cases, bringing witnesses. The grand vizier turned over many cases to the *Kaziaskers*. All business was done with despatch, and a large amount was accomplished. Decisions were briefly formulated, without discussion of the reasons for action. The *Reis Effendi* and lesser secretaries and clerks wrote down carefully all that was decided upon. After the sultan had signified his approval at the close of a Divan, the decisions were irrevocable.

During and also at the close of the session, which might last seven or eight hours,[3] a simple meal of bread, meat, rice, fruit, and water was served to all who were in attendance within and without the hall of the Divan. To meet the expense of this, four days' pay was reserved each year from the salaries of all who were expected to attend.[4] Order was kept most carefully among all who were present within and without the hall of the Divan, and absolute silence was preserved, except for such movements and conversation as were necessary to the transac-

---

[1] Postel, i. 123.
[2] Garzoni, 431.
[3] Postel, i. 123.
[4] Garzoni, 431.

tion of business. Any disturber of order and quiet was taken away and immediately bastinadoed.

After the day's work was done, which might be about noon in summer time or toward sunset in the winter, those officials of the Divan who had the right of audience went to the hall of audience to meet the sultan. They were the viziers, *Kaziaskers*, and *Defterdars* regularly, and the *Beylerbeys* and the *Agha* of the Janissaries when they had business;[1] the *Defterdars*, however, received audience on Sundays and Tuesdays only. The *Kaziaskers* entered first, and when their business had been approved they went to the gate and held court. The *Beylerbeys*, the *Defterdars*, and the viziers entered the audience chamber together. The *Beylerbeys* transacted their business and departed; the *Defterdars* did likewise, and went to the door of the treasury to give audience. The ordinary viziers, left behind in the presence of the sultan, usually said nothing unless asked; the grand vizier alone reported on the decisions of the day.[2] These the sultan usually approved as made, sometimes mitigating a decision or himself dictating a reply to an ambassador.[3] Suleiman was willing to give a free hand to Ibrahim, Rustem, and Mohammed Sokolli during their long periods of service.[4]

In time of war the Divan was held in the grand vizier's tent, which was usually pitched near the sultan's. As all the high officials, and the heads of bureaus with at least part of their clerks, were present with the army, much the same ceremony could be gone through with as in the capital. When the sultan was absent from the city on campaigns, the few officials of government who were left behind held a secondary Divan on Saturdays and Sundays. In case of emergency during war-time, or for some other special reason, a Divan might be held on horseback.[5]

The Divan of Suleiman was a splendid ceremony, and it transacted a great amount of administrative and judicial busi-

---

[1] Hammer, *Staatsverfassung*, 89; Trevisano, 118–119.
[2] Navagero, 98; D. Barbarigo, 26. See also above, p. 164 and note 3.
[3] Postel, i. 123.
[4] Trevisano, 120. See above, p. 164.
[5] Zinkeisen, iii. 125; Tiepolo, 164.

ness. A large proportion of the duties of the principal officials was attended to in its sessions rather than in private offices; and on particular matters there was a certain amount of deliberation, though the Ottomans were not a people of many words. The Divan was by no means a legislative chamber. It was in a sense a combination of a president's cabinet and a supreme court;[1] yet it was unlike both. Its presiding officer was appointed; all its decisions required the approval of the sultan, who was not present at its sessions; and all its members were responsible to him for good behavior on penalty of their lives. It was the highest court in the land, yet not so much a court of appeal as a court of first instance. It had no power to judge the validity of laws; yet it was not restricted in its jurisdiction, since it had cognizance of all civil and criminal cases that might be presented to it from any part of the empire. In its judicial aspect, again, its decisions had no validity without the approval of the sultan. With all its limitations, however, it was of great value to the Ottoman government. Below the sultan, but above all institutions of the empire, it bound together at the top the Ruling Institution and the Moslem Institution, and it united similarly all the component divisions of each; it was the pivot from which were suspended all the separate parts of the despotically constructed government. In it met the ablest men of the empire, chosen by selection after selection, each one charged with great responsibilities and possessing power to execute without delay what might be agreed upon. The Divan was excellently adapted to the general Ottoman system. It enabled the ruler, with a minimum of care, to keep the closest control over every part of the empire through extremely intelligent and capable agents, who were bound to him by gratitude, self-interest, ambition, and fear. It was a training-school of judges, administrators, and statesmen, since men ordinarily rose from place to place among its offices as they gained experience; here

---

[1] Heidborn, 141: " Le divan était à la fois une sorte de Conseil d'État, où se discutaient les affaires politiques importantes, et une Cour suprême autorisée à évoquer tout litige devant elle et à connaître notamment des procès entre Ottomans et étrangers qui dépassaient la valeur de 3000 aspres."

they imparted ideas and methods to each other, and made their abilities known to the highest officials, the grand vizier and the sultan, with whom lay the power of promotion. Nor was the Divan wholly destitute of legislative influence. All *Kanuns* were issued in the sultan's name and after his definite approval; yet the information on which they were based must regularly have come through members of the Divan, and members of the Divan with their subordinates must certainly have drawn them up and revised them into shape. Controlling administration and justice and influencing legislation, the Divan, under the leadership of the grand vizier, governed the Ottoman Empire for the sultan.

THE RULING INSTITUTION AS A WHOLE

That which for want of a better name has been called in this treatise the Ottoman Ruling Institution has now been discussed in all its general aspects. Space has been lacking for the presentation of many details, though the attempt has been made to introduce all such as would give necessary evidence or useful illustration. A few statements intended to summarize and bind together what has been said will complete the discussion of the institution.

The Ottoman Ruling Institution was in its most essential aspect a government for the Ottoman Empire. In this respect its form was a despotism, centered in one man, the sultan. Yet the despotism was greatly circumscribed by a rigid constitutional law, which was firmly grounded in strong religious belief and intense national conservatism. This law held the sultan within limited functions, but at the same time it gave him his right to rule. As a government under this law, the Ottoman Ruling Institution maintained public order, defended the empire against its enemies, and endeavored by conquest to enlarge its possessions and with them the domain of the Sacred Law. A large proportion of its energies was devoted to obtaining and distributing the means of its own support, to keeping its own machinery in order, and to maintaining its authority within the empire. The idea of labor for the public welfare or of effort toward progress was not present. Change came, not by conscious striving toward betterment, but by growth, development, and decay, the effects of which were adjusted when it became necessary. But within such limits, there was in the sixteenth century a distinct desire, founded on consciousness of greatness, pride of power, and loyalty to Islam, to have the government well-ordered and intelligently directed, and to cause it to bear upon its subjects as evenly and lightly as possible. Suleiman laid hold of many problems which had arisen, and through the agency of his ablest servants strove to set his house in order. That he did not succeed in accomplishing more permanent results was due to the fact that the task was too great for any man. The institution was too artificial to endure indefinitely.

The whole institution kept itself in power, and defended and enlarged the empire, by being organized as an army. With exceptions, all its officers of government were soldiers and all its army officers had governmental duties. It constituted a standing army of cavalry and infantry, aided by artillery, commissary, and transport services; and it controlled a much larger feudal and irregular army. Through the feudal army it kept the country in subjection. By garrisons it held the towns quiet. In case of rebellion, it threw a great force upon the insurgents, and beat them down with cruel and resistless energy. For foreign wars it gathered an enormous but well-controlled host, which was victorious in battle throughout the reign of Suleiman. It took by siege Belgrade and Rhodes, but it failed at Vienna and Malta. The weakness of the Ruling Institution as an army was its essential indivisibility. Only one great war could be waged at a time, although there were great enemies in two directions; hence an overwhelming defeat of the principal army would have been irreparably disastrous. But the army was to suffice for a long period; and for generations its worst foes were to be, not foreign armies, but internal rivalries and departures from its constitutive principles.

To maintain the pomp and ceremony which are attached to the idea of an empire, especially in the East, and to supply the sultan on a large scale with all the enjoyments which were considered due to his state, the Ottoman Ruling Institution was in another aspect a great court and household. Nearly all its members shared in the display of grand occasions, many went to the hunt with the sultan, and a large proportion of them had constant duties of ceremonial and personal service. Suleiman was known as the Legislator and the Conqueror, but beyond both these titles as the Magnificent; he shone as head of the government and the army, but still more as head of the court. Splendor and luxury, however, are expensive, and in the end his example was to be ruinous.

All the members of the Ruling Institution were set off as a nobility by exemption from taxation and by special jurisdiction; but, lest they might prove a danger to the institution, they were not allowed to transmit their nobility to their descendants. In the end, however, their special privilege was to become so desirable that the walls of separation would be invaded and the institution would be wrecked.

The Ottoman Ruling Institution, at once the government, the army, and the nobility of a great nation, was at the same time a genuine slave-family. Almost all its members were recruited as slaves and remained slaves throughout their days; their lives and their property were at the disposal of the sultan; they must obey without hesitation, as all slaves must obey. Yet their condition was far from being miserable. Their slavery conveyed no taint: one of them might be married to a protegée or even a daughter of the great master; their children would never be reproached because of the father's status. It was an honor to be the sultan's *kul*. Vast wealth and almost royal power and rule might be theirs; yet each member of the Ruling Institution was actually a slave.

The most characteristic feature of this institution lay in the fact that its recruits were almost all drawn from children (born within or without the empire) of Christian parents, and that before they were advanced they were expected to become Mohammedans. A twofold motive lay beneath this policy, — a desire to obtain single-hearted servants and to increase the number of believers in the Mohammedan faith. Sons of these converts were sometimes admitted to the Ruling Institution, but their grandsons practically never. Thus a constant stream of the ablest and fittest Christian children who were born in or near the Ottoman dominions were brought into the Ruling Institution, the Ottoman nation, and the Mohammedan fold.

The next most characteristic and the most abiding feature of the Ottoman Ruling Institution was its educational quality. The Christian slaves were all acquired while young, and were trained with the greatest care to become useful members of the institution, each in the capacity for which nature had best fitted him. They were provided with an education which, if not so general or so advanced as the usual training of modern times, was more nearly complete. Body and mind, social, moral, and religious nature, all received attention. The immediate object of this education was to fit the boys for the sultan's service in war and government; but they were also trained to adorn his ceremonies and his court, and to live by the principles and in the faith of Mohammed. When they were first admitted, their training was more or less like that in schools of an industrial, military, and cultural character; but it did not stop with the attainment of majority. Army, household, bureaus, local government, and Divan, all were conducted much like schools. Strict discipline was constantly maintained, slackness was severely punished, and industry and ability were richly rewarded. The results were well-nigh incredible; they constitute a wonderful demonstration of how little the human spirit is limited by the ignorance or the restricted and humble life of ancestors. With hardly an exception, the men who guided Suleiman's empire to a height of unexampled glory were sons of peasants and herdsmen, of downtrodden and miserable subjects, of unlettered and half-civilized men and women. It is not easy to decide which is more to be admired, the ability by which such young men rose, or the confidence with which they were chosen and expected to rise. If these men had not really risen, if they had remained boorish, ignorant, and narrow, though elevated to high position and authority, the facts would be less remarkable than they are. The evidence is, however, that they really became educated, cultured, and polished men: to this day their descendants have a manner and charm that can rarely be found among Western peoples. It is much easier to understand the whole process and its results in a modern democratic age and land than it was in feudal Europe of the sixteenth century. The Ottoman Ruling Institution was from start to finish ingeniously contrived to develop its members, within the limits of its purposes, to their utmost capacity. Great authority, great position, great financial rewards, were offered. Great punishments were not far away from those who might prove dangerous, treacherous, or even incompatible and inefficient.

As a result of its careful selection and training of men for society, war, and government, the Ottoman Ruling Institution, allowing for all imperfections of structure, was a very efficient and permanent entity. It was later to endure terrible shocks and losses without destruction; it was to suffer a partial separation of its component institutions into hostile bodies, and to witness serious departures from its rules and principles. But, despite attack from without and disintegration and decay within, it long stood firm; and, together with its dissimilar companion, the Moslem Institution of the Ottoman Empire, it has kept the vital spark of that empire alive for more than two centuries after extinction began to be thought imminent. Even today its abiding spirit gives promise of lighting a new and very different torch, which, having burned away the limitations and imperfections that caused the ruin of the older institution, will yet be the brighter for preserving a democratic faith in the capacity of the able individual, and a disposition to help him forward by education and to trust him with all the responsibility that he is able to bear. Most features of the Ottoman Ruling Institution cannot live in the twentieth century. Despotism, military rule, personal privilege, excessive imperial splendor, proselytism, and slavery have been dethroned in favor of political and religious liberty, equality, fraternity, separation of church and state, and government by the people. But the idea of an education which will develop the individual to the full extent of his capacities is thoroughly modern; and the disposition to entrust high offices to those who, without regard to ancestry, are the ablest, and who become by their own efforts and by carefully supervised training the best equipped, is in advance of the ordinary practice of Western democracies. Herein lies one of the strongest elements of hope for the future of the new Turkey, which may thus preserve continuity with the past.

The Ottoman Ruling Institution, still thus capable of imparting valuable ideas, was in its halcyon days a thing of immense moment in the world. Out of carefully selected but most heterogeneous materials it had built itself up as a firm, strong, and simple structure, which had gathered a chaotic mass of petty states and hostile peoples into a great and, by comparison, a well-governed and durable empire. In the reign of the great Suleiman no human structure existed which equalled this institution in wealth, splendor, power, simplicity and rapidity of action, and respect at home and abroad.

CHAPTER VII

THE MOSLEM INSTITUTION OF THE OTTOMAN EMPIRE

GENERAL DESCRIPTION

IN a survey of the institutional history of the Ottoman Empire, a study of the complex organization which was based upon and inspired by the Mohammedan religion would demand as large a space as that given to the Ruling Institution. In a discussion of the government of the empire, however, a much briefer treatment will suffice. The Moslem Institution as a whole will be sketched rapidly; fuller consideration will be given to its juristic and judicial features, which especially affected and entered into the government of the nation.

The structure of the Moslem Institution of the Ottoman Empire, as of the corresponding institutions in all Moslem lands, was and remains to the present time wholly different from that of any of the Christian ecclesiastical organizations. As a mere church it claimed far less place and influence than they do, but in other aspects it reached out far more widely. It included all those Mohammedans in the Ottoman Empire, outside of the Ruling Institution, who were in any way lifted above the level of the ordinary believer. Islam recognized no organized priesthood, no aristocracy, and no monks; yet the Ottoman Moslem Institution possessed groups that were much like each of the three. In addition it had a graded educational system, with a graded corps of teachers, it contained a hierarchy of jurist-theologians, and it supplied a classified body of judges, whose combined jurisdictions covered the whole empire. That which all persons who constituted this institution had in common was a special relationship to the Mohammedan religion, sometimes based on birth or piety, but usually established by intellectual training in connection with the Book and the Law of Islam. In contrast with the Ottoman Ruling Institution, the Moslem Institution cannot as a whole be regarded under several aspects. Like the former, it included component institutions; but these all grew up from the Mohammedan population and rested on one broad base, instead of being extended downward from the top. At the same time, the sultan was the head of this institution, whether it be considered as a whole or in reference to each of its component institutions. He and his government appointed its most influential personages, maintained careful oversight of its financial support, and kept record of the appointments of all its members who shared in this support. The two great institutions of the Ottoman Empire were therefore joined together at the top, and, as will appear, they touched at every other level both in financial and in governmental relations.

The fundamental difference of the two institutions lay in the fact that the members of the Ruling Institution were drawn almost exclusively from Christian families, and the members of the Moslem Institution even more exclusively from Mohammedan families. While it is likely that the majority of the Mohammedan families had sprung from Christian ancestors not many generations back, it is also true that Islam acts rapidly upon the spirit of converts. Accordingly the two institutions were very differently constituted. Between them arose a rivalry of tendency and influence which was to become extremely harmful to the Ottoman state.

In this treatise the financial side of the Moslem Institution will be considered, the four great groups of its membership will be discussed in the proportion of their relation to the government, and some attention will be given to the institution as a whole.

Financial Support of the Moslem Institution [1]

As already stated, a large proportion of the land of the Ottoman Empire, perhaps one-third,[2] was set aside as *vakf*, or religious

---

[1] Although this and other features of the Moslem Institution will be spoken of throughout this chapter in the past tense, much that is mentioned remains in existence in Turkey at the present time. The *vakfs* are discussed at length in D'Ohsson, ii. 437–567; and more briefly in Belin, *La Propriété Foncière*, 74–104. Heidborn, 306 ff., gives a well-analyzed account; and on p. 306, note 245, he mentions additional authorities.

[2] Ricaut, 213.

endowment. Much of this had been so devoted by sultans, and in such cases the imperial treasury could use for its own purposes none of the revenue or income from these lands. Other parcels of land had been set apart by private individuals, in these instances the treasury receiving for its own use the same revenues as before the endowment, while the surplus income from the land was devoted to the purposes specified by the giver. Each tract of such land was by the original act of endowment assigned to a particular object, and a *Muteveli* or administrator and a *Nazir* or inspector were appointed to take care of it. In a large proportion of cases a high official of the government or household, such as the grand vizier, the *Mufti*, the *Kapu Agha*, or the *Kizlar Agha*, was put in charge *ex officio* in one or the other capacity, on the theory that, being near the person of the sultan, he would be subject to constant control. In course of time the *Kizlar Agha*, the grand vizier, and the *Mufti* found it necessary to organize the properties under their charge by holding private Divans of the subordinate administrators and inspectors, and by appointing *Mufettishes*, or special judges, each with a staff of subordinates and travelling inspectors.[1]

Although every tract of land was assigned for a definite object and placed under specified guardians, the *vakfs* were a matter of public record, and the accounts of all were kept by the treasury department in the appropriate bureaus. The subjects who lived on *vakf* lands seem to have been better treated than those on lands of other sorts, just as in the West in the Middle Ages the serfs of the church were often better off than other serfs.[2] There were three classes of *vakfs*, — the regular *vakfs* of the mosques, the *vakfs* for charitable purposes, and the customary *vakfs* of the mosques. The last were chiefly in the nature of investments of the funds of the mosques, and were according to *Kanun* rather than *Sheri*.[3] In the second class were included endowments of schools, libraries, hospitals, bridges, fountains, caravan-

[1] D'Ohsson, ii. 540.
[2] Ricaut, 217. D'Ohsson, ii. 532, expresses a different opinion.
[3] Interest was allowable on the funds belonging to mosques, though otherwise forbidden: Ricaut, 218; D'Ohsson, ii. 550.

serais, public baths, convents for dervishes, and the like. The narrow provision of the Ruling Institution for public service was in this way supplemented.[1] The first class deserves further attention.

The chief material unit in connection with the Moslem Institution was the mosque. Each great mosque was a large house of worship, with a group of smaller institutions clustered about it, such as colleges, law schools, hospitals, insane asylums, and soup-kitchens. For the support of these and of all persons who conducted them, the income from the *vakfs* of the mosque was applied. In many cases the lands which had belonged to Christian churches before the Ottoman conquest were assigned as *vakfs* for the support of the mosques into which the churches were converted. For example, the grounds of the sultan's principal palace had belonged to the church, and were assigned as *vakf* to the mosque of Aya Sofia. When Mohammed II took them for his palace he pledged a revenue of one thousand and one aspers a day to the great mosque.[2] This church was one of eight in the city of Constantinople which were so treated.[3] The revenue of Aya Sofia was estimated at two hundred thousand ducats a year.[4] The income of the principal mosques being much larger than the expenses, a considerable portion of the surplus was used by the guardians for their own benefit, although they were supposed to receive no compensation, but to labor for the love of God. The fact is that many of the sultan's *kullar* provided an inheritance for their sons and descendants by setting apart for specific purposes lands in *vakf*, of which the desired persons should be administrators, it being clearly understood that a portion of the income should be retained by them.[5] The remainder of the surplus was held in a special treasury by the appropriate bureaus, or was reinvested in customary *vakfs*, or was lent to the government. The *vakfs* as a whole supported

---

[1] See below, p. 234, note 1.

[2] Ramberti, below, p. 243; Ricaut, 215.

[3] Hammer, *Geschichte*, ii. 237.

[4] Ricaut, 215. In D'Ohsson's time (ii. 538) it was estimated at 1,000,000 aspers. Nicolay, 68, says that it had been 300,000 ducats before the conquest.

[5] Morosini, 267; Zane, 406; Heidborn, 309.

all the official members of the Moslem Institution, except that the judges derived much of their income from fees and fines.[1] The treasury department received and controlled all the revenues from *vakfs*, and paid from the appropriate funds all who were duly certified as recipients of salaries and pensions.

All the *Ulema*, in connection with their support from semi-public funds, possessed the noble privilege of immunity from taxation. Since the rendering of justice was in their hands, they had their own justice. In addition, their property was not subject to confiscation; and, since they were not *kullar*, it passed by inheritance to their relatives and never to the sultan. All these privileges gave the learned class in the Ottoman Empire the prestige of nobility, besides great financial advantage.[2]

THE EDUCATIONAL SYSTEM

Like the Ruling Institution, the Moslem Institution contained and embodied an educational system which was of its essential structure. Through it, from the time of Mohammed II, the great majority of the members of the institution, including all who expected promotion, were required to pass; accordingly, they bore as a body the name of the *Ulema*, or learned men.[3] The schools, supported by *vakfs* and attached to mosques, were in three grades: the *mektebs* or primary schools, known in the sixteenth century as *okumak-yerleri* or reading-places; the ordinary *medressehs* or colleges; and the higher *medressehs* or law schools, of university grade. The *mektebs* taught Arabic reading and writing and the Koran; the *medressehs* gave a course of ten studies resembling the Seven Arts of the West;[4] the law

---

[1] Mohammed II fixed these fees: for example, 7 aspers for sealing a document, 12 for a signature, 32 for the marriage contract of a virgin, 15 for that of a widow, etc. See Hammer, *Staatsverfassung*, 100.

[2] D'Ohsson, iv. 599.

[3] The *Ulema* and other members of the Moslem Institution are described in D'Ohsson, iv. 482–686. Hammer, *Staatsverwaltung*, 372–412, gives a summary of D'Ohsson's treatment. Heidborn, 208–210, describes the educational system summarily.

[4] The ten studies were grammar, syntax, logic, metaphysics, philology, tropics, stylistics, rhetoric, geometry, and astronomy: Hammer, *Geschichte*, ii. 238.

schools taught the group of sciences connected with the Koran and the *Sheri* and including both law and theology.[1]

There was no compulsory education; nor could the system, by reason of the individual character of its foundations, be universal for Mohammedan children, But it may be supposed that any Moslem parent, the inhabitant of a town of some size, who desired his son to learn the rather difficult art of reading and writing Turkish and Arabic, or even to enter upon a learned career, was not devoid of an opportunity. Furthermore, where primary schools existed the instruction was free, and some students were even fed and lodged;[2] the students in the *medressehs* were also partially supported, and those in the law schools received a sufficiency. This system, which dated back at least to the twelfth century in Moslem lands, probably in the Ottoman Empire in the sixteenth century gave better opportunity for education to Moslem boys than was afforded to Christian children in any land until a much later date. The Ottomans believed thoroughly in education; but, unfortunately, their conservatism was in course of time to turn a beneficent institution into a harmful one. No change of consequence, either in methods of teaching or in subjects of study, was permitted from century to century; hence the training that had once carried its earnest pupils to the forefront of human knowledge was in time to hold them firmly at a stage which the rest of the world had long passed through and left far behind.

The *medressehs* were very numerous in the empire;[3] the mosque of the Conqueror had eight, that of Suleiman five. It was Suleiman who set the gradations of the system in their final

[1] Among these studies were advanced rhetoric and metaphysics, dogmatics, civil law, exegesis, jurisprudence, oral tradition, and written documents (Hammer, *Geschichte*, ii. 239). All schools above the *mektebs* came under the name *medresseh*. Heidborn distinguishes eight classes to which Suleiman added four colleges of yet higher degree. His implication (p. 210, note 5) that the student who aimed at the highest judgeships must study through eight or more *medressehs*, and then teach through a like series, can hardly be correct, since the ordinary human life would be too short for such a double round. Probably the steps of progress were not so precisely regulated or so numerous.

[2] D'Ohsson, ii. 464.

[3] Hammer (*Geschichte*, ix. 145–163) found 275 in Constantinople alone, of which 50 had been founded before the death of Suleiman.

form. All who aspired to any official position in the Moslem Institution must pass through a *medresseh* of some degree. On first entering they were called *Softas*, or more properly *Sukhtas*, as those who were *inflamed* with the desire for learning. The students were in different grades, but there seems to have been no fixed number of years of study; the instruction being largely individual, each could proceed as rapidly as he was able. On finishing, they received a sort of master's degree and were called *Danishmend*, which appears in several of the early sources as *Talisman*.[1] Such students as were content to teach primary schools, or to attend to ecclesiastical duties, needed to study no longer.

Those who aspired to become jurists or judges had to pursue a long course in law in the higher *medressehs*. At the end of this time they were examined personally by the *Mufti*, or chief jurist, and if successful they were dignified with the title of *Mulâzim*, or candidate. Those who did not aspire to the higher judicial positions ended their preparation at this point. The more ambitious sought appointment, for which they were now qualified, as *Muderisler*, or professors, in *medressehs* of low grade. The *Muderisler* received large salaries, which increased as they rose. They were in three classes, — the *Muderisler* of Constantinople, of Adrianople and Brusa, and of the other cities of the empire. The *Muderisler* of Constantinople numbered about four hundred; they were in ten grades, distinguished according to the subjects which they taught. Those of other cities than the capital, and those at the capital who did not pass through all the grades, became either jurists or judges of lesser degrees. Those who wished to reach the higher judgeships were obliged to pass through all ten grades. Since this was so long a process as regularly to bring a man to gray hairs before he reached the top, the rigid grading early began to be circumvented by the practice of inscribing the sons of *Ulema* as *Muderisler* while they were very young, substitutes being hired to teach in their places.[2] By the age of thirty or forty they would thus

---

[1] Chalcocondyles, 53; Ramberti, below, p. 244; Junis Bey, below, p. 265; etc.
[2] D'Ohsson, ii. 477; Heidborn, 213.

be able to attain high position. A continuance of this process, combined with the immunities and privileges of the *Ulema*, was in time to lead to great accumulations of wealth in the hands of a few families, who would be able to keep most of the high judicial offices within their own numbers.

CLERGY, SEIDS, AND DERVISHES

The clergy of the Ottoman nation were, as has been shown, of no great education, and they seem to have possessed less influence than the priests of any other religion.[1] They were in five classes: the *Sheiks*, or preachers; the *Khatibs*, or leaders of Friday services; the *Imâms*, or leaders of daily services; the *Muezzins*, who intoned the call to prayer; and the *Kaims*, or caretakers of the mosques.

The *Seids*, also known as *Emirs* or *Sherifs*, were a class apart among the Ottomans. They were not properly members of the *Ulema*, unless, like others, they passed through the schools; they owed their distinction rather to a real or assumed genealogy which carried their ancestry back to the Prophet Mohammed. They alone were privileged to wear a green turban. They were numerous; but the claims of many were doubted, and some of them seem to have possessed reputations that were far from savory.[2] They constituted the only hereditary nobility among the Ottomans, but their privileges appear to have been personal rather than financial: they were not to be struck, for example, on penalty of severe punishment, and they had their own justice. Great honor was shown to two members of this nobility, descendants of the Prophet: to the *Mir-Alem*, the sultan's standard-bearer, who was regularly a *Seid*, and had precedence of all the officers of the army; and to the *Nakib ol-Eshraf*, head of the *Seids*, who ranked second in the Moslem Institution, and at the ceremonies of Bairam had precedence even of the *Mufti*. The *Nakib ol-Eshraf* was appointed by the sultan for life; that

[1] Hammer, *Geschichte*, ii. 236: "The priesthood proper . . . is perhaps in no other state of less influence, but the teaching body is in no other kingdom (except China) of greater weight and political importance."
[2] Ricaut, 211.

member of the *Ulema* who was a *Seid* and who ranked highest when the place fell vacant was ordinarily chosen. He had a staff of officers and clerks in the capital and the provinces, and was head of the separate jurisdiction of the *Seids*. Under the sultan he held despotic authority over all *Seids;* and, when the sovereign ordered the punishment or death of one of them, the *Nakib ol-Eshraf* was commissioned to carry out the execution.

Dervishes also were not members of the *Ulema*. They were of many orders, though sixteenth-century observers seem to have been impressed with but four.[1] They represented in Islam the monks, the hermits, and the begging friars of Christianity. Through them heresies spread, uprisings were concocted, mobs were gathered, and holy war was preached. On more than one occasion they endangered the power of the government.[2] Many were honest, God-fearing folk, while others were scarcely more than tramps and wandering thieves.

Clergy, *Seids*, and dervishes represented the merely religious side of the Moslem Institution. Islam was fundamentally a religion without priests, monks, or nobles; and these persons never grew to possess permanent influence and power in the Ottoman state.[3]

JURISTS AND THE MUFTI

A number of the *Ulema* who had finished the law course, and who at some previous time had chosen to become counsellors and jurists rather than to take up the severer and more active judicial career, constituted a distinct body, the *muftis*, who were held in high esteem. One of these was assigned as associate to the judge of every important city, to the number of about two hundred in all, while others were counsellors for the *Beyler-beys* and *Sanjak Beys*. Appointed for life, they lived in retirement, having no initiative of action. When the judge, *Bey*, or any private citizen, confronted by a case or other matter

[1] Spandugino, 219; Menavino, 72 ff.; Nicolay, 121. Ricaut, 261 ff., knew eight or ten orders, which he describes at some length.
[2] Hammer, *Geschichte*, i. 154, ii. 357, iii. 67; Postel, i. 112.
[3] Heidborn, 269–274.

which involved a learned knowledge of the Sacred Law, submitted to one of them a question in writing, usually in the form of a hypothetical case, it was the duty of the *mufti*, after careful consideration of the question in the light of the law books of the school of Abu Hanifa, to give an answer that applied the Sacred Law to the matter concerned. These answers, which were called *fetvas*, were usually extremely concise and unaccompanied by reasoning; they were prepared and sealed in solemn form.[1] When a judge or a *Bey* proposed to his *mufti* a question touching a pending law case, the *mufti's* response ordinarily settled the case. Private citizens who obtained *fetvas* ordinarily did so to help their causes in pending law suits; here again a pertinent question and answer would usually settle the case. Since there was no class of professional lawyers, the *muftis* were a necessary and very useful body.

In ordinary cities the *mufti* ranked after the judge. This was not the case in Constantinople, where the sultan and his officers of government frequently had questions to present which touched matters of the highest public importance. As a consequence the *mufti* of Constantinople became *par excellence* the *Mufti*. Mohammed II assigned to him also the title of *Sheik ul-Islam*, the Ancient of Islam, which in later times was to become his ordinary title. The *Mufti* was not regularly chosen from among his fellows, but was usually advanced by the sultan from the active judicial service.[2] He had the right to appoint and promote all the other *muftis* of the empire. A special bureau called the *Fetva-khaneh* was created by Suleiman to assist the *Mufti* in preparing decisions.

The *Mufti* was definitely constituted by Suleiman the head of the *Ulema;*[3] and as such he outranked all officials of govern-

---

[1] Ricaut, 201.

[2] In Ricaut's time (p. 204) one of the *Kaziaskers* was regularly chosen for this position.

[3] D'Ohsson, iv. 500. Heidborn, 215, says that the title *Sheik ul-Islam* was first bestowed by Murad II upon the *mufti* of Adrianople, who was removed to Constantinople by Mohammed II after the capture; that Mohammed assigned the title *Reis ul-ulema*, or chief of the *Ulema*, to this officer, but that he reached great dignity only under Suleiman.

ment, except that he yielded place to the grand vizier on ordinary occasions. He was almost the equal of the sultan himself, since he was the expounder and representative of the Sacred Law, which was above the sultan. Bayezid II was accustomed to stand to receive the *Mufti*, and to give him a seat above his own.[1] Early in Suleiman's reign it was said, " The Turk shows his [*Mufti*] the greatest reverence of any man in his realm, because he represents justice and the image of God."[2] Sixteenth-century Westerners compared the *Mufti* with a " very great cardinal,"[3] but more often with the pope.[4] The *Mufti* had, however, no temporal authority and no active part in affairs; like his brethren in lesser cities, he could give responses only when his opinion was asked. He could, however, rightly be compared with the pope in dignity and in the magnitude of the matters with which he dealt. His alone was the right to proclaim that war should be begun, and to send out preachers to declare that the war was holy and incumbent on all Moslems. He was frequently consulted by the sultan as to the conformity of proposed *Kanuns* with the Sacred Law.[5] In his hands rested the extreme responsibility of pronouncing that a sultan had transgressed the Sacred Law and ought to be deposed. In short, though he could claim no divinely delegated power to create new rules of faith or law, he was the final earthly authority in the interpretation of the Sacred Law as completed by Mohammed the Prophet. He exercised a function similar to what in the United States of America is the highest office of the Supreme Court, — the power of defending the Constitution. In this capacity the *Mufti* often withstood the sultan. *Urf* was subordinate to *Sheri*, and in case of conflict the former must yield; therefore the sultan, who embodied the former, could not override the *Mufti*, who represented the latter. A century after the time of Suleiman it was said: —

[1] Spandugino, 113.
[2] Postel, i. 118.
[3] Spandugino, 112.
[4] La Broquière, 181; Ramberti, below, p. 247; Geuffroy, 241; Trevisano, 122; Busbecq, *Life and Letters*, i. 116; Bernardo, 364.
[5] Heidborn, 216.

" The *Mufti* is the principal head of the *Mahometan* Religion or Oracle of all doubtful questions in the Law, and is a person of great esteem and reverence amongst the *Turks;* his Election is solely in the Grand Signior, who chuses a man to that Office always famous for his Learning in the Law, and eminent for his vertues and strictness of Life: his Authority is so great amongst them, that when he passes Judgment or Determination in any point, the Grand Signior himself will in no wise contradict or oppose it. . . .

" In matters of State the *Sultan* demands his opinion, whether it be in Condemnation of any great man to Death, or in making War or Peace, or other important Affairs of the Empire; either to appear the more just and religious, or to incline the People more willingly to Obedience. And this practice is used in business of greatest moment; scarce a Visier is proscribed, or a *Pashaw* for pretence of crime displaced, or any matter of great alteration or change designed, but the Grand Signior arms himself with the *Mufti's* Sentence; for the nature of man reposes more security in innocence and actions of Justice, than in the absolute and uncontroulable power of the Sword. And the Grand Signior, tho he himself is above the Law, and is the Oracle and Fountain of Justice, yet it is seldom that he proceeds so irregularly to contemn that Authority wherein their Religion hath placed an ultimate power of Decision in all their Controversies." [1]

The power of the *Mufti* in the sixteenth century may be illustrated by one or two instances. In the early years of the century, shortly before the appearance of the Reformation movement in Western Europe, the Ottoman Empire was threatened by the presence of large numbers of heretics in Asia Minor, simultaneously with the rise of a strong Mohammedan heretical power in Persia. Selim the Grim disposed of the heretics in his dominions by wholesale execution,[2] and punished, though he failed to crush, the Persians by the defeat of Khaldiran and the annexation of a large part of their territory. After he had got rid of Mohammedan heresy in his dominions, he was impressed

---

[1] Ricaut, 200–202.　　　　[2] Hammer, *Geschichte*, ii. 401.

with the absence of unity occasioned by the presence of the Christian subjects.[1] Accordingly he decided to order all these Christians to accept Islam on pain of death. To say that he desired to execute the Christians of his dominions would be to put the emphasis in the wrong place. He seems rather to have had in mind such a process as was carried through in Spain in the course of the sixteenth century, as a result of which none were left in that land who professed another than the dominant religion.

But here the *Mufti* Jemali intervened decisively. He had readily given a *fetva* authorizing the extermination of the heretics as in accordance with the Sacred Law, and he was later to sanction the Persian and the Egyptian wars. In this case, Selim, it is said, deceived him by a hypothetical question into giving a response which might be interpreted to authorize the forcible conversion of the Christians. After the order was issued, however, Jemali, awakened to the situation, put the Greek Patriarch in possession of a sufficient defence by showing him that the Sacred Law provided that Christians who had accepted Mohammedan rule and agreed to pay *kharâj* and *jizyeh* (land tribute and poll-tax) were, aside from certain regulations, to be left unmolested in the exercise of their religion. This provision the Patriarch, as instructed by the *Mufti*, claimed to be an irrevocable and eternal compact; therefore, he urged, since Selim's intention was contrary to it, his purpose was unlawful and must be abandoned. The argument prevailed, and the Christians were not disturbed as to their faith.

It may be remarked that Selim's idea was an excellent one from the point of view of statesmanship, and would, in the end, have resulted in a great advantage to the Moslem Institution. As pointed out in the first chapter, the Christian churches in the Ottoman Empire constituted a group of organizations that were parallel and rival to the Moslem Institution; hence their removal would have left it a free field. Whether its unopposed action would, in the long run, have been an advantage to the empire and to the world is a matter for speculation which would be out

[1] *Ibid.* 536 ff.; Heidborn, 215, note 16.

of place here; but as a state the Ottoman Empire would have been notably unified by the clearing away of these institutions. They were old, strong, and of a tenacious vitality; in them centered the hopes and aspirations of the subject Christians; while they persisted, complete amalgamation of the population was impossible; they were to keep alive a sentiment of nationality and separatism that three centuries later was to break off great sections from the empire. It seems clear, then, that, had Selim been able to carry out his purpose, the history of the Levant since his time would have been very different from what it has been. But the *Mufti*, as guardian of the Sacred Law, was right. The position of the Christian subjects rested on a firm constitutional foundation.[1] The Prophet Mohammed himself, nine centuries before Selim, had made the religious and social unity of the Ottoman Empire forever impossible. He had also made political unity impossible at that time; for in the sixteenth century political, apart from religious, unity was not understood in either the East or the West. Only in the twentieth century was Turkey to arrive at a new hope of political unity through an attempt to remove religious differences from a position of great influence upon the state.

Another instance of the *Mufti's* power occurred in the reign of Suleiman, who, as a willing servant of the Sacred Law, freely recognized the greatness of the *Mufti's* position. The *Mufti* Ebu su'ud was one of the most distinguished ornaments of the Legislator's reign. He had passed through all the stages of advancement among the *Ulema*, and had been *Kaziasker* eight years when he was constituted *Mufti*. He wrote a great commentary on the Koran, and it was he who collected the best-known *Kanun-nameh* of Suleiman.[2] This man was closely connected with one of those sorrowful events which made the

[1] D'Ohsson, v. 104 ff.
[2] See Hammer, *Geschichte*, iii. 278 ff.; and Appendix III below. Heidborn, 215, contributes further details as to the great *Mufti's* advance in the *cursus honorum* of the Moslem Institution. He shows that he began his legal studies at 27 years of age, continued them until his 45th year, was made *Kazi* of Brusa, then of Constantinople, and in his 50th year (944 A.H.) *Mufti*. The last statement seems to be erroneous; for Hammer (as above) says that he became

reign of Suleiman, great as it was in victory, splendor, and learning, equally great in tragic ruin of hope. Suleiman must have passed through many hours of torturing indecision before he determined upon the execution of his eldest son, Mustapha; and in so great a matter he needed to consult the guardian of the Sacred Law. The story of the part which the *Mufti* played shall be told by Busbecq, who appears for the last time in the pages of this treatise: —

" Solyman had brought with him [to Amasia, where he joined the army] his son's death doom, which he had prepared before leaving home. With a view to satisfying religious scruples, he had previously consulted his mufti. This is the name given to the chief priest among the Turks, and answers to our Pope of Rome. In order to get an impartial answer from the mufti, he put the case before him as follows: — He told him that there was at Constantinople a merchant of good position, who, when about to leave home for some time, placed over his property and household a slave to whom he had shown the greatest favour, and entrusted his wife and children to his loyalty. No sooner was the master gone than this slave began to embezzle his master's property, and plot against the lives of his wife and children; nay, more, had attempted to compass his master's destruction. The question which he (Solyman) wished the mufti to answer was this: What sentence could be lawfully pronounced against this slave ? The mufti answered that in his judgment he deserved to be tortured to death. Now, whether this was the mufti's own opinion, or whether it was pronounced at the instigation of Roostem or Roxolana, there is no doubt that it greatly influenced Solyman, who was already minded to order the execution of his son; for he considered that the latter's offence against himself was quite as great as that of the slave against his master, in the case he had put before the mufti." [1]

The *Mufti's* power in reality went beyond the field of interpretation and entered upon that of legislation. It is well known

Mufti in 952 (1545 A. D.), after eight years' service as *Kaziasker*. Probably, then, he was made *Kaziasker* in 944 and *Mufti* in 952. After thirty years in that eminent position, he died in 982 (1574).

[1] Busbecq, *Life and Letters*, i. 116–117.

how much the Supreme Court of the United States of America has extended the powers of the federal government by the interpretation of the Constitution. The *Mufti* acted similarly, though with less freedom, in interpreting the Sacred Law. His power in this direction was recognized by some Ottoman Mohammedans: " The *Mufti* hath a spacious Field for his Interpretation; for it is agreed that their Law is temporary, and admits of Expositions according to times and state of things. And though they Preach to the People the perfection of their *Alchoran;* yet the wiser men hold, that the *Mufti* hath an expository power of the Law to improve and better it, according to the state of things, times and conveniencies of the Empire; for that their Law was never designed to be a clog or confinement to the propagation of Faith, but an advancement thereof, and therefore to be interpreted in the largest and farthest fetched sense, when the strict words will not reach the design intended." [1]

The *fetvas* of the *muftis* amounted in practice to a body of legislation which was intermediate between the *Sheri* and the *Kanuns:* they partook of the sacred character of the former, as being based directly upon it; they were, like the latter, of a modern and practical nature derived from recent application to actual cases. In the *fetvas*, however, nothing radical or startling could ever be attempted; novel features were obliged to be of a most inconspicuous character. The *fetvas* as a whole caused some development in the Sacred Law, but their combined additions were altogether too slight to keep it abreast of the march of events.

In reality, the *muftis* occupied the most influential position in the Moslem Institution and perhaps in the Ottoman state. Usually inferior to judges and officers of government in income and display, and giving no direct impulse to affairs, they nevertheless wielded the greatest continuous power in the state, — the quiet, steady, almost changeless, almost irresistible, force of Mohammedanism. They were " guardians of the laws " in as full a sense as any Greek could wish. Their authority rested,

[1] Ricaut, 202.

first, on the acceptance by the entire Moslem population of the absolute supremacy of the Sacred Law, and, second, on the recognition by the same population that they, who had acquired learning in the Law by long years of arduous mental labor, and who had chosen to continue in its study rather than take up its more active and lucrative application in service on the bench, were the persons through whom its supremacy on earth was rightly to be maintained. Thus by popular consent the *muftis* constituted the conservative, regulative force in the Ottoman state. They were destined to contribute very largely to the empire's durability, which, despite frightful shocks, disasters, and losses, was to continue far beyond the expectation of the world.

The *muftis* did their work only too well. The idea of the changelessness of the Sacred Law was essentially hostile to progress. Although considerable flexibility was possible under its provisions, the flexibility lay in its application to particular cases, and hardly at all in the law itself. When the Ottoman power began to rise, scholasticism was at its height, both in Christianity and in Mohammedanism. From this blighting theological and philosophical bondage, which tended to extend its deadening sway over all the activities of the human spirit, Christendom was delivered by the Renaissance and the Reformation. The Ottoman mind, on the contrary, continued to be held under it till the most recent years. That it remained so long in bondage, with scarcely a struggle to escape, was due very largely to the authority of the *Ulema*. They who accomplished much toward building the Ottoman state into a solid structure, and toward maintaining it against foes without and within, also held it nearly stationary while the rest of the world moved on.

THE JUDICIAL SYSTEM [1]

The judges who belonged to the corps of the *Ulema* had jurisdictions that were based upon territory, and that covered

---

[1] This description, based on D'Ohsson's account, may represent at some points a development later than the time of Suleiman. No sixteenth-century writer seems to have gone into the organization of the system in detail. Heidborn, 220 ff., treats with fulness the past and present judicial system of the Ottoman Empire.

the whole empire to an even wider extent than did the administration of the government. The Crimea and North Africa,
though under vassal governments, formed part of the Ottoman
judicial system.[1] The tribunals of the judges seem to have been
competent for all kinds of cases, whether civil or criminal, and
whether covered by the *Sheri*, the *Kanuns*, *Adet*, or none of these.[2]
But, as has been seen, they were not competent to try all persons.
The *kullar*, the *Seids*, and the members of the foreign colonies
had their separate systems of justice; even the subject Christians,
in matters between themselves, had their own ecclesiastical
tribunals to which they regularly resorted. Cases concerning
the administration of certain groups of *vakf* lands were tried in
special courts, which were, however, presided over by members
of the regular judicial body. The fief-holders had seigniorial
jurisdiction in certain matters; and the officers of local government seem also to have had independent right to decide cases
outside the sphere of the Sacred Law, whether covered by *Kanun*,
Adet, or unprovided for.[3] The judges of the Moslem Institution,
therefore, tried all cases involving the Sacred Law which arose
within the empire, and which were between Moslem and Moslem
or between Moslem and Christian (except when the Moslem was
a *kul* of the sultan or a *Seid*), as well as a large proportion of the
cases which were outside the sphere of the Sacred Law.

Nearly all judges were judges of cities, having jurisdiction
also over the surrounding territory; [4] exceptions were the *Mufet-*

---

[1] Hammer, *Staatsverwaltung*, 380.   [2] Postel, i. 117.

[3] The *Subashis* in particular were closely connected with the administration of
justice. Postel, i. 120, says loosely that *Pasha*, *Kazi*, and *Subashi* all mean
the same thing. Chesneau, 47, says that the sultan had two judges in every
city, a *Kazi* for civil cases and a *Subashi* for criminal cases. This is certainly
incorrect, for the Sacred Law provided for many criminal cases, while *Kanuns*
dealt with many civil cases. The *Sanjak Beys* and *Beylerbeys* held Divans, or
councils, resembling on a lesser scale the sultan's Divan (Heidborn, 143, note 17);
following the analogy of the *Kaziaskers*, the *Kazi* of the city in which each such
officer resided would sit in his Divan and decide the cases that came up touching
the Sacred Law, and would also hold independent court at other times. In cities
of lesser importance, the *Kazis* appear to have been the heads of the restricted
municipal governments (*ibid.*, note 16).

[4] A scheme of the higher offices in the judicial system in the early nineteenth
century is given in Hammer's *Geschichte*, ix. 1–10.

tishes of the *vakf* lands, the judge who accompanied the *Kapudan Pasha* on his annual cruise to the Aegean Islands, the two *Kaziaskers*, and the grand vizier. The judges were all carefully graded in five principal classes, three of which were each again subdivided into several groups. By another grouping, on a geographical basis, they were in two divisions under the *Kaziaskers* of Europe and Asia. The five classes were the greater *Mollas*, the lesser *Mollas*, the *Mufettishes*, the *Kazis*, and the *Naibs*. The general name for judge was *Kazi*, and the popular title of respect for them all was *Molla;* [1] but the official titles were as described above. In general, a *Danishmend* who aspired to the judicial career chose while in the law course, according to his ambition or ability, which of the five classes he would strive to enter and after entering one of them he could not pass to another. Each had its ladder of promotion.

The greater *Mollas* were in six groups: the *Kaziasker* of Rumelia; the *Kaziasker* of Anatolia; the judge of Constantinople; the judges of Mecca and Medina; the judges of Adrianople, Brusa, Cairo, and Damascus; and the judges of the three suburbs of Constantinople, — Galata, Scutari, and Eyub, — and of Jerusalem, Smyrna, Aleppo, Larissa, and Salonica. These seventeen were in later times nominated by the *Mufti* for approval by the grand vizier and confirmation by the sultan; in Suleiman's time the members of the last four groups were nominated by the *Kaziaskers* subject to the approval of the pashas.[2] Their positions were originally held for life, or until promotion, or during good behavior; and they rose by promotion from group to group. Each had a number of assistants, clerks, book-keepers, treasurers, and the like. They seem to have had superior jurisdiction over the inhabitants, and control of the lesser judges, in

---

[1] *Kazi* is the Turkish pronunciation of the Arabic word *kadi*, judge; *Molla* is the Turkish form of the Arabic word *maulā*, lord.

[2] Junis Bey (below, p. 265) and Postel, i. 119, state that the *Kaziaskers* nominated all *Kazis*. Junis Bey says: " Two *Cadilescher* talismans, one of Greece and the other of Natolia or Asia, and they each have revenues of 6 or 7 thousand ducats a year: who are executors of their law. . . . it is they who appoint the Kadis or podestas of all the lands of the Seigneur." Ramberti (below, p. 247) and Nicolay, 119, say that the consent of the pashas was necessary also.

the entire dominion of the officer of local government — *Beylerbey* or *Sanjak Bey* — who resided in their city.[1]   The *Kaziaskers* had each a large corps of subordinate officials.   They controlled the appointment of the judges of all other classes, subject to the confirmation of the sultan.   The five *Ulema* who held high office near the person of the sultan — his *Hoja* or teacher, the head physician, the head astrologer, and the two imperial *Imâms* — were reckoned as adjunct members among the *Mollas* of the first class. They had no small influence on the destiny of the empire, as being the most disinterested and trusted persons who had the ear of the monarch.

The lesser *Mollas* were the judges of the ten cities of second rank, — Marash, Bagdad, Bosna-serai, Sofia, Belgrade, Aintab, Kutaia, Konia, Philippopolis, and Diarbekr.

The *Mufettishes* were five in number, three representing the *vakfs* in Constantinople that were under the *Mufti*, the grand vizier, and the *Kizlar Agha*, and two representing all three of these exalted officials in Adrianople and Brusa.   Cases concerning *vakfs* that might arise elsewhere were taken before the nearest *Kazi*.

The *Kazis* proper included the vast majority of the judges, to the number, in D'Ohsson's time, of about four hundred and fifty, who were stationed in smaller cities.   About two hundred in Europe, in nine groups, and those in the Crimea and North Africa, were under the authority of the *Kaziasker* of Rumelia. About two hundred and twenty-five in Asia, in ten groups, and thirty-six in Egypt, in six groups, were under the control of the *Kaziasker* of Anatolia.[2]

The *Naibs* were in several groups, as judges of villages, lesser judges of cities, temporary substitutes for higher judges, and the like.   They ordinarily had no salaries, but lived upon fees and

[1] Ricaut, 205.
[2] Hammer (as above, p. 216, note 4) gives a list of 39 judges of rank above the *Kazis* proper, and 243 *Kazis* of Rumelia, 280 of Anatolia, and 34 of Egypt.   The total is thus 557 *Kazis* proper, and 596 judges in all.   In the subsequent list of 247 positions in Rumelia as rearranged under Mahmud II, five places in the Crimea are mentioned as seats of *Kazis in partibus*, but neither list appears to mention any in North Africa.

irregular earnings. A group of these were important in the sixteenth century as a kind of inspectors of public morals. They purchased their places, and lived upon fines — and sometimes, it is said, upon extortions — from persons who did not wish their private lives exposed.[1]

Exercising many of the functions of police and market judges, but not belonging to the *Ulema*, were the *Muhtesibs*, or lieutenants of police, of the various cities. Accompanied by soldiers and attendants, they patrolled the streets and inspected the markets, giving special heed to weights and measures. If they found that the law had been infringed, they inflicted punishment, whether financial or corporal, on the spot.[2] By reason of the duty of applying sumptuary regulations, the office was often lucrative.[3]

In every court a single judge sat, with his clerks and other subordinates. Cases were presented by the parties concerned, and decisions were usually rendered immediately and in very concise form. The judge coöperated with the *Subashi* of the city, who brought before the judge persons that were summoned and who executed the sentences of the judges,[4] an arrangement in which lay a certain likeness to the ecclesiastical courts of the West, which might condemn, but left the execution to the secular arm. Appeal went up to judges higher in the scale, and finally to the grand vizier.[5] Costs and fines were moderate, and were fixed by *Kanun;*[6] they constituted, however, a large part of the income of the judges and their subordinates. The judges were salaried, and some of them had in addition large amounts of irregular earnings. The judges attended to all the notarial work of the empire.

The *Subashis, Sanjak Beys,* and *Beylerbeys* had complete jurisdiction over all members of the Ruling Institution who

---

[1] Spandugino, 188; Postel, i. 127.
[2] Spandugino, 213; D'Ohsson, vi. 333.
[3] Postel, i. 126. This officer is called by Postel *Mortasi.*
[4] Menavino, 66; Spandugino, 211.
[5] Postel, i. 120, 124; Nicolay, 119. There was no regular organization of the procedure of appeal; nevertheless it was allowed (Heidborn, 389).
[6] Hammer, *Staatsverfassung*, 100. See above, p. 203, note 1.

resided in their districts, as well as a more or less undefined authority in cases controlled by *Kanun, Adet,* or otherwise outside the sphere of the Sacred Law.[1] In capital cases they never proceeded to execution without obtaining the approval of the judge of the city, in order to have the sanction of the Sacred Law.[2] The decisions of the judges in criminal cases were regularly submitted to without a murmur, since it was felt that the judges represented Mohammed, " wore the robe of God," and had power of " sovereign sentence." [3]

The highest courts were those of the *Kaziaskers,* the grand vizier, and the Divan. The *Kaziaskers,* besides attending to the cases that were brought before them in the Divan and at the palace gate after its close, held court at all other times in their own houses.[4] Mohammed II had provided that, when cases were brought primarily to them in the city of Constantinople, those which concerned Moslems should come before the *Kaziasker* of Rumelia and those which concerned non-Moslems before the *Kaziasker* of Anatolia. The titles of these judges show their original functions as judges of the armies of Rumelia and Anatolia, offices which they continued to exercise in time of war. In this capacity, also, appeals came up to them in time of peace from the *Subashis* and *Sanjak Beys* in matters touching *kullar.* The power of the *Kaziaskers* had been extended to include the headship of all the judges of their respective regions, and the appointment of all judges, subject to the approval of the pashas. In the Divan, and as " Pillars of the State," they ranked next to the viziers; they had the first right of audience with the sultan at the close of each Divan; and until the reign of Suleiman they had had all the authority over the *Ulema* that later came to the *Mufti.* They had immense incomes and were highly honored and esteemed.

---

[1] See above, p. 116.
[2] Spandugino, 211.
[3] *Ibid.*
[4] The Arabic words *kadi al asker* signify judge of the army. In the sixteenth century the pronunciation seems to have been *kadi l'esker;* nowadays it is *kazi asker.* The burdensome duty of holding court continually is mentioned in Spandugino, 96; D'Ohsson, iv. 581.

The grand vizier was actual head of the Moslem Institution as substitute for the sultan; accordingly his court was the highest court of appeal for all ordinary civil cases. It was also, however, like all other courts in the empire, a court of first instance. He decided great numbers of cases, large and small, for rich and poor alike. Justice was refused to no one; it was rendered either by the grand vizier's own decision, or by reference for prompt settlement to one of the *Kaziaskers* or to some other judge.[1]

The Divan's principal deliberative business as a court was the trial of capital cases of great officials. Although many such persons were executed, it is strenuously denied that Suleiman ever ordered death without a trial.[2] Nevertheless, the process was usually held in the absence of the accused person and without his knowledge; he might be at the end of the empire. In case of conviction a *Chaush* was sent to the condemned man's place of residence, bearing secretly a written commission, which was given to the nearest official who had power to execute. The condemned man had at best a few hours in which to settle his affairs and make his peace with God; then he was executed, and his head was given to the *Chaush* to be taken to the sultan as proof that the mission had been faithfully accomplished. It is said that forty or fifty heads sometimes reached the court of Suleiman in a single day.[3]

Early in his reign, when filled with pride by his victory over the rebel Ghazali, and feeling warm friendship toward Doge Loredano of Venice, he wished to send the rebel's head to the Doge by a special embassy, and was dissuaded only with great difficulty by the Bailo of Venice in Constantinople.[4] After Mohacs two thousand heads were set on poles about his tent.[5] To Western eyes it seems a blot upon the noble and generous character of Suleiman, that he treated the heads of his enemies and of condemned criminals after the fashion of his time and

---

[1] Postel, i. 123. Heidborn, 141–143, note 15, quotes from Ypsilanti an interesting description of a session of the grand vizier's court.

[2] Postel, i. 127, iii. 8.   [4] Hammer, *Geschichte*, iii. 11.

[3] *Ibid.* iii. 9.   [5] *Ibid.* 61.

country. Aside from the question of barbarity and cruelty, however, the policy of summary and certain execution of offenders was essential to the maintenance of the Ottoman Ruling Institution in power. It was a process of pruning, by which every dangerous growth was cut away. Had it not been done, the system would have seemed today more commendable, but it could hardly have failed to perish quickly. A century after Suleiman the remark was made that what preserved the Ottoman state was the quickness and severity of justice for crimes which had relation to the government.[1]

What was the general character of Ottoman justice? It is to be feared that it was often venal. A few years after Suleiman's death a Western writer expressed the opinion that the only incorruptible courts were those of the grand vizier and the Divan.[2] Another charged that Christian subjects had unfair treatment before the courts, in which they were not allowed to testify, since some of the Moslems considered it almost a meritorious religious act to turn a case against a Christian by false testimony.[3] It is probable, however, that the Ottoman courts in Suleiman's time were reasonably just. The judges were well-paid, highly honored, and carefully inspected by honest men who were sent out annually by the *Kaziaskers;*[4] nevertheless, many of them no doubt yielded to the same desire for money that afflicted the *kullar*. In at least one respect the Ottoman courts were highly to be commended: there was a minimum of trouble because of the " law's delay." Cases were always decided promptly, and in clear and simple terms. An unjust decision quickly given is often less expensive and less annoying in the long run than tardy justice.[5]

Some Western observers were as strongly impressed with the superiority of Ottoman justice over that in their own lands as they were with the superiority of discipline in the Ottoman

[1] Ricaut, 3.
[2] Garzoni, 430. See also Morosini, 273.
[3] Postel, i. 124. Matters were distinctly worse in Ricaut's time (pp. 140-141).
[4] Spandugino, 114.
[5] It has been suggested (Morosini, 273) that the promptness of justice had a connection with the early military character of the Moslems.

camp, or of promotion by merit in the Ottoman government service.[1] One of them said: " To understand at length their diligence in justice, it would be necessary to write more than I have done; and further, since there is nothing here [that is, in France] so near immortality as the processes and extortions which men do, it gives me shame to recite so great diligence among people proclaimed wicked; this it is, without any doubt, which makes them so to rule, conquer, and keep. . . . Of Sultan Suleiman, who rules at present, I do not wish to speak, for his deeds are not yet accomplished, and he cannot yet be praised, except for his humanity, justice, and fidelity." [2]

The law which the judges administered was primarily the Sacred Law, as given in the Koran and the traditions of Mohammed, but especially as codified by the great doctors of the school of Abu Hanifa, and as interpreted in collections of the *fetvas* of great jurists. Next the judges applied the *Kanuns* of the sultans, and the customs and immunities of the regions in which they served.[3] Finally, they had a considerable field in which to make use of equity: " The good sense and prudence of judges trained in reasoning," says Postel, " supplies and decides many things that are not written." [4] The only resemblance to the Anglo-Saxon system of case law seems to have been the use of the *fetvas* of the *muftis*. Since the hearing of ordinary cases was summary and decisions were rendered very briefly, no extended reports were possible. The absence of printing, which was not introduced into Turkey until the eighteenth century, aided further toward making a general use of the decisions of judges as precedents practically impossible. In those days judges relied upon their own knowledge of law and custom, on the few books they might possess, on their sense of equity, and, in matters of difficulty, on the opinions of the local *muftis*. Since the judges were not each surrounded by a group of trained and keenly watchful lawyers, but acted alone except for their own subordinates, there was more opportunity for unjust decisions by a dishonest judge than among English-speaking peoples. Or, to

[1] Spandugino, 211, 255.
[2] Postel, i. 127, iii. 87.
[3] *Ibid.* i. 117.
[4] *Ibid.*

state the matter differently, Ottoman justice depended more upon the integrity of judges than does Anglo-Saxon justice. Although the Sacred Law was rigid, its application to the individual case was adjustable, and adjustment was ordinarily accomplished by the decision of one man. Judges therefore possessed great power over the fortunes of individuals, a fact which in part explains the great deference and honor that was shown them.

THE MOSLEM INSTITUTION AS A WHOLE

A few words of summary will sketch the outlines of the complete Moslem Institution in the Ottoman Empire. It represented and maintained the entire system that was based upon the life and work of the Prophet Mohammed. This system claimed to be sufficient for all sides of the temporal, as well as for the eternal, life of all individuals, and for the life of the state which they constituted; it also provided a place for subject peoples and resident foreigners of other religious affiliations. The power of the institution extended over the whole empire, even beyond the limits of political control.

The Moslem Institution was firmly grounded in the allegiance, the fundamental beliefs, and the affections of the entire Moslem-born population of the empire. It is true that not all Moslems believed exactly alike, nor did they all practise the Sacred Law according to the system of Abu Hanifa. But they were all fiercely and proudly Moslems, and devoted to the supremacy of the Mohammedan system in this world, as expressed in an institution which might not be what every one wished, but which revealed and maintained the power of Islam. All the Moslems of the empire were in a sense members of the institution. In the sixteenth century any one of them might hope to see his son mount to a very high place within the organization, since industrious study combined with native ability was all that was demanded. Opportunities in the way of schools were present nearly everywhere; and a student who once had shown his aptitude would be carried forward, without expense to his relatives, by funds which had been provided by sultans and pious individuals " for the good of their souls." The Moslem Institution was fundamentally democratic. It was united in complete solidarity and perfect harmony with all in the empire who were attached to the doctrines of the Prophet. All believers were equal before God, and all were supposed to have equal opportunity to rise to places of honor in the system.

Distinction and membership in the institution proper rested upon birth in the case of the descendants of Mohammed, upon profession of piety and special religious service in the case of the dervishes, but upon learned knowledge of the Sacred Law in all positions of public influence and importance. The three highly-honored classes of teachers, jurists, and judges were trained in the same superbly-planned educational system, in the same text-books and the same ideas. Whether in Constantinople or Cairo, the Crimea or Algiers, Budapest or Bagdad, old, grave, wise, and learned professors, jurists, and judges taught, interpreted, and enforced the same wide-reaching and changeless Sacred Law. As teachers, the *Ulema* conveyed to children and youth, in impressible years, that which they had themselves received. The same learned persons, after fixing each part of the whole round of legal studies in their minds by periods of teaching, were advanced to places where they dealt not with boys, but with men, where their work affected not the fortunes of individuals, but the destinies of the empire. Yet their influence was exerted strenuously in the same direction throughout, to impress and perpetuate the changeless body of ideas in the Sacred Law. Professors, jurists, and judges alike were, in all that they did and throughout their lives, fundamentally teachers. The *Ulema* taught all the Moslems of the empire, from the young child to the aged sultan. They maintained schools for the young; places of worship, courts, and offices of consultation for adults. Every important officer of administrative government had a judge and a *mufti* at his elbow. Not only was the sultan himself in close relations with the *Kaziaskers* and the *Mufti*, but he had always a spiritual adviser to whom he showed great deference, and who bore the significant title of the sultan's *Hoja*, or teacher. There was an aspect in which the Moslem Institution, based upon the Moslem population of the empire, fitted the government as hand fits glove.   This figure, moreover, can be pressed beyond the mere comparison of shape; the hand is of much the same efficiency with or without the glove, while the glove is useless without the hand; furthermore, the hand may live to wear a succession of gloves.

CHAPTER VIII

COMPARISON OF THE TWO GREAT INSTITUTIONS

The Ottoman Ruling Institution, and the Moslem Institution of the Ottoman Empire might be compared, contrasted, and reflected upon at great length. In this discussion, however, it must suffice to select and comment upon a few of their salient likenesses, differences, and interactions, without attempting to separate such features sharply.

Likenesses

Both institutions were constructed out of old and well-seasoned materials. Many of the ideas in each can be followed back until their origin is lost in prehistoric obscurity; hardly a feature in either but had a clear derivation from, relationship to, or suggestion in, some prototype of pre-Ottoman days. Only the final structure of each, the proportion and composition of its parts, and the effect of the completed whole was worked out in the Ottoman Empire. If an attempt be made, in a very general way, to distinguish the main lines of influence which led up to the two institutions, it may be said that the Ruling Institution had its nucleus of ideas from the Turks of the steppe lands. Influenced by old Persian neighbors and Chinese rulers, the original group of ideas was brought into the Moslem Empire and Asia Minor by the predecessors of the Seljuk Turks and by the Seljuk Turks themselves. Coming into contact in Asia Minor with the ideas of the Byzantine Empire, and to some extent with those of the crusaders from the West, the system took on a large number of new features; and the Ottomans continued the process in Asia Minor and Southeastern Europe until the time of Suleiman. The Moslem Institution began with the ideas of the Arabs as combined by Mohammed with Jewish, Middle Persian, and Christian influences. Political notions were rapidly incorporated from those prevailing in Byzantine Syria and Egypt, and perhaps to a greater extent from those in the Sassanian Persian Empire. A compact system of ideas began early to be developed, and in the twelfth and thirteenth centuries it reached final scholastic shape. Together with its institutional embodiments, it began to pass to the Ottomans in their earliest days; and, as the nation grew, it grew into the Moslem Institution of the Ottoman Empire, fresh power being given to it by Selim's conquest of the old Moslem lands, and especially by his acquisition of the over-lordship of the Holy Cities. The two lines of tendency which led to the two great Ottoman institutions were first brought into contact when, in the seventh century, the Arab conquest of Persia advanced the Moslem frontier into Central Asia. From that time to the reign of Suleiman reciprocal influence was exerted, although the Moslem ideas affected the Turkish much more than the Turkish did the Moslem.

Both of the great Ottoman institutions were founded upon groups of ideas and not upon racial descent. This subject, discussed above in the Introduction, has been shown to be true to an extreme in the Ruling Institution, which drew its members from every direction except from the existing stock of the nation. The Moslem Institution embodied a religion of universal claim. Though originally given to the Arabs, the Moslem faith was intrinsically independent of race, as its subsequent history revealed. Belief, and not blood, became the sole test of membership. This common hospitality of its two great institutions to all who might wish to join them laid firmly the foundation of the Ottoman nation, and made possible the greatness and the permanence of its dominion.

Both Ottoman institutions were self-perpetuating through education. Each had a great educational system which was adapted to its special character, and which was life-long in extent. The Ruling Institution trained its pupils physically as well as mentally, whereas the Moslem Institution neglected physical education in favor of a greater amount of intellectual training. Otherwise their work was largely parallel. One institution took its pupils from the children of Christian subjects and neighbors, and trained them to conquer and to rule. The other took its pupils from the children of Moslems and trained them to know, practise, teach, and enforce the Moslem rules of law and life. The one system raised the ablest Christian-born individuals to the highest positions, and the other raised the ablest Moslem-born individuals similarly. Both continually brought in new material at the bottom, and continually worked upon all their material to increase its value. Each offered such rewards and promotions as to induce its members to put forth their most strenuous exertions, that they might develop their own powers and visibly help their institution. Whatever faults of plan and structure the institutions may have had, they were able to survive all dangers and disasters largely through the trained ability of the individuals whom their educational systems had brought to the front.

Both institutions rose to an apex, through the Divan and the grand vizier, in the sultan, who was the head and center of each. Yet the ideas by which the two institutions were joined to their head were in striking contrast. The sultan was master and owner of the Ruling Institution; he was the divinely-appointed chief of the Moslem Institution. The members of the former obeyed him as slaves; the members of the latter obeyed him as free Moslems commanded by the Sacred Law to render allegiance to the chief interpreter and defender of that law. The former knew no power greater than the sultan's; the latter relied upon the Sacred Law as above the sultan. The Ruling Institution was extended downward in each of its parts from the sultan's authority, and in organization and membership depended for existence upon his will. The Moslem Institution rose upward from the people, and was attached almost artificially to the sultan's authority. Suleiman regulated the grades of higher advancement in it, but the sultans who came after him touched the organization of the institution scarcely at all. Very seldom, moreover, by comparison, did the sultans punish the members of this institution; for the most part its work went on quite independently of them. But the sultan was the head of both institutions: every member of each looked upward along converging lines which met at the foot of his throne. The highest promotions in each were made by him directly, the honored men being put into positions near their sovereign.

DIFFERENCES

The fact that the Ruling Institution was recruited from Christian slaves and the Moslem Institution from Moslem freemen led to a profound difference of spirit. The Christian slaves, newly converted to Mohammedanism, were not as a body so closely attached to the Sacred Law as were the Moslem freemen. Their loyalty being rather to one man, their master and benefactor, they felt a servile devotion which was very different from the reasoned allegiance of those who had always been free. A *Mufti*, fortified by the Sacred Law, would firmly oppose the will of the sovereign in a case where a grand vizier would scarcely dare venture a mildly contrary suggestion. The Sacred Law, despite the introduction of all later influences, still breathed forth something of the freedom of the Arabian desert: in one or two generations, as has been seen, it could render its followers unfit to be slaves. Thus the spirit of the Ruling Institution was far less independent of personal authority than that of the Moslem Institution.

As to the authority of old ideas the contrary was true. The fundamental distinction of parties in modern states seems to rest upon a greater or less relative inclination to follow old paths or to enter upon new ones. Both institutions of the Ottoman state would in modern times be classed as strongly conservative, but of the two the Moslem Institution was by far the more so. Conservatism, in fact, was of the very essence of the Sacred Law. The early Turks had also loved their *Adet*, but not so much as to be unwilling quickly to adopt the new if they saw in it distinct advantage; the rise of the Ottoman power was, indeed, marked by the constant incorporation of new ideas, devices, and methods.[1] As the Moslem influence grew, however, changes became increasingly more difficult to make; and when they were made it was by the activity of the Ruling Institution, usually against the resistance or the inert passivity of the Moslem Institution.

[1] The use of cannon is perhaps the most conspicuous example.

The fact that the Ruling Institution fought and governed while the Moslem Institution thought and judged was, of course, highly significant: the former embodied the active, the latter the contemplative, principle of the nation. Here again is involved a difference of Turk and Saracen. In the steppe lands the Turk fought, obeyed, and gave orders; after the fever of conquest was abated, the Saracen, under Islam, thought, preserved intellectual independence, and worshipped. With the two characters placed side by side, it was in the nature of things that in the long run muscle would be controlled by mind.

By comparison with the Moslem Institution, the Ruling Institution possessed a great structural disadvantage, in that it was much more artificial and therefore much less stable. It admitted its members as slaves, but they were not hereditary slaves; most of them were free-born subjects of the empire or of the neighboring Christian states. A class of hereditary slaves would not have possessed the requisite mettle. Now, the acquisition of a large number of free-born children who can be made into slaves is hardly a process that can be continued indefinitely. Conquest had its limits for the Ottoman Empire, for boundaries were reached beyond which lay states whose powers of self-defense developed increasingly; accordingly, recruiting by capture became increasingly difficult. But the levying of children as tribute was strongly against human nature; and in the long run it, too, must lead to decline, for under its operation the best were taken and inferiors were left. Furthermore, not only were children separated from their parents against the wishes of the parents, but the recruits, when they grew up, were not encouraged to form family ties. Even when they did so, they were unable to advance their children as they had been advanced themselves, and they could not be sure of conveying their property to their descendants. Thus in several respects the Ruling Institution ran counter to the idea of the family. On the other hand, the advantages given to the sultan's *kullar* became too great not to be coveted; and it was not natural that the free-born Moslems should continue to let outsiders be the only recipients of so much wealth, power, and privilege. The Moslem population forced its way in, and the plan of the Ruling Institution was upset. The Moslem Institution, on the contrary, was recruited voluntarily from an increasing population; hence, as its advantages became attractive, it was benefited rather than harmed by pressure for admission. Its able men, while they must labor if they would advance, were free, unhindered in their family relationships, and under little fear of being deprived of property or life.

INTERACTIONS

The two institutions, running everywhere parallel, with their members in constant association one with the other, could not fail to act reciprocally upon each other. It is not easy, however, to discriminate likenesses that were due to mutual influence from those that were caused by common circumstances; nor is it easy to distinguish pre-Ottoman interactions from those which operated after the beginning of the fourteenth century. A few probabilities may be expressed, however.

It is a matter of frequent remark that men, institutions, and peoples are apt to impart to each other their faults and vices more readily than their good qualities. Whether or not this be true, the two Ottoman institutions certainly seem to have taught each other some evil qualities. Luxury, venality, and unnatural vices were all strongly discountenanced by the Sacred Law; but all were fostered in the members of the Ruling Institution by the very conditions of the system, and by the sixteenth century all had come to be charged against the members of the Moslem Institution as well. On the other hand, the conservatism of the Moslem Institution and its resistance to progress came more and more to characterize the Ruling Institution. Members of the *Ulema* taught even the pages of the palace and the princes on the intellectual side of their training, thereby exerting a constant influence which in the course of time operated powerfully on the Ruling Institution from top to bottom, till it, too, began to acquire a changelessness which resisted improvement and progress. With such a character once established, the end of the empire's greatness was at hand. In a rapidly progressing world, a stationary position means a relative decline.

The two institutions contributed strongly to each other's power and permanence. The Ruling Institution defended the Moslem Institution by the sword, and carried out among the people the decisions of its wise men. It also protected the latter's sources of regular revenue, and thus enabled the *Ulema*, secure of a living, to devote themselves to the study and teaching of the Sacred Law. The Moslem Institution, on the other hand, kept the Moslem population obedient and submissive to the sultan's authority as expressed in the Ruling Institution. It taught that the Sultan was divinely appointed and therefore always to be obeyed, no matter what his character was or how oppressive his rule might become, so long as he did not transgress the Sacred Law; and that it was for the *Ulema* alone to decide when he had made such a transgression. Accordingly the two institutions, so long as they acted in harmony, were absolutely impregnable in their position among the Moslems of the empire.

THE RELATIVE POWER OF THE INSTITUTIONS

These two institutions constituted, as it were, the two great parties in the Ottoman state.[1] The Moslem Institution was always strongly Islamic, and extremely conservative in all respects. The Ruling Institution was originally liberal both religiously and in its receptivity of new ideas, but it departed from its liberal tendency in much the same proportion that the Moslem Institution increased in power.

To trace the ups and downs of the influence of the two institutions from the beginnings of Ottoman history would be an interesting problem. Much depended of course, as must always be the case in a despotic state, on the character of the sultan. With an active conquering sultan like Mohammed II or Selim I, the Ruling Institution would gain upon its rival; with a pious or mild sultan like Murad II or Bayezid II, the Moslem Influence would increase in importance. Selim I's vast conquests in Moslem territories, and his acquisition of the protectorate of the Holy Cities and of the title of caliph, prepared the way for a

[1] Halil Ganem, i. 201.

later advance in the power of the Moslem Institution which was not in harmony with his own personal influence. Suleiman had a fiery active period of youth when the liberal policy was stronger in his mind, and a quieter old age when the Moslem influence became predominant; it is not unlikely that a consciousness of his position as caliph grew upon him with advancing years. But in general, through all the reigns, the power of the Moslem Institution grew; the only difference from reign to reign was in the rate of speed. The Ruling Institution also grew in power before the world and the Ottoman nation as long as the empire continued to expand rapidly; but it did not grow relatively so fast as did the Moslem Institution.

The reasons for the more rapid growth of Moslem influence lay chiefly in the fact that that influence was cumulative. As to its financial basis, the Moslem Institution, like the Christian church in the West, gained lands and wealth continually, and never lost any; for sultans took great pride, and high officials vied with each other, in founding mosques, schools, colleges, and other charitable and semi-public institutions supported by *vakfs*.[1] In general moral and political influence, also, the institution gained rapidly through its system of education; for, like the medieval Christian church again, it held in its hands all the means and methods of intellectual development. Every new primary school, college, and law school, — and they were many in the days of glory, — strengthened the influence of this institution. In this field, indeed, its power acted constantly upon its rival. Old *Hojas* taught the pages in the palace, advised the sultan's mother, and trained the young princes and the sons of high officials. Thus within the nation the external show of the Moslem Institution, and its sway over the minds of men, grew without ceasing.

---

[1] Spandugino, 207: " And the Turkish lords generally, as well great as small, study only to build churches and hospitals and to enrich and make hostelries for lodging travelers, to improve the roads, to build bridges, to construct baths, and several other charitable works which they do in such a way that I suppose the Turkish lords are beyond comparison greater alms-givers than our Christian lords; and in proportion as they have good zeal, they use great hospitality. They voluntarily lodge Christian, Turk, and Jew alike." See also Morosini, 270.

The Ruling Institution, on the other hand, lost relatively. In the early days, when recent converts were exceedingly numerous and the religious spirit of the young nation was weak, the Turkish-Aryan organization was far stronger than the Semitic influence. Sultans, however, were constantly giving away state lands as endowment for new mosques and colleges; and, worse still, so much of the educational system of this institution as was not controlled by its rival was directed only toward its own membership and not toward the nation at large. Accordingly, although the Ruling Institution grew in wealth and power, it did not keep pace with the Moslem Institution, which, after two and a half centuries of gain, was able to overtake it about the time of Suleiman's reign. His gifts of great mosques, numerous colleges, and vast endowment,[1] his arrangement in final perfection of the *cursus honorum* which led up from the primary schools to the office of *Mufti*, and the personal leaning of his later years toward the influence of the *Ulema*, settled permanently the preponderance of the Moslem Institution.

At the same time, the Moslem Institution could never destroy its rival. Theoretically it had no need of such a counterpart. Mohammed and the early caliphs had no such institution. The Sacred Law developed with no mention of a secular government, and with no hint of any deficiency in its own provisions that would make it inadequate to guide a nation by its own strength; but, within thirty years from the death of Mohammed, Muavia had set up a secular government at Damascus, and since then every Moslem state had had one. Many a Moslem state, also, had had a ruler who was not of lawful blood; for the Sacred Law affirmed that the *Imâm*, or divinely appointed ruler, must be of the tribe of the Koreish.[2] According to that unenforced provision, Suleiman himself had no right to the throne. The fact is that the Moslem Institution very early became too unworldly to live unsupported by a secular power. It was a strong but

---

[1] He built seven mosques (Hammer, *Geschichte*, iii. 456), four colleges at Mecca (*ibid.* 459), four colleges around the Suleimanieh Mosque (*ibid.* 470), and endowed them all, etc.

[2] See above, p. 150.

tender hand, which must always wear a glove. After it had acquired a permanent ascendency in the state, therefore, the Moslem Institution was compelled to keep its rival in place, and to allow it always strength enough to defend and support the empire which nourished both.

Bound together closely in an alliance which neither enjoyed, but which was necessary for the preservation of both, the Ruling Institution and the Moslem Institution constituted the twofold inner framework of the Ottoman Empire, to which it owed all its might and energy, its grandeur and repute, its continuity and durability.

APPENDICES

APPENDIX I

THE SECOND BOOK OF THE AFFAIRS OF THE TURKS

Written in 1534, supposedly by Benedetto Ramberti
Translated from the Italian

[From *Libri Tre delle Cose de Turchi*, as printed in *Viaggi* . . . *alla tana*, Venice, 1543, pp. 131–146.]

As from a laborious and very dangerous sea into a safe and very quiet port, one enters the city of Constantinople, after the great trouble and inconvenience of the ride which he has endured over the long road.[1] This city (to continue until I have here made an end of particular description) was anciently called Byzantium, and afterwards was called New Rome, and then Constantinople from the first Constantine. Byzantium, as it is reported, was in the region where Pera is now, and was so named from the river Byzantium, which afterward, by reason of an earthquake such as are frequent in that region, changed its course elsewhere. But I do not believe this, nor does it seem to me to agree with the description of Polybius and other writers, who call those here Chalcedonians; these, when they might themselves in ancient times have built upon this site, did not care for it, but built in Asia, not having discerned the convenience and beauty they were leaving to others; who might deprive them even of their own site, as indeed happened.

The city is 18 miles in circuit. It has seven little hills, not very high. It is surrounded by wretched walls, and is full of houses, not many of which are good, being made of clay and wood and only a few of stone. It is full of groves, that is, of places wild and uninhabited, where cypresses grow, and other such trees.[2] In Constantinople, then, is the palace of the Turkish Signor, which is a singular structure and very large, as will be told later.

There is the palace of the ladies of the Signor, the palace of the Janissaries, the Patriarcate, the palace of the Emperor Constantine, which is in part ruined, the church of St. Sophia, which is a structure most beautiful and divine; this was built by the Emperor Justinian from the oldest and finest columns and marbles, as one can see now;

[1] Ramberti came overland from Ragusa on his journey from Venice to Constantinople.

[2] The writer seems not to have observed that these groves were cemeteries.

239

in part of it the Turkish Signor has made stalls for his horses. There is the mosque of Sultan Mohammed, which has an *Imaret* attached to it that is like a hostel; in which they lodge any one, of any nation or law, who may wish to enter, and they give him food for three days,— honey, rice, meat, bread, and water, and a room in which to sleep. They say that from day to day there are more than a thousand guests from various nations. Near this they have baths and some fountains, most beautiful and delightful to behold. There are the mosques of Sultan Bayezid, Sultan Selim, and other Signors, which are very beautiful and exceedingly well-built. This makes it clear that, when they wish, they know also how to build houses and palaces that are magnificent and sumptuous.

There is the Hippodrome, that is, the place where in ancient times horses were made to run as in a theater and circus: in the center of this Hippodrome there stands a needle, which is a column made in the form of a needle, very beautiful and wrought very well and without mortar, made of living rocks joined together in such a manner that they rise through more than fifty cubits, tapering in the shape of a needle, which rests on four marble balls.[1] There is a column of bronze in the shape of a serpent with three heads.[2] There is a bronze Hercules brought from Hungary,[3] and in the center there is a colossal structure made of different beautiful marbles, in which is engraved the history of all the above-mentioned objects, and of other things which used to stand in the Theater and Hippodrome. There are throughout the city many vestiges of antiquities, such as aqueducts, arches, porphyry columns, fountains brought from the Danube and other near-by rivers.[4] Many gardens about the houses of the great. Many mosques of private lords, and baths which are attached to the mosques of private men and of public magistrates.

On the other side of the sea from the Seraglio Point are the hills of Asia, and the journey is of a little more or less than two miles; this Asia is to-day called by a single name Anatolia; and there are on the shore there some fortresses called Scutari. Then Kadikeui, situated

---

[1] The writer evidently did not know that this Egyptian obelisk consists of a single stone. It actually rests on four bronze cubes.

[2] This was the support of the tripod of the priestess at Delphi. The heads have been broken off, and are now in the treasury of the Old Seraglio at Constantinople.

[3] This was overthrown at the downfall of Ibrahim in 1536.

[4] This remarkable statement is probably the source of Nicolay's similar idea (p. 77). The Danube is more than two hundred miles distant from Constantinople.

on a bay of the Hellespont,[1] where one can see many vestiges of antiq- uities; and I, when I went there, saw underground where men were working, a well of the finest marble with an aqueduct which came to the center of the well, and a canopy of fine marble supported by four beautiful columns. And in other places there appear many vestiges of old churches, both of Christians and of heathen, places indeed most beautiful, most pleasant, most fruitful. The situation of Constanti- nople is such that not only can it not be described adequately, but it can hardly be grasped in thought because of its loveliness. Cer- tainly it is rather to be considered divine than otherwise. Nor is there any one who has seen it who has not judged it worthy to be ranked above all other situations in the world.

There are in the city besides the Turks, countless Jews, or Marrani expelled from Spain;[2] these are they who have taught and who are teaching every useful art to the Turks;[3] and the greater part of the shops and arts are kept and exercised by these Marrani. There is a place which is called *Bezestan,* where they sell and buy all sorts of cloth and Turkish wares, silks, stuffs, linens, silver, wrought gold, bows, slaves, and horses; and in short all the things that are to be found in Constantinople are brought there to market: this, except for Friday, is open every day.

Constantinople is in Thrace: this has as its boundaries on the east the Propontis and the mouths of the greater sea, on the west part of Bulgaria and part of Macedonia, on the north Bosnia, on the south the Aegean Sea with part of Macedonia which lies toward the river Nishava, called in ancient times the Nesus.[4]

This most noble city is inhabited by Turks: these as the more reliable authors have written, and as many of the Turks themselves have confirmed to me, had their origin in Scythia, which now is a part of Tartary, a northern region divided into two parts by the river Don: one of these parts is in Europe, and one in Asia.[5] The European part is bounded on one side by Pontus, and on the other by the Riphean Mountains, and at the back by Asia proper and the river

[1] Rather, of the Sea of Marmora.

[2] *Marrani*: Jews and Moors of Spain, baptized, but remaining true to their own religion.

[3] This statement and the following one are certainly exaggerations.

[4] Either the writer's geographical knowledge or the text is in confusion. The description here, as well as that which follows, cannot be made to fit the map.

[5] The boundary between Europe and Asia is now, of course, placed far to the east of the Don.

Taspus. In Ptolemy these two Scythias are called the one *intra Imaum montem*, and the other *extra Imaum*. They departed then from Scythia (as is said above) and began to make invasions and raids into their present confines: then proceeding farther, in a short time they became lords of a good part of Asia, but because they did not know how to keep only one chief among them, they had no foundation or firmness. This circumstance having been considered by one who was called Othman, a man of low rank among them, but of lofty and valorous mind, he thought that, by having the arm and the favor of some men of intelligence and authority, he could easily rule all this people and the conquered territory, and increase it further upon good opportunity: then having revealed this his thought to three persons, who seemed more suitable than others for this business, he promised that those by means of whom he might acquire the dominion to which he aspired, he would always maintain, both themselves and their descendants, in great state and dignity, and suitably to the great benefit which he had received from them: besides this that he would never harm their blood nor that of their posterity through laws that would lay hands upon them even if they should transgress grievously.[1] They accepted the condition and conspired together for the sovereignty; which they obtained by astuteness, artfulness, threats, and the slaughter of many. These three were called, the one Michael, a Greek who had turned Turk; from him the Marcalogli [2] are descended; one of them is now Sanjak in Bosnia. The second was Malco, a Greek renegade; from him have come the Malcozogli, and there is now only one, who is Sanjak in Greece. The third was Aurami, a native Turk; his descendants were called the Eurcasli; it is not now known that any of these remain. In case the Ottoman family should fail, these would pretend to the sovereignty, and therefore they are highly respected.

This Othman came to power about the year 1300, and lived in lordship twenty-eight years:[3] Orchan succeeded him and lived twenty-two years in the kingship. Then Murad who reigned twenty-three years. Then Bayezid. Then Chiris Celeby, or, as others wish,

[1] Compare Junis Bey, below, pp. 272, 273.

[2] Michaloghli.

[3] More accurately, Othman, beginning in 1299, ruled 27 years; Orchan, 33 years; Murad I, 30 years; Bayezid I, 13 years; Mohammed I (*Chelebi*) in undisputed rule 8 years, after 11 years of civil war; Murad II, 30 years; Mohammed II, 30 years; Bayezid II, 31 years; Selim, 8 years, until his death in 1520, when Suleiman came to the throne.

Calepino, who lived about six years. Then Mohammed, who reigned fourteen years.[1] Then Murad II who reigned 31 years. Then Mohammed II who reigned 32 years and was the first Emperor of Constantinople. Then Bayezid II who reigned 31 years. Then Selim eight years: to him succeeded Sultan Suleiman, his only son, who reigns at present. Of this succession it is written otherwise in some histories, where they treat of wars and peaces, which have been made by our republic in times past with this family: but since I have recounted these in other places, it now suffices to have noticed the common opinion of those who have written of the affairs of the Turks up to this time. And so I will go on to describe the court of this Signor: it is arranged in the following manner.[2]

SULTAN SULEIMAN has a palace in the angle of Constantinople by the two seas:[3] this is in circuit about three miles: and in it are his residence and his court, which is called the PORTE. This palace, because it was begun to be built by Sultan Mohammed, he willed when dying that it should be rent-paying property of his mosque, and that it should pay a thousand aspers a day, which are twenty ducats; and this has been observed to the present.[4]

He has in the aforesaid palace countless highly ornamented chambers, but one among the others is set apart for himself: in this he sleeps, and he has there six youths who serve his person.[5] Of these six, two are deputed for the service of the chamber and the Signor during the day, and then in the night the same ones come to keep guard when he sleeps: these stand ever vigilant, the one at his head and the other at his feet, with two lighted torches in their hands: these two then in the morning when they clothe the aforesaid Signor, put into one of the pocket-purses of his caftan a thousand aspers, and into the other twenty golden ducats; whatever of this money is not given away by the Signor during the day, remains to those who undress him at night; they never find much in the garments, according to report. And always when he goes forth to enjoy the chase or for some other purpose, besides the aforesaid money which he carries, he is accustomed always

---

[1] Celeby and Calepino are forms of *Chelebi*, the Gentleman, which was an appellation of Mohammed I; these three names, therefore, refer to the same person.

[2] At this point the writer begins to follow the pamphlet of Junis Bey.

[3] Seraglio Point is thrust out into the Bosphorus just before it meets the Sea of Marmora.

[4] The land on which Mohammed's palace was built had belonged to the church of St. Sophia under the Byzantine Empire. See above, p. 202.

[5] Junis Bey speaks of eight youths, but names six, as below.

to have behind him the *Khazinehdar-bashi*, or chief treasurer; this man carries with him a great sum of money to be given away.

The duty of the aforesaid six youths, who are changed according to the will of the Signor, is: of one to be *Papuji*,[1] or him who bears the shoes, of another *Silihdar*, who bears the bow and arrows, of another *Chokadar*, who bears the garments, of another *Sharabdar*, who bears the pitcher of water, of another *Iskemleji*, who carries the stool, and then of the sixth to be *Oda-bashi*, or chief of the Chamber. These have a fixed salary of 15 to 20, and the *Oda-bashi* of 30 aspers per day. Next comes

The eunuch *Kapu Aghasi*,[3] or chief of the gate, who has 60 aspers per day.

The *Khazinehdar-bashi*, a eunuch, chief treasurer, 60 aspers.[2]

The *Kilerji-bashi*, chief of the butlers, 40 aspers.

The *Seraidar-bashi*,[3] a eunuch, chief of the palace when the Signor is away; he has 50 aspers. Twelve eunuchs subject to the aforesaid, with 10 to 15 aspers each.

There are next about five hundred youths aged from eight to twenty years, who reside in the palace and are the delight of the Signor: they have each from ten to twelve aspers per day; they are instructed in various arts according to their genius, but especially in reading, writing, and in the doctrine of their laws, and in riding. The masters are old *Danishmends*,[4] called *Hojas*, or doctors of the laws. These boys at the season of Bairam, which is like our Easter day, are clothed by the Signor, some with silk and some with cloth, without any uniformity; and each has a golden bonnet, a scimitar, and a bow: they never leave the aforesaid palace until they have reached the age when the Signor thinks them fit for offices: and then he makes them *Spahi-oghlans*, or *Silihdars*, or of higher degrees according to their worth and the favor which they have gained with the Signor. Each ten of them are guarded by a eunuch called *Kapu-oghlan*, or chief of youths,[5] and each has a slave's frock, in which he sleeps rolled up in such a manner that he does not touch another

---

[1] After Junis Bey. The word here is " *Chiuchter*."

[2] There were two treasurers of the household, bearing the same name. One labored within the palace, and one without. See above, p. 127

[3] There is confusion here. The *Kapu Aghasi* and the *Seraidar-bashi* were the same person. The chief of the gate is rightly called the *Kapuji-bashi*. Junis Bey shows similar confusion (below, p. 263). See above, p. 126; and Redhouse, 1435.

[4] " *Talismani*." See above, p. 205.

[5] " *Capoglano*." The derivation is faulty; the literal meaning is " gate-youth."

who may be near him. They reside in a large hall, full of great lights and spacious, and their eunuchs sleep in the middle of this hall. They have a garden in the palace, which extends more than a mile, in which reside about thirty-five gardeners, called *Bostanjis*, who are *Ajem-oghlans:* [1] these gardeners have from three to five aspers each per day; they are clothed in blue cloth, and given a shirt. Then when they leave the palace, they become Janissaries, or *Solaks*, or *Kapujis*, or something else according to their quality.

The *Bostanji-bashi*, or chief gardener, has fifty aspers a day and many perquisites.

The *Kiaya*,[2] who is, as it were, a lieutenant for the gardeners, has 20 aspers per day; and each ten [gardeners] have a chief called *Boluk-bashi*. From this garden, which is very large and well-tended, full of excellent fruit-trees of every sort, they obtain so much every year that from the product of it alone they make the living expenses of the Signor, and also get something more. Near the garden are always stationed two small galleys; these are rowed by the gardeners when the Signor goes on a pleasure-trip, and the *Boluk-bashi* holds the helm.[3]

The *Ashji-bashi*, chief cook, with fifty cooks under him. He has 40 aspers per day, the cooks under him four, six, or eight aspers each.

The *Helvaji-bashi*, or chief confectioner, with 40 aspers, and he has thirty companions with five to six aspers per day each.

The *Chasnijir-bashi*,[4] chief of the cupboards, with eighty aspers: morning and evening he brings with his own hand the dish of the Signor, and he has under him a hundred *Chasnijirs* with from three to seventy aspers each.[5]

The *Mutbakh-emini*,[6] or steward, with 40 aspers. He has a secretary with 20 aspers a day.

A hundred *Ajem-oghlans*, who transport on carts the wood of the palace. They have three to five aspers, and are provided with clothing.

---

[1] " *Gianizzerotti.*" Junis Bey, below, p. 263, speaks of 400 gardeners, which is probably more nearly correct.

[2] " *Protogero.*" *Kiaya*, or by transliteration *Ketkhuda*, is the Turkish word. See above, p. 96, note 4.

[3] This should read " the *Bostanji-bashi* ": Junis Bey, 263.

[4] The chief taster.

[5] Junis Bey, 264, says five to six aspers each.

[6] Intendant or steward of the kitchen.

Ten *Sakkas*, who carry water on horse-back in leathern sacks, with three to five aspers each.

The expenses for the table of the Signor, and of the youths with their eunuchs and others to about a thousand, amount to five thousand aspers a day.

Three *Kapuji-bashis*, or captains of the gate, who have a hundred aspers a day and are clothed every year: and they have under them two hundred and fifty *Kapujis*, who have five to six aspers each; and each *Kapuji-bashi* with a third of the *Kapujis* is obliged to keep guard at the gate of the Signor, changing from day to day. And when any ambassador or other person goes to kiss the hand of the Grand Signor, all these are given presents of clothes or of money according to the degree of him who is introduced.

A *Kapuji-kiaya*, who is, as it were, a lieutenant of the *Kapujis*, has forty aspers a day.

Four Vizier Pashas, or chief counsellors: the greatest has ordinarily twenty-four thousand ducats a year and the others sixteen to eighteen thousand; but they have also so much feudal income that they receive three times as much as the provision in money.[1] To this should be added the garments which the Signor gives them, the presents of ambassadors and of others, the perquisites of the office they hold, which are unlimited. At present they are only three. The first is Ibrahim, born a Christian at Parga. The second Aias of Khimara. The third Kassim of Croatia, a kidnapped Christian. To these there is added a fourth at present,[2] who is Khaireddin Bey Barbarossa of the Albanian nation, formerly a corsair and now king of Algiers in Barbary. These Pashas live and dress very superbly. They have: Ibrahim six thousand and more slaves, Aias two thousand, Kassim fifteen hundred, and Barbarossa about four thousand. To all these slaves they give pay, horses, garments, golden bonnets and silver chains,[3] according to their offices and degrees. And these serve their Pashas under the same arrangements by which the Signor is served by his [slaves]. They have also twenty-five or thirty chancery secretaries to the Signor, men of great repute, with twenty-five to thirty aspers per day each: they keep

---

[1] The word translated " feudal income," or " feudal grant," is " *timar*." See above, p. 100 ff.

[2] This sentence was evidently inserted after the previous part of the paragraph had been written. See below, p. 255.

[3] " *Centola*."

more or fewer slaves as they can. These Pashas have entry to the Signor for affairs of state; and it is in fact they who govern the whole after their own fashion.

There is next the *Mufti*, or the interpreter and chief of the laws; they do not trouble him about anything except the affairs of religion and their faith, and he has the position which our Pope had in ancient times.[1]

Two *Kaziasker Danishmends*, or doctors of the laws for the army, one for Greece, the other for Anatolia. Their position is of great importance. They sit at the Porte and have precedence of the Vizier Pashas: on this account they are much esteemed. They are executors of the laws, and with the consent of the Pashas they appoint and remove the *Kazis*, who are like podestas for the whole country. They have feudal income of about six thousand ducats a year each. They keep two hundred to three hundred slaves each, and they are accompanied by ten secretaries appointed by the Signor and two *Mochtur-bashis*, who hold the office of ushers: [2] these live from perquisites, of which they have a great many.

Two *Defterdars*, or treasurers, or rather, as we would say, governors of the revenues. One of these has the receipt and the care of those revenues which come from a third of Greece, or from that part which is toward the Danube, and besides, from Asia, from Syria, and from Egypt, with feudal income of ten thousand ducats a year, although with the perquisites he gets twice as much. The other has the care of the other two-thirds of Greece: but when the Signor takes the field this man remains in Constantinople as his vicar and lieutenant; and he has six thousand ducats of feudal income, but gets three times as much; and their position is of great dignity. They have under them fifty clerks with many helpers: these keep the accounts of the *Khazineh*, or treasury of the Signor; and these clerks are appointed by the Signor with pay of fifteen to fifty aspers per day each. The *Defterdars* have, the first a thousand slaves and the second five hundred, and the clerks from two to twenty slaves each.[3]

Two *Rusnamehjis*, chief clerks, who receive the money and disburse it as needed, with twenty-five companions besides themselves.

[1] This remark seems to contain a comparison between the relation of the pope to the Roman emperor and that of the *Mufti* to the sultan. Such a comparison would, however, be inexact. See above, p. 209.

[2] " *Cavalleria*." Junis Bey, below, p. 265, calls them *cursori*.

[3] Junis Bey, 266, says 15 to 20 slaves each.

The two have forty aspers each, and the twenty-five have eight to ten aspers a day.

Two *Veznedars*, or weighers of aspers and ducats, with twenty-five to thirty aspers each.

Six *Sarrafs*, or bankers, who know gold and silver [coins], and they have ten to fifteen aspers each.

One *Nishanji-bashi*, who signs the ordinances and public writings with the monogram of the Signor. His position is like that of grand chancellor and is of great repute. He sits at the Porte below the *Beylerbeys*. He has eight thousand ducats of feudal income, and travels in great honor with more than three hundred slaves.

An outside *Khazinehdar-bashi*, or household treasurer, with ten *Khazinehdars* under him. He has fifty aspers, and they ten to fifteen per day.

A *Defter-emini*, who has charge of the feudal grants: he keeps the register of those who receive feudal grants. He has forty aspers a day, and under him are ten clerks with ten to fifteen aspers per day each.

Eighty *Muteferrika*, or lancers of the body-guard [1] of the Signor, these always carry lances when he takes the field; they recognize no other head than the Signor himself. And when by artifice or merit they acquire favor, they are made *Aghas*, or generals. The least has ten, the greatest eighty, aspers per day.

A *Chaush-bashi*, or chief sergeant of the army. He is of so great credit with every one, that when he is sent by the Signor to some Pasha, *Sanjak*, or *Kazi*, with the order to have the head of such and such a one cut off, he is obeyed without their requiring a letter from him, or a command in writing; not otherwise than if the Signor himself were there, and gave command. He has a hundred aspers a day, and under him he keeps a hundred slaves,[2] with twenty-five to forty aspers each.

The *Mihter-bashi*, or chief of those who pitch the tents and spread the rugs, who sweep the court-yards and attend to other similar duties; he has forty aspers, a *Kiaya* with twenty-five aspers, sixty *Mihters* with five to eight aspers each; and they are clothed every year by the Signor.

---

1 " *Spezzate.*"

2 That the other *Chaushes* were slaves not of the *Chaush-bashi*, but of the sultan, is shown by the amount of their pay. See Junis Bey's testimony, below, p. 265.

An *Agha*, or general of the Janissaries. He has for pay a thousand
aspers and over per day, and six thousand ducats of feudal grant
per year. When this *Agha* holds court, which is two or three times
per week, he is obliged to give the Janissaries to eat, a meal of bread,
rice, mutton, honey, and water. He has under him a *Kiaya* or
Secretary of the Janissaries, who is, as it were, a vicegerent; he has
two hundred aspers per day of pay in cash, and thirty thousand of
feudal grant per year.[1] And there is a clerk of these Janissaries,
called the *Yaziji* of the Janissaries,[2] with a hundred aspers a day.
A *Seymen-bashi*, chief of the harriers.[3] He has a hundred aspers and
has from the number of the Janissaries about two thousand under
him.
A *Zagarji-bashi*, head of the hounds.[4] He has fifty aspers a day,
and has under him about seven hundred of the Janissaries.
The Janissaries number about twelve thousand: they have each
from three to eight aspers of pay per day. Each ten has its *Oda-bashi*, and each hundred has its *Boluk-bashi*. And these heads of
ten or of a hundred go on horseback. And the *Oda-bashis* have
forty, and the *Boluk-bashis* sixty aspers a day. The remainder of
the Janissaries go on foot. They are clothed once a year by the
Signor with coarse blue cloth. They have their residence in two
barracks in Constantinople given by the Signor. Those who have
no wives reside in these. Those who are married reside at various
places in the city. For their living expenses each contributes so
much a day, and they have a steward and a cook, who provide their
necessary living: and those who have less pay than the others are
obliged to serve those who have more pay than they. Every
hundred of them when they take the field transport a tent. They
go on foot, and part of them are musketeers, and part halbardiers,
and part use the scimetar alone. Every three lead a horse which
carries their clothing. And when they come to old age, or when for
some other reason the service of one of them does not please the
Signor, they are stricken from the book of the Janissaries, and are
sent as *Hissarlis*[5] or castle guards; and those of their officers who are
deposed for such a reason, are sent as castellans with a feudal grant
equivalent to the pay which they had previously, in such a way that

[1] Junis Bey, below, p. 266, says that the *Kiaya* of the Janissaries has 300
ducats of feudal grant per year, which would equal about 15,000 aspers.
[2] " *Giannizzeriasis.* "   [4] " *Bracchi.* "
[3] " *Livreri.* "   [5] " *Assareri.* "

none of them suffers hardship. Such of them as succeed in war are made *Voivodes*,[1] and raised to high positions. They come as boys to this soldiery and are taught by the experienced ones. They choose healthy ones, well-built, but nimble and dextrous, lively above all, and more often cruel than compassionate. In them rests the force and all the firmness of the army of the Turk; they, because they are always exercising and living together, all become as it were a single body, and of a truth they are terrible.[2]

From the Janissaries are chosen a hundred and fifty *Solaks*, who are footmen of the Signor, with fifteen to twenty aspers a day each: they march surrounding the person of the Signor every time he goes forth.

Two *Solak-bashis*, chief officers of the *Solaks*, who go on horseback, with thirty aspers per day. And these and the *Solaks* are in obedience to the *Agha* of the Janissaries.

An *Agha* of the *Spahi-oghlans*, an office of great honor. He has from feudal grant and pay ten ducats a day, and he has a large number of slaves, with a *Kiaya* under him, or lieutenant: this man has from feudal grant and pay a hundred aspers a day. And also a *Yaziji*, or secretary, with thirty aspers, and with large perquisites.

The *Spahi-oghlans*, or youths on horseback, who may be called *Spahi-oghlan*, are more than three thousand; and they have twenty to forty aspers each; and every twenty have a *Boluk-bashi*. These serve on horseback, each with five or six slaves and a like number of horses. And they always journey, and also encamp, at the right hand of the Signor. They are great people. From them the Signor is wont to choose his chief men. They are first put as boys into the palace, and when they grow up they succeed well if they attain this grade: it is like a ladder to mount to higher positions.

An *Agha* of the *Silihdars*, who has thirty thousand aspers a day,[3] and under him a lieutenant, a secretary, a *Kiaya*,[4] with thirty aspers and more each.

There are three thousand *Silihdars*. They moreover ride and encamp at the left hand of the Signor. They have twenty to

---

[1] This Slavonic word seems to be used here simply in the sense of " army officers."
[2] " *Immensi*."
[3] This is an error. Probably the number intended is three hundred. Junis Bey, below, p. 267, gives two hundred and fifty.
[4] Only two officers should be named here. The lieutenant (*Protogero*) and the *Kiaya* were the same. Junis Bey gives this correctly.

twenty-five aspers per day each, and they have four or five slaves and a like number of horses, with feudal income for their living. They are trained by the same education with which the *Spahis* are brought up: nor is there any difference between them, except that the *Spahis* go on the right, and these on the left, of the Signor.

Two *Ulufaji-bashis*, or chief officers of soldiers, with two thousand *Ulufajis*, who go on the right hand and the left of the Signor. The chief officers have a hundred and twenty aspers, and the others eight to sixteen aspers; then under them [1] they have a *Kiaya*, a secretary, and a lieutenant,[2] with slaves and with horses, some more and some fewer.

Two *Aghas*, chief officers of the *Ghureba-oghlans*, or poor youths [3] with eighty aspers each. *Kiayas*, thirty aspers. Secretaries, twenty-five. And they have under them about two thousand *Ghureba-oghlans* with seven to fourteen aspers per day: these have slaves and horses.

Two *Emir-al-Akhors*,[4] or masters of the stable, a greater and a lesser. The greater has five hundred aspers, the lesser two hundred, with lieutenant and *Kiaya* [5] and others, who have thirty to forty aspers each.

Sixteen thousand altogether of *Serraj*, who have charge of bridles [6] and saddles; *Ceyssi*, or stable servants; *Carmandari*, who take care of the mules; *Deveji*, who take care of the camels, and *Cavriliji*, who herd the cattle and horses in various places. These have two to twenty aspers per day each.

Thirty to forty *Peiks*, or runners on foot, men who when boys have had their spleens removed: [7] and they run post on foot with great speed. These when the Signor goes forth remain continually near, so that he may employ them according to his needs.

Select horses about four thousand for the person of the Signor; on these the pages of the palace and the eunuchs ride for exercise in their turns.

[1] Under each *Agha*, or chief officer.
[2] The *Kiaya* and the lieutenant are the same.
[3] This derivation is from a secondary meaning; the primary meaning is " foreign youth." See above, pp. 98, 99, note 1.
[4] " *Bracor-bashi.*"
[5] This should read " *Kiaya* and secretary."
[6] " *Brene.*"
[7] This is the common report in Western writers as regards the *Peiks*. See Menavino, 155; Nicolay, 100.

A *Chakirji-bashi*, chief Vulturer, and a *Shahinji-bashi*, chief Falconer. The first has a hundred and fifty aspers, and the other has eighty; with *Kiayas*, lieutenants,[1] and others, with ten to twenty-five aspers each per day. Under these are about two hundred *Zanijiler*,[2] only a hundred of whom have ten aspers a day, and the others have feudal income, or exemption from taxation. And they take the field when the Signor has need.

A *Jebeji-bashi*, chief armorer. He has sixty aspers, a *Kiaya* and a secretary with twenty aspers each. He has under him about one thousand five hundred *jebejis*, with seven to twelve aspers. These all go on foot when the Signor takes the field.

A *Topji-bashi*, chief of artillery. He has seventy aspers, a *Kiaya* [and] secretary with twenty aspers: and under him are two thousand *Topjis* with six to ten aspers, and they go on foot.

An *Arabaji-bashi*, chief wagoner. He has forty aspers, a *Kiaya* [and] secretary with twenty aspers: and under him three thousand *Arabajis* with three to six aspers each.

A *Mihter-bashi*, or chief of trumpeters and drummers. He has thirty [aspers] per day, and under him two hundred *Mihters*, part of them on foot and part on horseback with three to five aspers per day.

An *Emir-Alem Agha*, who carries the standard of the Signor. He has two hundred aspers a day, and is captain of all the musicians.

An *Arpa-emini*, who is Provider of the grain, with a Lieutenant and a Chancellor.[3] He has sixty aspers, the Lieutenant thirty and the Chancellor twenty: this *Arpa-emini* has under him twenty persons who receive among them all about eight hundred aspers.

A *Shehr-emini*,[4] or Commissioner of public works, who takes care of the streets of Constantinople, and also of the road when the Signor goes forth to war: and he has charge also of public buildings, fountains, and aqueducts. He has fifty aspers, and keeps under him four hundred men: among all of these is given a thousand aspers. He has also a *Kiaya* and secretary with about thirty-eight aspers each.[5]

---

[1] *Kiayas* and secretaries.
[2] This refers to those whom Junis Bey, below, p. 268, calls *Zainogiler*, a body of lancers, who are here erroneously classed with the falconers. Junis Bey's figures are 20,000 in all, 1000 receiving pay in money. Are they the Voinaks (above, p. 131) ?
[3] Junis Bey, " *cursor*," a messenger or porter.
[4] Literally, " intendant of the town."
[5] Junis Bey says 57.

A *Berat-emini*, who is deputed to distribute the ordinances of the Signor in writing and who receives the fees; and he has forty aspers, with two secretaries, and two superintendents with twenty aspers each.

A *Terjuman*,[1] or interpreter of all the languages. This position is highly reputed in proportion to the worth and intelligence of him who holds it. He has five hundred ducats of fixed income each year, and has also a like sum from feudal grant, and more than four times as much of extraordinary income; and he is wont to be highly respected.

Proceeding now further as I have begun, I shall leave it for another time and eye to reduce this Porte to better order and put everything in its proper place. I find that to all the above-mentioned things should be added a PALACE of the ladies of the Signor.[2] This is very large, with a circuit of about a mile and a half; and it is provided with different chambers and other rooms, where the sons of the Signor reside separately with their mothers, and with a great number of eunuchs for their guard and service. There also reside the Sultanas, that is the mothers and the wives of the Signors; and there are three hundred damsels, placed there virgins, and given to the government of many matrons. To all of these damsels the Signor has it taught to embroider different designs, to each he gives pay of ten to twenty aspers per day; and twice every year at the two Bairams he has them clothed in stuffs of silk. And when one of these pleases him he does what he wishes with her, and when he has lain with her he gives her a golden bonnet and ten thousand aspers, and has her placed in a separate apartment from the others, increasing her ordinary pay.[3] In the aforesaid Palace there is an *Agha* of the Eunuchs: to these are given a hundred and twenty aspers for all. Three *Kapuji-bashis*, and with them a hundred *Kapujis* and Janissaries at the gate: among all these is given six hundred aspers a day. Ten *Sakkas*, who carry water, forty aspers in all. And the damsels are served and educated up to the age of twenty-five years. The teachers are the matrons, the servants are the youngest among them; and when they have arrived at twenty-

---

[1] Usually called by Western writers " Dragoman."

[2] This was the " Old Palace " of Mohammed the Conqueror, and stood where the *Seraskierat*, or War Office now stands.

[3] Suleiman is said to have been faithful to Roxelana after he had made her his wife. See above, p. 56.

five years, if it does not please the Signor to keep them for his own use, he marries them to *Spahi-oghlans*, and to others of the slaves of the Porte according to the degree and condition of both parties; and in their place he substitutes others.

There is also a palace near Pera for about four hundred boys, who have pay of six to ten aspers, and are clothed with silk twice a year. These have an *Agha* and eunuchs, as have those in the great palace, [and] *Kapujis*, *Ajem-oghlans* and a hundred teachers of various arts. Among all these is distributed eight hundred aspers a day. They are not so noble, or of so beautiful appearance or show of intelligence as are those who reside with the Signor; but from these also many become great, and some of them are taken into the great palace. And similarly in Adrianople there is a palace of three hundred boys under pay, an *Agha*, eunuchs, *Kapujis*, Janissaries, and teachers, about two hundred in all, who have all together two thousand eight hundred aspers a day. These are of third grade, but they are carefully taught and well kept like all the others, and from them according to the spirit and worth which they show promotions are made. There is also in that region another palace, recently built, with a large and beautiful garden: this is located on the river Maritza, and in it reside about three hundred *Ajem-oghlans;* on these [palaces] they spend every year two hundred thousand aspers for each, and they have an *Agha* with forty aspers and a lieutenant and secretaries with thirty aspers each per day. In various other places in Adrianople there are gardens: in these reside continually as on deposit one thousand five hundred *Ajem-oghlans* with *Agha* and secretaries, and on these they spend six thousand aspers a year [1] or a little more.

There is also an *Agha* of the *Ajem-oghlans*, or Janissary recruits, who resides in Constantinople; he has sixty aspers per day, and under him are about five thousand *Ajem-oghlans:* these they clothe twice a year, and on their teachers and chiefs they spend ten thousand aspers [2] a year. They put them on ships and buildings to carry wood and perform other tasks. They become cooks or servants of the Janissaries, and finally they become Janissaries.

And every four years the Turkish Signor sends into Greece and into Anatolia to seize boys, sons of Christians, ten or twelve thousand each time: these he sends into Anatolia in the region of Brusa

---

[1] This should read " per day." Junis Bey, below, p. 269.

[2] This should read 100,000: *ibid.*

or Caramania to dig the earth, so that they will become accustomed to hard labor, and so that there they may learn the Turkish language. These boys remain in such a place and occupation three or four years: then they are ordered to be gathered again, and are given to the government and discipline of the *Agha* of the *Ajem-oghlans*. For these the Signor does not have any expenses so long as they reside in Anatolia, because they are clothed and have their living from those whom they serve by plowing the ground and doing other work for them.

It seemed best to me to make mention in this place of all the palaces, because they are as it were of the same body as that of the Signor, and all the expenses of these are computed in the book of the expense of the great palace, or that of the Signor. To these expenses are added those, which are incurred in clothing twice each year the Pashas, the *Kaziaskers*, the *Defterdars*, the *Beylerbeys*, and the *Nishanji*, and the expenses which are incurred for the extraordinary presents of the Signor. These in all amount to and go beyond a million aspers a year.

There is also an Arsenal in the region of Pera, small and of short circuit: this has on the sea-front ninety-two vaults, and so little area and ground within that not merely no galleys but not even materials and timbers can be contained there. In it usually work each day about two hundred men; although there are under pay two hundred patrons with two thousand aspers per day for all.[1] A thousand *Azabs*, who have among them four thousand aspers. Foremen, or masters fifty in number, who have in leisure, that is, when not working, six aspers, and when working, twelve aspers each. An Intendant, forty aspers. A Secretary, twenty-five aspers, with ten clerks under him, who have a hundred aspers. All these fulfil their duties when there is great need; but they understand ill the trade and art of building galleys. For this reason they do not turn out good and ready ones like ours; and what few there are are overseen by Christians, who are well paid.

Over this Arsenal and all these persons, there is one who is called the *Beylerbey* of the sea; that is to say, Lord of lords, an office created at the time when I was in Constantinople; since in the past he who was *Sanjak* of Gallipoli was wont to be called Captain of the Sea. And Khaireddin Bey called Barbarossa was the first who had this title; he was then made fourth Pasha. To him is given the

---

[1] Junis Bey, below, p. 270, says 200,000 per year.

government of all the fleets, and he has for income every year a feudal grant of fourteen thousand ducats, besides that from Rhodes, Euboea, and Mytilene; so that he receives twice as much more.

I find nothing else that pertains to arrangements for the rule and watch of the sea which are worthy of note: wherefore I will now come to those of the land; these are in truth well and usefully ordered.

There is first one called the *Beylerbey* of Greece: in this are included all the lands which the Turkish Signor possesses in Europe: this *Beylerbey* is greater than all the others. He has from feudal grant sixteen thousand ducats a year, and gets more than double this. He sits at the Porte after the Pashas,[1] and is of great repute with everybody. He has under him besides his slaves, who number more than a thousand, a *Defterdar* with feudal income of three thousand ducats a year; a hundred clerks who keep the books and accounts of the feudal grants assigned to *Subashis, Kazis, Spahis,* and others; among all of whom are distributed ten thousand ducats a year.

Thirty-six *Sanjaks*: these are in obedience to him, and have for feudal income from five to twelve thousand ducats a year each. They are distributed through the provinces: in these they reside only so long as pleases the Signor: he changes them, as seems best to him, from one province to another. Their duty is to rule the *Spahis*, and to have them trained in arms, and to keep them in obedience.

Four hundred *Subashis*, who have among them all from feudal income four hundred thousand ducats, and have about five hundred slaves each.[2]

Thirty thousand *Spahis:* these are horse soldiery set apart some to the service of the *Beylerbey*, and some to that of all the *Sanjaks* of Greece. They have from feudal grant two hundred ducats each, and each of them, for every hundred ducats of feudal income, is obliged to maintain an armed man, with horse and lance. And then they have besides the armed man two or four or five servants and horses. These *Spahis* are all slaves of the Signor, and sons of slaves, and of *Spahis*.

Twenty thousand *Timarjis* who have ten to forty ducats of feudal income each year, and because they do not reach a hundred

---

[1] At the meetings of the Divan.
[2] This should read fifty each: Junis Bey, below, p. 271.

ducats, they are not called *Spahis*. These have each a horse and two or three servants, and they serve distributed through all the *Sanjaks* of Greece. The feudal grants are by assignment of land; the income of this assignment they get partly from rent, but the greater part from the tithes of all the income, which Turks as well as Christians pay, and from the poll-tax, which is twenty-five aspers per head from Christians alone, and from the imposts laid on animals, fruit-trees, and other things. These imposts, moreover, are in addition to those which they pay ordinarily to the Signor.

Sixty thousand *Akinji*, or mounted adventurers, inscribed for the lands of Greece and obliged to go to war without payment. But they are exempt from any burden, and cities and villages are bound to give them, when they pass through, living expenses only.

There are in all Greece, that is, in all the countries which the Turkish Signor possesses in Europe, sixty-eight thousand villages of Turkish and Christian people, subject to public burdens.[1]

There follow next six *Beylerbeys* of Asia, and a separate one of Egypt. The first of these is called the *Beylerbey* of Anatolia which was anciently Asia Minor: he has from feudal income fourteen thousand ducats, but gets a great deal more. This man has under him and in his government Pontus, Bithynia, Asia proper, Lydia, Caria, and Lycia: these provinces under a single name are called at present Anatolia. This man's place at the Porte is after the *Beylerbey* of Greece. And he has under him, besides his own slaves, who are more than a thousand, twelve *Sanjaks* with feudal income of from four to six thousand ducats each. Ten thousand *Spahis*, with five to ten aspers a day, and also more or less feudal income according to their degree. Next after these follows

The *Beylerbey* of Caramania, which was anciently Cilicia and Pamphylia, with feudal income of ten thousand ducats. This man has under him seven *Sanjaks* with four to six thousand ducats of feudal income each, and five thousand *Spahis*, with five to ten aspers a day each and feudal income besides.

The *Beylerbey* of Amasia and Tokat, which was Cappadocia and Galatia, with feudal income of eight thousand ducats. Four *Sanjaks* with four to six thousand ducats of feudal income each. Four thousand *Spahis* with five to ten aspers a day each and feudal income.

---

[1] " *Che fanno fattione.*"

The *Beylerbey* of Anadole, which is a region between Syria, Caramania, and Tokat, which was anciently Paphlagonia, and is the half of Armenia Minor. He has ten thousand ducats of feudal income, and under him seven *Sanjaks* with four to five thousand ducats of feudal income. Seven thousand *Spahis*, with five to ten aspers per day and feudal income. In this province of Anadole, they say that when the Signor is there, besides the paid troops thirty thousand persons are obliged to ride without any pay, but only with expenses from the villages.

The *Beylerbey* of Mesopotamia, under whom is the remainder of Armenia Minor and part of the Major, the other parts belonging to the Persians and the Kurds. This borders with Bagdad, or Baldach, which was anciently Babylonia. He has of feudal income thirty thousand ducats: and besides his own slaves, who number two thousand, he has under him twelve *Sanjaks* with feudal income of four to six thousand ducats a year, and ten [1] *Spahis* with ten to fifteen aspers per day each, and with large feudal income because of being at the confines of the Persians: with these they are continually in conflict.

A *Beylerbey* of Damascus and Syria and Judea, with feudal income of twenty-four thousand ducats; he has more than two thousand slaves, and under him twelve *Sanjaks* with feudal income of five to seven thousand ducats, and twenty thousand *Spahis* with ten to fifteen aspers per day each and with good feudal income.

A *Beylerbey* of Cairo: he holds jurisdiction as far as Mecca, or as far as into Arabia: this Arabia is possessed by the Turkish Signor in the way in which he possesses Albania, where he is not yielded such obedience as he is accustomed to receive from all his other states and countries. But [Arabia] Felix stands in somewhat greater obedience than the rest. He has for feudal income thirty thousand ducats, with numerous slaves: these amount to more than four thousand; sixteen *Sanjaks* with feudal income of six to eight thousand ducats each; and sixteen thousand *Spahis* with fifteen to twenty aspers each per day.

Near Mecca, and the countries of the Persians, are some Arabic lords who do not obey any one. The rest [2] then borders the Persians as far as Mesopotamia, in which is Bagdad.[3] Passing

---

[1] This should read " ten thousand " : Junis Bey, below, p. 272.
[2] Of the Turkish possessions in Asia.
[3] " *Maldac*."

Mesopotamia it borders the Persians again to the plain of Naximan, then touches Erzinjan [1] and Erzerum, which are the chief places of Armenia Major. This Armenia borders with the Iberians and Georgians. In these Armenias, Major and Minor, are many Kurds, people of the mountains and warlike, those of [Armenia] Major obedient partly to the Turkish Signor, and partly to the Persian; those of [Armenia] Minor to no one. Next Trebizond borders with the Georgians and Mingrelians, and with part of the Iberians, which people were anciently called Colchians. And Ajemia,[2] which anciently was Assyria, belongs to the Persian: he is absolute master of it.

There are in all Anatolia, or in all the countries which the Turkish Signor possesses in Asia, villages of Turks and Christians to the number of more than seventy-two thousand, not counting those which are in Egypt, which are many.

The *Sanjaks* truly [set forth]: these (as I said above) have under government the provinces entrusted to the *Beylerbeys;* they are men of much and very great reputation and esteem, especially in the affairs of war; they are named as below by the names of the places which are given to their government. And first the *Beylerbey* of Greece holds as his sanjakate the places about Salonika. Then follow the others of Kaffa, Silistria, Nicopolis, Vidin, Semendria, Servia and Belgrade,[3] Zvornick, Bosnia, Hersek, which is the Servia called the Duchy,[4] Scutari, Avlona, Yanina, Karli Ili, Lepanto, Morea, Negropont, Trikkala, Gallipoli, Kirk-Kilisse or Forty Churches, Viza, Chirmen, Kostendil, Vishidrina, Prisrend, Okhrida, Alaja Hissar, Elbassan, Voinuch, Chiuchene, Zaiza. These are usually counted thirty-five, but five are regions united to neighboring places, namely Philippopolis, Sofia, Durazzo, Albania, and Uskup.

ANATOLIA, or Asia Minor: Pontus, Bithynia, Lydia, Caria, and Lycia. The sanjakate of the *Beylerbey* is at Kutaia. And the others are in Hoja-ili, Boli, Kastamuni, Angora, Kanghri,[5] Tekke-ili, Menteshe-ili, Aidin-ili, Alayeh,[6] Bigha, and Manissa,[7] which is that of Sultan Mustapha, the oldest son of the Signor. This place is opposite the middle of Chios near the sea.

---

[1] " *Esdum.*" Junis Bey, below, p. 272, has " *exdrun.*"
[2] More correctly, *Irak Ajam*, north-central Persia.
[3] Junis Bey, 273, counts these as two, and the whole number as thirty-six.
[4] Herzegovina.   [6] " *Hallayce* " or " *Allaye.*"
[5] " *Cangri.*"   [7] The ancient Magnesia.

AMASIA, and Tokat, which is Paphlagonia, Galatia, and Cappadocia. The sanjakate of the *Beylerbey* is in Amasia, of the others in Chorum, Janik, Kara-hissar, Samsun, Trebizond.

CARAMANIA, which is Cilicia opposite Cyprus and Pamphylia. The sanjakate of the *Beylerbey* is in Konia. The others have theirs in Naranda, Hissar, Eski-hissar, Versag-ili, Sivri-hissar.

ANADOLE, or Armenia Minor. The sanjakate of the *Beylerbey* is in Marash. Those of the others in Sarmussacli, Albistan-ovassi,[1] Adana, Tarsus.

DIARBEKIR, or Mesopotamia, and part of Armenia Major, of which the remainder belongs to the Persians and the Kurds. The sanjakate of the *Beylerbey* is in Diarbekir. And the others have theirs in Kara Amid, Arghana, Toljik, Hassan-Kief, Mardin, Kharput, Mosul, Erzerum, Baiburt, Bitlis, and Naximan-ovassi.

SYRIA, and Judea. The sanjakate of the *Beylerbey* is in Damascus. Of the others in Malatia, Divirigi, Aintab, Antioch, Aleppo, Tripoli, Hama, Homs, Safita, Jerusalem, Gaza.

EGYPT, with part of Arabia Deserta as far as Jeddah;[2] Mecca, with all of Arabia Felix, where are many Arab lordlings, who are partly in devotion to the Turkish Signor, partly to no one. The sanjakate of the *Beylerbey* is in Cairo, and of the others. . . .[3]

All the aforesaid *Sanjaks*, *Beylerbeys*, Pashas, and other officials have salary or feudal income, as I have said above, by fixed arrangement, that is, regularly: but they obtain from extraordinary sources about as much more. And they live with very great expenses for slaves: these they are accustomed to clothe and they give them also wages besides, so that they will not steal.

How great the revenues of this Signor are, may be estimated from the expenses. These revenues are obtained from the Kharâj, which is paid by the non-Turkish subjects; this gives a million and a half ducats: from the tax on animals, which gives eight hundred thousand ducats: from mines, which give six hundred thousand ducats: from countless other duties, salt-taxes, commendations, inheritances, gifts, the revenues of Egypt over and above the expenses, rents, and tributes. And they are so great that they not only meet the expenses, which amount besides the feudal income in ready money drawn from the Treasury to more than twelve thou-

---

[1] The plain of Albistan.
[2] " *Alziden.*"
[3] Evidently the writer intended to fill these in, but failed to secure the names.

sand ducats a day; [1] but there remains over a great sum of money from the surplus of each year. And it is believed that all the revenues amount to fifteen millions in gold: five of which enter the Treasury, and the other ten remain for the servants of war. [2]

[1] This amounts to about four million ducats a year.

[2] The reference is, of course, to the feudal *Spahis* and their officers, who then received according to this estimate two-thirds of the revenues of the empire.

APPENDIX II

PAMPHLET OF JUNIS BEY AND ALVISE GRITTI

Printed in 1537.   Presented in the original Italian.

OPERA NOUA LA QUALE DECHIARA

tutto il gouerno del gran Turcho & tutta la Spesa che il gran Turcho ha sotto di lui cosi in pace como in guerra
& il numero de le Persone & nome & gouerno de le sue Don
ne & Garzoni che lui tene
nel Serraglio serrati &
de tutta la Entrata che
lui ha a lanno & no
mina tutti li Si-
gnori de le sue
prouincie:
E il nome de tutte le sue terre chelha
sotto se : & la ordinãza del suo Cam
po quãdo ua ala guerra como
ua in ordinanza tutte le
persone a sorte per
sorte & come
uanno e
che arme portano.   Nouamente stam-
pata nel M D X X X V I I.

IL Signor grãde cioe il grã Turcho ha uno serraglio principale doue
tene la sua sedia, & ha una camera deputada per lui doue dorme,
& al gouerno dessa ha 8. gioueni ch' lo uestano e sue stano doi al
giorno deputati ala guardia, & seruitii suoi, & la notte li fanno la
guardia uno da capo, laltro da piede con due torce accese: & q̄l
li doi che li hãno fatto la guardia la notte lo uestano la mattina, &
li mettano ne la Scarsella del dulimano cioe de la casacha sua aspri
Mille uno aspro ual soldi do di Milano, & in laltra duchati 20 doro:
questi dinari sel Signor nõ li dona uia quel giorno restano a colori

ch'lo spogliano la sera, & q̄sti giouani hāno uno capo ch'si domāda Oddabassi cioe capo de li camarieri uno Papugi che li porta le scarpe, laltro Selictare che porta larco & frezze, laltro Ciochadar ch'li porta le ueste, laltro Seracter che li porta il mastrapā zoe il rami dalacq̄, laltro schēni ch' porta la sedia questi sono li nomi che hanno li otto gioueni, & il capo de questi cioe Oddabassi ha aspri 30. al di di soldo, & li altri 8. gioueni hano chi 15. chi 20. aspri per uno secondo il loro grado.

El Capagasi e monuco cioe castrato & e portinaro de la porta del gran Turco ha aspri 60. di soldo.

El Capiagabasi cioe il capo del Serraglio doue sta il Turcho quādo il Signor e fora de Cōstantinopoli ha aspri 50. & ha sotto lui 12 mōuchi cioe castrati che hāno aspri 16. al di per uno di soldo & spesa.

El Casnādarbasi e monucho, cioe Tesorero de la Saluaroba del Signor ha aspri 60. al di di soldo.

Ha in el serraglio il Sgnor gioueni de anni 8. fino in 20. ṅumero 700. che hāno di soldo al giorno chi 10. chi 14. secondo il suo grado & sono uestiti dal Signor q̄sti hàno maestri che li insegnano a legere e scriuere & la lege loro, & como escano del serragliò hanno nella porta cioe ne la sua corte officii chi Spacoglài chi Selictari chi Solachi & altri stipēdii secondo gratia e ualore loro.

Spacoglani sono gétilhomini che cortigiano il Signor quādo caualca: & li Selictari sono q̄lli che uano alla mā sinistra del Signor q̄ndo ua in campo: & li Solachi sono stafferi del Signor, & li suoi maestri sono Talasimāi uecchi detti Cogia dotti nella lege loro, cioe sacerdoti & questi putti sono ogni 10. in gouerno d'uno monucho detto Capogliano, ognuno ha uno schiauinotto nel qual dormino détro la notte de sorte che non si toccano insiemo & stanno in uno salotto & li Monuchi dormeno in mezo desso salotto & stanno lc lume acccse tutta la notte.

Ha uno giardino nel serraglio che uolge circa doi miglia doue stanno circa 400. putti giardineri detti Bustāgi sono Ianicerotti, & hanno uno capo che si domanda Bustāgibassi che e sopra tutti li giardini del Signor ch' sono moltie lui ha aspri 40. il di di soldo & altre molte regalie & a li giardineri chi 3. chi 5. aspri al di & sono ognuno uestiti del Signor di pāno azuro turchesco & una gamisa e uno paro di braghe do uolte a lanno & quādo escano del serraglio che sono grādi diuentano Ianizari cioe guardiani del Signor.   Solachi cioe stafferi & Capigi cioe Portinari: & il ditto Bonstāgibassi e qllo ch'e timonero quãdo al Signor ua in Fusta hãno uno ptoiro cioe loco tenente che ha aspri 20. al di & ogni 10 de detti hãno uno capo ditto Balucasi che ha aspri 20. il di & questi putti uãno per tutto dentro del Serraglio & mai escano fino che non sono homeni.

El Signor ha due Fuste che li nauegano li sopraditti giardineri, & lo capo loro sta al timone con le quale il Signor ua a spasso assai per canale & a li giardini lor.

El calualgibasi capo de le cõfettioni ha aspri 40. il di con 30. homini sotto di lui & hanno chi 5 chi 6, aspri al di.

El Vechilargibasi capo deli despésieri ha aspri 40. il di cõ uno scriuano cõ aspri 20 il di di soldo.

El Cessignirbassi capo de li cardẽceri ha aspri 80. il di & questo porta la sera & mattina il piato al Signore & ha sotto di lui homini 100. che hanno chi 5 chi 6. aspri al di di soldo.

Vno Asgibassi capo de li coghi ha aspri 40. al di & ha da circa 80. coghi sotto di lui che hãno chi 5. chi 6. chi 8. aspri il di, & ha da 80. Ianicerotti da 10. in 20. anni ditti baltagi cioe taglia legne che tagliano le legne per la cucina del signore & per tutto il serraglio che hanno da 3. in 5. aspri il di per uno & sono uestiti dal Signore.

Ha circa 20. garzoni Ianicerotti carretteri che portano con li carri le legne nel serraglio & hanno aspri 3. in 5. al di & sono uestiti dal Signore.

Sacha 10. cioe acquaroli che portano lacqua con li caualli nel serraglio hanno 3. in 5. aspri il di & uestiti dal Signore.

Vna stalla con 200. caualli per la psona del Signore con 100. homini al gouerno suo che hanno aspri 5. in 8. al di soldo per uno. Vnaltra stalla con 4000. caualli per li schiaui soi con 2000. homini al suo gouerno che hãno da 3 in 5 aspri di di soldo & spesa.

Il gran Turcho ha molti giardini & si uendano li frutti & del tratto di essi si fa le spese a lui per essere entrate licite, & il suo serraglio paga di liuello aspri 1000. al giorno a la moschea cioe a la gesia del padre de suo padre Soltan memet.

Spesa nel piato del Signor aspri 5000. & per li garzoni soi aspri 2500. ogni giorno.

Vno Capigilarchi caiasi idest gouernator & capo de tutti li capigi cioe di portineri de la porte ha aspri 500. il di: & 3 capigibassi de la porta del signore hanno aspri 100. il di & uestiti, sotto q̄ste sono Capigi cioe Portinari numero 250. chi hanno aspri 57. il di per uno, & questi fanno la guardia a la porta del Signor di 24. in 24. hore, &

quando qualche Ambasciator ua a basciare la mano al Signor bisogna chel presenta tutti costori. Vno Capigi la che chi si Protoiro idest locotenente di Capigi ha aspri 40. il giorno,
El Ciausbasi capo de li ciausi cō 100. ciausi sotto lui q̄sti sono homini grādi & quādo uāno pfare morire alcuno sia dassai quāto si uoglia sono obediti senza altra cōmissione in scritto, & q̄ndo il Signor caualca uāno semp' ináci a ui faciādo fare largo, hāno di soldi da aspri 25. sino in 40. al di secūdo lor grado & il ciaubasi ha aspri 200.
El Mecterbasi capo de quelli che destendano li padiglioni & tapedi & spazzar la porta & altre simile cose ha aspri 40. il di con il suo Protoiro che ha aspri 20. il di con 60. homini sotto di lui che si domandano Mecteri che hanno aspri 5. in 6. il di per uno & sono uestiti.
Sono ordinatamēte 4. Bascia soi cāzelleri e cōseieriel primo ha duchati 24000 di entrata a lanno: li altri tre hāno chi 16000. chi 18000. duchati a lanno & li sono date entrate doue cauano il tutto, & hāno molte altre regalie & p̄senti.
Abrain eora de la pargha albaneso e morto, hora li e Aiisbassa de la sinita ch' e il prícipale Albāeso uno altro mostafa bas cia che mamalucho di Alchayro & uno Casin bascia ch'e, Crouato & Cayradibeii cioe Barbarossa ch'era greco di metelí Isola & niuno puo essere bascia se non Christiani renegati. Ayas ha numero 600. schiaui. Mostafa ne ha numero 200: Casin crouato ne ha numero 150. Barbarossa ne ha da numero 100. A liquali danno soldo caualli scufie doro & spade fornire dargento & di questi essi Bascia fanno la corte loro & sono uestiti da essi Bascia.
Doi Cadilescher talasimani uno de la Grecia laltro de la natolia cioe Asia, & ha di entrata ducati 6 in 7 milia a lanno per uno : q̄sti sono executori de la lege loro & hano 10. homini executori per uno dati dal Signor sono q̄lli che metteno li Cadi cioe podesta per tutto il paese del Signor & quādo uanno dal Signor entrano auanti deli Bascia hanno per uno mocturbasi cioe cursor, & como cauallieri de li executori & questi tutti uiuano di regalie, hāno lo Cadilescheri 200. in 300. schiaui per uno che se ne fanno la lor corte.
Doi Defterderi cioe thesoreri uno di Asia laltro di Europa che scodano tutte le entrade del Signor & gouernano quasi il tutto hanno di entrada ducati sie in sette milia a lanno per uno, & hanno 200. schiaui per uno & ne fanno la lor corte.
Hanno q̄sti Defterderi 50. scriuani per uno con li cogitori quali tengano conto del thesoro del Signor, questi scriuani sono posti dal Signor

con soldo di 15. in 50. aspri al di per uno secondo il grado loro & hāno 15. in 20. schiaui per uno.

Secretarii 25. posti dal Signor che hanno 25. in 30. aspri il di & suoi schiaui sono doi Rosanamagi idest capi de li scriuani che reuedano li cōti & ch' receuano dāno fora con 20. cōpagni sotto loro doi, hanno aspri 40. il di & li 25. compagni hāno aspri 8. in 10. al di per uno di soldo.

Cinque Seraferi idest Bancheri che uedano tutto li danari che si scodano hanno aspri 10, in 15. al di di soldo.

Vno Tescheregibassi che segna tutti li commandamenti del Signor ha di entrata ducati 7000. & 300. in 400. schiaui.

Vno Casmandarbassi di fora con 10. Casandari il capo ha aspri 50. il di & ha aspri 10. in 15. al di di soldo sintéde sopra la saluaroba del Signore di fuora del serraglio.

Vno Defterdaro emino cioe douanero sopra le intrade & tene il libro de li timarati ha aspri 40. il di con lo scriuano che ha aspri 10. in 15. al di.

Vno Agha de Ianiceri cioe Capitano de tutti li Ianiceri che ha intrata duch. 7000. lāno, & ha aspri 10000. per far pasto a li Ianizari quādo el da audiétia in casa sua che 2. o 3. uolte la settima na le da & ha 400. schiaui sotto se questi Ianizari sono la guardia del Signor tutti schiopetteri & uanno a piede.

Vno Gachaia de Ianizari cioe locotenéte ha 200 aspri di & ducati 300. di timaro cioe entrata a lanno con 25. schiaui suoi.

Vno Scriuan di Ianizari che tien contro de loro Ianizari ha aspri 100. al di & circa a 200 schiaui.

Secmébassi capo di brachi da caza ha aspri 100. il di & ha del numero di Iāizari 200 sotto di lui.

Il Zarcagibassi capo de li liureri da cazza ha aspri 50 il di & ha del numero di Ianizari 700. sotto di se che menano li cani a spasso quādo bisogna.

Sono li Ianizari numero 12000. li quali hanno da 3. sino in 8. aspri il di di soldo & ogni 10. hanno il suo Odabassi cioe capo de numero dece & ogni cento hanno il suo capo che si domanda Bolucbassi, & li capi loro quando uanno in cāpo uāno a cauallo & hāno aspri 40. in 60. al* di per vno secondo il grado loro.

De li Ianizari si caua da 150 solachi che sono staferi dil Signor & 2 solachibassi capi de q̄lli & tutti sono sotto lagha de Ianizeri, & sono vestiti vna volta alanno dil Signor di pāno azuro, & hāno le

---

* At this point the smaller type begins. See below, p. 315.

stantie loro in 2 lochi in Constantinopoli fatto fabricare dil Signor & li stano q̄lli che non hāno moglie li maritati stano sora cō le dōne loro, & nel vitto ogniuno mette tāto al di & hano dispēsieri choghi & q̄lli che hāno pocho salario seruan al altri, & ogni 100 di loro quādo vano in cāpo portano vno padiglione, & sono soldati apedi schpeteri & alabarderi e simitarre. Quādo li ditti venghano in desgratia dil Signoro in veghieza si mādan a sario zoe castelli che sono guardiani & si cassano del libro de Ianizari & hāno entrate equalmente al suo primo soldo & li capi loro similmente vano castellani con timaro vtsupra.

Vno agha di Spachoglani capo cioe di destri giouene gentilhomo che a tra timaro e soldo ducat 10 il di con reghalie & 400 schiaui.

Vno Iaxagi scriuano de questi spacoglani ha àspri 30 il di con reghalie & 30 schiaui.

Vno Cacaia de ditti zoe protoiro a tra timaro soldo aspri 100 al di.

Sono li Spachoglani 3000 che hano aspri 20 in 40 il di secondo il grado loro & ogni 20 hano vno capo domandato Bolucbassi & questi seruano a caualo con 5 o 6 schiaui & altri tanti caualli per vno questi vano sempre ala man destra dil Signor, & alogiano appresso a lui in campo.

Vno Agha deto Selicterbassi capo de li sinistri che sono ala mā sinistra dil Signor ha aspri 250 il di & vno Protoiro cioe loco tenēte & vno scriuano co aspri 30 il di per vno questo Aga e capo di 3000 Selictari a cauallo che stano a la man sinistra dil Signore & hano aspri 20 in 25 al di p vno & hano 4. o. 5. schiaui & altri tanti caualli & lui capo a 200 schiaui soi.

Doi Holofagibassi da la man destra & sinistra uno per banda capi de li soldatia aspri 120 al di & hano 200 Holofagi sotto se cō aspri 16 il di pervno il suo logo tenente cō aspri 20 e vno scriuano cō aspri 20 & vano a cauallo con 2. o 3. caualli & tanti schiaui.

Doi Aga capo de li carippoglani zoe poueri gioueni che hano aspri 30 il di per vno cō il suo protoiro & scriuano con aspri 15 in 30 al di & sono li Carippoglani numero 2000 che hano da 7 sino in 14 aspri al di per vno li capi hano 25 schiaui per vno.

Doi Bracorbassi zoe maestri di stalla vno grande vno picolo il grāde a aspri 500 il di, & il picolo ne a 200 al di di soldo con protoiro & scriuano con 30 sino in 40 aspri il di per vno.

Sedici milia Sarachi zoe famigli che cōzano brene & selle Caysli zoe fanti di stalla Carmādari zoe mulateri deuegi zoe gābeleri che vano dreto a gambeli circirgli zoe mandreri che pascolano le mādre de li caualli in varii lochi hano di soldo da 2 sino ī 20 aspri il di pervno secōdo il grado loro chi pui che meno.

Caualli da caualcare per il Signor & soi puti & monuchi zoe castrati numero 4000.

Vno Zarchigibassi capo de li astori che al di soldo apri 150 il di & schiaui & vno Zarchigibassi capo di falconeri che a aspri 80 il di & schiaui con il sou protoiro & scriuano con aspri 25 per vno al di.

Vintimilia zainogiler homini a cauallo di lāza & mili soli de questi hāno soldo aspri 10 il di & resto hāno timari o vero exemption di angarie per essere homeni dil Signor & vano in campo.

Vno hebegibassi capu de le armature a aspri 60 il di con il suu protoiro & scriuan con aspri 20 per vno di soldo & à da 160 Ebegi zoe famigli sotto se con 7 fino in 10 aspri il di per vno, & vano a pede.

Vno Topgibassi capo de li bombarderi che ha aspri 60 il di con protoiro & scriuan con aspri 20 pervno & a 2000 Topgi sotto se zoe bombarderi cō 6 sino in 10 aspri il di soldo per vno o vano a pede.

Vno Arabagibassi capo de li careteri a aspri 40 il di con protoiro & scriuano con aspri 20 per vno & a 1000 Arabagi zoe careteri sotto se con 3 sino in 6 aspri il di per vno.

Vno Mecterbassi capo de li trombeteri & tamburini a aspri 30 il di con protoiro & scriuan con aspri 12 p vno di soldo al di & a 12 millia compagni sotto se che hano di soldo 3 sino in 5 aspri il diper vno parti vano a piedi & parti a cauallo & altre regalie.

Imralem aga Capitanio che porta il stendardo dil Signor a di soldo aspri 200 al di & e sopra tutti li mecteri zoe trombetti & tamburini & banderali.

Vno Arpaemin prouiditore de le biaue per il campo con vno protoiro & vno cursor le emin a aspri 60 il di protoiro a aspri 30 il cursor aspri 20 al di di soldo & a 20 persone sotto di lui con aspri 800 al di fra tutti quelli 20 persone.

Vno Saremin prouiditore de comun a cōzare le strade & fabricare in Constantinopli a aspri 50 il di, & a sotto di lui 400 homeni cō aspri 1000 al di fra tutti cō protoiro & scriuano cō aspri 57 il di per vno.

Vno Baratemin che dispensa tutti li comandamēti & che scode li denati de li ditti a aspri 40 il di & a 2 scriuani & doi soprastanti con aspri 60 il di per vno di soldo.

Vno Seraglio di donne in Constantinopli che circōda vno miglio e mezo cō stantie & camere doue stano li figlioli separati luno da laltro cō loro madre & monuchi, & soltane zoe molier dil Signor & li sono da 200 in 300 dōzelle sotto la custodia di molte matrone

veghi alequa il Signor fa insegnare a arica mar̄ diuersi lauori & a
cadauna li da di soldo asp 10 fino in 20 per vna secondo il grado
loro & ogni anno doi volte a li bairami zoe a le sue pasque li veste
tutte di setta, & lequal donzelle quādo piace alcuna desse al Signore
lui sta con lei & fa il fatto suo, & como la hauta li dona vna schufia
doro che val duc. 200 & aspri 10 millia di cōtadi & la fa stare in vna
camera separata da le altre & li cresse i soldo suo & q̄lla che fa
prima fioli quella e la sua moglie prima.

In ditto seraglio & de tutti li altri monuchi zoe castrati che sono in
detto seraglio a aspri 60 il di di soldo & stano in questo seraglio 20
monuchi & hano aspri 120 il di tra capigibassi zoe portinari &
Ianizari nu. 100 a le porte p guardia hāno aspri 500 al di fra tutti & numero 10 Sacha che portano laqua dētro zoe aquaroli &
hāno aspri 40 al di fra tutti di soldo.

Quando le donzelle sono in eta de anni 25 il Signor le maritta a li
schiaui di la porta zoe di la sua corte & in loco loro ne mete de le
altre & le piu giouan e seruano a le altre.

A vno seraglio appresso a perea de garzoni nu. 400. in circa che hano
di soldo da 6 fin in 10 aspri il di p vno & li veste dói volte alanno
di panno di seda si como fa a le dōne & vno Agha zoe capo del
seraglio & 20 monuchi como nel altro seraglio & capigi & Ianizeri
& maestri che imparano voltegiare a cauallo & īparano a sonare in
tutto numero 100 homeni che hāno aspri 600 al di di soldo tra tutti
& laga a aspri 60 il di di soldo & 10 sacha con aspri 40 il di di soldo
fra tutti li aquaroli.

Vno Seraglio in Andranopoli nouo con vno bel giardino appresso a
la mariza fiumera nel qual stano Ianizerotti numero 300 & hāno
aspri 12 al di per vno Andranopoli e 5 zornate lōtan da Constantinopoli.

Vno capo de detti zardineri a aspri 40 il di con vno protoiro & vno
scriuano che tengono cōto de ditto zardino con aspri 30 per vno al
di.

In diuersi lochi il Signor ha piu giardini in liquali son asai Ianizerotti
garzoni & soi capi hāno di soldo aspri 6000 al di fra tutti questi
giardini.

Vno aga de agiamoglani Capitanio zoe gioueni greci in Cōstātinopoli
a aspri 60 il di & a 4 in 5000 Iantizerotto sotto lui & li da di soldo
tra tutti alāno ne a di spesa aspri 100 millia & liveste due fiate
alanno & hano li loro capi como li altri & questi se metano sopra
fabriche & condutte legne co nauigli in Constantinopoli per il

Signor & altre stente poi si fano coghi & famegli di Ianizeri & in fino si fano Ianizeri.

Ogni 4 anni il Signor manda a tore di gretia & di Natolia piu figlioli de christiani per il paxe zoe p leville & doue vno padre ha 2 fioli li piglian vno fiol p forza & lo fano turco & cosi a ognuno christiani p il suo paese fano zoe soi subditi & ne piglia 10 ī 12000 a la volta liquali puti li sano stare in la Natolia zoe in asia a zapare la terra acio imparano la lingua turcha & cosi stentano 3. o vero 4. anni & poi li manda a scriuere sotto laga di agiamoglani ditto vtsupra & di questi il Signor non ne a spesa alcuna per che sono vestiti & fatto le spese da quelli a che seruano per che li mete a stare cō altri sino chano imparato la lingua & poi quando sono scritti li da soldo per la prima 2. in 3 aspri per vno & secōdo li mete in altri officii li cresce il salario.

Ha di spesa in li altri seragli di viuere aspri 5000 il di ditto di sopra.

Veste due fiate alanno li Bassa zoe confieri defterderi zoe texoreri beglerbeii zoe Signor de Soignori nesangibei zoe quello che sopra di frutti dil Signor & presenti di spexa aspri 5000 per volte.

Vna Arsenale doue ten le sue galere che a volti 100 zoe 30 di galere grosse che si domandano maone p portare caualli & il resto sono galere futile.

Tene continuamenti numero 200 patroni de galere pagati che hāno soldo fra tutti aspri 200000 alanno di spexa.

Tene continuo mille homeni axapi zoe marinero di galeri & ne a di spexa alāno fra tutti aspri 400000.

Maistri ouero proti numero 50 che sono sopra a far lauorare le galere zoe farle chi inocio hanno soldo aspri 6 il di & quando lauorano hāno aspri 12 il di.

Emino zoe capo de questi a aspri 40 il di vno scriuan che ten conto ha aspri 28 al di con 10 scriuani sotto lui con aspri 80 al di fra tutti.

El Zustiniano zoe vno zentilomo Venetiano che serue il Turcho & e sopra a far fare galere ancora lui spexe straordinaria ha di soldo aspri 50 il di.

Vno Beglerbei dil mar zoe Signor de Signori capo sopra le terre maritime che a di entrata duc, 14000 & traze piu dil duplo sopra rodi metelino negropōte & il tributo di sio isole in mar.

Il Beglerbei di la gretia zoe capo di tutto il paese di la gretia magior de tutti li altri a di entrada ducati 260 millia a lanno & traze il duplo & a schiaui 1000.

Vno protoiro zoe loco tenente di la gretia a ducati 4000 di entrada a lanno & a schiaui 300.

Vno Deftero zoe texorero de le entrate di la gretia che loro domandano timari a ducati 3000 de entra da a lanno & ha 900 schiaui soi seruitori.

Cento scriuani che tengono li libri & cōti dil Signor a di entrada fra tutti a lanno ducati 10000.

Trentasette Sanzachibei zoe contadi Signori per il paese che han di entrada di 5 in 12 millia ducati a lanno secondo il grado loro chi piu chi meno & hāno vno per laltro in tutto duca, 260 millia a lanno & 300 schiaui per vno.

Quatrocento Subasi per il paxe dil Signor zoe Capitanio di Iustitia che hāno duc. 100 alanno per vno di entrada & hāno 50 schiaui per vno soi famigli.

Trenta millia Spachi che hanno di entrada luno per laltro ducati 200 per vno alanno & ciaschaduno de ditti per ogni ducati 100 che hāno di entrada deue tener vno homo armato di lanza a cauallo & oltra le lanze hanno tre o 4 famigli per vno & altri tanti caualli zoe li Spachi.

Vintimillia Trimarati zoe q̄lli che scodano le entrate per il paese hano duc 40 de di entrata alanno p vno & per che non ariuano a li 100 ducati dintrada nō si chiamano spachi & sono homeni a cauallo & vano in campo.

Li Spacoglani li sopradetti timari cioe entrade de le decime de tutte le entrade cosi de christiani como di turchi splenza aspri 25 per testa da li christiani & da langaria de li animali & altra quanto pagano dil Signor zoe piu o meno secondo diuersi paesi.

Sesantamillia Iaching zoe ventureri scritti per il paese obligadi andare in campo quando piace al Signor senza soldo & quando vano a la guerra le ville & cita li dano il modo dil viuere.

Tutti li spachi sono schiaui & figli de schiaui del Sig.

Sette Beglerbei zoe Signor de signori sopra bassavno che se chiama di la natolia ilquale era antichamēte in assia minore il qual a di entrata ducati 24000 & ne traze assai piu & a sotto se il ponte labitinia azia ppia Lindia carian, licia prouincie & a schiaui 1000 soi seruitori & a sanzachi 12 sotto lui zoe Signoroti cō entrada da 4 in 6000 ducati alanno per vno & schiaui 500 pervno & Spachi 1000 sotto se cō soldo da 5 in 10 aspri al di pervno secōdo la cōdition loro & q̄ste Beglerbei e di piu authorita de li altri & e forte nominato per il paese questi Spachi nō hano tanta entrata como vtsupra per essere piu abondantia la.

Beglerbei de caramania chera silicia & pamlilia prouincie ha di entrata ducati 10 millia & a 7 sanzachi sotto se con soldo ditte & spachi numero 500 sotto cō soldo como laltro beglerbei & schiaui mille.

Beglerbei di auādoule che e tra la soria & Caramania & tocato era gia Pamphlagonia che e la mita di larmenia minore ha di entrada ducati 10 millia alanno & sette sanzachi che hano di entrada da 4 in 5000 ducati alāno & a schiaui 100 & Spachi 700 sotto lui quando il Signor hera fora si dice questo Beglerbei faceua persone da caualcare senza soldo numero 30 millia.

Beglerbei di la mexopotania sotti ilqual e il resto di larmenia minor & parte di la magiore che laltra parte e dil Sophi & dacordo a di entrata ducati trenta millia & schiaui due millia & sanzachi 12 con entrata vt supra & spachi diece millia cō soldo vtsupra & confina con baldach zoe la babilonia vera.

Baglerbei di Damascho & Soria & Giudea a di entrada ducati 24 millia & schiaui due millia & sanzachi 12 con entrata vtsupra & a Spachi numero vintimillia sotto di lui.

Beghlerbei di Alcario ha di entrata ducati trentamillia & schiaui quarto millia Sāzachi 16 con entrada vr supra pervno & Spachi sedeci millia sotto lui & Ianizeri tre millia & va fina alamecha cioe fina a la arabia liquali ello possede como si fa deli albanesi per forza benche la arabia felize stia in magior obedientia.

Tra lamecha & Sophi sono alcuni Signori arabi poi il resto confina con il Sophi fina in la mexopotania in laqual e baldach zoe Babilonia poi passato la mexopotania cōfina il Suphi ne la pianura di nassimō poi exdrun & extum che sono in la armenia mazore laqual cōfina con Zorgiani & hiberi & ne larmenia mazor & minor sono assai cordi obedienti quelli de la mazor parte al Signor Turcho & parte al Sophi Re di persia & trabixonda lucho de Imperio in mar magior cōfina con mengreli zoe mengrelia doue non si spende danari & ancora confina cō giorgiani che antichamente si dimandauano colchi azamia chera asiria e dil Sophi.

Armenia magior e minor sono christiani assai di quelli di san Thomaso trabixonda sono greci & mengreli sono christiani & giorgiani sono christiani.

Ottoma hebe in sua cōpagnia ad acqstare il dominio vno michali greco fatto turco dal qual son dissexi li mazalogli zoe mamaluchi de laqual stirpe ne vno hora sanzaco in bosina zoe Conte devna prouiucia.

Malco greco renegato alqual sono nasiuti li malcozogli, & di quella stirpe ne vno & e Sanzaco in gretia. Aurami che si chiamano Eurcassi de laqual stirpe non si sa che ne sia alcun hora.

Tutti questi generatione promisse ottoman di nō mettere mai mane nel sangue loro ne mancharli mai di magistrato & ancora si conserua la promessa fatali & questi furono quelli che aiutorno la caxa ottomana.

Intrada dil gran Turcho de caragi zoe tributatii caua ducati 1300000 da la Natolia & grecia caua ducati 1600000 di Egipto caua duc. 700000 de Soria caua ducati 150000 de mexopotania ducati 250000 questi danari caua si non di terra ferma senza le Isole che sotto lui & li douane di Constantinopli e pera.

Le entrate che se dice disse il Signor Aluise Gritti che sono piu presto piu che meno & la spexa di la porta zoe di la corte dil Signor penso che cōsuma tutta la entrada o poco meno.

Li Beglerbei di egitto stano sotto il beglerbei di Alcairo per la magior parte & li sono Sanzachi sino in lamecha doue sta larcha de macomet Zingil Ghebur Iurcan & Tibris fiumi dil Paradiso Terestro.

Li Beglerbei & li Sanzachi a chi piu chi meno secōdo la autorita sua & son pagati de li territori doue st no escetto quelli che pigliano soldo dil gran Turcho la entrada de li ditti non si po sapere a ponto bisogna per arbitrio pensarla zoe de quelli di egitto.

QVI SI DICHIARA TVTTI LI SANZACHI

zoe contadi che sono sotto li Beglerbei & si nomina li paexi doue sono & Prouincie doue stano e prima.

Li Sanzachi zoe Contadi che sono sotto il Beglerbei di la Gretia prima.

1 Gretia.
2 Cafa.
3 Silistria.
4 Nicopoli.
5 Vidin.
6 Suornich.
7 Bossina.
8 Ersech del Ducato.
9 Samandria belgrado.
10 Seruia.
11 Belgrado.
12 Schutari.
13 Valona.
14 Carlali.
15 Negroponte.
16 Lepanto.
17 Morea.
18 Trighala.
19 Galipoli.
20 Quaranta Giexie.
21 Vissa.
22 Crimen:
23 Ochria.
24 Giostaudil.
25 Vlzitrin.
26 Pisdren.
27 Alzasar.
28 Albasan.
29 Voinuch.

30 Ciuchene.
31 Zaiza.
Filipopoli.
Sofia.

Durazo.
Albania.
Schopia.

Li Sanzachi che sono sotto il Beglerbei di la Natolia zoe Asia minor.
1 Giotachie.
2 Cogia olli.
3 Bolli.
4 Castamoni.
5 Anghori.

6 Caugri.
7 Tescheli.
8 Metesseli.
9 Haeid neli.
10 Allaye.
11 Buga.
12 Manguixa il statto.

Li Sanzachi che sono sotto il Beglerbei di Cappadocia.
1 Amassia.
2 Cioriun.

3 Giauich.
4 Caraister.
5 Sauisum.
6 Trapixonda.

Li Sanzachi che sono sotto il Beglerbei di Caramania.
1 Siogna.

2 Naranda.
3 Assar.
4 Eschi assar.

Li Sanzachi che sono sotto il Beglerbei di Auandoule.
1 Maras.
2 Sarmus Sachi.

3 Albistanouasi.
4 Adaria.
5 Tersis.

Li Sāzachi che sono sotto il beglerbei di mesopotāia.
1 Dierbech.
2 Carachmit.
3 Argni.
4 Solgich.
5 Casangieph.

6 Meridim.
7 Carput.
8 Mussul.
9 Exrun.
10 Haiburth.
Dittilis.   Nassim nouasi.

Li Sanzachi che sono sotto il Beglerbei di Soria.
Damasco.
Malatia.
Dirmighi.
Antep.
Antiocha.

Aleppo.
Tripoli.
Cama ama.
Cams.
Sefetto.
Ieroxalem.
Gazara.

Questi sono i lochi che ha sotto il Turco.

Questo sie la ordenanza dil Cāpo dil Signore zoe dil gran Turcho quādo và a la guerra primamente vna quātita di spacoglani gētilomini con lanza & spada.

Inanze al primo bassa li va numero 15 caualli ornati p la sua persona con vno Ianizero per banda.

E poi tre garzoni vestiti doro con schufie doro rosse vno li porta larcho vno li porta le veste & vno li porta il ramin da laqua.

E poi vno Aga con schufia doro zoe Capitanio.

E poi doi garzoni senza milza arente al bassa.

E poi mille Ianizeri schopeteri a piedi.

E poi da 60 Sanzachi zoe stendardi a cauallo.

E poi trombetti e tamburin insiema a cauallo.

E poi il campo a refuso de diuersi generationi e de diuersi lanze tutti a cauallo.

E poi gambelli muli bagaie del campo.

E poi Gentilomeni Spachi a cauallo con spada & archo e frize solle.

E poi li cari de lartelaria.

E poi caualli numero 30 con briglie doro per la persona dil Signor.

E poi tutti li capi de li Ianizari zoe Boluchbassi Odabassi a cauallo con barete doro aguze con vno penagio di garzette bianche in zima con lanze & con le banderolle zalle.

E poi 12 milia Ianizeri con schiopetti alabarde apedi.

E poi li solachi apedi staferi dil Signor cō archi e frize

E poi il gran Turcho sollo in mezo di Solachi.

E poi 3 garzoni con schufie doro vestiti di pāno doro che li portano archo e frize e laqua & veste.

E poi 2 monuchi sēza coioni a cauallo dreto al signor

E poi Imralemaga ch' porta il stēdardo dil Signor tutto verde sollo.

E poi 6 Sanzachi zoe bandere vna rossa vna biācha vna verde due diuixa vna rossa e bianca & vna verde e rosso a cauallo.

E poi trombeteri & tamburi a cauallo.

E poi il campo arefuxo con li dulipante a cauallo cō lanze e spada con le banderole rosse.

A la banda destra dil Signor Spacoglani a cauallo cō lanze con banderole zalle.

A la banda sinistra dil Signor Selictari a cauallo con lanze con banderolle rosse e bianche.

E poi gambelli & mulli e bagaie dil campo e pagi.

E poi Spachi con lanze a cauallo con dulipāti biāchi.

E poi vno bassa solo con soi Stafeti.

E poi 22 Sanzachi zoe stendardi a cauallo.

E poi trombeteri tamburi a cauallo.

E poi il campo a refuso de diuerse sorte con dulipant & barette rosse de piu sorte generatione.

E poi gambelli e muli e bagaie dil campo insema.

E poi tutti li Iachingi zoe ventureri.

Questo libro e stato cauato da Ionus bei il qual era greco & hora e turcho & e interpetro grande dil Signor & dal Signor Aluise gritti fiol dil Duxo di Venetia & tutto e vero.

APPENDIX III

INCOMPLETE TABLE OF CONTENTS OF THE KANUN-NAMEH, OR COLLECTION OF EDICTS, OF SULEIMAN THE MAGNIFICENT AS ARRANGED BY THE MUFTI EBU SU'UD

Translated from the Turkish

[From folios 69–70 of the Turkish MS. Fluegel No. 1816, Imperial Library, Vienna: "Fundamental Laws of Sultan Suleiman, according to the arrangement of the Mufti Ebu-Su'ud." The table does not begin till folio 27 of the manuscript. The page references are to Hammer's *Staatsverfassung*, where a translation of the paragraphs may be found.]

APPENDIX IV

THE GOVERNMENT OF THE MOGUL EMPIRE IN INDIA[1]

"The uncommon abilities of most of the princes, with the mild and humane character of all, rendered Hindostan the most flourishing empire in the world during two complete centuries."—Dow.

GENERAL COMPARISON OF OTTOMAN AND INDIAN CONDITIONS

WHEN Baber first rode down through the grim gates of India's northwest mountain-wall, the accession of Suleiman lay but a year in the future; the Mogul won the battle of Panipat but four months before the Turk was victorious at Mohacs. Thus the founding of the Mogul Empire nearly coincided with the meridian splendor of the Ottoman power, and its decisive battle of establishment with the victory which led to the last great extension of Ottoman authority into Europe. Not Baber or even Akbar, Suleiman's contemporaries, but Aurangzeb, whose reign began a century after Suleiman's death, affords the closest comparison with the Turkish monarch; yet the third battle of Panipat in 1761 marked the virtual destruction of the Mogul Empire, whereas the second battle of Mohacs in 1687 meant but the first noteworthy step of the Ottoman retreat. The house of Timur has disappeared from history, while the house of Osman still reigns over wide territories; less than two and a half centuries of genuine sovereign rule were enjoyed by the Moguls, while six centuries have not sufficed to measure the independent existence of the Ottomans.

The Mogul emperors perhaps never ruled so large a territory as the Ottoman sultans, but their lands were far more productive; moreover, having from five to ten times as many subjects as their Western cousins and an income in proportion, they could surpass even the Magnificent Suleiman in display and largesse. The inferior persistence of their dominion, therefore, suggests inferior strength and stability in their institutions, a suggestion to which even a limited investigation lends much support.

[1] The object of this appendix is to set forth in outline the features of the Mogul government, in order to suggest comparison with that of the Ottoman Empire. Completeness neither of research nor of exposition has been attempted. A list of the authorities consulted, most of which are secondary, will be found at the end of the appendix.

The Moguls shared with the Ottomans their relation to the ideas of the Mongol and Turkish Tatars of the steppe lands, and to those of the Persians and the Arabs. They were more directly and vitally influenced by the Tatars and Persians, and less directly by the Arabs. Farther than this their relations were not to the comparatively organized and energetic civilization of the Mediterranean but to the more speculative and passive culture of India. Over the lands into which they entered as conquerors lay the shadow not of sternly practical Roman legalism, but of Hindu and Buddhist contempt for things mundane.

They founded a despotism, but one that was never, even under Aurangzeb, so closely related to the Sacred Law of Mohammed as was the government of Suleiman. They ruled a variety of lands in a variety of relationships, but never with the stern control exercised by the *Kaisar-i-Rûm* (Roman emperor), the name which they gave to the Turkish ruler at Constantinople. They enforced the obedience of many peoples, who spoke many languages and practised many forms of religion; yet they never held these peoples under any such iron system of subjection as that which dominated the Christian subjects of the sultan, even to the seizure of their children for tribute.

Since the passing of those prehistoric times when all human ideas were solidified together into a single " crust of custom," every nation has probably had two leading institutions, more or less closely connected, — the one of religion and the other of government. The foregoing pages have shown how powerful and pervasive were the Ottoman Ruling Institution and the Moslem Institution in the Ottoman Empire. In the parallel organizations of the empire of the Moguls, however, it is not possible to discern comparable unique individuality, systematic structure, and ordered efficiency. Some allowance must be made for a comparative lack of information, since not many Western observers have described the more distant empire; but this fact can hardly alter the conclusion materially. The institutional structure of the Mogul Empire was decidedly inferior to that of the Ottoman Empire in solidity, system, and persistent energy.

THE PERSONNEL OF THE MOGUL GOVERNMENT

Baber's following consisted of the comrades of his many years of fighting, an army of cavalry, artillery, and musketry composed in ancient Turkish fashion of high-spirited men attached to their chief by impressive leadership and open-handed generosity. Courage, military prowess, and the nominal profession of Islam were the necessary qualifications; differences of race, education, and Moslem doctrine were disregarded. Warriors of Turki stock, Persians of Shiite leanings, hardy Afghans, " Roman " artillery engineers from Stambul, were equals in the rough brotherhood of Baber's camp. The principle of subordination, at least among persons of consequence, was not that of slaves to their master, but of tribesmen to their chief, of vassals to their honored suzerain.

When Turks had first invaded India, five centuries before, slavery as a means of recruiting and training soldiers and governors was in full swing. Mahmûd of Ghazni was the son of a father who had risen through slavery. The thirteenth century saw enthroned at Delhi a dynasty of slave kings which antedated by several decades the Mamelukes of Egypt. Late in the fourteenth century Firoz III owned 180,000 slaves, of whom 40,000 constituted his household. The Mameluke government endured for more than two and a half centuries, until overthrown by the more centralized and efficient slave system of the Ottomans; but in Central Asia and ultimately in India a new force speedily rendered the slave method, save for some survivals, antiquated and impossible.

The dominance of the Mongols was based on the discipline of an army of freemen who were intelligent enough willingly to render absolute obedience to their officers as the well-tested condition of certain success. With the break-up of the vast Mongol Empire, the lands now in Russian Central Asia, Afghanistan, and Persia lapsed toward the horde organization of nomad Tatars, but became more and more modified by Moslem feudalism. Under such conditions, Timur, high-born and adventurous, chivalrous and literary, fanatical and cruel, achieved an empire that was large and splendid, but personal to himself, and destined to vanish almost with its founder. Yet he presaged a time when in Asia and Europe alike there should come, after the disintegrating individualism of the fourteenth and fifteenth centuries, a period of the gathering together of lands and peoples into large units under strong personal governments.

Baber, descendent of Timur in the sixth generation, descendant also of Genghis Khan, came at the beginning of the new era. Less ruthless than either of his great ancestors, less legal than the " Inflexible One," less Moslem than the " Scourge of Asia," but possessed of much of the leadership and military genius of both, he stands forth, by reason of his memoirs, as one of the best known conquerors of history. His love of carousing, his family affection, his literary bent, his toleration of heretics and infidels, his bold leadership, his liberality in dividing spoil, presented qualities and suggested modes of activity which were to characterize all his descendants down to the puritanical Aurangzeb.

Thus the family life of the house of Baber was far more normal than that of the house of Osman. In contrast with an almost unbroken line of Ottoman slave mothers and wives, whose names with those of their daughters have hardly survived, many of the Mogul imperial ladies are well known. Witness the princess Gul-Badan, daughter of Baber, who like her father wrote memoirs; the empress Nur-Jehan, who ruled India for a time; and the empress Mumtaz-Mahal, for whom her devoted husband built the fairest of all mausoleums. Turki princesses, ladies of high Persian descent, and daughters of Hindu *Rajahs*, were taken into the imperial harem, where, though women and eunuchs were present " from Russia, Circassia, Mingrelia, Georgia, and Ethiopia," no emperors sprang from slave mothers during the period of greatness. With such a policy in the family which constituted a chief element in the unity of the Mogul Empire, it was but natural that officers and soldiers, statesmen and public servants, should be accepted with a like catholicity. The best fighters, of course, continued to be those who came down newly from the high country beyond the northwest passes; and since such of these as met success were apt to send for relatives and friends, there was continual recruiting from among Tatars, Persians, Afghans, and Arabs, — all Moslems, but of various sects. " Rûmis " from the Ottoman Empire were especially useful in the artillery service. Some of them were doubtless European renegades, but " Firinjis " or Franks were likely to come more directly from Portugal and other European countries. Yet by no means all the brave were from foreign lands. Many Rajputs under their own *Rajahs* served the Mogul emperors most acceptably, and when treated without prejudice they were faithful. The high officers of government were usually Persians; but Akbar was nobly served by the great Todar Mal, and appointed *Rajahs* to govern the Punjab and Bengal. About one in eight of his paid cavalry chiefs was a Hindu; and of the lesser civil-service positions the mere necessity for numbers, apart from superior skill and training, required that many should be held by Hindus.

It is not that slavery had disappeared from the Mogul system. Traces of the old method can be discerned as late as the eighteenth century. In fact, Muhammad Khan, a Bangash *Nawab* of Farrukhabad, maintained what was practically a replica in miniature of the Ottoman system. Hindu boys between the ages of seven and thirteen, some of them sons of Rajputs and Brahmins, were seized, bought, or accepted as *chelas* or slaves to the number of one or two hundred a year. They were taught to read and write, and were specially rewarded when the task was completed. Five hundred *chelas* from eighteen to twenty years of age were trained as a regiment of musketeers. From among the older *chelas* were chosen the officers of the household, generals of the army, and deputy governors of provinces. The *Nawab* arranged marriages between *chelas* and the daughters of *chelas*. He encouraged them to acquire personal property, which he could claim in time of need; but he forbade them to found towns or build masonry structures, lest occupying these they might tend toward independence. Muhammad Khan did not, however, depend exclusively on his Hindu slaves; he sent money to his own Bangash tribe, and thus obtained a colony of Afghans to whom he gave high military positions and upon some of whom he bestowed his daughters in marriage. Other vassals of the emperor made use of a similar slave system; and it is not unlikely that the emperor himself recruited his permanent infantry with the help of slavery, and that he promoted some slaves to high positions. But the absence of definite information in this direction is in most striking contrast to its abundant presence in the records which deal with the Ottoman Empire in the sixteenth century.

In theory the officers of government were so far the servants of the emperor that their accumulated personal property belonged to him at their death; but in practice the opulence and the generosity of the sovereign led him often to leave such wealth in the hands of the officers' children. When this was not done, employment in the public service was assigned to sons and pensions were granted to widows.

Titles of nobility were awarded for life to distinguished officials; the chief officers of the central government and governors of great provinces were called *Emirs* (*Omrahs* in many Western writings, probably a plural of majesty), generals of the army were *Khans*, and distinguished soldiers of lesser rank were *Bahadurs* or knights. Khondamir says that Humayun organized a system of twelve orders or arrows, according to which the entire imperial household was graded. "The twelfth arrow, which was made of the purest gold, was put in the auspicious quiver of this powerful king, and nobody could dare to touch it. The eleventh arrow belonged to His Majesty's relations and brethren, and all the sultans who were in the government employ. Tenth, to the great *mushaikhs, saiyids,* and the learned and religious men. Ninth, to the great nobles. Eighth, to the courtiers and some of the king's personal attendants. Seventh, to the attendants in general. Sixth, to the *harems* and to the well-behaved female attendants. Fifth, to young maid-servants. Fourth, to the treasurers and stewards. Third, to the soldiers. Second, to the menial servants. First, to the palace guards, camel-drivers, and the like. Each of these arrows or orders had three grades; the highest, the middle, and the lowest." Appointments and promotions were, as at Constantinople, based upon valor and manifest ability. Through all the period of greatness the ladder of advancement was kept so clear that vigor, courage, and prowess could mount from the lowest ranks to the steps of the throne.

RELATION OF GOVERNMENT TO RELIGIOUS PROPAGATION

When the Ottoman Turks conquered their European territories, as well as parts of their Asiatic dominions, they for the first time introduced the Moslem religion. This was not the case with the Mogul advance into India. Beginning with Mohammed ben Kasim's invasion of Sind in 712 A.D., and starting afresh with Mahmûd of Ghazni in 1000 A.D., the Moslem political control, accompanied by the conversion of a portion of the native population, had spread step by step until, when Baber came after eight centuries, there remained little of India that was not actually or had not at some time been under Moslem rule. No data appear to exist for determining the actual proportion of the total population that was Moslem during the Mogul period. Guesses have been made ranging from a possible one in four to Bernier's estimate of one in hundreds. The only basis of any value would perhaps be that obtained by working backward from the British censuses. In 1911 the Mohammedans constituted about twenty-one per cent of the population of India, and their number was increasing at a slightly more rapid rate than the average. It may be supposed that the increase of the Moslem proportion was greater during the days of the Mogul Empire, when it was especially profitable to change, and when there was a strong inward flow at the northwest; but since the Mogul decline the rate of relative progress has probably always been slow. Perhaps the proportion about 1761 was somewhat less than one in five, and in 1526 it may have been not more than one in from ten to twenty. Bernier's guess would certainly seem to have been wild, for it is inconceivable that so small progress would have been made in a thousand years and so great in the next two hundred. No doubt the Moslem contingent was then, as it is now, unevenly distributed, being in high proportion in the northwest and diminishing gradually with the distance from the mountain passes. At points on the seacoast where trade had been active, the Moslem influence had come early by way of the sea; hence there also the percentage was greater. In Suleiman's empire, comprising as it did a large amount of old Moslem territory and including even the Holy Cities, the proportion of Moslems was, of course, much higher; but it diminished rapidly from south to north, until in Hungary it must have been extremely attenuated.

In the absence of an elaborate slave system in India, there was not the steady public machinery of conversion which operated powerfully in the Ottoman Empire. Furthermore, it would seem that before the reign of Aurangzeb no emperor cared to promote conversion to Islam by financial or political rewards. Akbar, in fact, removed the *jizyeh*, or poll-tax, which had previously, as in all other truly Moslem lands until recent times, laid special burdens upon unbelievers, and the tax was not reimposed until the time of Aurangzeb. Akbar also forbade the enslavement of captives and of their wives and children. For a century, therefore, the government lent little encouragement to change of faith. Down to the accession of Aurangzeb there was a clear contrast between Ottoman and Mogul policy in the attitude toward the Moslem religion: the Moguls held far less than the Ottomans to the idea of the conquest of the world for Islam, or to the conversion of unbelievers, as an object of governmental endeavor. Aurangzeb alone had such zeal as characterizes the average descendant of Osman; he desired no infidels in his service, and regarded the Deccan as the *Dar-ul-harb* which he wished to make part of the *Dar-ul-Islam*. There can be no doubt, however, that under all the Mogul emperors the social pressure usual in Moslem lands continued to encourage conversion privately, while the slavery which Islam normally sanctions was also contributing to the increase of the faithful. Moreover, it is not likely that all the officers of the liberal emperors were as tolerant and as indifferent to Moslem progress as were their superiors.

The Army

At Delhi, as at Constantinople, no sharp line could be drawn separating government and army. The Mogul conquest was achieved by an army, and the army became a government. Amalgamation with older systems of course introduced groups of under-officials who had no military duties; but those who would be great had to be capable of military command, men who might be familiar with the pen but who must know how to wield the sword.

The Mogul army organization seems, in the midst of confused testimonies, to have borne a considerable resemblance to that of the Ottomans. The emperor was commander-in-chief, and as late as Aurangzeb regularly commanded in person in great campaigns. He had a personal army of 12,000 to 15,000 paid infantry and 12,000 to 40,000 paid cavalry. These corresponded in number and function, but not at all in political importance, to the Janissaries and *Spahis* of the Porte among the Ottomans. In great campaigns the standing army was supported by the feudal cavalry, estimated at from 200,000 to 400,000, and by indefinite numbers of irregular infantry, drawn from a mass estimated at four millions. The army was strong in artillery, and possessed in trained elephants a force of which the Ottomans could not make use.

The emperor's infantry were, at least from Akbar's time, matchlockmen; they seem to have been the only trustworthy and efficient foot-soldiers. It would appear that their clumsy weapons, improved by Akbar himself, were not changed up to the time of Aurangzeb; for Bernier reports that in his day the muskets were rested on forks and fired by men who squatted on the ground, and who feared that the flash might damage their eyebrows and beards. On account of the method of payment it is not possible to estimate closely the number of the emperor's cavalry, or *Mansabdars*. Men who agreed to furnish from five to five thousand troopers were taken into his service, and pay (*mansab*) was assigned for the stipulated number; but even in Akbar's time, according to Badauni, it was possible to present followers hired only for the occasion, and yet to draw lifelong pay for their services. In later years there ceased to be even approximate correspondence between the amount of pay and the number of troops furnished. The *mansab* was then regarded as a salary, or even as a pension.

The more numerous feudal cavalry consisted of the holders (with their followers) of *jagirs*, or grants, of the revenue of districts of larger or smaller size, in return for which they served without other pay, except in case of unduly prolonged campaigns. Holders of large areas were accustomed to administer them in person, whereas those who held smaller sections would often leave the administration to the governors of provinces, who in time tended to appropriate the revenues. Aurangzeb, however, pursued the policy of assigning service in regions remote from the appointee's *jagir*, and of retaining wives and children at the court as pledges of fidelity. Hindu *Rajahs* were easily brought into the system by being invested with analogous rights in their hereditary territories. Apart from these cases, the appointments, as in Turkey, were not regarded as hereditary, but were apt to be given to fresh recruits of ability from beyond the mountains. It was customary to make small assignments to sons of dead *Jagirdars*, and to increase their allowances upon proof of merit. *Jagirdars* and *Rajahs*, like Timariotes and *Zaims*, had jurisdiction and other governmental duties in the areas assigned to them, and thus carried a large part of the task of local government. Ultimately many of the higher positions became hereditary in families which worked toward independence in the days of decline.

The artillery seems to have been surprisingly strong under Baber and Humayun, and to have declined later. Baber is said to have had seven hundred guns at Panipat, which he chained together after the method employed by Selim I at Kaldiran. Humayun is reported to have had at Kanauj seven hundred guns discharging stone balls of five pounds weight, and twenty-one guns discharging brass balls ten times as heavy. Aurangzeb, it is said, transported seventy pieces of heavy artillery and two or three hundred swivel guns, mounted on the backs of camels. For fortress defence and siege operations the Moguls had a few enormous guns, some of which are said to have required for transport two hundred and fifty and even five hundred oxen! In addition to these resources, it appears, if testimonies can be trusted, that Akbar kept five thousand war elephants, each of which was accounted equal in time of battle to five hundred horsemen; and Hawkins says that Jehangir had twelve thousand elephants of all descriptions. Aurangzeb is reported to have maintained in the palace stables the more modest number of eight hundred elephants.

The early Mogul armies were efficient and successful. Aurangzeb, however, conducted about the Deccan in his twenty-four years' war of conquest a horde that resembled a migration rather than an army. For each fighting man there were at least two camp-followers; the march was without discipline and order, like the movement of a herd of animals; and the camp was a city five miles long, or, as others say, seven and a half miles, or twenty miles in circumference. One European observer even reported that the encampment was thirty miles about, and contained five million souls! Among these he counted seven hundred thousand soldiers, of whom three hundred thousand were cavalry. With all due allowance for exaggeration, the Mogul army clearly tended to become exceedingly numerous, but of increasing weakness and inefficiency. A battle in 1526 between Baber and Suleiman would have been a worthy contest, but the army of Aurangzeb would probably have been defeated easily by the Ottoman troops which bit the dust before Prince Eugene.

THE COURT

Splendid as was the display of Suleiman's *entourage*, it lacked the financial basis which the Moguls possessed from Akbar to Aurangzeb. Gold and silver, gems, silks and muslins, were far more abundant in the eastern land. A more highly developed architecture, showing far greater richness of detailed ornamentation, served in India to construct not only temples of religion and tombs of great personages, but also marvellous palaces and pleasure-houses for the emperors. Many thousands of attendants supplied every possible luxury and rendered every conceivable service.

No systematic description of the organization of the imperial household has come to hand. Scattered allusions reveal the presence of very numerous groups of officials, agents, and servants of all grades. Teachers, physicians, scholars, valets, chamberlains, butlers, cooks, kitchen servants, musicians, poets, generals, captains, guards, equerries, hostlers, herdsmen, elephant-drivers, and stablemen, ministers of state, judges, treasurers, secretaries, swarmed about the great halls and myriad chambers of the palaces at Agra, Delhi, and Fatehpur-Sikri. These, with the tradespeople who made their living by supplying the household but who were less directly attached to the emperor, constituted a migratory city of large size, which followed the emperor from residence to residence and in time of campaign swelled almost unbelievably the following of his enormous army.

As for the court life which went on at the center of this vast and multi-colored setting, this was necessarily twofold, by that custom of all Moslem lands according to which the sexes must be segregated. Daily assemblages, gatherings at the mosques on Fridays, great ceremonies for special occasions, and the imperial hunts contained none but men as participants. If women saw any part of such festivities, it was from a distance and through thick veils or close-wrought lattices. Khondamir says that Humayun divided his attendants into three great classes, concerned respectively with government and war, with learning and literature, and with music and personal grace and beauty. The latter were called "people of pleasure . . . because most people take great delight in the company of such young-looking men, of rosy cheeks and sweet voices, and are pleased by hearing their songs, and the pleasing sound of the musical instruments, such as the harp, the sackbut, and the lute." Humayun devoted Sundays and Tuesdays to dealings with the first class, holding audience and attending to government duties on those days. Saturdays and Thursdays were days when "the tree of the hope" of literary and religious persons "produced the fruit of prosperity by their obtaining audience in the paradise-resembling court." Mondays and Wednesdays were devoted to pleasure parties, when old companions and chosen friends were entertained by musicians and singers. On Fridays were convened "all the assemblies," whatever this may mean; and the emperor sat with them as long as he could.

The splendor of the court may be illustrated by two or three extracts. Nizam-uddin Ahmad relates that Akbar, journeying in the fifteenth year of his reign, accepted an invitation to rest at Dipalpur. "For some days feasting went on, and upon the last day splendid offerings were presented to him. Arab and Persian horses, with saddles of silver; huge elephants, with chains of gold and silver, and housings of velvet and brocade; and gold and silver, and pearls and jewels, and rubies and garnets of great price; chairs of gold, and silver vases, and vessels of gold and silver; stuffs of Europe, Turkey, and China, and other precious things beyond all conception. Presents of similar kind also were presented for the young princes and the emperor's wives. All the ministers and attendants and dignitaries received presents, and every soldier of the army also participated in the bounty."

Sir Thomas Roe describes a curious annual ceremony of the Mogul emperors as carried through by Jehangir. "The first of September was the King's Birth-day, and the solemnitie of his weighing, to which I went, and was carryed into a very large and beautiful Garden, the square within all water, on the sides flowers and trees, in the midst a Pinacle, where was prepared the scales, being hung in large tressels, and a crosse beame plated on with Gold thinne: the scales of massie Gold, the borders set with small stones, Rubies and Turkeys, the Chaines of Gold large and massie, but strengthened with silke Cords. Here attended the Nobilitie, all sitting about it on Carpets until the King came; who at last appeared clothed or rather loden with Diamonds, Rubies, Pearles, and other precious vanities, so great, so glorious; his Sword, Target, Throne to rest on, correspondent; his head, necke, breast, armes, above the elbows, at the wrists, his fingers every one, with at least two or three Rings; fettered with chaines, or dyalled Diamonds; Rubies as great as Wal-nuts, some greater; and Pearles such as mine eyes were amazed at. Suddenly he entered into the scales, sate like a woman on his legges, and there was put in against him many bagges to fit his weight, which were changed six times, and they say was silver, and that I understood his weight to be nine thousand rupias, which are almost one thousand pounds sterling: after with Gold and Jewels, and precious stones, but I saw none, it being in bagges might be Pibles; then against Cloth of Gold, Silk, Stuffes, Linen, Spices, and all sorts of goods, but I must believe for they were in sardles. Lastly against Meale, Butter, Corne, which is said to be given to the Banian." The extract neglects to state that the ceremony was followed by the distribution as largesse of all the valuables weighed against the royal person with its heavy adornments.

Bernier describes an audience of Aurangzeb. " The king appeared seated upon his throne at the end of the great hall in the most magnificent attire. His vest was of white and delicately flowered satin, with a silk and gold embroidery of the finest texture. The turban of gold cloth had an aigrette whose base was composed of diamonds of an extraordinary size and value, besides an oriental topaz which may be pronounced unparalleled, exhibiting a lustre like the sun. A necklace of immense pearls suspended from his neck reached to the stomach. The throne was supported by six massy feet, said to be of solid gold, sprinkled over with rubies, emeralds, and diamonds. It was constructed by Shah-Jehan for the purpose of displaying the immense quantity of precious stones accumulated successively in the Treasury from the spoils of ancient *Rajahs* and *Pathans*, and the annual presents to the monarch which every Omrah is bound to make on certain festivals. At the foot of the throne were assembled all the Omrahs, in splendid apparel, upon a platform surrounded by a silver railing and covered by a spacious canopy of brocade with deep fringes of gold. The pillars of the hall were hung with brocades of a gold ground, and flowered satin canopies were raised over the whole expanse of the extensive apartment, fastened with red silken cords from which were suspended large tassels of silk and gold. The floor was covered entirely with carpets of the richest silk, of immense length and breadth."

As regards the female side of the court, although this had almost a separate organization and was, in keeping with Moslem and Indian tradition, to a large extent secluded, yet the imperial ladies possessed a measure of freedom through two centuries which allowed several of them to stand forth as distinct individuals, and a few to influence affairs profoundly. Jehangir assigned to the women of the household the sixth and fifth orders, or arrows, of rank. Akbar is said to have kept five thousand women in his harem. As usual, however, only a few of these were wives or votaries of the imperial pleasure; most of them constituted an elaborate organization for the housekeeping and entertainment of the few great ladies, the mother, aunts, sisters, wives, and favorites of the emperor. As already indicated, these women were of all kinds, — free-born and slave, Moslem, Christian, and pagan, Turki, Afghan, Persian, Hindu, Armenian, Slavic, Circassian, Georgian, and Ethiopian. Their communication with the outside world was kept up through their relatives and through eunuchs.

A few of the imperial ladies may be mentioned. The princess Gul-Badan, third daughter of Baber and Dil-Dar, wrote a history of the deeds of her half-brother, Humayun. In her later life she went with other great ladies on pilgrimage to Mecca, taking seven years for the journey; one-half of this time she spent in Arabia, where she performed the rites of the pilgrimage four times. After twenty more years filled with works of piety and charity she died at the age of eighty. Her nephew, Akbar, with his own hand helped bear her to the tomb.

Most powerful of all the Mogul imperial ladies was the Persian Nur-Jehan, or Nur-Mahal, wife of Jehangir. Born in poverty and actually cast away by her parents, she rose to the throne of command. Mohammad Hadi says that " by degrees she became, in all but name, undisputed sovereign of the empire, and the king himself became a tool in her hands. He used to say that Nur-Jehan Begam has been selected, and is wise enough, to conduct the matters of state, and that he wanted only a bottle of wine and a piece of meat to keep himself merry. Nur-Jehan won golden opinions from all people. She was liberal and just to all who begged her support. She was an asylum for all sufferers, and helpless girls were married at the expense of her private purse. She must have portioned above five hundred girls in her lifetime, and thousands were grateful for her generosity." Not only could she rule the empire effectively, if not always wisely and impartially, but she could lead armies. Defeated at last by Shah-Jehan, she put on perpetual robes of mourning for her dead husband and spent her last eighteen years in devoted seclusion.

Mumtaz-Mahal, niece of Nur-Jehan and wife of Shah-Jehan, did not aspire to political control. She held fast the heart of her imperial husband and became the mother of his fourteen children. The incomparable Taj Mahal, built by the emperor after her untimely death, bears eternal witness to great love followed by great grief.

Last may be mentioned two of the daughters of Mumtaz-Mahal, Jehan-Ara and Raushan-Ara. These ladies, like Charlemagne's daughters too great for matrimony, stirred up much trouble in the imperial household. Jehan-Ara was her father's favorite in his decadent old age, and an active partisan of her brother Dara. Of vast influence for many years, she was at length overshadowed by Raushan-Ara, who supported Aurangzeb and rose to greatness with his advancing fortunes. Bernier was well-nigh overcome by a distant view of this lady's majesty. " I cannot avoid dwelling on this pompous procession of the Seraglio. Stretch imagination to its utmost limits, and you can imagine no exhibition more grand and imposing than when Raushan-Ara Begam, mounted on a stupendous Pegu elephant, and seated in a *meghdambhar* blazing with gold and azure, is followed by five or six elephants with *meghdambhars* nearly as resplendent as her own, and filled with ladies attached to her household (and succeeded by the most distinguished ladies of the court) until fifteen or sixteen females of quality pass with a grandeur of appearance, equipage, and retinue, more or less proportionate to their rank, pay, and office. There is something very impressive of state and royalty in the march of these sixty or more elephants; in their solemn and as it were measured steps, in the splendour of the *meghdambhars*, and the brilliant and innumerable followers in attendance; and if I had not regarded this display of magnificence with a sort of philosophical indifference, I should have been apt to be carried away by such flights of imagination as inspire most of the Indian poets, when they represent the elephants as conveying so many goddesses concealed from the vulgar gaze."

THE GOVERNMENT PROPER

" The authority of the Great Mogul was despotic by all its origins: by the fact of the conquest, by the Turkish tradition, by the tradition of the old royalties of the country ";[1] and also, it may be added, by the practice of Islamic governments since the abandonment of Medina as the seat of the caliphs. The conquering chief owned all the conquered land, and the wealth and labor and lives of its inhabitants were at his disposal. As for the restriction of despotism by the Sacred Law, the house of Baber did not feel this strongly until late. On the other hand, even a drunkard like Jehangir had a keen sense of the responsibility of his high position. The emperor considered it his duty to maintain order, reward faithful service, and sit daily on the bench of justice to redress the wrongs of his people. Aurangzeb is reported by Bernier to have expressed his feeling of responsibility by saying: " Being born the son of a king and placed on the throne, I was sent into the world by Providence to live and labour, not for myself, but for others; . . . it is my duty not to think of my own happiness, except so far as it is inseparably connected with the happiness of my people. It is the repose and prosperity of my subjects that it behoves me to consult; nor are these to be sacrificed to anything besides the demands of justice, the maintenance of the royal authority, and the security of the State." One of his letters to his imprisoned father contains these words: " Almighty God bestows his trusts upon him who discharges the duty of cherishing his subjects and protecting the people. It is manifest and clear to the wise that a wolf is no fit shepherd, neither can a faint-hearted man carry out the great duty of government. Sovereignty is the guardianship of the people, not self-indulgence and profligacy. The Almighty will deliver your humble servant from all feeling of remorse as regards your Majesty." The sole fountain of legislation, the emperor observed economy in the issuance of it, making use, so far as possible, of established Islamic practice and immemorial custom. Yet from time to time, by administrative regulations, ordinances, and decrees, he sought to improve the methods of government. Aurangzeb, so much like Suleiman in many other respects, like him also ordered and financed the compilation of a code of the Sacred Law. It does not appear, however, that any such quantity of personal

---

[1] Lavisse and Rambaud, *Histoire Générale*, vi. 879.

legislation was issued by him or by any other Mogul emperor as by the great Ottoman.

The succession to the Mogul throne never became regular, since neither by Mongol nor by Moslem custom was any one method prescribed. Nor did the more kindly disposition of the house of Baber ever permit the publication of such a decree as that of Mohammed II for the execution of brothers upon the accession of a sovereign. Accordingly the resources of the empire were apt to be wasted in civil wars between father and son, and between older and younger brothers. Even the sons of Baber engaged in civil war: Kamran, aided by Askari and Hindal, fought against Humayun. Akbar's brothers were so young that he had no rival at the time of his accession. His two elder sons drank themselves to death; but this did not prevent Selim, who became the emperor Jehangir, from rebelling against his father and hastening the latter's death. Jehangir's two sons rebelled against him in turn. Shah-Jehan's four sons, Dara, Shuja, Murad, and Aurangzeb, fought together until the last encompassed the death of the others, besides keeping his father a prisoner during the last seven years of life. The mournful story need not be carried beyond the fierce civil war which followed the death of Aurangzeb, in which two of his sons were slain. Clearly, the Ottoman method was more practical if less humane. So unstable was the personal situation of the emperor that, if he failed to show his face in public daily, the empire fell into commotion and civil war became imminent. From the uncertainty of the succession the state, at least, derived this benefit, that the fittest of the candidates for power was likely to obtain the throne. Nevertheless, as Dow says, " to be born a prince " of the Mogul Empire was " a misfortune of the worst and most embarrassing kind. He must die by clemency, or wade through the blood of his family to safety and empire."

As the army was the defence and prop of the Mogul government, so finance was its sustenance. Here again the regulations of the Sacred Law were but scantily observed. Akbar, aided by Todar Mal and extending the methods of the Afghan Sher Shah, reduced to order and regularity the existing revenue system, which in the course of centuries of varying rule had become much confused. By ancient custom of India, the sovereign as primary owner of the land was entitled to one-third of the crops in kind. It was Akbar's task to change the system to a more modern money régime, a step in progress which the Ottomans have not been able to take even to the present day. In classical times as in late years, India, importing less of other commodities than she exported, steadily absorbed gold and silver. It is likely that a large share of the wealth of the newly-discovered Americas had already by Akbar's day made its way to India through the increasing Portuguese trade, and that Columbus, Cortes, and Pizarro thus unwittingly gave him the means of modernizing his land revenue. Several great tasks were involved in the change. All the cultivated land of India had to be measured, its quality judged, its average annual produce for the first nineteen years of Akbar's reign calculated, and the amount of the government's share for each tract reduced to current money. At first, it was attempted to renew the settlement annually; but, since this proved very difficult in a large and conservative land, a ten-year basis was eventually adopted. When the British came to power they found the revenue in a state of confusion which indicated that at some time during the Mogul period the evaluation had ceased to be made regularly, modifications of the last assessment having then been introduced successively, until all system had disappeared.

The imperial revenue was collected by a separate hierarchy of officials. The great provinces were divided into districts, or *sirkars*, in each of which a *Diwan* was chief financial agent. His office was the *Defter ali*, and his clerks were *Mutasidis*. In lesser districts the collectors were *Amils* or *Karoris*, the treasurers *Fotadars*. *Karkums* were appointed to settle disputes and audit accounts. The crown revenue might be farmed out, in areas of a size comparable to the *jagirs*, to officials known as *Zamindars* or *Talukdars*, who in the days of decline strove to make their position hereditary. In the local unit, or *pargana*, the government was represented by a *Kanungo*, who kept the records of assessments and payments. Akbar took measures also to bring under cultivation waste and abandoned lands, and appointed for this purpose *Karoris*, whose efforts were attended with much success. In the best days the imperial financial officers acted as a check upon the civil and military officials, upholding alike the interests of emperor and common people. Evidence exists, however, that even in the time of Akbar there was financial corruption, and that revenue officials were not lacking who plundered the people and defrauded the emperor.

The granting of *jagirs* to officers and *Rajahs*, of pensions to learned men and others, and of land in full title, free from revenue, for religious foundations seems to have diverted from the royal treasury about two-thirds of the possible land revenue. On the other hand, it has been estimated that the emperor received from customs, tolls, miscellaneous taxes, and presents an amount equal to what he got from the land. Careful calculations have resulted in ascribing to Akbar a revenue of over two hundred million dollars annually, and to Aurangzeb as much as four hundred and fifty million dollars. Suleiman's revenue would then have been not the tenth part of Akbar's and Louis XIV's not the tenth part of Aurangzeb's.

This revenue was expended upon the standing army, the court, the support of learned and religious persons, a series of building operations which were perhaps costly beyond parallel, bountiful gifts at certain seasons, and regular charities. It would appear, farther, that the expenses of the provincial governments were deducted from the imperial land revenue after it had been estimated but before it was paid into the treasury. In spite of the lavish outflow, however, an enormous treasure seems to have been accumulated. By Mandelslo it was estimated in 1638 at the incredible sum of one and a half billion crowns, equivalent to about the same number of dollars!

It was probably because of the greatly increased revenue which Akbar obtained by his new method that he found it possible to remit the *jizyeh* or capitation tax on non-Moslems, and also the tax on pilgrims, which had made the earlier Moslem rule obnoxious to the Hindu population. On the other hand, it may have been not merely religious zeal, but also financial stress caused by the civil wars preceding his accession, by the Rajput revolt, by the long struggle in the Deccan, and by the pious remission of many taxes not authorized by the Sacred Law, including the tax on Hindu temple lands, that influenced Aurangzeb to reimpose the capitation tax, and thus open wide the rifts in his disintegrating empire.

In the days of its greatness, the budget of the Mogul Empire, alike in income and expenditure, reached a height which had rarely if ever been attained before. That of the East Roman Empire under the Macedonian dynasty, and of the Saracen Empire in the days of Harun Al-Rashid, may have rivalled it; but it is probable that only the great Western powers, enriched by the industrial revolution in the late nineteenth and early twentieth centuries, have ever reached a financial magnitude beyond that of the empire of Aurangzeb.

Humayun divided the responsibilities of government among four ministers, and a fourfold division persisted at least as late as Aurangzeb. By a curious form of logic the classification of duties and the names of the four departments were based, not on convenience, but on relation to the four elements: earth, air, fire, and water. The *Khaki* department had the care of agriculture, buildings, and domain lands; the *Hawai*, of the wardrobe, the kitchen, the stables, and the like; the *Ateshi*, of the artillery and the making of war material and other things in which fire was employed; and the *Abi*, of the emperor's drinks, and canals, rivers, and water-works. When Khondamir wrote, about 1534, one man had oversight of all four departments; but the development of a regular supreme official of great power, like the grand vizier of the Ottoman Empire, seems never to have taken place, no doubt because the imperial house did not abandon the tradition of personal government.

Humayun set aside two days of the week for business of state. Drums were beaten to summon officials and give notice that the hall of audience was open. Any subject might appear and ask for justice. Suits of fine apparel and purses of money were at hand to reward the worthy, and executioners stood by with drawn swords to punish the guilty. Guns were fired at the close of the audience to notify officials that they might retire. Aurangzeb held general court in the great hall of audience for two hours on regular days. Persons who had petitions to present held them up, and these were taken by the emperor, read by him, and often granted on the spot. On at least one day in the week he sat with the two *Kazis* of the city, and on another day he heard privately ten cases of persons of low rank. In the evening the chief officers were commanded to be present in a smaller hall, where Aurangzeb sat to " grant private audiences to his officers, receive their reports, and deliberate on important matters of state." This gathering resembled the Divan of Suleiman, but it lacked most of the latter's judicial work; in India such work was done by the chief judges sitting separately, or by the emperor in the great audiences. Furthermore, it was the sovereign and not a grand vizier who presided in this council. The assembly was deliberative in matters of policy and general administration, and judicial in that it had jurisdiction of cases which involved officers of high rank.

For purposes of local government the empire was divided into *subahs*, or provinces, each under a *Nawab* (a plural of majesty, from *naib*, often called " nabob " by Westerners), or governor. Under Akbar the number of *subahs* varied from fifteen to eighteen. Like the *Beylerbeys* of the Ottoman Empire, the *Nawabs* tended to increase in number, the size of their provinces diminishing accordingly.

The *Nawab* was almost a little emperor in his province. He held audiences, commanded the army, conferred lesser titles, appointed and dismissed most officials, and was the highest judicial authority. His power was limited, however, by the emperor's right to recall him, by the right of appeal in judicial cases from him to the emperor, and by the fact that the financial and judicial officers were separately appointed and were responsible only to the throne. The *Nawab* and his court were supported by lands granted in *jagir*. He might suspend the *jagirs* of officers pending imperial decision. He was responsible for the security and order of his province, and had *Faujdars* under him in the several districts, who exercised military command and the powers of chief of police and police judge, their position resembling somewhat that of the *Sanjak Beys* of the Ottoman system. The chief financial officers in each province were the *Diwans*, who, as explained above, collected the imperial revenue and had oversight of all lesser revenue officers. They and their deputies possessed judicial powers in cases concerning finance and land titles. The chief judge of the province, subject however to appeals to the governor, was the *Nizam*. He heard the serious criminal cases, and his deputy, the *Daroga Adaulat al Aulea*, attended to most of the important civil ones. Local *Kazis*, aided by *Muftis*, *Mohtesibs*, and *Kutwals* or mayors, kept order in the smaller cities and districts. *Rajahs* who had made terms with the emperor exercised powers very similar to those of the *Nawabs*. Their positions were secured by heredity, however, and in their provinces the imperial financial and judicial officers had no jurisdiction. They simply owed military service and a certain amount of tribute, failing in which they might be reduced by force of arms. The Ottoman system contained no subjects who were at once so secure of their positions, so nearly independent, and so powerful as the *Rajahs*. Kurdish, Albanian, and Arabian chieftains were perhaps as secure and as independent, but they were of very small wealth and might; while the Voivodes of Wallachia and Moldavia were not so secure or so independent.

The condition of the common people under this government is to be known mainly by inference. Various documents and acts show the benevolent intentions of emperors and high officials toward the masses. Whether from wise prevision or from genuine charitable feeling, there appears to have been much solicitude lest the cultivators of the soil should be reduced to utter penury or driven from their lands. Akbar, for instance, issued strict orders that on military expeditions nothing should be taken from the people without careful assessment and immediate or subsequent payment. Nevertheless, at the best the result of the general policy was to leave the cultivator little more than a bare living. The whole system drained away wealth to a few great cities and a comparatively few persons. If but few complaints rose from the masses, it was because their lot was no worse than that of their forefathers had been for many generations. Aside from the periods of civil war, the Moguls gave peace and order. Akbar removed internal tolls two centuries before such a thing was accomplished in France, and thus made of the land a single economic unit, with the result that in his reign India as a whole enjoyed such prosperity as she has known at very few other periods in her history.

Before the time of Aurangzeb special care was taken to conciliate the Hindus. Akbar adopted definitely the policy of equal treatment for all, a degree of toleration not to be found in the contemporary Europe of William the Silent and Henry of Navarre. The government strove to abolish or mitigate such Hindu practices as were abhorrent to Mohammedanism, and at least one Moslem practice which offended the Hindus. Child-marriage, the ordeal, and animal sacrifice were forbidden. Widows were to be burned on the funeral pyres of their husbands only with their own full consent, and those who preferred to live might marry again. In the Rajput tributary states Hindu law of course prevailed. Probably in the regions under direct Mogul rule Hindus were judged by their own law when Moslems were not concerned and perhaps even by their own judges. It is true that the Hindus had to wait until Akbar came to be released from the personal disabilities imposed by earlier Moslem conquerors, that their temple lands were taxed until the time of Aurangzeb, and that Brahmans, pundits, and fakirs were perhaps only in Akbar's presence treated with respect equal to that accorded *Sheiks, Seids,* and *Ulema.* But the emperors and their officers gave like justice to all; they permitted every man to worship according to the rites of his forefathers, and apparently never had a thought, as had Selim the Cruel, of giving to all non-Moslem subjects the choice between Islam and death. There was little ground for discontent until Aurangzeb began to apply a harsher policy.

The Moslems and the Moslem Church

In comparison with conditions in the Ottoman Empire, Moslems and non-Moslems in the India of the early Moguls were far more nearly on a level. This was due not merely to the toleration and indifference of the emperors, but even more to the circumstances of the conquest, under which both groups were treated alike, since Baber at Panipat in 1526 subdued the Moslem Lodi Sultans of Delhi, and at Kanwaha in 1527 the Hindu Rajput confederacy. Indian-born worshippers of Allah and of Brahma, Vishnu, and Siva were mingled in the same vast mass of conquered subjects, equally separated from the victorious invaders. There was also, in all probability, a much greater difference of race between Baber's highlanders and the Moslems that he found in India than between the latter and the Hindus; for many inter-marriages had taken place, and many natives of India had joined the followers of the Prophet. Time, of course, diminished this distinction.

Suleiman was distinctly the head of the Moslems of his empire. Through his appointee the *Sheik-ul-Islam*, through his *Hoja*, the *Kaziaskers*, the *Nakib-ol-Eshraf*, and other learned and saintly personages, he kept in close touch with the religious chiefs of the Mohammedan population. All who prayed toward Mecca, at least from the older portions of the Ottoman Empire, were attached by many ancient ties to the house of Osman. Their ancestors had perhaps been converts through its activities, had certainly fought for it, and had seen its gradual and vigorous rise to greatness. No such vital bonds joined to the Moguls the great mass of their Moslem subjects. These remembered the glories and favors of lost dynasties, and were indebted to the new sovereigns only for defeats and humiliations which depressed them toward the level of the Hindus, whom they had for centuries held to be far inferior to themselves. They had no *Sheik-ul-Islam*, honored by the sovereign with a seat above his own, whose decisions might determine the fate of the ruler or of the empire. Almost as much to them as to the Hindus the emperor was a stranger and a foreigner, to whom should be rendered, because of his power, full submission and instant obedience, but not loyal affection and wholehearted devotion. There was ever an absence of solidarity between the house of Timur and those Moslem subjects who had not come into India in the service of that house, and this was not least among the elements of weakness that shortened the life of the empire. When

Rajputs had been stirred to revolt, when Mahrattas had grown great, when bronzed and capable Moguls had been supplanted by " pale persons in petticoats," who were left to rally about the tottering throne ? More than two and a half centuries have elapsed since the Ottomans ceased to draw systematically from the strength of the Christian population, and yet the fighting stock of their Moslem subjects has never failed or grown weak or faltered in its loyalty; but Aurangzeb's successors found few upon whom to rely, and of this few a very small proportion who would sacrifice their own fortunes freely, who would be faithful unto death.

The Moguls found in India *Sheiks*, *Dervishes*, *Seids*, and *Ulema*, mosques, schools, and pious foundations in abundance. In fact, the developed system of Mohammedanism had extended itself over India with visible results very much like those in all other Moslem lands, among them the Ottoman Empire. From the ranks of those educated in Moslem lore were taken teachers, judges, and counselors-at-law.

There must have existed for the children of the Moslem population *mektebs*, ordinary *medressehs*, and law schools, in which the Arabic language and the sciences built upon the Koran, as well as the Persian language and literature were taught. No doubt, also, the imperial household contained systems of education, arranged for the two sexes separately and prepared to train imperial and noble children and young attendants, servants, and slaves in the knowledge which was thought best adapted to fit them for life. It is interesting to notice what impression the teaching regularly given to a young prince made (if Bernier can be trusted) upon the keen intellect of Aurangzeb. When the latter became emperor, his old teacher, it appears, confidently presented himself at Delhi for reward. What, then, must have been his surprise to receive such a deliverance as this from the lips of majesty!

" Was it not incumbent upon my preceptor to make me acquainted with the distinguishing features of every nation of the earth; its resources and strength; its mode of warfare, its manners, religion, form of government, and wherein its interests principally consist, and, by a regular course of historical reading, to render me familiar with the origin of States; their progress and decline; the events, accidents, or errors, owing to which such great changes and mighty revolutions have been effected ? . . . A familiarity with the language of surrounding nations may be indispensable in a king; but you would teach me to read and write Arabic; doubtless conceiving that you placed me under an everlasting obligation for sacrificing so large a portion of time to the study of a language wherein no one can hope to become proficient without ten or twelve years of close application. Forgetting how many important subjects ought to be embraced in the education of a prince, you acted as if it were chiefly necessary that he should possess great skill in grammar, and such knowledge as belongs to a Doctor of Law; and thus did you waste the precious hours of my youth in the dry, unprofitable, and never-ending task of learning words! . . . Ought you not to have instructed me on one point at least, so essential to be known by a king, namely, on the reciprocal duties between the sovereign and his subjects ? Ought you not also to have foreseen that I might at some future period be compelled to contend with my brothers, sword in hand, for the crown, and for my very existence ? Such, as you must well know, has been the fate of the children of almost every king of Hindustan. Did you ever instruct me in the art of war, how to besiege a town, or draw up an army in battle array ? Happy for me that I consulted wiser heads than thine on these subjects! Go! withdraw to thy village. Henceforth let no person know either who thou art or what is become of thee."

In this rebuke, whether it comes chiefly from Bernier or from Aurangzeb, is excellent criticism upon the stereotyped Moslem education, and material enough to cheer the hearts of modern advocates of a closer relation between subjects of instruction and the business of life.

The lack of solidarity between the mass of the Moslems of India and the Mogul government, together with the religious indifference of several emperors, prevented the Moslem church there from reaching the full measure of the dignity, influence, and authority of the Moslem Institution in the Ottoman Empire. Humayun's division of the household into three classes shows that he gave highest rank not to the clergy but to princes of the blood, with nobles and ministers of state and military men. " The holy persons, the great *Musheiks* (religious men), the respectable *Seids*, the literati, the law officers, the scientific persons, poets, besides other great and respectable men formed the second class." The orders, or arrows, of nobility show a little more definitely the place of the Moslem learned men, since they are assigned to the tenth order, after the monarch and the princes of the blood and the *Rajahs*.

In the palace-city of Fatehpur-Sikri, Akbar built a great hall, the Ibadat-Khana, to which he repaired on holy nights with *Sheiks*, *Seids, Ulema*, and nobles. Finding that his followers could not keep the peace when mingled indiscriminately, he assigned one of the four sides of the hall to each group. Here he was accustomed to listen to theological discussions; and it appears that what he heard tended to destroy his respect for the faith of the Prophet, and to predispose his mind toward the eclectic religion which he instituted later. Says Badauni: "The learned doctors used to exercise the sword of their tongues upon each other, and showed great pugnacity and animosity, till the various sects took to calling each other infidels and perverts." In course of time Akbar obtained a document signed by the principal *Ulema*, to the effect that a just ruler is higher in the eyes of God than a doctor of the law (*Mujtahid*), that Akbar was a just ruler, and that therefore his decrees in matters of religion were binding upon the world. This declaration placed Akbar distinctly above the Moslem church and at least on a level with the prophet Mohammed; and he seems even to have played with the idea that he was himself God. Certainly he hoped to unify all creeds by his " divine faith." His son and grandson were not much interested in religion, and not at all inclined to assume actively the religious headship of the empire; under them, the Moslem church had to take care of itself. Religious interest appeared again in Aurangzeb, not in any spirit of free inquiry, but in a rigid conformity to the rules of the Sacred Law. From those youthful days when he preferred the meagre life of a saint to the splendors of princely state, down to the long-deferred close of his troubled career, Islam knew no more faithful observer of its rites and prescriptions. In Aurangzeb's reign and in his alone did the Moslem religion take such a place in India as in the Turkey of Suleiman's time.

The learned Moslems of the Mogul Empire never had as the head of their hierarchy a personage of such dignity and power as the *Sheik-ul-Islam* of Constantinople. The *Sadr Jehan* appears to have been concerned chiefly with the granting of land from the treasury to learned and religious persons in lieu of pensions. The hierarchy of judges seems to have been complete, at least in territory that was directly administered, with two officials at court who corresponded to the *Kaziaskers* of Suleiman, and with *Kazis* of high rank in the chief city of each province and of lesser rank in other cities; but the functions of these officers appear to have been more closely restricted than in the Ottoman Empire, by reason of the superior jurisdictions of the emperor and the governors, and of the criminal and financial jurisdictions of the *Nizams* and *Diwans* and their deputies. As there is little mention of the *muftis*, it would seem that their rôle was not very important.

The Moslem church in India was not of the very fabric of empire. The imperial family and most of their associates in government adhered to it; but it had no thorough control of education and justice, and no power to sanction war or pronounce the deposition of an emperor. It did not curb the spirit of the nation or lay a heavy hand upon progress; but, as it was relatively unable to hinder by its weaknesses, so it could not contribute its abiding strength. The Mogul Empire is but a memory. The Moslem church of India thrives and grows under the rule of aliens of another faith.

BOOKS CONSULTED IN THE PREPARATION OF APPENDIX IV

BADEN-POWELL, B. H. A short account of the land revenue and its administration in British India. 2d edition. Oxford, 1907.

BAYLEY, SIR E. C. The local Muhammadan dynasties. Gujarát. London, 1886. — A sequel to Elliot's History of India.

BERNIER, FRANCOIS. Travels in the Mogul empire, A.D. 1656–1663. Westminster, 1891. — [As quoted by Lane-Poole and others.]

CRICHTON, A. S. The Mohammedans as rulers of India. In *The Moslem World*, i. 99–116. London, 1911.

DOW, ALEXANDER. The history of Hindostan. 3 vols. London, 1770–1772.

ELLIOT, Sir H. M., and DOWSON, JOHN. The history of India, as told by its own historians. 8 vols. London, 1867–1877. — Vol. v (1873) contains extracts from Khondamir, Badáúní, Nizam uddin Ahmad, etc.

GUL-BADAN BEGAM. The history of Humāyūn (Humāyūn-nāma). Translated by Annette S. Beveridge. London, 1902.

HOLDEN, E. S. The Mogul emperors of Hindustan. New York, 1895.

HUNTER, SIR W. W. A brief history of the Indian peoples. 23d edition. [Oxford, 1903.]

IRVINE, WILLIAM. The army of the Indian Moghuls; its organization and administration. London, 1903.

—— The Bangash Nawabs of Farrukhabad. J. R. A. S., Bengal, 1878, 340 ff.

KEENE, H. G. The fall of the Moghul empire of Hindustan. New edition. London, 1887.

—— The Turks in India. London, 1879.

LANE-POOLE, STANLEY. Aurangzíb. (Rulers of India series.) Oxford, 1893.

LANE-POOLE, STANLEY. Bábar. (Rulers of India series.) Oxford, 1899.
—— Mediæval India under Mohammedan rule (A.D. 712–1764). New York, 1903.
LYALL, SIR A. C. The Moghul empire. In *Cambridge Modern History*, vi. 506–529. New York, 1909.
MALLESON, G. B. Akbar. (Rulers of India series.) Oxford, 1908.
RAMBAUD, ALFRED. Organisation de l'empire mongol. In Lavisse and Rambaud's *Histoire Générale*, vi. 878–883. Paris, 1895.
RITCHIE, LEITCH. A history of the oriental nations. 2 vols. London, 1848.
ROE, SIR THOMAS. Journal of his embassy to the court of the Great Mogul. 1615–1619. In Hakluyt Society's publications, 2d series, vols. i–ii. London, 1899. — [As quoted by Lane-Poole and others.]

APPENDIX V

BIBLIOGRAPHICAL NOTES

I. Sources of Ottoman Governmental Ideas

THREE traceable lines of influence can be followed from the earliest times until their appearance in the Ottoman government of the sixteenth century. The oldest began in Egypt, and continued down through various dynasties until the Roman conquest, after which it began to enter the Roman imperial government. From this it passed to the Byzantine and thence to the Ottoman system. Locally again it followed a more direct course through the Fatimides and Mamelukes until the time of Selim I's conquest of Egypt. The slave government of the Mamelukes offers an interesting subject for comparison with the Ottoman Ruling Institution. It would be superfluous to give references for this line of development, except perhaps to mention Sir William Muir's book, *The Mameluke or Slave Dynasty of Egypt* (London, 1896), and Stanley Lane-Poole's *Egypt in the Middle Ages* (London, 1901).

The second line, which seems to have contributed a greater number of elements, came down in the Bagdad-Euphrates valley through various governments to the Saracen and Seljuk empires, from which it passed to the Ottomans. Here again no general references need be given. Perhaps the most useful book in connection with the subject is D. B. McDonald's *Moslem Theology, Jurisprudence, and Constitutional Theory* (New York, 1903).

The third and most direct line of influence is through the Tatars of the steppe lands. In A. H. Keane's *Man, Past and Present* (Cambridge, England, 1899) there is a full and clear discussion of the anthropological relationships of the Turks. E. H. Parker's *A Thousand Years of the Tartars* (London, 1895) gives an account which is based closely upon the Chinese sources, but which would be helped by the addition of as many of the two or three thousand notes which he did not print as would show the sources of his information. The Chinese story of the great Tatar empire of the sixth century A.D. may be found in Stanislas Julien's *Documents Historiques sur les*

Tou-Kious (Paris, 1877). W. Radloff's *Alttürkischen Inschriften der Mongolei* (Leipsic, 1894–95) discusses the earliest known Turkish monuments, which date from the eighth century. Emil Bretschneider's *Medieval Researches from Eastern Asiatic Sources* (2 vols., London, 1888, new edition, 1910) gives an account of the Uigurs, whose greatness came in the eighth and ninth centuries and whose name persisted until at least the twelfth century, as is shown by the oldest known Turkish book, which is in their dialect.

This old book has been printed, with original Syriac text, transliteration into Roman characters, and German translation, by Arminius (Hermann) Vambéry, under the title *Uigurische Sprachmonumente und das Kudatku Bilik* (Innsbruck, 1870). The *Kudatku Bilik*, the " Wisdom that Blesses," written at Kashgar in 1068 by Yusuf Khass Hajil, is really an " Art of Government," composed for the instruction of a Turkish prince. It contains in rhymed couplets, arranged in chapters, a large amount of advice on governmental matters, much of it being in the form of proverbs. The book throws a great deal of light on the fundamental Ottoman character. Vambéry has also made a study, on a philological basis, of the civilization of the Tatars, entitled *Die Primitive Cultur des Türko-tatarischen Volkes* (Leipsic, 1879).

A book equally remarkable with the *Kudatku Bilik* is the *Siasset Namèh*, written in 1092 for the Seljuk sultan Melek Shah by the great vizier Abu 'Ali al Hasan b. Ishaq (known better by his title, the Nizam al-Mulk), and printed in the original Persian, with a French translation, by Charles Schéfer, Paris, 1893. This " Book of Government " reveals to some extent three things, — the methods of government of Sassanian times, the actual government under Melek Shah, and the Seljuk government as the Nizam al-Mulk would have it. It also sheds much light upon Ottoman institutions.

The best general book on the Turks in Central Asia and their activities down to the occupation of Asia Minor is undoubtedly Léon Cahun's *Introduction à l'Histoire de l'Asie: Turcs et Mongols* (Paris, 1896). The same ground is covered briefly by Cahun in Lavisse and Rambaud's *Histoire Générale*, vol. ii. ch. xvi. There is a great deal of information about the Persians and the Seljuk Turks in E. G. Browne's *Literary History of Persia* (2 vols., London, 1902–1906). Maximilian Bittner has made a valuable study of the Turkish language, entitled *Der Einfluss des Arabischen und Persischen auf das Türkische* (Kaiserlichen Akademie der Wissenschaften, *Sitzungsberichte der Philosophisch-Historischen Classe*, vol. cxlii. pt. iii. Vienna, 1900).

Sir W. M. Ramsay's books are valuable for a study of the settlement of the Turks in Asia Minor, particularly his *Historical Geography of Asia Minor* (London, 1890), *The Geographical Conditions determining History and Religion in Asia Minor* (with comments by D. G. Hogarth, H. H. Howorth, and others, *Geographical Journal*, September, 1902, xx. 257–282), and *Studies in the History and Art of the Eastern Provinces of the Roman Empire* (Aberdeen, 1906). Volume v of H. F. Helmolt's *Weltgeschichte* (Leipsic, etc., 1905) is useful for its attempt to trace the elements of Ottoman culture which were derived from Byzantine and other sources. William Miller's *The Latins in the Levant* (New York, 1908) gives a clear picture of the confused and divided state of affairs to which the Ottomans put an end in their rough way.

II. THE OTTOMAN GOVERNMENT IN THE SIXTEENTH CENTURY

Abundant material for a study of the sixteenth-century Ottoman government has been provided and preserved; for the great place which the expanding empire held in the world developed an immense interest in its affairs on the part of the West, and made it worth the while of many of its Western residents to prepare descriptions of its outstanding features, among which its peculiar government was treated with special fulness. The writings of these men of various Western nationalities are in a way more helpful than a similar number of books from native writers would be, because the foreigners could usually take nothing for granted, but were compelled to draw a complete picture. They could not, on the other hand, get at the inner springs of the Ottoman activity as well as natives could; nor do any of them, with the exception of Menavino, seem actually to have read and known the Ottoman laws. Fortunately, Ottoman historians began to write abundantly shortly before the reign of Suleiman. For Suleiman's own time, the collections of his *Kanuns* (since he was noted as a legislator) contain much material which helps toward an understanding of his government; moreover, writers of a later date have been drawn with special interest toward his reign, as the climax of Ottoman greatness. At the same time, no one but Zinkeisen has attempted to give an extended account of the Ottoman government as it was in the sixteenth century.

No reasonably complete bibliography of books relating to Turkey has been made. The following lists are worthy of mention as giving information in regard to the material for a study of Turkish history and institutions before the year 1600: —

Richard Knolles gives a bare list of his authorities, to the number of about twenty-five, at the beginning of his *Generall Historie of the Turkes*, London, 1603.

J. H. Boecler published at Bautzen in 1717 a *Commentarius Historico-Politicus de Rebus Turcicis*, in which he gives, at pp. 14–41, a list of 317 works on Turkish history and affairs, including 45 folio volumes, 128 quartos, 98 octavos, and 45 duodecimos.

Joseph von Hammer discusses his authorities in the preface to volume i of his *Geschichte des Osmanischen Reiches* (Pest, 1827); and in volume x, pp. 57–336 (1835), he prints a list containing 3,025 titles of works relating to Ottoman history which were to be found in Europe outside of Constantinople.

Amat di San Filippo, in his *Biografia dei Viaggiatori Italiani*, etc. (2 vols., Rome, 1882), gives accounts of many of the early Italian writers on Turkish affairs.

Henri Hauser, in his edition of Du Fresne-Canaye, described below (p. 319), prints as Appendix II an *Essai d'une Bibliographie des Ouvrages de XVIe Siècle relatifs au Levant*. The list, which does not pretend to completeness, contains about 60 different titles.

The catalogue of the library of Count Paul Riant, published in two parts at Paris in 1899, also contains the titles of a great number of books and pamphlets which relate to the subject under discussion. Most of this material has been transferred to the Ottoman collection of the Library of Harvard University, through the generosity of Messrs. J. R. Coolidge and A. C. Coolidge, — a gift, it may be added, that has made the preparation of the present treatise possible. There are also many titles on early Ottoman history in the catalogue of Charles Schéfer's Oriental library (published at Paris in 1899), from which the same donors have contributed 445 volumes to the Harvard Ottoman collection.

The list given in the *Cambridge Modern History*, i. 700–705, in connection with Professor J. B. Bury's chapter on " The Ottoman Conquest," is fuller than most of those just mentioned. It omits some valuable authorities, however, such as Schiltberger, Menavino, Ramberti, and Busbecq.

It is possible to get contemporaneous views of the Ottoman Empire at a date earlier than the beginning of the sixteenth century, though they are all incomplete. The first accounts go back to the battle of

Nicopolis in 1396. Froissart (*Chroniques*, ed. Lettenhove, xv. 319 ff., Brussels, 1871), in a description of the battle and succeeding events which was based on accounts given by Jacques du Fay and Jacques de Helly, gives some idea of the Turkish army and the sultan. A better account for the present purpose is that by Johann Schiltberger (translated into English by J. B. Telfer, and published by the Hakluyt Society as *The Bondage and Travels of Johann Schiltberger*, London, 1879). Schiltberger, then a youth of sixteen, was taken prisoner at Nicopolis, and after serving as slave to Bayezid I for six years, was captured by Timur at the battle of Angora, 1402. He was retained as captive, not without important responsibilities and wide journeys, for twenty-five years longer, when he succeeded in escaping. It is a matter for regret that he says very little of his life at the sultan's court, since he held a position which corresponded to that of page in later times.

Another general account of the Turkish polity comes from the pen of Bertrandon de la Broquière, first gentleman-carver (*écuyer tranchant*), councillor, and chamberlain of Duke Philip the Good of Burgundy. In the course of a trip through the Levant he met Murad II in Rumelia in 1433. His observations show that many features of the Turkish system were then already in operation, — as the four pashas, the slave system, the pages, the imperial harem, the Janissaries (*Jehanicéres*), the feudal army, the Divan, etc. La Broquière's memoirs are edited by Charles Schéfer, under the title *Le Voyage d'Outremer*, as volume xii of *Recueil de Voyages et de Documents pour servir à l'Histoire de la Géographie depuis le XIIIe jusqu'à la fin du XVIe Siècle* (Paris, 1892). The same volume contains an opinion in regard to the military power of the Turks by Jehan Torzelo, dating from the year 1439.

Still another report was written by a Transylvanian whose name remains unknown, but who was a slave in Ottoman private families from 1436 to 1453. Evidently he had before his capture been a theological student who held some of the ideas that preceded the Reformation movement. His book had a great vogue after the year 1509, under various titles, such as: Ricoldus, *De Vita et Moribus Turcarum*, Paris, 1509 (the attachment to the name of Ricoldus is purely accidental); *Libellus de Ritu et Moribus Turcarum*, Wittenberg, 1530 (with a preface by Martin Luther); S. Frank, *Cronica-Abconterfayung*, etc., Augsburg, 1531; *Tractatus de Moribus*, etc. The Wittenberg edition has been used in this treatise, and is referred to as *Tractatus*. Although most of the book is theological and argumentative, it affords a great deal of information. Among other things, it contains what is probably the earliest mention of the tribute children as the regular means of recruiting the Janissaries (*Ginnitscheri*).

The next good contemporary account of the Ottoman system is given in the history of Chal(co)condyles (written in Greek), of which there are many editions and translations. The one used here is the French translation, *Histoire de la Décadence de l'Empire Grec et Établissement de celui des Turcs*, Rouen, 1670. This writer, whose story comes down to 1465, speaks out of his own observation in describing the Ottoman camp and government.

The oldest authentic *Kanuns* are in the *Kanun-nameh* of Mohammed II, which is translated by Hammer in his *Staatsverfassung* (Vienna, 1815), 87–101.

The earliest book that was devoted to a description of Ottoman manners, religion, and government is by Teodoro Spandugino Cantacusino. Born of an Italian father and a Greek mother, he spent his life alternately in the East and the West. His book describes the empire as it was under Bayezid II, who died in 1512, his information about the government being obtained from two very high renegade officials, probably Messih Pasha and Hersek-Zadeh Ahmed Pasha. The earliest edition was printed in French at Paris in 1519 under the title *Petit Traicté de l'Origine des Turcqz;* later editions, with and without his name, or under the name of B. Gycaud, bear the title *La Généalogie du Grant Turc à Présent Regnant*, etc. The edition used here is a reprint of the first French issue, edited with notes by C. Schéfer, Paris, 1896. This writer is sometimes quoted as Spandugino, and sometimes as Cantacusino. The first form is used in the present treatise.

A book that is even more valuable in some ways is Giovanni Antonio Menavino's *Trattato de Costumi et Vita de Turchi*. The edition used here was printed in Florence in 1548. Menavino came of a wealthy Genoese family. About the year 1505, when he was twelve years of age, handsome, bright, and well educated for his years, he was captured near Corsica by corsairs, and set aside as a gift suitable for the sultan. Taken to Bayezid II, he pleased the old sultan greatly, and was placed at once in the school of pages, where, as his book shows throughout, he must have profited greatly by the teaching that he received. He describes the religion, customs, and government of the Ottomans in much detail. In 1514 he was taken by Selim I on the expedition against Persia; but he managed to escape to Trebizond, whence he made his way to Adrianople, Salonika, and thence home to Genoa.

A group of excellent sources for studies of both the government and the history of the Ottoman Empire in the sixteenth century is found in the reports which the Venetian *Bailos* and orators extraordinary presented to their Senate.

Venice, says Ranke, " frequently sent her most experienced and able citizens to foreign courts. Not content with the despatches on current affairs regularly sent home every fourteen days, she further required of her ambassadors, when they returned after an absence of two or three years, that they should give a circumstantial account of the court and the country they had been visiting." [1] Since Constantinople was in the sixteenth century the station of first importance in the Venetian diplomatic service, it is safe to assume that the sons whom she sent there were her most intelligent.

A number of these Venetian reports, which do not, however, reach far into Suleiman's reign, are summarized by Marini Sanuto the Younger in his volumious *Diarii*, 1496–1533 (58 vols. in 59, Venice, 1879–1903). The reports of Alvise Sagudino in 1496, and of Andrea Gritti in 1503, are quoted by Schéfer in the introduction to his edition of Spandugino's work, noticed above. Rinaldo Fulin, in his *Diarii e Diaristi Veneziani* (Venice, 1881) reprints Sanuto's abstract of the Itinerary of Pietro Zeno, orator at Constantinople in 1523.

The Venetian reports for the reign of Suleiman are all, so far as preserved and known, collected in the invaluable work of Eugenio Alberi, *Relazione degli Ambasciatori Veneti al Senato* (15 vols., Florence, 1839–1863). The three volumes of the third series (published 1840, 1844, 1855, respectively), as well as a portion of the fifteenth volume or Appendix, are devoted to Turkish reports. Volume i of this series is also separately printed as *Documenti di Storia Ottomana del Secolo XVI* (Florence, 1842). A few writings are included in these volumes which were not reports to the Venetian senate.

In all, thirty-nine documents are thus presented, of which sixteen fall within the reign of Suleiman. Unfortunately there is a gap between the years 1534 and 1553, a period for which there should be eight or ten documents of great value bearing on the Ottoman dealings with France, Austria, Spain, and Persia.

---

[1] Leopold Ranke, *The Ottoman and the Spanish Empires*, Preface, 1.

These volumes contain much helpful apparatus, such as a glossary of Turkish words (vol. i); notes on the Venetian embassies to the Porte in the sixteenth century, with a list of the Venetian representatives (vol. ii); biographical notes concerning the writers (all three volumes); chronological tables, genealogies, etc. (Appendix). The Venetians were particularly interested in the financial side of the Ottoman government, its mechanism, its army, and its fleet. Many character descriptions of great personages enliven the pages. The last pages of the Appendix contain a chronological index of the *Relazione* and the other writings included; also an alphabetical list of them by authors, and chronological lists by countries. The subjoined list of reports from Constantinople is taken from page 435, and will serve as a means of locating many references in the foregoing pages. The more valuable reports are distinguished by asterisks.

VENETIAN REPORTS FROM CONSTANTINOPLE

as given in Alberi's *Relazione*, 3d series, 3 vols. and Appendix
(Florence, 1840–1863)

Writer	Date	Volume	Page
Gritti, Andrea	1503	iii	1
Giustiniani, Antonio	1514	"	45
Mocenigo, Alvise	1518	"	53
Contarini, Bartolomeo	1519	"	56
Minio, Marco	1522	"	69
Zen, Pietro	1524	"	93
Bragadino, Pietro	1526	"	99
Minio, Marco	1527	"	113
Zen, Pietro	1530	"	119
*Ludovisi, Daniello	1534	i	1
*Navagero, Bernardo	1553	"	33
Anonimo	"	"	193
*Trevisano, Domenico	1554	"	111
*Erizzo, Antonio	1557	iii	123
*Barbarigo, Antonio	1558	"	145
Cavalli, Marino	1560	i	271
Dandolo, Andrea	1562	iii	161
Donini, Marcantonio	"	"	173
*Barbarigo, Daniele	1564	ii	1
Bonrizzo, Luigi	1565	"	61
Ragazzoni, Jacopo	1571	"	77
*Barbaro, Marcantonio	1573	i	299
Barbaro, Marcantonio	"	Append.	387
Badoaro, Andrea	"	i	347
*Garzoni, Costantino	"	"	369

VENETIAN REPORTS FROM CONSTANTINOPLE (*continued*)

Writer	Date	Volume	Page
Alessandri, Vincenzo	1574	ii	103
Anonimo	1575	"	309
*Tiepolo, Antonio	1576	"	129
*Soranzo, Giacomo	"	"	193
Venier, Maffeo	1579	i	437
Anonimo	1582	ii	209 [1]
Anonimo	"	"	427
Contarini, Paolo	1583	iii	209
*Morosini, Gianfrancesco	1585	"	251
Michiel, Giovanni	1587	ii	255
Venier, Maffeo	"	"	295
*Moro, Giovanni	1590	iii	323
*Bernardo, Lorenzo	1592	ii	321
*Zane, Matteo	1594	iii	381

An interesting small pamphlet is the *Auszug eines Briefes . . . das Türckich Regiment unn Wesen sey*, which was printed in a South-German dialect in 1526. It purports to be a letter from a German settled at Adrianople to his cousin in Germany, telling of his life as subject Christian under the sultan. The literary arrangement is so good, and the statements diverge so uniformly toward the dark side, that this would seem to be a pamphlet written in Germany for the purpose of arousing alarm and activity after the battle of Mohacs.

Hieronymus Balbus, bishop of Gurk, published at Rome in 1526 a little book of two essays addressed to Clement VII. The second part, " continens Turcarum Originem, Mores, Imperium," etc., was also commended to the Archduke Ferdinand. The work makes up for a conspicuous lack of definite and accurate information by means of abundant scriptural and classical quotations and allusions, vituperation of the Turks, and assertion of their military ineffectiveness. It is chiefly valuable as an evidence of the " Turkish fear."

A book that had a wide influence is *Turcicarum Rerum Commentarius* addressed by Paolo Giovio, or Paulus Jovius, bishop of Nocera, to Emperor Charles the Fifth, and dedicated at Rome in 1531. It was published in several languages; the edition used here is the Latin one, Paris, 1539. The book is historical except for the last ten pages, which contain a description of the Ottoman government with particular reference to its military resources. Giovio published also in

---

[1] The report at this page, though ascribed to Jacopo Soranzo, 1581, and so referred to in the foregoing footnotes, was really written in 1582 by some one in his suite.

two volumes at Florence, in 1550–1552, *Historiarum sui Temporis Tomus Primus* [*et Secundus*].

V. D. Tanco, or Clavedan del Estanco, a Spanish gentleman, wrote in his native tongue a book that was translated into Italian and published at Venice in 1558 under the title *Libro dell' Origine et Successione dell' Imperio de' Turchi.* The basis of the work is the *Commentarius* of Jovius, just noticed; but this has been intelligently combined with information from Froissart, Aeneas Sylvius, and others. The latest date mentioned is 1537, and the death of Ibrahim in 1536 is not known.

A very valuable and interesting work is the *Libri Tre delle Cose de Turchi,* etc., published by Aldus in Venice in 1539, and reprinted often thereafter. It appears also as one of the component parts of the work published by Aldus in 1543, *Viaggi fatti da Vinetia, alla tana . . . in Costantinopoli,* known sometimes simply as *Viaggi alla tana,* or " Travels to the Don." The book appeared anonymously, but it has been attributed with much confidence to Benedetto Ramberti (see Alberi, *Relazione,* 3d series, iii. 8; *Archiv für Oesterreichische Geschichte,* 1897, lxxxiii. 9; *Revue Critique,* 1896, i. 20–21). Ramberti accompanied Ludovisi to and from Constantinople during the first six months of 1534. The book was written in the same year; for it shows that Barbarossa was made pasha while it was in process of composition (see above, Appendix I, p. 246, and, for the fact that Barbarossa was back in Algiers, May 9, 1534, see Ursu, *La Politique Orientale de François I*, Paris, 1908, p. 79), and in a long characterization at the close of the third book it represents Luigi (Alvise) Gritti, who was assassinated in Hungary late in 1534, as still living.

The first book of the three describes the journey overland from Ragusa to Constantinople; the third book contains observations of no great value on the power and policies of the Turks. The second book is the *pièce de résistance.* It opens with a brief description of Constantinople and a rapid sketch of the origin and history of the Ottoman Turks. An account of the Turkish government follows, beginning with the inside service of the household of the sultan, proceeding to the outside service, then taking up the chief officers of government, the Janissaries, the *Spahis* of the Porte and the auxiliary branches of the army. The harem, the palaces of the pages, the *Ajem-oghlans,* and the arsenal are next described; then the feudal army is explained as it was constituted in Europe and in Asia; and, finally, a list of the sanjakates of the empire is given. The Italian used is fairly good, and the style is very simple, often degenerating to the mere cataloguing of officers. Throughout the book the financial aspect of the government is emphasized strongly, the incomes of all persons mentioned being carefully stated. This second book of Ramberti is of so great importance to the present treatise that it is given in translation as Appendix I. The text used is that of the *Viaggi . . . alla tana* (Venice, 1543).

Standing in exceedingly close relationship to the second book of Ramberti is a twenty-two page pamphlet bearing the name of Junis Bey (Ionus Bei). Written in broad Venetian dialect and printed on coarse paper in type of a poor quality, not kept clean, it is in two portions, respectively of eight and fourteen pages, which are distinguished by the use of larger and smaller type. The title-page bears the inscription " reprinted in 1537." The sixth page begins the list of pashas with the statement that " Ibrahim of Parga is dead," and then gives the name of his successor in the office of grand vizier. On the seventeenth page it is said that the territories of the *Beylerbey* of Mesopotamia " border " those of Bagdad which belong to Persia (Bagdad was taken by Suleiman in the winter of 1535 and 1536); on the eighteenth occurs the remark that Alvise Gritti " says " such and such a thing; and at the close the book is attributed to " Ionus bei " and " Signor Aluise gritti." Now, Junis Bey was in Venice from December 6, 1532, to January 9, 1533 (thesis of Theodore F. Jones, p. 168, Harvard College Library); Gritti was assassinated in 1534; Junis Bey was again in Venice from January 15 to February 17, 1537 (Jones, 209). It seems reasonable to conclude, therefore, that the first edition of the pamphlet was printed at Venice in 1533 at the time of Junis Bey's first visit, and that at the time of his second visit in 1537 the first eight pages were recast with a few changes, and in certain unsold copies substituted for the older pages, the remainder being left as it stood originally, despite the erroneous reference to Gritti.

It is very clear that Ramberti had before him while preparing his " second book " a document almost identical with this pamphlet. Beginning with his description of the sultan's household service, the order of treatment is practically the same, and even the words and phrases are often the same, except for differences of dialect. His language frequently suggests that he is expanding on some material before him. It is worthy of note, however, that not only Ramberti's use of Italian, but also his use of Turkish, is frequently better than that of Junis Bey. Moreover, in his list of officials he includes the *Mufti* and the chief dragoman (*Terjuman*), whom Junis Bey leaves out, the latter omission being the more remarkable in that Junis Bey held that office himself. On the other hand, where there are differences in numbers, Junis Bey is more apt to be correct than Ramberti. It seems not unlikely that both works were derived from a manuscript, more nearly complete and correct than either, in the possession of Alvise Gritti, which the latter allowed the two writers to use, Junis Bey probably in 1532 and Ramberti in 1534. Alvise Gritti was well known to both. Natural son of the doge Andrea Gritti, he had won high favor with Ibrahim, who entrusted him with great responsibilities. In fact, it may not be too bold a conjecture to suggest that some of the information contained in his manuscript came from the celebrated Grand Vizier himself. Aside from this possibility, a minute survey of the Ottoman government, prepared by Gritti himself or with his collaboration, either for his own use or for the information of his kinsfolk the Venetians, possesses a presumption in favor of its accuracy and truthfulness. Accordingly the closing words, " all is true," may be accepted with little reserve.

These two works, by Ramberti and Junis Bey, were much used by other writers on Turkish affairs. Postel shows a close acquaintance with them, and Geuffroy frequently does little more than present a translation. Ramberti was incorporated into a number of the collected works in regard to the Turks which appeared in various languages after the middle of the sixteenth century and thus entered into systematic histories. Since the pamphlet of Junis Bey is very rare, its text is presented in Appendix II, above. Besides matter very similar to that of Ramberti, it contains near the end an account of the order of march of the sultan's army when he went to war.

Guillaume Postel is perhaps the broadest-minded of the sixteenth-century observers. He gives evidence of having had a legal training, and of having reflected along political and constitutional lines. Nicolay, in his preface, informs us that Postel knew Latin, Greek, Hebrew, Chaldean, Syriac, and Arabic, as well as the principal Western languages. He was sent by Francis I with the momentous embassy of La Forêt, and was therefore in Constantinople about the year 1535. He seems to have made a later visit for the purpose of acquiring manuscripts; but the substance of his book, as appears from numerous references, dates from the first visit. The volume was printed at Poitiers in 1560, but was not published till 1570. It contains three parts, separately paged: —

I. *De la République des Turcs;* II. *Histoire et Considération de l'Origine, Loy, et Coustume des Tartares . . . Turcs,* etc., III. *La Tierce Partie des Orientales Histoires, ou est exposée la Condition, Puissance, & Revenue de l'Empire Turquesque,* etc. The first part gives, among other things, an excellent account of the page system and of Ottoman law and justice. The third part is built upon the information in Ramberti and Junis Bey; it describes the page system further, and adds a good account of the *Ajem-oghlans* and the Janissaries. By a reference it shows acquaintance with Giovio.

Antoine Geuffroy, knight of St. John, issued in 1542 his *Briefve Description de la Court du Grand Turc.* Four years later this was published in English by R. Grafton under the title *The Order of the Great Turcks Court of Hye Menne of War;* ánd from thirty to fifty years later it appeared, combined with other material, in large volumes in the Latin and German tongues under the name of N. Honigerus or Haeniger, with a Latin translation by G. Godelevæus, entitled *Aulae Turcicae, Othomannicique Imperii Descriptio,* etc. The work of Geuffroy thus had a great vogue. It was a sound, intelligent description of the empire, built upon the information in Ramberti and Junis Bey. By references and allusions it shows acquaintance with Froissart, Spandugino, and Giovio. The references to Geuffroy in the foregoing pages are to the reprint in Schéfer's edition of Jean Chesneau, described below.

Bartholomew Georgevitz, pilgrim to Jerusalem, issued a small book, *De Turcarum Moribus Epitome,* which passed through many editions in two or three languages, the first dating not later than 1544, and the latest not earlier than 1629. The chapters are on various topics and from various sources. The first, on the rites and ceremonies of the Turks, is abridged from Spandugino. The second, on the Turkish soldiery, is by Georgevitz himself; it is perhaps the most valuable, and shows by the age assigned to Prince Mustapha that it was written about 1537. The fourth chapter gives useful Turkish phrases, and is interesting as showing how Turkish words were pronounced in the sixteenth century. The fifth chapter gives a full account of the treatment of slaves of private citizens, written by one who had been a slave, apparently Georgevitz himself. The edition referred to in this treatise was printed at Paris in 1566.

Jérome Maurand accompanied Captain Pinon on his mission to Constantinople in 1544. A few years later he wrote, in Italian, an account of his journey, which was translated by Léon Dorez as

Itinéraire de Jérome Maurand d'Antibes à Constantinople, and published at Paris in 1901 as vol. xvii of *Recueil de Voyages*, etc.

Before 1549, Ibrahim Halebi, the jurist, prepared by command of Suleiman the codification of the Sacred Law which bears the name of *Multeka ol-ebhar*, and which formed the foundation of D'Ohsson's great work.

Jean Chesneau went to Constantinople with D'Aramont, ambassador of Henry II of France, and accompanied him on Suleiman's campaign against Persia in 1549. His narrative, which is not very illuminating or accurate, was edited by Charles Schéfer and published at Paris in 1887, under the title, *Le Voyage de Monsieur d'Aramon*, as vol. viii of *Recueil de Voyages*, etc. Bound in the same volume are five letters in the Italian language, written from Constantinople in 1547 by the ambassador Veltwyck to Archduke Ferdinand of Austria; there is also (at pp. 227–248) a reprint in French of the first edition of Geuffroy.

Nicolas de Nicolay of Dauphiné, royal geographer and extensive traveler, who wrote a book called *Discours et l'Histoire Véritable des Navigations, Pérégrinations et Voyages faicts en la Turquie*, is not the least interesting of sixteenth-century authorities on Turkey. His account of his voyage from Marseilles to Constantinople in the year 1551 in the train of the Seigneur d'Aramont, ambassador of Henry II, and the drawings from life with which he embellishes his book, show his capacity for exact observation. In his descriptions of the customs and government of the Ottoman Empire, however, he does not reveal the possession of much first-hand information. Menavino is here his principal source of knowledge. The first edition of his book appeared at Lyons in 1567; it was translated into several languages and reproduced often. An enlarged edition, published at Antwerp in 1586, is the one referred to in the foregoing pages. The plates in the book, about sixty in number, have been said to be the work of Titian; but this is apparently incorrect, for the preface merely states that Nicolay drew from life on the spot and afterwards had the drawings reproduced " *avec fraiz & labeur incroyable.*"

From a literary point of view, Ogier Ghiselin de Busbecq is by all odds the most interesting of sixteenth-century sources for the study of Ottoman history and government. The charm of his style should not obscure the facts that he was a keen and exact observer possessed of a true scientific spirit, and that he reflected carefully on what he saw. He wrote on Turkey during his period of service as ambassador from

Charles V to Suleiman between 1555 and 1562. One of his four Turkish letters was printed in Antwerp in 1581, and since that time at least twenty-seven editions and reprints have appeared in seven languages. The edition of his *Life and Letters*, in two volumes, translated from the original Latin by C. T. Forster and F. H. B. Daniell (London, 1881), has been used in this treatise, as has also his *De Re Militari contra Turcam instituenda Consilium*, as printed in a complete edition of his writings published at Pest in 1758, pp. 234–277.

Philippe Du Fresne-Canaye, a young Huguenot gentleman, was sent by his family to Venice for safety in the troubled days after the massacre of St. Bartholomew; and he took advantage of his nearness to the Levant to visit Constantinople in 1573. He had prepared himself for his visit by reading Ramberti, Postel, Nicolay, and others, but he does not seem to have learned much that was not in those authorities. His *Voyage du Levant* was edited for publication in Paris in 1897 by Henri Hauser, as vol. xvi of *Recueil de Voyages*, etc. Hauser's Appendix II contains the bibliography of sixteenth-century works relating to the Levant which is mentioned above (p. 308).

The *Kanun-nameh* of Suleiman, collected by the *Mufti* Ebu su'ud, who died in 1574, contained a number of the Sultan's *Kanuns* relating mainly to financial and feudal matters. A translation of the incomplete table of contents of the Turkish manuscript copy of this *Kanun-nameh* (which is in the Imperial Library at Vienna, Fluegel No. 1816) is given above as Appendix III. Many of the *Kanuns* are translated in Hammer's *Staatsverfassung*, pp. 396–424, where they are erroneously attributed to Achmet I.

A little anonymous book, *The Policy of the Turkish Empire*, published at London in 1597, contains an interesting preface. The remainder of the book deals only with the Turkish religion, and is drawn mainly from Menavino, with some incorporation from Spandugino and Georgevitz.

At the conclusion of Richard Knolles's *Generall Historie of the Turkes* (London, 1603), is to be found " A Briefe Discourse of the Greatnesse of the Turkish Empire," written probably in the year of publication, since the story comes down to the accession of Achmet I in 1603. The lands of the empire, "of all others now upon earth farre the greatest," are described, its revenues are set forth, the Timariotes, the Janissaries, the chief officers of state, and the fleet receive notice, and the Turkish power is compared with that of all

320   APPENDIX

states which touch its frontiers. It is to this part of Knolles's work (as printed in the 6th edition of his History, with Ricaut's continuation, London, 1687, ii. 981–990) that most of the references in the foregoing pages are made.

Pietro Della Valle, known as Il Pellegrino, or The Pilgrim, wrote *Viaggi . . . in la Turchia, la Persia, e l'India*, which was published in two volumes (four parts) at Rome in 1658–1663. He was in Constantinople in 1614 and 1615, and took advantage of every opportunity to witness a ceremony. Observant of costumes and jewels, he could not esteem the Turkish officials highly, because they were all slaves. The references in this treatise are to the second edition of the first part, published in 1662.

Many collections based on the above-mentioned writings and on others were issued after the middle of the sixteenth century, and many surveys of the Ottoman Empire were prepared as time went on. Of the latter, three stand forth as of sufficient importance to throw light on sixteenth-century conditions: —

Sir Paul Ricaut, a resident of Turkey for many years, issued late in the seventeenth century *The History of the Present State of the Ottoman Empire*. He explains that he obtained his information from Turkish records from high officials, from members of the *Ulema*, and from a Pole who had passed through the school of pages and had spent nineteen years in all at the Ottoman court. Ricaut was evidently a student of political philosophy; he seems to have relied especially upon Tacitus, the civil law, Machiavelli, and Lord Bacon. His book was printed in several languages, has been much quoted since, and deserves the fame it received. The sixth English edition, published in London in 1686, is used here. The book is also printed at the end of the second volume of his edition of Knolles's *Turkish History*, London, 1687.

Ignatius Mouradgea D'Ohsson, born in Turkey and long a resident there, prepared between 1788 and 1818 his great *Tableau Général de l'Empire Othoman*. He based his work on the *Multeka ol-ebhar* (see above, p. 318) which with its comments he rearranged and translated, adding to it a great many observations of his own. The book appeared in two forms, the huge folio edition being a magnificent example of the bookmaker's art. The smaller edition of the book (7 vols., Paris, 1788–1824) has been used here. The last three volumes were published under the supervision of his son after his death. Six of the seven volumes are based on the *Multeka;* the seventh contains a full description of the government, including the court, the ministers, the bureaus, the army, etc.

Joseph von Hammer published at Vienna, in 1815, *Des Osmanischen Reichs Staatsverfassung und Staatsverwaltung*, in two volumes. The former is very largely a collection of documents, such as *Kanuns*, *fetvas*, and extracts from the *Multeka*. A large amount of valuable material is presented; but it is only partly digested, and the author often does not indicate clearly whence he drew his extracts. The second volume goes over much the same ground as D'Ohsson's seventh volume. Another work of Hammer's, his *Geschichte des Osmanischen Reiches* (10 vols., Pest, 1827–1835), has furnished the historical background for this treatise. This work is extremely valuable from the fact that it is based upon numerous inaccessible Turkish sources; but it is largely uncritical, and it does not make sufficient use of Western authorities.

Leopold Ranke published at Hamburg in 1827 the first volume of his excellent work, *Fürsten und Völker von Sud-Europa*. He was the first to discern the value of the Venetian reports, and by their aid he reached far greater accuracy than had yet been attained in attempts to describe these great South-European empires when at the height of their power. The English translation by W. K. Kelly, entitled *The Ottoman and the Spanish Empires in the Sixteenth and Seventeenth Centuries* (London, 1843), has been used in the present treatise.

The third volume of J. W. Zinkeisen's *Geschichte des Osmanischen Reiches in Europa* (Gotha, 1855) has been used for its discussion of the Ottoman government in the sixteenth century. It is based too exclusively on the Venetian reports, which Zinkeisen seems to have regarded as always trustworthy, and it makes little or no use of Turkish sources.

Stanley Lane-Poole, in his *Story of Turkey*, London, 1886, chapters xiv and xvi, gives a very good summary of the structure of the Ottoman household and administration, condensed from D'Ohsson's seventh volume.

In Lavisse and Rambaud's *Histoire Générale*, iv. 747 ff., there is a brief account, by Rambaud, of the organization of the Ottoman Empire in general. Though not accurate in every respect, it gives, on the whole, an excellent picture.

A. Heidborn published at Vienna and Leipsic in 1909 a careful, well-planned, and extremely valuable work entitled *Manuel de Droit Public et Administratif de l'Empire Ottoman*. Although the principal purpose of the book is to explain present-day conditions, the historical background is outlined at many points. Unfortunately there is neither table of contents nor index; but perhaps these will be supplied when the work is extended farther. The chapters of the present volume deal with the territory of the state, the sources and fundamental principles of the legislation in force in the Ottoman Empire, the head of the state, nationality, the administrative organization, and justice. The chapter on justice occupies more than half the book, and treats fully the judicial organization, civil and criminal law, and procedure.

In addition to the works described above, the appended alphabetical list contains the names of a few authors whose works, though occasionally quoted in this treatise, call for no special comment; and also the names of a number of writers who have dealt with the government of Turkey, but who have not been quoted because their information either is of secondary importance or derivation, or deals with a later time, when conditions had been changed.

III. Alphabetical List of Works Cited

Achmet I. See Kanun-nameh of Achmet I.
Alberi, Eugenio. Relazione degli ambasciatori Veneti al senato. 15 vols. (in 3 series). Florence, 1839–1863. — See pp. 311–313.
Alessandri, Vincenzo. Relazione, 1574. In Alberi's Relazione, 3d series, ii. 103–127. Florence, 1844.
Angiolello. Mss. in Bibliothéque Nationale, Fonds Italien, No. 1238.
Auszug eines briefes . . . das türckich Regiment und Wesen sey. n. p. 1526. — See p. 313.
[Aventinus, Johannes.] Türckische Historien, oder Warhaftige Beschreibunge aller Türcken Ankunfft, Regierung, u. s. w. Translated from the Italian by Heinrich Müller. Frankfort, 1570. — Earlier edition, with slightly different title, 1563-[1565].
Badoaro, Andrea. Relazione, 1573. In Alberi's Relazione, 3d series, i. 347–368. Florence, 1840.
Balbus, Hieronymus. H . . .B. . . . ad Clementem VII . . . de civili & bellica fortitudine liber . . . cui additus est alter continens Turcarum originem, mores, imperium, etc. Rome, 1526. — See p. 313.
Barbarigo, Antonio. Sommario della relazione, 1558. In Alberi's Relazione, 3d series, iii. 145–160. Florence, 1855.
Barbarigo, Daniele. Relazione, 1564. Ibid. ii. 1–59. Florence, 1844.
Barbaro, Marcantonio. Relazione, 1573. Ibid. i. 299–346. Florence, 1840.
—— Relazione, 1573. Ibid. Appendix vol., 387–415. Florence, 1863. .
Bassano, Luigi. See Du Zare.

BAUDIER, MICHEL. Histoire généralle du serrail, et de la cour du grand seigneur empereur des turcs. Paris, 1626.

BELIN, A[LPHONSE]. Du régime des fiefs militaires dans l'Islamisme, et principalement en Turquie. *Journal Asiatique.* 6th series, xv. 187–301. Paris, 1870.

—— Étude sur la propriété foncière en pays musulman, et spécialement en Turquie. Paris, 1862.

BÉRARD, VICTOR. La révolution turque. Paris, 1909.

BERNARDO, LORENZO. Relazione, 1592. In Alberi's *Relazione*, 3d series, ii. 321–426. Florence, 1844.

BITTNER, MAXIMILIAN. Der Einfluss des Arabischen und Persischen auf das Türkische. Kaiserlichen Akademie der Wissenschaften. *Sitzungsberichte der Philosophisch Historischen Classe*, vol. cxlii. pt. iii. Vienna, 1900. — See p. 306.

BOECLER, J. H. Commentarius historico-politicus de rebus Turcicis. Bautzen, 1717. — See p. 308.

BON, OTTAVIANO. Il serraglio del gransignore (1608). [Edited by Guglielmo Berchet.] Venice, 1865.

BONRIZZO, LUIGI. Relazione, 1565. In Alberi's *Relazione*, 3d series, ii. 61–76. Florence, 1844.

BRAGADINO, PIETRO. Sommario della relazione, 1526. In Alberi's *Relazione*, 3d series, iii. 99–112. Florence, 1855.

BRETSCHNEIDER, E[MIL]. Medieval researches from Eastern Asiatic sources. 2 vols. London, 1888; another edition, 1910. — See p. 306.

BROSCH, MORITZ. The height of the Ottoman power. *Cambridge Modern History.* Vol. iii. ch. iv. London, 1904.

BROWNE, E. G. A literary history of Persia. [2 vols.] London, 1902–1906. — See p. 306.

BURY, J. B. The Ottoman conquest. *Cambridge Modern History*, vol. i. ch. iii. London, 1902.

BUSBECQ, OGIER GHISELIN DE. Exclamatio: sive De re militari contra Turcam instituenda consilium, etc. In *Augerii Gislenii Busbequii Omnia quae extant*, 234–277. Pest, [1758]. — See p. 319.

—— Life and Letters. Translated by C. T. Forster and F. H. B. Daniell. 2 vols. London, 1881. — See p. 318.

CAHUN, LÉON. Introduction à l'histoire de l'Asie: Turcs et Mongols. Paris, 1896. — See p. 306.

—— Les révolutions de l'Asie. In Lavisse and Rambaud's *Histoire Générale*, vol. ii. ch. xvi. Paris, 1893. — Formation territoriale de l'Asie. *Ibid.*, vol. iii. ch. xix. Paris, 1894.

CAMBRIDGE medieval history (The). Planned by J. B. Bury; edited by H. M. Gwatkin and J. P. Whitney. Vol. i. Cambridge, England, 1911. — See PEISKER.

CAMBRIDGE modern history (The). Edited by A. W. Ward, G. W. Prothero, and Stanley Leathes. 12 vols. and Index. London, 1902–1911. — See BROSCH, BURY.

CANTACUSINO. See SPANDUGINO.

CAVALLI, MARINO. Relazione, 1560. In Alberi's *Relazione*, 3d series, i. 271–298. Florence, 1840.

CHAL(CO)CONDYLES, L[AONICUS]. Histoire de la décadence de l'empire grec et éstablissement de celui des Turcs. Translated from the Greek by B[laise] de Vigenere. Rouen, 1670. — See p. 310.

CHARDIN, SIR JOHN. Travels into Persia and the East-Indies. London, 1686.

CHARRIÈRE, E[RNEST]. Négociations de la France dans le Levant. 4 vols. Paris, 1848–1860.

CHESNEAU, JEAN. Le voyage de Monsieur d'Aramon (1549). Edited by Charles Schéfer, in *Recueil de Voyages*, etc., vol. viii. Paris, 1887. — See p. 318.

CONTARINI, BARTOLOMEO. Sommario della relazione, 1519. In Alberi's *Relazione*, 3d series, iii. 56–68. Florence, 1855.

CONTARINI, PAOLO. Relazione, 1583. *Ibid.* 209–250. Florence, 1855.

CRONICA — ABCONTERFAYUNG, etc. Augsburg, 1531. — The same as TRACTATUS, *q. v.*

DANDOLO, ANDREA. Relazione, 1562. In Alberi's *Relazione*, 3d series, iii. 161–172. Florence, 1855.

DAY, CLIVE. A history of commerce. New York, 1907.

DELLA VALLE, PIETRO (IL PELLEGRINO). Viaggi . . . in . . . la Turchia, la Persia, e l'India. 4 pts. in 2 vols. Rome, 1658–1663 (pt. i, La Turchia, 1662, is 2d edition). — See p. 320.

DJEVAD BEY, AHMED. État militaire ottoman. Vol. i. bk. i. Le corps des Janissaires. Translated from the Turkish by Georges Macridès. Paris, etc., 1882.

DOCUMENTI di storia ottomana del secolo XVI. Vol. i. Florence, 1842. — The same as Alberi's *Relazione*, 3d series, i (1840). See p. 311.

D'OHSSON, IGNATIUS MOURADGEA. Tableau général de l'empire othoman. 7 vols. Paris, 1788–1824. — See p. 320.

DONINI, MARCANTONIO. Relazione, 1562. In Alberi's *Relazione*, 3d series, iii. 173–208. Florence, 1855.

DOREZ, LÉON. See MAURAND.

DU FRESNE-CANAYE, PHILIPPE. Le voyage du Levant (1573). Edited by Henri Hauser in *Recueil de Voyages*, etc., vol. xvi. Paris, 1897. — See p. 319.

DU ZARE, LUIGI BASSANO. Consuetudines & ratio vitae Turcorum. Rome, 1545.

EBU SU'UD. See KANUN-NAMEH of Suleiman.

ELIOT, SIR CHARLES. Turks. *Encyclopedia Britannica*. 11th edition, xxvii. 468–473. Cambridge, 1911.

ERIZZO, ANTONIO. Relazione, 1557. In Alberi's *Relazione*, 3d series, iii. 123–144. Florence, 1855.

ESTANCO. See TANCO.

FEBURE, MICHELE. L'état présent de la Turquie. Paris, 1675.

FROISSART, SIR JOHN. Oeuvres (chroniques). Edited by Kervyn de Lettenhove. 25 vols. (in 26). Brussels, 1867–1877. — See p. 309.

FULIN, RINALDO. Diarii e diaristi veneziani. Venice, 1881. — See p. 311.

GARZONI, COSTANTINO. Relazione, 1573. In Alberi's *Relazione*, 3d series, i. 369–436. Florence, 1840.

APPENDIX 325

GEORGEVITZ, BARTHOLOMEW. De Turcarum moribus Epitome. Paris, 1566. — See p. 317.
GERLACH, STEPHAN. Tage-buch (1674). Quoted in Zinkeisen's *Geschichte des Osmanischen Reiches*, iii. 222 ff. Gotha, 1855.
GEUFFROY, ANTOINE. Briefve description de la court du grand Turc (1542). Edited by Charles Schéfer in *Recueil de Voyages*, etc., viii. 227–248. Paris, 1887. — See p. 317.
GIBBON, EDWARD. The history of the decline and fall of the Roman empire. Edited by J. B. Bury. 7 vols. London, 1906.
GIOVIO, PAOLO (JOVIUS, PAULUS). Historiarum sui temporis tomus primus [et secundus]. 2 vols. Florence, 1550–1552. — See p. 314.
—— Turcicarum rerum commentarius. Paris, 1539. — See p. 313.
GIUSTINIANI, ANTONIO. Sommario della relazione, 1514. In Alberi's *Relazione*, 3d series, iii. 45–50. Florence, 1855.
GODELEVÆUS, G. [translator of GEUFFROY, *q. v.*]. Aulæ Turcicæ, Othomannicique imperii descriptio. Basel, 1569. — See p. 317.
GOLDZIHER, IGN[ATIUS]. Muhammedanisches Recht in Theorie und Wirklichkeit. *Zeitschrift für Vergleichende Rechtswissenschaft*, viii. 406–423. Stuttgart, 1889.
—— The progress of Islamic science in the last three decades. *Congress of Arts and Science, St. Louis, 1904* (ed. H. J. Rogers), ii. 497–517. Boston, etc., 1906.
GRAFTON, R. [translator of GEUFFROY, *q. v.*]. The order of the great Turcks court of hye menne of war. London, 1546. — See p. 317.
GRASSI, ALFIO. Charte turque, ou organisation religieuse, civil et militaire, de l'empire ottoman. 2 vols. Paris, 1825.
GRITTI, ALVISE (or LUIGI). See JUNIS BEY.
GRITTI, ANDREA. Relazione, 1503. In Alberi's *Relazione*, 3d series, iii. 1–43. Florence, 1855.
GYCAUD, B. La généalogie du grant Turc á present regnant. — The same as SPANDUGINO, *q. v.*
HALIL GANEM. Les sultans ottomans. (Études d'Histoire Orientale.) 2 vols. Paris, 1901–1902.
HAMMER, JOSEPH VON. Geschichte des osmanischen Reiches. 10 vols. Pest, 1827–1835. — See p. 321.
—— Des osmanischen Reichs Staatsverfassung und Staatsverwaltung. 2 vols. (vol. i, Staatsverfassung; vol. ii, Staatsverwaltung). Vienna, 1815. — See p. 321.
HAUSER, HENRI. Essai d'une bibliographie des ouvrages de XVIe siècle relatifs au Levant. In *Recueil de Voyages*, etc., xvi. 316–320. Paris, 1897. — See p. 308. See also DU FRESNE-CANAYE.
HEIDBORN, A. Manuel de droit public et administratif de l'empire ottoman. Vienna, etc., 1909. — See pp. 321, 322.
HELMOLT, H. F. Weltgeschichte. 9 vols. Leipsic, etc., 1899–1907. — See p. 307.
HOLDICH, T. H. Asia. *Encyclopaedia Britannica*. 11th edition, ii. 748–749. Cambridge, 1910.
HONIGERUS (or HAENIGER), NICOLAUS [German translator of GEUFFROY, *q. v.*].

HUNTINGTON, ELLSWORTH. The fringe of verdure around Asia Minor. *National Geographic Magazine*, xxi. 761–775. Washington, 1910.

IBRAHIM HALEBI. Multeka ol-ebhar. See MULTEKA.

IDRIS, Turkish poet-historian. Quoted in Hammer's *Geschichte*, i. 91. Pest, 1827.

IONUS BEI. See JUNIS BEY.

JOHNSON, MRS. [SUSANNAH WILLARD]. Narrative of . . . captivity. Springfield, 1907. — Reprinted from the 3d edition, Windsor, Vt., 1814; 1st edition, Walpole, N. H., 1796.

JONES, THEODORE F. Venice and the Porte, 1520–1542. Thesis in the Library of Harvard University.

JORGA, N[ICOLAE]. Geschichte der Türkei. Vols. i–iv. Gotha, 1908–1912.

JOVIUS, PAULUS. See GIOVIO.

JULIEN, STANISLAS. Documents historiques sur les Tou-Kioue (Turcs), traduite du chinois. Paris, 1877. — See p. 305.

JUNIS BEY (IONUS BEI), and ALVISE GRITTI. Opera noua la quale dechiara, etc. Venice, 1537. — See pp. 315, 316, and Appendix II.

JUYNBOLL, T. W. Handleiding tot de Kennis van de mohammedanasche Wet. Leyden, 1903.

KANUN-NAMEH, of Achmet I. In Hammer's *Staatsverfassung*, pp. xvii–xix. Vienna, 1815.

—— of Mohammed II. Translated *ibid.* 87–101. Vienna, 1815. — See p. 310.

—— of Suleiman. Collected by the Mufti Ebu su'ud, 1574; translated in part, *ibid.* 384–427. Vienna, 1815. — See p. 319 and Appendix III.

KEANE, A. H. Man, past and present. Cambridge, England, 1899. — See p. 305.

KEENE, H. G. The Turks in India. London, 1879.

KNOLLES, RICHARD. Generall historie of the Turkes. London, 1603. — See p. 319.

—— The same, entitled " Turkish History," with continuation by Paul Ricaut. 3 vols. London, 1687–1700. — Knolles's work runs, with continuous pagination, a little way into vol. ii (pp. 837–990). — See p. 320.

KOCHI BEY. Turkish historian. Quoted in Hammer's *Geschichte*, iii. 490, etc. Pest, 1835.

KOHLER, J. Die Wirklichkeit und Unwirklichkeit des islamitischen Rechts. *Zeitschrift für Vergleichende Rechtswissenschaft*, viii. 424–432. Stuttgart, 1889.

KUDATKU BILIK (Art of Government). By Yusuf Khass Hajil, 1068. See VAMBÉRY, Uigurische Sprachmonumente, etc.

LA BROQUIÈRE, BERTRANDON DE. Le voyage d'outremer (1433). Edited by Charles Schéfer, in *Recueil de Voyages*, etc., vol. xii. Paris, 1892. — See p. 309.

LANE-POOLE, STANLEY. A history of Egypt in the Middle Ages. London, 1901. See p. 305.

—— The story of Turkey. London, 1886. — See p. 321.

LAVISSE, ERNEST, and RAMBAUD, ALFRED. Histoire générale du IVe siècle à nos jours. 12 vols. Paris, 1893-1901. — See CAHUN, RAMBAUD.
LEFEVRE, M. See FEBURE.
LIBELLUS de ritu et moribus Turcarum. Wittenberg, 1530. — The same as TRACTATUS, etc., q. v.
LODGE, RICHARD. The Close of the Middle Ages, 1273-1494. London, 1906.
LONICERUS, Philippus. Chronicorum Turcicorum. 2 vols. (in one). Frankfort, 1584.
LUDOVISI, DANIELLO. Relazione, 1534. In Alberi's Relazione, 3d series, i. 1-32. Florence, 1840.
MACDONALD, D. B. Moslem theology, jurisprudence, and constitutional theory. New York, 1903. — See p. 305.
MARSH, H. A new survey of the Turkish empire. London, 1664.
MAURAND, JÉROME. Itinéraire d'Antibes à Constantinople (1544). Edited and translated by Léon Dorez, in Recueil de Voyages, etc., vol. xvii. Paris, 1901. — See p. 317.
MAURER, CASPAR. Türckishe chronica, oder historische Beschreibung von der Türcken Ursprung. Nuremberg, 1660.
MENAVINO, GIOVANNI ANTONIO. Trattato de costumi et vita de Turchi. Florence, 1548. — See p. 310.
MERRIMAN, R. B. Gomara's annals of Charles V. Oxford, 1912.
MEYER, EDUARD. Geschichte des Altertums. 2d edition. Vol. i (in 2 pts.). Stuttgart, etc., 1907-1909.
—— Persia. Encyclopedia Britannica. 11th edition, xxi. 202-224. Cambridge, 1911.
MICHELI, GIOVANNI. Relazione, 1587. In Alberi's Relazione, 3d series, ii. 255-294. Florence, 1844.
MILLER, WILLIAM. The Latins in the Levant. New York, 1908. See p. 307.
MINIO, MARCO. Relazione, 1522, 1527. In Alberi's Relazione, 3d series, iii. 69-91, 113-118. Florence, 1855.
MOCENIGO, ALVISE. Sommario delle relazioni, 1518. Ibid. 51-55. Florence, 1855.
MOHAMMED II. See KANUN-NAMEH of Mohammed II.
MONTESQUIEU, BARON DE. Esprit des lois.
MORO, GIOVANNI. Relazione, 1590. In Alberi's Relazione, 3d series, iii. 323-380. Florence, 1855.
MOROSINI, GIANFRANCESCO. Relazione, 1585. Ibid. 251-322. Florence, 1855.
MUIR, SIR WILLIAM. The Mameluke or slave dynasty of Egypt, 1260-1517. London, 1896. — See p. 305.
MÜLLER, HEINRICH. See AVENTINUS.
MULTEKA OL-EBHAR. By Ibrahim Halebi, 1459. — See p. 318.
MYERS, P. V. N. Medieval and modern history. Revised edition. Boston, [1905].
NAVAGERO, BERNARDO. Relazione, 1553. In Alberi's Relazione, 3d series, i. 33-110. Florence, 1855.

NICOLAY, NICOLAS DE. Discours et histoire véritable des navigations, pérégrinations, et voyages faicts en la Turquie. Antwerp, 1586. — See p. 318.

NIZAM AL-MULK. See SIASSET NAMÈH.

PARKER, E. H. A thousand years of the Tartars. London, 1895. — See p. 305.

PEISKER, T. The Asiatic background. Cambridge Medieval History, i. 323–359. Cambridge, 1911.

PÉLISSIÉ DU RAUSAS, G. Le régime des capitulations dans l'empire ottoman. 2 vols. Paris, 1902–1905.

PÉSCHEL, OSCAR. The races of man and their geographical distribution. New York, 1882.

POLICY (The) of the Turkish empire. [Anonymous.] London, 1597. — See p. 319.

POSTEL, GUILLAUME. [Pt. i] De la république des Turcs; [pt. ii] Histoire et consideration de l'origine, loy, et coustume des Tartares . . . Turcs, etc.; [pt. iii] La tierce partie des orientales histoires, etc. 3 pts. in 1 vol. Poitiers, 1560. — See pp. 316, 317.

RADLOFF, WILHELM. Die alttürkischen Inschriften der Mongolei. Leipsic, 1894–1895. — See p. 305.

RAGAZZONI, JACOPO. Relazione, 1571. In Alberi's Relazione, 3d series, ii. 77–102. Florence, 1844.

RAMBAUD, ALFRED. L'empire ottoman (1481–1566). In Lavisse and Rambaud's Histoire Générale, vol. iv. ch. xix. Paris, 1894. — See p. 321.

[RAMBERTI, BENEDETTO.] Libri tre delle cose de Turchi. Venice, 1539. — See pp 314–316, and Appendix I.

RAMSAY, SIR W. M. Geographical conditions determining history and religion in Asia Minor. Geographical Journal, xx. 257–282. London, 1902. See p. 307.

—— Historical geography of Asia Minor. London, 1890.

—— Studies in the history and art of the eastern provinces of the Roman empire. Aberdeen, 1906.

RANKE, LEOPOLD. The Ottoman and the Spanish empires in the sixteenth and seventeenth centuries. Translated by W. K. Kelly. London, 1843. — See p. 321.

RAWLINSON, GEORGE. The story of Parthia. New York, 1893.

—— The seventh great oriental monarchy. 2 vols. New York, 1882.

—— The sixth great oriental monarchy. London, 1873.

RECUEIL de voyages et de documents pour servir à l'histoire de la géographie depuis le xiiie jusqu'à la fin du xvie siècle. Edited by Charles Schéfer and Henri Cordier. 21 vols. Paris, 1882–1907. — See CHESNEAU, DU FRESNE-CANAYE, GEUFFROY, HAUSER, LA BROQUIÈRE, MAURAND, TORZELO.

REDHOUSE, SIR J. W. A Turkish and English lexicon. Constantinople, 1890.

REVUE Africaine: journal des travaux de la société historique algérienne. 55 vols. Alger, [1856]–1911.

APPENDIX 329

RIANT, COUNT PAUL. Catalogue de la bibliothèque. Prepared by L. de Germon and L. Polain. 2 pts. Paris, 1899. — See p. 308.

RICAUT, SIR PAUL. The history of the present state of the Ottoman empire. 6th edition. London, 1686. — See p. 320.

RICOLDUS. De vita et moribus Turcarum. Paris, 1509. — The same as TRACTATUS, etc., q. v.

ROBERTSON, WILLIAM. The emperor Charles V. 4 vols. London, 1811.

SAN FILIPPO, AMAT DI. Biografia dei viaggiatori italiani. 2 vols. Rome, 1882. — See p. 308.

SANUTO, MARINO (the younger). Diarii [1496–1533]. 58 vols., with an additional volume of *Prefazione.* Venice, 1879–1903.

SCHÉFER, CHARLES. Catalogue de la bibliothèque orientale. Paris, 1899. — See p. 308. See also CHESNEAU, LA BROQUIÈRE, SIASSET NAMÈH, SPANDUGINO, TORZELO.

SCHILTBERGER, JOHANN. Bondage and Travels. Translated by J. B. Telfer. Hakluyt Society. London, 1879. — See p. 309.

SIASSET NAMÈH, traité de gouvernement composé pour le sultan Melik-Châh par le vizir Nizam oul-Moulk [1092]. Translated by Charles Schéfer. Paris, 1893. — See p. 306.

SNOUCK HURGRONJE, G. Le droit Musulman. *Revue de l'Histoire des Religions,* xxxvii. 1 ff., and 174 ff. Paris, 1898.

SORANZO, GIACOMO. Relazione, 1576. In Alberi's *Relazione,* 3d series, ii. 193–207. Florence, 1844.

[SORANZO, JACOPO.] Relazione e diario, 1581. *Ibid.* 209–253. Florence, 1844. — See p. 313, note 1.

SPANDUGINO CANTACUSINO, TEODORO. Petit traicté de l'origine des Turcqz [Paris, 1519]. Edited by Charles Schéfer. Paris, 1896. — See p. 310.

STEEN DE JEHAY, LE COMTE F. VAN DEN. De la situation légale des sujets ottomans non-musulmans. Brussels, 1906.

SULEIMAN. See KANUN-NAMEH of Suleiman.

TANCO, V. D. (ESTANCO, CLAVEDAN DEL). Libro dell'origine et successione dell'imperio de' Turchi. Venice, 1558. — See p. 314.

TAVERNIER, J. B. Nova ed esatta descrizione del seraglio del gran Turco. Milan, 1687.

TIEPOLO, ANTONIO, Relazione, 1576. In Alberi's *Relazione,* 3d srics, ii. 129–191. Florence, 1844.

TISCHENDORF, P. A. VON. Das Lehnswesen in den moslemischen Staaten, insbesondere im osmanischen Reiche. Leipsic, 1872.

TORZELO, JEHAN. [Opinion on the military power of the Turks, c. 1439.] Edited by Charles Schéfer, in *Recueil de Voyages,* etc., xii. 263 ff. Paris, 1892.

[TRACTATUS.] Libellus de ritu et moribus Turcorum ante LXX annos aeditus [1460]. Wittenberg, 1530. — See pp. 309, 310.

TREVISANO, DOMENICO. Relazione, 1554. In Alberi's *Relazione,* 3d series, i. 111–192. Florence, 1840.

TÜRCKEN, BERNARDIN. Getrewe und wolmeynende kurtze Erinnerung von der Türcken Ordnung, in iren Kriegen vñ Veldtschlachten. Burgel, 1542.

330 APPENDIX

UBICINI, A[BDOLONYME]. État présent de l'empire ottoman. Paris, 1876.

URBINUS, THEOPHILUS. Türckisches Städt-Büchlein. Nuremberg, 1664.

URSU, J[ON]. La politique orientale de François I (1515–1547). Paris, 1908.

VAMBÉRY, HERMANN (ARMINIUS). Die primitive Cultur des turko-tatarischen Volkes auf grund sprachlicher Forschungen. Leipsic, 1879. — See p. 306.

—— Uigurische Sprachmonumente und das Kudatku Bilik. Innsbruck, 1870. — See p. 306.

VENIER, MAFFEO. Relazione, 1579, 1587. In Alberi's *Relazione*, 3d series, i. 437–468, ii. 295–307. Florence, 1840–1844.

VIAGGI fatti da Vinetia, alla tana . . . in Costantinopoli. Venice, 1543. — Contains Libri Tre, etc., of RAMBERTI, *q. v.*

YOUSSOUF FEHMI. Histoire de la Turquie. Paris, 1909.

YUSUF KHASS HAJIL. Kudatku Bilik (Art of Government). See VAMBÉRY, Uigurische Sprachmonumente, etc.

ZANE, MATTEO. Relazione, 1594. In Alberi's *Relazione*, 3d series, iii. 381–444. Florence, 1855.

ZEN (or ZENO), PIETRO. Itinerario, 1523. In Fulin's *Diarii*, 104–136. Venice, 1881.

—— Relazione, 1524, 1530. In Alberi's *Relazione*, 3d series, iii. 93–97, 119–122. Florence, 1855.

ZINKEISEN, J. W. Geschichte des osmanischen Reiches in Europa. 7 vols. and Index, Hamburg and Gotha, 1840–1863. — See p. 321.

GLOSSARY OF TURKISH WORDS

The pronunciation of the words defined should be approximately phonetic, the vowels by the continental system, the consonants as usually in English. Forms not defined are variant Western spellings. Gh is silent except at the beginning of a word. Plurals of nouns originally Turkish are formed by affixing -ler or -lar. The plurals in -s used in the foregoing pages are Anglicized.

Achiar, or Aconiziae, see Akinji.
Adet, established custom, 152, 161.
Agha, a general officer.
Aghiar, see Akinji.
Agiamoglani, see Ajem-oghlan.
Ajem-oghlan (untrained youth), a cadet or apprentice Janissary, 79 ff.
Akinji, the irregular cavalry, 105.
Alai Bey, a colonel of the feudal cavalry, 103.
Alcangi, Alcanzi, or Alengi, see Akinji.
Allophase, see Ulufagi.
Ameji, a receiver of petitions, etc., 183.
Aquangi, see Akinji.
Arpa-emini, intendant of forage, 132.
Ashji-bashi, a chief cook, 245.
Azab, the irregular infantry, 105.

Bailo (Italian), a Venetian minister resident at Constantinople.
Bairam, the name of two great Moslem festivals, 136.
Balucasi, see Boluk-bashi.
Bascia, see Pasha.
Bash, a head, a chief.
Bassa, see Pasha.
Berat, an ordinance, or document conferring a dignity or privilege.
Berat-emini, a distributor of ordinances, 253.
Beylerbey (lord of lords), a general of feudal cavalry and governor of a province or group of provinces, 103.

Beylikji, a director of the three chancery bureaus, 183.
Beylik Kalemi, a bureau of the Chancery, 183.
Bezestan, a market house in Constantinople, built by Mohammed II.
Bin(m)bashi (chief of a thousand), a colonel.
Boluk-bashi, a captain of the Janissaries, 249.
Bostanji, a gardener.
Bostanji-bashi, the head gardener of the Sultan's palace — a high official, 130.

Cacaia, see Kiaya.
Cadilescher, see Kaziasker.
Cahaia, or Caia, see Kiaya.
Calvalgibassi, see Helvaji-bashi.
Capagasi, see Kapu-aghasi.
Capiagabasi, see Kapuji-bashi.
Capi (oglan), see Ghureba (oghlan).
Caragi, see Kharâji.
Caripicus, see Ghureba.
Caripp (oglan), see Ghureba (oghlan).
Caripy, see Ghureba.
Carmandari (Italianized), muleteers, 251.
Carzeri, see Kharâji.
Casnandarbasi, see Khazinehdar-bashi.
Cavriliji (Italianized), a herdsman, 251.
Ceyssi, see Seis.
Chakirji, a vulturer, 252.
Chasnejir, a taster, 245.
Chasnejir-bashi, a chief taster, 245.

331

Chaush, an usher, 130.
Chaush-bashi, chief of the Chaushes — a high official, 183.
Checaya, or Chechessi, see Kiaya.
Chelebi, a gentleman.
Cheri-bashi (chief of soldiery), a petty officer of feudal cavalry.
Chiccaia, or Chietcudasci, see Kiaya.
Chokadar, a page of high rank, 127.
Ciarcagi, see Ghureba.
Ciaus, see Chaush.
Cogia, see Hoja.
Coureyschs, see Koreish.

Danishmend, a master of arts, 205.
Dar ul-harb, home or land of war, 29.
Dar ul-Islam, home or land of Islam, 64.
Defterdar, a treasurer, 167 ff., 174.
Defter-emini (intendant of account-books), a recorder of fiefs, 172.
Deli, crazy (appellation of a scout or a captain of the Akinji).
Dervish, a member of a Moslem religious order, 207.
Deveji, a camel-driver, 251.
Devshurmeh, a gathering or collecting (of the tribute boys), 51.
Divan, the Ottoman council of state, 187 ff.; a council of a great officer, 216, note 3.
Dulbend, or Dulipante (Italianized), a turban.

Emin (plural Umena), an intendant, 132.
Emir, a descendant of the prophet Mohammed, 206 ff.; a commander, a governor.
Emir-al-Akhor, a grand equerry, 131.
Ersi kharâjiyeh, tribute lands, 31.
Ersi memleket, state lands, 31.
Ersi 'ushriyeh, tithe lands, 31.
Eski, old.

Fetva, a response from a Mufti, 208, 223.
Fetva-khaneh, the drafting bureau of the Sheik ul-Islam, 208.
Fikh, the practical regulations of the Sacred Law, 153.

Firman, an administrative ordinance' 157.

Gachaia, see Kiaya.
Gharib(oglan), see Ghureba(oghlan).
Ghureba (foreigner), a member of the lowest corps of the standing cavalry, 98 and note 5.
Gonnullu, a volunteer soldier or sailor, 102.
Gul-behar, rose of spring (a feminine proper name), 57 note 3.

Hebegibassi, see Jebeji-bashi.
Hekim-bashi, a chief physician, 129.
Helvaji-bashi, a chief confectioner, 245.
Hoja, a teacher; the Sultan's adviser, 128.
Holofagi, see Ulufagi.
Humayun, imperial.

Iaching, see Akinji.
Ianicerotti (Italianized), the Ajem-ogh-lans.
Iaxagi, see Yaziji.
Ikinji Kapu-oghlan, a white eunuch in charge of the second gate of the place, 128.
Imâm, the Caliph or lawful successor of Mohammed, 28, 150, 235; a leader of daily prayers, 206.
Imbrahor, Imbroor, Imrakhor, or Imror, see Emir-al-Akhor.
Iskemleji, a page of high rank, 244.
Itch-oghlan (inside youth), a page in one of the Sultan's palaces, 73 ff.

Jebeji-bashi, a chief armorer, 252.
Jerrah-bashi, a chief surgeon, 129.
Jizyeh, a poll or capitation tax on non-Moslems, 175.

Kadi, see Kazi.
Kadi al asker, or Kadi l' esker, see Kaziasker.
Kaim, a caretaker of a mosque, 206.
Kalem, a bureau of the Treasury, 168 ff.
Kanun, an imperial decree, 152, 158.

Kanuni, legislator, 27.

Kanun-nameh, a book or collection of laws, 158 ff.

Kapu Aghasi (general of the gate), the white eunuch in charge of the principal palace, 126.

Kapudan Pasha, an admiral, 189.

Kapuji, a gatekeeper, 130.

Kapuji-bashi, a head gatekeeper, 126.

Kapujilar-kiayasi, a grand chamberlain, 190.

Kazi, a judge, 215 ff.

Kaziasker (judge of the army), one of the two chief judges of the Ottoman Empire, 220 ff.

Ketkhuda, see Kiaya.

Kharâj, a tax or tribute in money or kind on lands belonging to non-Moslems, 175.

Kharâji, a non-Moslem who pays the kharâj, 41.

Khass Oda (private chamber), the highest chamber of pages, 75, 126.

Khass, a very large fief, 100.

Khatib, a leader of Friday prayers, 206.

Khazinehdar-bashi, a treasurer-in-chief, 127.

Khazineh-odassi (chamber of the treasury), the second chamber of pages, 127.

Khojagan, a chief of a treasury bureau, 168.

Khurrem, happy, joyful (a feminine proper name), 57.

Kiaya (common form of ketkhuda), a steward or lieutenant, 96 note 4, 125.

Kiaya-bey, the lieutenant of the grand vizier, 182 ff.

Kiaya Katibi, a private secretary of the Kiaya-bey, 184.

Kilerji-bashi, a chief of the sultan's pantry, 127.

Kiler-odassi (chamber of the pantry), the third chamber of pages, 127.

Kizlar Aghasi (general of the girls), the black eunuch in charge of the palace of the harem, 125.

Koreish, the Arabian tribe of which Mohammed the prophet was a member, 150, 235.

Kul, a slave; one of the sultan's slave-family, 47 ff.

Masraf-shehriyari (imperial steward), substitute for the intendant of kitchen, 132.

Mawuna, or Maone (Italianized), a sailing vessel.

Mecter, see Mihter.

Medresseh, a secondary school or college, 203 ff.

Mekteb, a school, 203.

Mektubji, a private secretary of the grand vizier, 184.

Mihter, a tent-pitcher; a musician.

Mihter-bashi, the chief tent-pitcher, 132.

Mir Alem, the imperial standard bearer, 131, 206.

Miri-akhor, see Emir-al-Akhor.

Molla, a judge of high rank, 217.

Mosellem, a fief holder by ancient tenure, 105.

Muderis, a professor in a Medresseh, 205.

Muezzin, one who calls Moslems to prayer, 206.

Mufettish, a special judge dealing with endowments, 201, 218.

Mufti, a Moslem legal authority; in particular, the Sheik ul-Islam, 207 ff.

Muhtesib, a lieutenant of police, 219.

Mujtahid, a doctor of the Sacred Law.

Mulâzim (candidate), a graduate of the higher Medressehs, 205.

Mulk, land held in fee simple, 31.

Munejim-bashi, a chief astrologer, 129.

Muste emin, a resident foreigner, 34.

Mutbakh-emini, intendant of the kitchen, 132.

Muteferrika, the Noble Guard, 129.

Muteveli, an administrator of an endowment, 201.

Naib, an inferior judge, 218.

Nakib ol-Eshraf, the chief of the Seids or descendants of the prophet Mohammed, 206.

Nazir, an inspector of an endowment, 201.

Nishanji, a chancellor, 182 ff.

Nizam al-mulk, basis of the order of the kingdom (title of a vizier of Melek Shah), 306.

Oda (a room), a chamber of the pages or of the harem recruits; a company of the Janissaries.

Oda-bashi (head of chamber), the page of highest rank, 244; a corporal of the Janissaries, 249.

Oghlan, a youth.

Okumak-yerleri (reading-places), primary schools, 203.

Orta, a company of the Janissaries. (*See also* Oda.)

Ouloufedgis, *see* Ulufaji.

Papuji, a page of high rank, 244.

Pasha, a very high official.

Peik, a member of the body-guard of halbardiers, 130.

Podesta (Italian), a municipal judge.

Quaia, or Queaya, *see* Kiaya.

Ramazan, the Moslem month of fasting.

Rayah, non-Moslem Ottoman subjects, 159.

Reis Effendi, or Reis ul-Khuttab, a recording secretary, 174; a recording secretary of the Divan, later an important minister of state, 182 ff.

Reis ul-Ulema (head of the Ulema), an early title of the Sheik ul-Islam, 208 note 3.

Rekiab-Aghalari (generals of the stirrup), a group of high officers of the outside service of the palace, 131.

Rusnamehji, a chief book-keeper of the Treasury, 168.

Ruus Kalemi, a bureau of the Chancery, 183.

Sakka, a water-carrier.

Sanjak, a flag or standard, a district.

Sanjak Bey, a high officer of feudal. cavalry and governor of a Sanjak, 103.

Saremin, *see* Shehr-emini.

Sarraf, a banker.

Schēni, *see* Iskemleji.

Seferli-odassi (chamber of campaign), the fourth chamber of pages, 128 note 1.

Segban-bashi (master of the hounds), the second officer of the corps of Janissaries, 96, 132 note 3.

Seid, a descendant of the prophet Mohammed, 206.

Seis, a groom, 251.

Selicter, *see* Silihdar.

Seracter, *see* Sharabdar.

Serai, a palace.

Seraskier, a commander-in-chief.

Serraj, saddlers, 251.

Seymen-bashi, a popular form of Segban-bashi, *q. v.*

Shahinji, a falconer, 252.

Sharabdar (drink-bearer), a page of high rank, 127.

Shehr-emini, intendant of imperial buildings, 132.

Sheik, a preacher; a head of a religious community, 206.

Sheik ul-Islam, the Mufti of Constantinople and head of the Moslem Institution, 208 ff.

Sheri (or Sheriat), the Moslem Sacred Law, 152 ff.

Sherif, a descendant of the prophet Mohammed, 206.

Silihdar (sword-bearer), a member of the second corps of standing cavalry, 98 and note 5; the page who carried the sultan's arms, 127.

Sillictar, *see* Silihdar.

Sipah, or Sipahi, *see* Spahi.

Sofi, woolen; a dervish (an appellation of the Shah of Persia).

Softa, an undergraduate in a Medresseh, 205.

Solak (left-handed), a janissary bowman of the sultan's personal guard, 129.

Spachi, *see* Spahi.

Spacoillain, *see* Spahi-oghlan.

Spahi, a cavalry soldier; a member of the standing or feudal cavalry, 47, 98 ff., 100 ff.

Spahi-oghlan (cavalry youth), a member of the highest corps of the standing cavalry, 98 and note 5.

Spai, *see* Spahi.

Subashi, a captain of the feudal cavalry and governor of a town, 103.

Sukhta (inflamed), *see* Softa.

Sulastrus, *see* Silihdar.

Sultana, a princess or queen mother, 125; (the true Turkish form uses a proper name or the word Valideh, followed by Sultan).

Suluphtar, *see* Silihdar.

Tahvil Kalemi, a bureau of the Chancery, 183.

Talisman, *see* Danishmend.

Tapu, a tenant's lease or title deed, 31.

Terjuman, an interpreter (dragoman).

Terjuman Divani Humayun, a chief interpreter of the sultan, 183.

Teshrifat, ceremony, 134.

Teshrifatji, a master of ceremonies, 184.

Teskereh, a document.

Teskereji, a master of petitions, 184.

Teskereji-bashi (chief of document-writers), the Nishanji, 184, 185.

Timar, a fief of small income, 100; feudal income.

Timarji, the holder of a Timar.

Tughra, the sultan's monogram, 185.

Ulema (plural of âlim, a learned man), the whole body of Moslems learned in the Sacred Law, 203 ff.

Ulufaji (paid troops), a member of the

third corps of the sultan's standing cavalry, 98 and note 5.

Umena, plural of Emin.

Urf, the sovereign will of the reigning sultan, 152, 162.

'Ushr, a tithe on lands belonging to Moslems, 175.

Vakf, a religious endowment, 31, 201 ff.

Valideh, a mother.

Veznedar, an official weigher of money, 132.

Vizier (burden-bearer), a minister of state, 163 ff.

Voivode (Slavic), an officer, a governor.

Yachinji, *see* Akinji.

Yaya, a fief holder by ancient tenure, owing infantry service, 105.

Yaziji, a scribe or secretary.

Yedi-kuleh (seven towers), a strong castle against the land wall of Constantinople, 172.

Yeni-cheri (new soldiery), the corps of the Janissaries, 91 ff.

Yeni Oda (new chamber), the lowest chamber of pages in the principal palace, 75, 127.

Zagarji-bashi (master of the harriers), a high officer of the Janissaries, 132 note 5.

Zanijiler (Italianized), lancers or Voinaks (?), 252.

Zarabkhanc-cmini, intendant of mints and mines, 132.

Ziam, the holder of a Ziamet.

Ziamet, a large fief, 100.

Zimmi, a tributary non-Moslem subject, 34.

INDEX

INDEX